FLORIDA CONSTITUTIONAL LAW

IN A NUTSHELL®

ROBERT M. JARVIS
Professor of Law
Nova Southeastern University

WEST
ACADEMIC
PUBLISHING

Nutshell Series, In a Nutshell and the Nutshell Logo are trademarks registered in the U.S. Patent and Trademark Office.

© 2020 LEG, Inc. d/b/a West Academic
   444 Cedar Street, Suite 700
   St. Paul, MN 55101
   1-877-888-1330

West, West Academic Publishing, and West Academic are trademarks of West Publishing Corporation, used under license.

Printed in the United States of America

ISBN: 978-1-62810-216-1

The lobby of Florida's current capitol building in Tallahassee. The state seal (pictured here upside down) is in the foreground, while the opening words of the Florida Constitution appear on the wall above it. (Photograph by Mark Wallheiser / courtesy of Getty Images)

For Judge Rex J Ford

PREFACE

Since 1990, I have been teaching Florida Constitutional Law ("FCL") at Nova Southeastern University ("NSU") in Fort Lauderdale. Previously, the subject was taught by Associate Dean Rex J Ford. Just before he left to join the federal government, I audited his Spring 1989 course. His lectures continue to inspire me.

Throughout my time teaching FCL, no suitable study aid has existed. As a result, students repeatedly have asked me to write one. Accordingly, this book belongs as much to them as it does to me. It is my hope that it will serve as a useful guide to the constitution's meaning and, at the same time, bring its words to life (hence the reason for the inclusion of so many anecdotes).

During my work on this book, I received constant encouragement from Mac Soto and Stephanie Galligan at West Academic Publishing, as well as from Adriana Marinau, a friend who took unstinting interest in my progress. As always, my wife Judi provided unflagging support.

My NSU colleagues Rob Beharriell, Phyllis Coleman, Richard Grosso, Mike Masinter, Beth Parker, Becka Rich, Gail Richmond, and Alison Rosenberg regularly pitched in, as did Dean Jon Garon, who provided me with a research stipend.

Professors Edward LaRose (Stetson) and Patrick McGinley (Barry) kindly reviewed various chapters before they went to press. Associate Dean Tim Chinaris (Belmont) helped me with a particularly tricky research issue. Thanks also are due to bar review representatives Ashley Ahearn and Anna Taraszki (Kaplan), Nachman Gutowski (Themis), and Madison Nesbitt (Bar/Bri).

Nutshells, by design, are compact, with strictly-enforced word limits. This has required me to make difficult choices regarding what to cover, what to omit, and how much detail to include. Unsurprisingly, I have paid the most attention to those matters that, year after year, have bedeviled or beguiled my students. In this regard, Lauren Turner (NSU Class of 2015) deserves special thanks for sharing with me her detailed outline.

As I was nearing completion of the book's first draft, Professor Sandy D'Alemberte (FSU) passed away. His contributions are too many to list here—suffice it to say that anyone who has ever encountered the Florida Constitution is a beneficiary of his labors. Professors Clifford Alloway (Miami), John Cooper (Stetson), and Thomas Marks (Stetson), as well as Florida House of Representatives Clerk Allen Morris, also are due recognition for their work in our shared enterprise.

The research for this book closed on December 31, 2019. Ch. 23 explains how to locate amendments adopted after this date; case law updates can be obtained by using Westlaw.

Lastly, comments and suggestions are invited and can be sent to me at jarvisb@nova.edu.

OUTLINE

PART II. INDIVIDUAL RIGHTS

PART III. STATE GOVERNMENT

PART IV. LOCAL GOVERNMENTS

PART V. GOVERNMENT FINANCES

TABLE OF CASES

References are to Pages

TABLE OF CONSTITUTIONAL SECTIONS

**Florida Constitution
(as amended through November 6, 2018)**

———————

*Page references indicate the starting point
of the principal discussion*

"Florida constitutional law, across its long duration, is quite thick, a rich, agglomerative medium manifestly inviting intense investigations of alternative approaches."

—*Professor Patrick O. Gudridge*
64 University of Miami Law Review 879, 881 (2010)

FLORIDA CONSTITUTIONAL LAW

IN A NUTSHELL®

PART I
BASICS

CHAPTER 1
INTRODUCTION

A. OVERVIEW

The Florida Constitution is the basic ("organic") law of the State of Florida. Its principal purpose is to act as a check on governmental power. This is made clear by Art. I, § 1: "All political power is inherent in the people. The enunciation herein of certain rights shall not be construed to deny or impair others retained by the people." Similar language has appeared in each of Florida's constitutions.

B. BASICS

Florida's constitution consists of a preamble followed by 12 articles:

Art. I: Declaration of Rights

Art. II: General Provisions

Art. III: Legislature

Art. IV: Executive

Art. V: Judiciary

Art. VI: Suffrage and Elections

Art. VII: Finance and Taxation

Art. VIII: Local Government

Art. IX: Education

Art. X: Miscellaneous (a hodgepodge of sections concerned primarily with gambling, health care, and property rights)

Art. XI: Amendments

Art. XII: Schedules

A copy of the Florida Constitution (along with an index) appears in every edition of the Florida Statutes. *See* Fla. Stat. § 11.242(4)(b)–(c). The constitution also can be found on-line at various web sites, including:

https://www.flsenate.gov/Laws/Constitution

http://www.leg.state.fl.us/statutes/index.cfm? submenu=3

https://dos.myflorida.com/media/698540/florida-constitution.pdf

http://sb.flleg.gov/nxt/gateway.dll?f=templates& fn=default.htm$vid=html:FLCC

As an aid to readers, the constitution includes footnotes, known as "catch lines," after each section that has been amended since 1968. The first catch line appears after Art. I, § 2 and reads as follows:

Am. S.J.R. 917, 1974; adopted 1974; Am. proposed by Constitution Revision Commission, Revision No. 9, 1998, filed with the Secretary of State May 5, 1998; adopted 1998; Am. proposed by Constitution Revision Commission, Revision No. 6, 2018, filed with the Secretary of State May 9, 2018; adopted 2018.

Thus, § 2 has been amended three times since 1968: in 1974, 1998, and 2018. The 1974 change was proposed by the Florida Legislature ("S.J.R." stands for Senate Joint Resolution), while the 1998 and 2018 changes were proposed by the Constitution Revision Commission.

In 1998, all gender-specific pronouns were removed from the constitution. Due to an oversight, Art. V, § 2(d) still uses such language: "The chief judge shall be responsible for the administrative supervision of the circuit courts and county courts in *his* circuit." [Emphasis added.]

C. HISTORY

Florida has had six official constitutions and multiple unofficial ones. They can be found, along with related works, in the HeinOnline "State Constitutions Illustrated" database (https://home.heinonline.org/). Another useful (but less comprehensive) resource is the Florida Memory Collection's "Florida's Early Constitutions" web page (https://www.floridamemory.com/Collections/Constitution/).

1. FORERUNNERS

Florida became a state on Mar. 3, 1845. Prior to that time, it was a Spanish possession (1513–1763); two British colonies (1763–83); two Spanish possessions (1783–1821); and a U.S. territory (1821–45).

(a) Royal Decrees (Pre-1800)

Florida was discovered by the Spanish explorer Juan Ponce de León in 1513, who named the area "La Florida" (the place of flowers). In 1565, the Spanish admiral Pedro Menéndez de Avilés founded the city of St. Augustine, the first permanent settlement in Florida (and the oldest in the United States).

In 1573–74, King Phillip II published three ordinances concerning Spain's overseas possessions. These pronouncements addressed the respective roles of the government and the Catholic Church; the types of public buildings to be constructed; and the treatment of native populations.

In 1763, King George III issued a proclamation regulating the recently-acquired colonies of British East Florida and British West Florida. (Spain was forced to cede Florida to Great Britain after losing the French and Indian War. For administrative reasons, Great Britain split Florida into two colonies.)

In addition to setting their boundaries, the proclamation ordered the colonies' new governors (Scottish military officers James Grant and George Johnstone) to establish legislatures and courts and ensure friendly relations with the local Indian tribes.

In 1783, as part of the Treaty of Paris (the agreement ending the American Revolutionary War), Great Britain was required to return Florida to Spain (which had been a U.S. ally). The loss of Florida, a desolate and isolated outpost, caused little consternation across the British Empire.

(b) Republic of West Florida Constitution (1810)

During Spain's second occupation of Florida (during which, like the British, it administered East Florida and West Florida as separate entities), U.S. citizens began to move into the region, leading to friction between Spain and the United States. Matters grew increasingly tense after the Louisiana Purchase (1803), which, rather than clarifying the countries' disputed borders, added to the confusion surrounding them.

In Sept. 1810, settlers living in the far reaches of West Florida rebelled against Spanish rule and established the independent Republic of West Florida ("RWF"). In Oct. 1810, they promulgated a constitution modelled after the U.S. Constitution.

In Dec. 1810, the United States forcibly annexed the RWF. Today, what had been the RWF lies in eastern Louisiana in an area known as the "Florida Parishes." These eight counties comprise nearly 11% of Louisiana and are home to both the state capital (Baton Rouge) and a museum dedicated to the RWF (http://www.jacksonlamuseum.com/).

(c) Constitution of Cádiz (1812)

In 1810, Spain's first legislature—the Cortes—began meeting in Cádiz. (As an absolute monarchy under the Habsburgs and then the Bourbons, Spain had never had such a body.) In Mar. 1812, the Cortes approved the country's first constitution. Formally known as the Constitution of Cádiz, this highly progressive instrument granted Spain's overseas possessions (including Florida) expansive political rights.

(d) Patriots' Constitution (1812)

While the Cortes was putting the finishing touches on the Constitution of Cádiz, a group of 300 Georgia settlers known as the "Patriot Army" was establishing the "Republic of East Florida" on Amelia Island. For the next 14 months, they fought to oust the Spanish from East Florida.

In July 1812, the Patriots adopted a constitution that included a legislative council, a chief executive, and a court system. Its preamble made the Patriots' goal clear: "[W]e hope through [God's] providence shortly to become a territory and a component part of the Government of the United States."

In 1813, the insurgency collapsed when the United States, not wanting to provoke a war with Spain, stopped supporting the Patriots.

(e) Congressional Establishment Act (1821)

In 1819, Spain agreed to sell Florida to the United States for $5 million pursuant to the Adams-Onís Treaty. *See* 8 Stat. 252. (The treaty also required the United States to recognize Spain's claims to California and Texas.) The United States did not pay any money to Spain. Instead, it agreed to become responsible for the numerous "spoliation" claims pending against Spain, many of which involved

Spanish seizures of U.S. vessels and cargoes. *See, e.g., Comegys v. Vasse*, 26 U.S. (1 Pet.) 193 (1828).

Due to delays on Spain's part, the treaty did not go into effect for two years. When it did, Pres. James Monroe named Gen. Andrew Jackson Florida's military governor. On July 17, 1821, Jackson formally accepted West Florida from Col. José María Callava in a short turnover ceremony in the Plaza Ferdinand in Pensacola. (Volunteers now annually re-enact this event for tourists.) One week earlier, Col. José Coppinger had turned over East Florida to Col. Robert Butler.

To prepare for the takeover, Congress on Mar. 3, 1819 adopted "An Act to Authorize the President of the United States to Take Possession of East and West Florida, and Establish a Temporary Government Therein." *See* 3 Stat. 523. On Mar. 3, 1821, this law was superseded by "An Act for the Establishment of a Territorial Government in Florida." *See* 3 Stat. 637. For the next 24 years, this frequently amended statute served as Florida's de facto constitution. Among other things, it merged East Florida and West Florida; delineated the territory's boundaries; created two superior courts (at Pensacola and St. Augustine); provided for the presidential appointment of the territory's officers; declared the laws of the United States to be applicable in Florida; extended most of the rights contained in the U.S. Constitution to Florida's inhabitants; prohibited the importation of foreign country slaves into Florida; and granted the territory one non-voting congressional delegate.

2.   1838 CONSTITUTION

In Feb. 1837, Florida's territorial council passed a law titled, "An Act to Take the Sense of the People of this Territory on the Policy and Propriety of Becoming a State." *See* 1837 Fla. Terr. Acts 49. It directed:

> [A]t the next election [May 1, 1837] for [the] Delegate to Congress for this Territory, it shall be the duty of the Judges, or inspectors of the election aforesaid at every place or precinct, where any such election may be held, to put the question to every voter . . . whether said voter wishes a "State" or Territorial Government, and the Judges . . . shall before any ballot is put into the Box, write on the back of every ballot the answer of the voter. . . .

Id.

On July 27, 1837, Gov. Richard Call reported "there was given a majority of 1005 votes for a State Government." In fact, the actual margin of victory was 30 votes less than Call reported: 2,139 to 1,164. While most of the "yes" votes (1,152) came from Middle Florida (Tallahassee), home to the territory's bankers, merchants, and planters, most of the "no" votes (614) came from East Florida (St. Augustine), whose residents were bearing the brunt of the Second Seminole War (1835–42) and feared an increase in taxes. In West Florida (Pensacola), there was strong support (69.3%) for statehood.

To gain admission, Florida was required to submit a proposed constitution to Congress (this practice had been established by the Northwest Ordinance of 1787, 1 Stat. 51). Thus, in Feb. 1838 the territorial council passed a law titled, "An Act to Call a Convention for the Purpose of Organizing a State Government." *See* 1838 Fla. Terr. Acts 15. In pertinent part, it read:

> *Sec.* 1.   [A]n election shall be held in the several counties of this Territory on the second Monday of October next [*i.e.*, Oct. 8, 1838] . . . for members of a Convention to devise and adopt the most efficient, speedy and proper measures for the formation and establishment of an independent State government for the people of Florida, and to form and adopt a Bill of Rights and Constitution for the same, and all needful measures preparatory to the admission of Florida into the National Confederacy. . . .

> *Sec.* 5.   [The] Convention shall be held on the first Monday of December next [*i.e.*, Dec. 3, 1838] at the city of St. Joseph. . . .

> *Sec.* 8.   [A]ll white, male inhabitants, citizens of the United States, above the age of twenty-one years who have resided in the Territory of Florida for the space of six months immediately proceeding the day of election, shall be entitled to vote . . . and all white, male inhabitants, citizens of the United States, above the age of twenty-one years, who have resided in the Territory of Florida for twelve months immediately proceeding the day of election, shall be eligible as delegates. . . .

Id. at 15–17.

In 1838, St. Joseph, a Panhandle town with an estimated 12,000 residents (an official count does not exist), was the largest in Florida, even though it had been founded just three years earlier. Upon being selected, it immediately began building a meeting space (dubbed "Convention Hall") for the delegates. A dozen new hotels also were erected.

The convention opened as scheduled with 46 delegates in attendance. They quickly organized themselves into 18 committees. Drawing inspiration from the U.S. Constitution, various state constitutions (principally the 1819 Alabama Constitution), and the day's leading treatises (including Justice Joseph Story's *Commentaries on the Constitution* (1833)), the committees accomplished their respective tasks in short order. One issue, however, proved so contentious that it turned the expected two-week gathering into a six-week ordeal.

Due to their booming economy (built on cotton), Middle Florida residents were ardent bank supporters. In the rest of Florida, which was struggling, residents viewed banks with suspicion, especially after the Panic of 1837, which had ignited a national recession and imperiled the territory's finances (see Ch. 22 of this book). As a result, the convention was sharply divided over the "banking question." In the race for convention president, for example, Robert Reid, a bank foe, beat former governor William DuVal, a bank ally, by a single vote. After much back and forth, the anti-banking delegates prevailed. As a result, the constitution placed numerous restrictions on banks.

On the morning of Jan. 11, 1839, the convention voted 55–1 (including 12 proxy votes) to approve the constitution. (The lone dissenter was Richard Fitzpatrick, the delegate from Dade County. Fitzpatrick was South Florida's largest landowner, an enthusiastic proponent of slavery, and a diehard bank supporter.) In the afternoon, 41 delegates signed the constitution.

On May 6, 1839, the constitution was adopted 2,070 to 1,975. (Some sources report the tally as 2,071 to 1,958.) Although opposition to the banking article played a key role in the constitution's near-defeat, many voters remained opposed to the whole idea of statehood. Still others favored statehood but believed Florida should enter the Union as two states instead of one (this sentiment was particularly strong in St. Augustine).

For the next six years, Florida waited to be admitted. The hold-up was the lack of a companion "free" state, an unofficial requirement since the Missouri Compromise of 1820 (3 Stat. 545). Although Florida had been "paired" with Iowa, the latter's admission repeatedly was held up by disagreements over its boundaries.

Congress finally agreed to admit Florida without Iowa. *See* 5 Stat. 742 (making Florida the 27th state on Mar. 3, 1845). In keeping with tradition, a star representing Florida was added to the U.S. flag on July 4, 1845.

The 1838 constitution went into effect upon Florida's admission. Although the original has been lost, a copy is in the State Archives in Tallahassee.

The town of St. Joseph no longer exists, a victim of a series of misfortunes: a storm (1839); a yellow fever epidemic (1841); a fire (1841); a hurricane (1841); and a tidal wave (1844). Like most port cities, St. Joseph had a reputation for alcohol, gambling, and prostitution. As a result, clergymen claimed God's wrath had destroyed it.

Today, the area where St. Joseph stood is a state park called "Constitution Convention Museum State Park." It features a large monument (erected 1922—see https://www.floridamemory.com/items/show/711 54) and a museum (opened 1955—see https://www. floridastateparks.org/parks-and-trails/constitution-convention-museum-state-park) that includes a life-size diorama recreating the constitution's signing (see https://www.floridamemory.com/items/show/371 66). In 1909, the City of Port St. Joe was founded approximately two miles from St. Joseph. It bills itself as the "Constitution City" and its motto is "Birthplace of the Florida Constitution." *See* http://www.cityofportstjoe.com/.

3. 1861 CONSTITUTION

On Nov. 6, 1860, Abraham Lincoln was elected president of the United States. Three weeks later, the Florida General Assembly passed a bill authorizing a secession convention. *See* 1860–61 Fla. Laws 15. The law required delegate elections to be held on Dec. 22,

1860; made the convention's opening day Jan. 3, 1861; and chose Tallahassee as the host city.

The "Florida Convention of the People" commenced on Jan. 5, 1861, with 69 delegates in attendance. One reason it did not begin on time was because Pres. James Buchanan, in a last-ditch effort at national reconciliation, declared Jan. 4, 1861 a day of prayer and reflection. (Many of the delegates spent it attending services at St. John's Episcopal Church, where Bishop Francis Rutledge delivered a fiery sermon encouraging secession.)

When matters finally did get underway, Judge John McGehee of Madison County was elected convention president. As everyone knew, the question was not whether Florida would secede but when it would do so. While many delegates favored an immediate departure, others wanted to wait until other Southern states acted.

On the convention's sixth day (Jan. 10), the delegates voted 62–7 for immediate secession, declared Florida "a sovereign and independent Nation," and adopted a new constitution (which was made effective immediately). By now, Mississippi and South Carolina had left the Union. Within weeks, Alabama, Georgia, Louisiana, and Texas followed. On Feb. 8, 1861, the Confederate States of America ("CSA") was born when deputies meeting in Montgomery, Alabama agreed on a provisional constitution. *See* https://avalon.law.yale.edu/19th_century/csa_csapro.asp. A permanent one was adopted on Mar. 11, 1861. *See* https://avalon.law.yale.edu/19th_century/csa_csa.asp.

On Apr. 12, 1861, the Civil War began when CSA troops opened fire on Fort Sumter in Charleston. Subsequently, Arkansas, North Carolina, Tennessee, and Virginia seceded, bringing the total number of CSA states to 11.

In most respects, Florida's 1861 constitution retained the 1838 constitution's language. However, a few notable changes were made, including:

1) increasing the number of votes needed to override gubernatorial vetoes;

2) ordering the legislature to provide the governor with a Tallahassee residence;

3) doubling the terms of senators (to four years) and representatives (to two years);

4) limiting legislative sessions to 30 days (unless extended by a 2/3 vote);

5) softening the more draconian provisions affecting banks; and,

6) eliminating the legislature's right to amend the constitution.

4.   1865 CONSTITUTION

On Apr. 9, 1865, the CSA formally surrendered. Five days later, Lincoln was assassinated. These two events signaled both the end of the Civil War and the start of what would become a bitter effort to restore the CSA states to the Union.

Due to its distance from the front lines, almost no fighting took place in Florida. The state's only significant military engagement—a CSA victory known as the Battle of Olustee—occurred on Feb. 20, 1864 near present-day Lake City.

Indeed, Florida was so far removed from the war that it did not learn that the CSA had lost until Union troops marched into Tallahassee on May 10, 1865. Nine days later, Acting Governor Abraham Allison resigned, leaving Florida with no civilian government. On May 22, 1865, Gen. Edward McCook placed Florida under martial law.

On July 13, 1865, Pres. Andrew Johnson appointed William Marvin to be Florida's provisional governor. Marvin had been a federal judge in Key West from 1847 to 1863, when he left Florida to ride out the war in New York City. Upon returning to Florida, he announced that an election would be held on Oct. 10, 1865 for 55 delegates to a constitutional convention. Only those eligible to vote on Jan. 10, 1861, and who had been granted amnesty by the federal government, were permitted to participate. The first condition barred all blacks; the second condition barred most whites.

Of the state's 8,512 eligible voters, 6,707 cast ballots for delegates. The candidates they elected were decidedly pro-CSA. Indeed, two had been members of the 1861 secession convention: James Gettis of Hillsborough County and John Morrison of Walton County.

The convention began in Tallahassee on Oct. 25, 1865 with 42 delegates. After electing former Florida senate president Erasmus Tracy (D-Fernandina

Beach) the convention's president, the delegates got down to work. What they ended up producing looked very much like the 1861 constitution. Indeed, except for a grudging acknowledgment that "slavery has been destroyed in this State by the Government of the United States," the new constitution took pains to ensure that blacks remained second-class citizens.

Thus, the right to vote was reserved to "every free white male person of the age of twenty-one years and upwards . . . and none others. . . ." Legislative representation was to be determined by counting "the whole number of white inhabitants [and] three-fifths of the number of colored people. . . ." Judges were instructed to exclude "the testimony of colored persons . . . unless made competent by future legislation." Yet another provision declared, "The Jurors of this State shall be white men[.]"

In addition to the constitution, the delegates passed nine ordinances and five resolutions that made their feelings clear. Resolution No. 5, for example, called on Marvin to "exert himself to have removed from the interior of the State, at as early a day as possible, the Colored Troops of the United States. . . ."

Having finished its work, the convention adjourned on Nov. 7, 1865. Before it did so, it declared the new constitution in effect.

As part of its reorganization of the government, the constitution called for new elections to be held on Nov. 29, 1865. David Walker, a former mayor of Tallahassee, ran unopposed for governor and was sworn in on Dec. 20, 1865. Eight days later, Florida became the 30th state to approve the 13th Amendment (banning slavery).

As far as Johnson was concerned, Florida was again a U.S. state. Crucially, however, Congress, which had adjourned in Mar. 1865 but now was back in session, had not, as required by the constitution, been asked for its approval. *See* Art. IV, § 3, cl. 1 ("New States may be admitted by the Congress into this Union. . . .").

For much of 1866, the legal status of Florida and the other former CSA states remained unsettled. To many, however, the question was largely academic, especially when, on July 7, 1866, Tennessee became the first former CSA state to ratify the 14th Amendment (guaranteeing equal rights to all citizens). However, on Oct. 27, 1866, Texas rejected the amendment. Florida (Dec. 3, 1866) and the rest of the former CSA quickly did likewise.

Citing the rejections as proof that the former CSA states were not yet ready to rejoin the Union, Congress on Mar. 2, 1867 passed the Military Reconstruction Act ("MRA"). *See* 14 Stat. 428. The MRA divided the former CSA states (except Tennessee) into five military districts. Florida, along with Alabama and Georgia, was made part of the Third Military District under Gen. John Pope.

The MRA set three conditions for re-entry: 1) the former CSA states (now termed "provisional" states) had to adopt new constitutions; 2) the new constitutions had to conform to the U.S. Constitution and be approved by Congress; and, 3) the former CSA states had to ratify the 14th Amendment.

5. 1868 CONSTITUTION

On Apr. 8, 1867, Pope and Col. John Sprague began implementing the MRA by dividing Florida's 39 counties into 19 electoral districts. Although many whites insisted that this arrangement gave blacks an unfair advantage, the pair ignored their complaints.

Campaigning was intense and continued right up to the election (Nov. 14–16, 1867). To ensure that blacks were not turned away, federal troops were stationed at every polling place. Overwhelmingly (14,300 to 203), voters approved holding a new constitutional convention.

Although Democrats had controlled Florida since the state's founding, 43 of the convention's 46 delegates were Republicans. Many were recent arrivals from the North. Viewing them as opportunists, white Floridians labeled them "carpetbaggers." White Floridians who collaborated with them were "scalawags."

Florida's fourth constitutional convention got underway in Tallahassee on Jan. 20, 1868. Because of its racial diversity, the convention was derisively labeled the "black and tan" convention. This was something of a misnomer, as blacks made up just 38% of the convention even though Florida was 49% black.

On the convention's opening day, 29 delegates were in attendance—the rest were still en route. Immediately, two factions emerged: the "mule teamers," who wanted radical change, and the "moderates."

Because most of the delegates who were present were mule teamers, they had no trouble getting their preferred candidate, Daniel Richards, elected convention president. Richards, white and originally from New York, had come to Florida in 1866 as a Republican Party strategist.

As more delegates arrived, the balance of power began to shift. On Feb. 1, Thomas Osborn, a native New Yorker and former Union colonel who had come to Florida in 1865, convinced 20 moderates to join him in setting up a "rump" convention in Monticello, some 25 miles from the capital.

Osborn's departure left 22 delegates in Tallahassee. On Feb. 6, 1868, they sent a draft constitution to Gen. George Meade in Atlanta. A short time earlier, Meade had succeeded Pope as commander of the Third Military District.

In the meantime, Osborn and his followers managed to pick up four more delegates. As a result, they returned to Tallahassee on Feb. 10. Aided by federal troops, they took control of the convention and on Feb. 19 installed Horatio Jenkins as the convention's new president. Jenkins, a Massachusetts native and former Union general, had arrived in Florida in 1865.

With Jenkins in the chair, the convention prepared a second draft constitution, which nine delegates refused to sign and eight initialed "under protest."

After sending it to Meade, the convention adjourned on Feb. 25.

There were three main differences between the two drafts: 1) the method used to choose state and county officers; 2) the loyalty oath to be taken by former CSA members (to regain their voting rights); and, 3) the number of state representatives each county was granted. While the radicals wanted elected officers, a broad loyalty oath, and representation based solely on population, the moderates favored appointed officers (to limit the number of black officeholders), a narrow loyalty oath (to re-enfranchise as many whites as possible), and representation that was based only partially on population (to curb the power of black counties).

In most other respects, the two constitutions were the same. Both gave men over the age of 21 the right to vote regardless of "race, color, nationality, or previous condition [of servitude]"; pledged that the public schools would be open to all students "without distinction or preference"; required "jurors [to] be taken from the registered voters of the respective counties"; dropped the 1865 constitution's prohibition on blacks testifying in court; and promised that "all the inhabitants of the State" would be counted equally in future censuses. In addition, the right to bear arms, which had been omitted from the 1865 constitution to prevent blacks from owning guns, was declared to be a right of "the people."

The most novel provision—never actually used—concerned the Seminoles:

The tribe of Indians located in the southern portion of the State, and known as the Seminole Indians, shall be entitled to one member in each House of the Legislature. . . . The tribe shall be represented only by a member of the same, and in no case by a white man. . . .

The campaign to ratify the constitution (the federal government placed only the moderates' version before the voters) was marked by fraud. Nevertheless, on May 4–6, 1868, it was approved 14,520 to 9,491. By a slightly larger margin, Republican Harrison Reed (a moderate) was elected governor. Originally from Massachusetts, Reed had been sent to Florida in 1863 by the U.S. Treasury Department.

Reed assumed office on June 8, 1868. On the following day, the Florida Legislature approved the 14th Amendment. On July 4, 1868, with the MRA's conditions having been met, Meade officially recognized Florida's return to the Union.

6. 1885 CONSTITUTION

Between 1868 and 1876, Florida was firmly in the hands of pro-black Republicans. In 1876, however, three events occurred that marked the beginning of the end of their rule:

1) In March, the U.S. Supreme Court gutted the 15th Amendment (which had given black men the right to vote) by holding that it did not prohibit "grandfather tests,"

literacy tests, or poll taxes. *See United States v. Reese*, 92 U.S. (2 Otto) 214 (1876).

2) In November, Democrat George Drew narrowly (195 votes) beat Marcellus Stearns, the Republican incumbent, in Florida's gubernatorial race. Although the Democrats had engaged in widespread fraud, the Florida Supreme Court refused to overturn the results. *See State ex rel. Drew v. McLin*, 16 Fla. 17 (1876).

3) Also in November, Democrat Samuel Tilden and Republican Rutherford Hayes squared off in the U.S. presidential election. Although Tilden beat Hayes by 254,235 votes, in Feb. 1877 Florida, Louisiana, and South Carolina agreed to give their 19 Electoral College votes to Hayes in an unwritten deal known as the "Compromise of 1877." This made the final tally 185–184 for Hayes. In exchange, Hayes agreed to remove federal troops from all three states (the only ones still under military occupation). When the last U.S. soldiers left Baton Rouge on Apr. 24, 1877, Reconstruction ended.

By 1884, the Democrats had regained full control of Florida's government. As a result, in Feb. 1885 they ordered a new constitutional convention to be held. *See* 1885 Fla. Laws ch. 3577. To staff it, Floridians went to the polls on May 5, 1885 and elected 108 delegates: 82 Democrats, 23 Republicans, and three Independents. Only seven delegates were black (6.5%), even though blacks made up 47% of Florida's population.

The convention opened in Tallahassee on June 9 and ran until Aug. 3, 1885. As their first order of business, the delegates chose Samuel Pasco to be the convention's president. Pasco was typical of the convention's other Democrats, who, because of their reactionary views, were derisively known as "Bourbon Democrats" (a reference to the Bourbon kings who had been overthrown during the French Revolution but managed to return to power in 1815).

The Democrats wanted three things from the new constitution: a governor with limited powers; cheap state government; and an end to black rights. Thus, as part of their many changes, the delegates:

1)   Created an elected six-person state cabinet, thereby guaranteeing that governors would be forced to wage endless turf battles. Moreover, while governors could serve only one term (after which they had to sit out a term), no such limits were placed on cabinet members.

2)   Eliminated various state offices, including the lieutenant governor; specified how much money legislators could be reimbursed for their travel costs; and left it to the legislature to decide how much the Florida Supreme Court could spend on library books.

3) Authorized poll taxes; banned mixed-race marriages; and required segregated schools.

Along with the constitution, the convention promulgated three ordinances, the first of which provided:

This Constitution shall be submitted to the people of the State of Florida for ratification on the first Tuesday after the first Monday in November, A. D. 1886. . . . [I]n case of its ratification . . . it shall go into effect on the first day of January, A. D. 1887.

On Nov. 2, 1886, the voters approved the new constitution 31,803 to 21,243.

7. 1968 CONSTITUTION

In 1921, the National Municipal League ("NML") released its "Model State Constitution." According to the NML, state constitutions were most effective when they limited themselves to basic and enduring principles (leaving more prosaic matters to statutes). The NML also called for conciseness, flexibility, and readability. Although Florida's 1885 constitution possessed none of these qualities, the NML's report failed to spark any interest in Florida.

The first serious push to update the 1885 constitution came in 1947, when the Florida State Bar Association released a 101-page report titled, "A Proposed Constitution for Florida." Its many changes included banning segregated schools and lowering the voting age to 18.

In a widely-read 1955 law review article, two researchers at the University of Florida also made the case for a new constitution:

> Despite the enormous differences in the economic, social, and governmental composition of the state, the government operates under a Constitution framed in light of the experience of the very attenuated activities of the late nineteenth century. This situation would not have worked any hardship but for the fact that the Constitution contained many provisions designed solely for the period then at hand. The result is the Constitution we know today—a long, frequently amended, and in part unsatisfactory, basic law. . . .

Manning J. Dauer & William C. Havard, "The Florida Constitution of 1885: A Critique," 8 *U. Fla. L. Rev.* 1, 9 (1955).

In the same year that Dauer and Havard's article appeared, Gov. LeRoy Collins persuaded the legislature to create the Florida Constitution Advisory Commission. Using its recommendations as a starting point, in 1957 the legislature passed 14 joint resolutions that collectively proposed a near-total overhaul of the constitution (only the recently-amended judiciary article was left untouched). Each amendment stated that it would be effective only if the voters approved all of them.

In *Rivera-Cruz v. Gray*, 104 So. 2d 501 (Fla. 1958), the Florida Supreme Court struck down all the proposals. According to the court, while the legislature could propose individual amendments, the revision of multiple sections had to come from a constitutional convention. To reverse this result, the constitution was amended in 1964 to allow legislative revisions.

In 1965, the Florida Legislature authorized the creation of a Constitution Revision Commission ("CRC"). In Jan. 1967, the CRC finished its work. All signs therefore pointed to a new constitution being put before the voters by the end of the year. This timetable was delayed, however, by the need to reapportion the legislature following a series of court orders.

The legislature finally took up the CRC's recommendations during a special session that began on June 24, 1968 (its opening had been delayed by the June 6 assassination of Sen. Robert F. Kennedy (D-N.Y.)). On July 3, 1968, the legislature adopted, by votes of 94–16 (house) and 37–9 (senate), three resolutions:

House Joint Resolution 1-2X constituted the entire revised constitution with the exception of Articles V, VI, and VIII. Senate Joint Resolution 4-2X proposed Article VI, relating to suffrage and elections. Senate Joint Resolution 5-2X proposed a new Article VIII, relating to local government. Article V, relating to the judiciary, was carried forward from the Constitution of 1885, as amended.

Reviser's Explanatory Note to the Current Florida Constitution. (The legislature's failure to come to an agreement on Art. V, necessitating its omission, was rectified in 1972. *See* Ch. 15 of this book.)

Following the vote, Rep. Murray Dubin (D-Miami) told a *Miami Herald* reporter: "I think we've launched a rocket into the future." Picking up on this comment, a campaign poster soon appeared showing an arrow leading from a horse-and-buggy to a spaceship under the headline, "A New Constitution Responsive to the Needs of the People."

At the Nov. 5, 1968 general election, the ballot listed H.J.R. 1-2X as Amendment 1; S.J.R. 4-2X as Amendment 2; and S.J.R. 5-2X as Amendment 3. All passed by similar margins: 645,233 to 518,940; 625,980 to 497,752; and 625,347 to 508,962.

Only 16 counties voted for the amendments—the other 51 voted against them. With just a handful of exceptions, the "pro" counties were all located along Florida's highly urbanized eastern coast. Remarkably, every county voted consistently (*i.e.*, it either supported or rejected all three amendments).

The 1968 constitution became effective on Jan. 7, 1969. Since then, it has been amended 134 times. *See* Ch. 23 of this book.

Despite the NML's advice, Florida's current constitution is highly technical, filled with minute detail, and incredibly obtuse. And while its length (64,971 words) pales in comparison to Alabama's (388,882 words—the country's longest), it far exceeds Utah's (8,565 words—the country's shortest). (The average state constitution is 39,000 words. The U.S. constitution runs 7,591 words.)

Links to all 50 state constitutions can be found at https://ballotpedia.org/State_constitution. A link to the U.S. constitution can be found at https://ballotpedia.org/United_States_Constitution. For a helpful guide to state constitutions, see Thomas C. Marks, Jr. & John F. Cooper, *State Constitutional Law in a Nutshell* (2d ed. 2003). For a helpful guide to the U.S. constitution, see Jerome A. Barron & C. Thomas Dienes, *Constitutional Law in a Nutshell* (9th ed. 2017).

D.   PREAMBLE

Except for the 1861 constitution, Florida's constitutions always have begun with a preamble (the 1861 constitution began with the state's secession order). The current preamble—the shortest of the five—reads as follows: "We, the people of the State of Florida, being grateful to Almighty God for our constitutional liberty, in order to secure its benefits, perfect our government, insure domestic tranquility, maintain public order, and guarantee equal civil and political rights to all, do ordain and establish this constitution."

Being introductory in nature, the preamble neither creates rights nor imposes duties. Nevertheless, it does indicate the constitution's origin, purpose, and scope.

E.   DECLARATION OF RIGHTS

Like all its predecessors, the 1968 constitution's first article is the Declaration of Rights (a requirement of the 1787 Northwest Ordinance). The

Florida Supreme Court has explained its importance by writing:

> Primacy of position in our State Constitution is accorded to the Declaration of Rights. It comes first, immediately after the preamble. . . .
>
> It is significant that our Constitution . . . commences by specifying those things which the state government must not do, before specifying certain things that it may do. . . . Thus no department, not even the legislative, has unlimited power under our system of government.

State v. City of Stuart, 120 So. 335, 347 (Fla. 1929) (en banc).

Although the Declaration of Rights is more expansive, there are many parallels between it and the U.S. Constitution's Bill of Rights.

F. INTERPRETING THE FLORIDA CONSTITUTION

Art. X, § 12 contains directions for construing the constitution. None of Florida's previous constitutions have included such a provision.

Regrettably, the definitions contained in paragraphs (a) and (g) are of only minimal help. The same is true of the rules of construction found in paragraphs (b) and (c).

Paragraph (h) states: "Titles and subtitles shall not be used in construction." Thus, the constitution's headings and sub-headings are to be used only as "finding aids." *See, e.g., Tague v. Florida Fish and Wildlife Conservation Commission*, 390 F. Supp. 2d 1195 (M.D. Fla.), *aff'd*, 154 F. App'x 129 (11th Cir. 2005) (rejecting plaintiff's argument that Art. I, § 6, which concerns union membership, guarantees each citizen a job because its sub-title is "right to work").

Paragraph (f) provides: "The terms 'judicial office,' 'justices' and 'judges' shall not include judges of courts established solely for the trial of violations of ordinances." This is a reference to municipal courts, which still existed in 1968 but were eliminated as part of the 1972 revision of Art. V (see Ch. 15 of this book). As such, this paragraph is obsolete.

Lastly, paragraphs (d) and (e) define the number of votes needed to win elections (plurality) and pass legislation (either a majority of those voting or a greater number, depending on the text).

Many recent amendments include their own definition sections. A good example is Art. X, § 30 (adopted 2018), which defines (in paragraph (b)) the term "casino gambling" as well as the words "gaming" and "gambling."

Although the Florida Constitution is not a statute (despite often reading like one), it is construed using standard statutory interpretation techniques:

When reviewing constitutional provisions, this Court "follows principles parallel to those of statutory interpretation." *Zingale v. Powell*, 885 So.2d 277, 282 (Fla.2004). First and foremost, this Court must examine the actual language used in the constitution. *Crist v. Fla. Ass'n of*

Criminal Def. Lawyers, 978 So.2d 134, 140
(Fla.2008); *Fla. Dep't of Revenue v. City of
Gainesville*, 918 So.2d 250, 256 (Fla.2005). "If
that language is clear, unambiguous, and
addresses the matter in issue, then it must be
enforced as written." *Fla. Soc'y of
Ophthalmology v. Fla. Optometric Ass'n*, 489
So.2d 1118, 1119 (Fla.1986). The words of the
constitution "are to be interpreted in their most
usual and obvious meaning, unless the text
suggests that they have been used in a technical
sense." *Wilson v. Crews*, 160 Fla. 169, 34 So.2d
114, 118 (1948) (quoting *City of Jacksonville v.
Glidden Co.*, 124 Fla. 690, 169 So. 216, 217
(1936)). Additionally, this Court "endeavors to
construe a constitutional provision consistent
with the intent of the framers and the voters."
Zingale, 885 So.2d at 282 (quoting *Caribbean
Conservation Corp. v. Fla. Fish & Wildlife
Conservation Comm'n*, 838 So.2d 492, 501
(Fla.2003)). Constitutional provisions "must
never be construed in such manner as to make it
possible for the will of the people to be frustrated
or denied." *Id.* (quoting *Caribbean Conservation*,
838 So.2d at 501).

Lewis v. Leon County, 73 So. 3d 151, 153–54 (Fla.
2011). *See also International Association of
Firefighters Local S-20 v. State*, 257 So. 3d 364 (Fla.
2018) (Lewis, J., dissenting) (if two provisions
conflict, the one later in time controls); *Brinkmann v.
Francois*, 184 So. 3d 504 (Fla. 2016) (if a provision is
ambiguous, its drafting history may be consulted);
Graham v. Haridopolos, 108 So. 3d 597 (Fla. 2013) (if

multiple provisions address the same subject, they should be read in pari materia—*i.e.*, in a consistent manner); *Lawnwood Medical Center, Inc. v. Seeger*, 990 So. 2d 503 (Fla. 2008) (all words must be given effect); *Bush v. Holmes*, 919 So. 2d 392 (Fla. 2006) (recognizing the applicability of the principle expressio unius est exclusio alterius—"the expression of one thing implies the exclusion of another").

Because interpreting a constitutional provision involves a question of law, appellate courts use the de novo standard of review. *See JBK Associates, Inc. v. Sill Bros., Inc.*, 191 So. 3d 879 (Fla. 2016).

G. RELATIONSHIP BETWEEN THE U.S. CONSTITUTION AND THE FLORIDA CONSTITUTION

As noted at the outset of this chapter, the Florida Constitution places limits on the power of the state government. In contrast, the U.S. Constitution gives certain limited ("enumerated") powers to the federal government. As the Florida Supreme Court observed in *Cotton v. County Commissioners of Leon County*, 6 Fla. 610, 619 (1856): "Whilst the Federal Constitution contains only specific grants of powers, coupled with a general reservation, the State constitution makes a general grant of all the political power of the people, restricted only by specific reservations."

Due to the Supremacy Clause of the U.S. Constitution (Art. VI, cl. 2), the U.S. Constitution (and, by extension, federal law) stands above the

Florida Constitution. Thus, in any conflict between the two, the latter must give way. *See Gray v. Winthrop*, 156 So. 270 (Fla. 1934) (en banc).

In addition to resolving interstitial conflicts, the U.S. Constitution, through a process known as "incorporation," now also regulates how states treat their citizens by requiring them to conform their behavior to the Bill of Rights.

At one time, the U.S. Supreme Court rejected incorporation, reasoning that the Bill of Rights applied only to the federal government. *See, e.g., The Slaughter-House Cases*, 83 U.S. (16 Wall.) 36 (1873). The adoption of the 14th Amendment (1868), which contains two clauses that explicitly mention state governments (the "due process" clause and the "privileges or immunities" clause, both found in § 1) eventually caused the Court to change its mind. *See Gitlow v. New York*, 268 U.S. 652 (1925).

Today, nearly the entire Bill of Rights has been incorporated—the only exceptions are the Third Amendment (quartering of soldiers); Fifth Amendment (grand juries); Sixth Amendment (jurors' residences); and Seventh Amendment (civil jury trials).

In two instances, the Florida Constitution expressly "links" itself to the U.S. Constitution. Thus, decisions under Art. I, § 12 (searches and seizures) must conform to the Fourth Amendment, see, e.g., *State v. Markus*, 211 So. 3d 894 (Fla.), *reh'g denied*, 2017 WL 944231 (Fla. 2017), while decisions under Art. I, § 17 (death penalty) must conform to the

Eighth Amendment. *See, e.g., Valle v. State*, 70 So. 3d 530 (Fla.), *cert. denied*, 564 U.S. 1067 (2011). For a further discussion, see Ch. 7 of this book.

The U.S. Supreme Court has recognized that state courts possess special expertise when it comes to interpreting and applying their own constitutions. One consequence of this fact is that the Court will not review a final decision of a state court, notwithstanding the presence of a federal question, if the state court based its decision on state law and that law is both independent of the federal issues and adequate to support the judgment. This is known as the "adequate and independent state grounds" doctrine. *See PruneYard Shopping Center v. Robins*, 447 U.S. 74 (1980).

H. THE FLORIDA BAR EXAM AND THE FLORIDA CONSTITUTION

For many years, the Florida Bar Exam ("FBE") had to include an essay question on Florida Constitutional Law ("FCL"). In 1988, the Florida Supreme Court eliminated this requirement. *See In re Florida Board of Bar Examiners*, 524 So. 2d 643 (Fla. 1988). The court also authorized the bar examiners to test FCL in conjunction with other subjects.

Between 1989 and 2019, the FBE was given 62 times. Of these tests, 49 included a FCL question, with the most-tested sections being equal protection (Art. I, § 2), search and seizure (Art. I, § 12), and homestead protection (Art. X, § 4). To view the most recent questions, see the Florida Board of Bar

Examiners' web site: https://www.floridabarexam. org (under "Study Guides").

Because it is regularly tested on the bar exam, every Florida law school offers either a 2- or 3-credit elective course on the Florida Constitution. For many years, Cumberland law school in Alabama also had such a course (to accommodate students planning to practice in Florida).

I.   TRIBAL CONSTITUTIONS

Both of Florida's federally-recognized Indian tribes have their own constitutions. The Miccosukees' (ratified 1962) is available at http://www.indigenous people.net/micconst.htm. The Seminoles' (ratified 1957) is available at https://www.loc.gov/law/help/ american-indian-consts/PDF/58060124.pdf.

J.   SELECTED BIBLIOGRAPHY

1.   ARTICLES

Dauer, Manning J. & William C. Havard, "The Florida Constitution of 1885: A Critique," 8 *University of Florida Law Review* 1 (1955)

Gudridge, Patrick O., "Complexity and Contradiction in Florida Constitutional Law," 64 *University of Miami Law Review* 879 (2010)

Hoskins, F.W., "The St. Joseph Convention: The Making of Florida's First Constitution," 16 *Florida Historical Quarterly* 33 (July 1937) (Part I), 16:97 (Oct. 1937) (Part II), 16:242 (Apr. 1938) (Part III), 17:125 (Oct. 1938) (Part IV)

2.   CASEBOOKS

Alloway, Clifford C., *Florida Constitutional Law* (D & S Publishers, 3d ed. 1983)

Cooper, John F. & others, *Florida Constitutional Law: Cases and Materials* (Carolina Academic Press, 5th ed. 2013)

McGinley, Patrick John, *Analyzing Florida's Constitution* (Carolina Academic Press, 2020)

3.   MONOGRAPHS

Adkins, Mary E., *Making Modern Florida: How the Spirit of Reform Shaped a New State Constitution* (University Press of Florida, 2016)

Mirow, M.C., *Florida's First Constitution: The Constitution of Cádiz—Introduction, Translation, and Text* (Carolina Academic Press, 2012)

The Florida Bar, *Constitutional Litigation in Florida* (1973)

4.   RESEARCH AIDS

Busharis, Barbara J. & others, *Florida Legal Research* (Carolina Academic Press, 4th ed. 2014)

Gustafson, Jill & others, "Constitutional Law," 10–10A *Florida Jurisprudence 2d* (West-Thomson Reuters, 2016)

West's Florida Statutes Annotated, Volumes 25–26A (various dates)

5.   SURVEYS

Alloway, Clifford C., in *University of Miami Law Review*, at 8:158 (1954), 10:143 (1956), 12:288 (1958), 14:501 (1960), 16:685 (1962) (with Richard B. Knight)—continued by Barry N. Semet, 18:888 (1964)

Hawkins, David C., in *Nova Law Review*, at 14:693 (1990), 15:1049 (1991), 16:167 (1991)

Levinson, L. Harold, in *University of Miami Law Review*, at 28:551 (1974), 30:277 (1976) (with Patricia Ireland)

6.   SYMPOSIA

"Florida's 2017–2018 Constitution Revision: It's Your Turn to Decide," 92 *Florida Bar Journal* 10 (Sept./ Oct. 2018)

"Issues of Constitutional Significance in Twenty-First Century Florida," 18 *Florida Coastal Law Review* 1 (2016)

"Twenty-Five Years and Counting: A Symposium on the Florida Constitution of 1968," 18 *Nova Law Review* 715 (1994)

7.   TREATISES

D'Alemberte, Talbot, *The Florida State Constitution* (Oxford University Press, 2d ed. 2016)

Morris, Allen, *The Florida Handbook* (Peninsular Books, 1947–2012), updated version available at https://www.myfloridahouse.gov/contentViewer.

aspx?Category=PublicGuide&File=FloridaHand
book.html

Vallandingham, Christopher A., "Tracking Down Legal Sources on Prestatehood Florida," in 1 *Prestatehood Legal Materials: A Fifty-State Research Guide, Including New York City and the District of Columbia* 249 (Michael Chiorazzi & Marguerite Most eds., Haworth Information Press, 2005)

8.   WEB SITES

Florida State University, "State Constitutional Law: Florida," at https://guides.law.fsu.edu/stateconlaw

Nova Southeastern University, "Florida Legal Research: State Constitution," at https://nsufl.lib guides.com/c.php?g=112218&p=724868

Stetson University, "Florida Constitutional Law," at https://www.stetson.edu/law/library/fl-constitutional-law.php

9.   MISCELLANEOUS WORKS

Colburn, David R. & Lance Dehaven-Smith, *Government in the Sunshine State: Florida Since Statehood* (University Press of Florida, 1999)

MacManus, Susan A. & others, *Politics in Florida* (Florida Institute of Government, 5th ed. 2019)

The History of Florida (Michael Gannon ed., University Press of Florida, 2013)

CHAPTER 2
POLITICAL STRUCTURE

A. OVERVIEW

Political scientists define a "state" as an entity that exerts control over a defined place and people, has a common language and heritage, and is readily identifiable through its use of distinctive marks and symbols. In accordance with this understanding, Art. II of the Florida Constitution sets outs the basic framework of Florida's government. It is augmented by several additional sections that appear, haphazardly, elsewhere in the constitution.

B. BORDERS

Florida's 1838 constitution provided, "The jurisdiction of the State of Florida shall extend over the Territories of East and West Florida." This simple formula was retained in the 1861 constitution. Since the 1865 constitution, Florida has described its borders in far more precise terms. *See also* Fla. Stat. §§ 6.08 and 6.081 (Florida-Alabama boundary) and 6.09 (Florida-Georgia boundary).

The current constitution sets out the state's borders in Art. II, § 1. Oddly, paragraph (a) makes the Gulf Stream the state's eastern border: "[T]hence due east to the edge of the Gulf Stream or a distance of three geographic miles whichever is the greater distance." The Gulf Stream is an undulating ocean current that begins in the Gulf of Mexico and stretches to Canada before crossing over to Europe.

As a result, Florida's eastern border, although never less than three miles, can on any given day extend as far as 70 miles.

In *Benson v. Norwegian Cruise Line Ltd.*, 859 So. 2d 1213 (Fla. 3d Dist. Ct. App. 2003), *appeal dismissed*, 885 So. 2d 388 (Fla. 2004), a shipboard physician was sued for malpractice. The doctor moved for dismissal because the vessel had been at sea. The trial court granted her motion but was reversed on appeal. At the time of the incident, the ship was 11.7 miles east of Florida. The Gulf Stream that day was 14 miles off the state's coast. As such, the appellate court ruled that the doctor had been legally present in Florida.

Paragraph (a) further provides that the state's western border extends three marine leagues (10.4 miles) from the coast. This provision has been upheld twice by the U.S. Supreme Court. *See United States v. Louisiana*, 363 U.S. 1, *reh'g denied*, 364 U.S. 856 (1960); *Skiriotes v. State of Florida*, 313 U.S. 69, *reh'g denied*, 313 U.S. 599 (1941). In both cases, the Court relied on the fact that this border was included in the state's 1868 constitution, which Congress approved when it readmitted Florida following the Civil War.

Art. II, § 1(b), added in 1962, further complicates the subject. It provides: "The coastal boundaries may be extended by statute to the limits permitted by the laws of the United States or international law." This is the only section of the constitution that mentions international law.

Paragraph (b) has not been directly construed by the courts. However, in *State v. Stepansky*, 761 So. 2d 1027 (Fla.), *cert. denied*, 531 U.S. 959 (2000), the Florida Supreme Court held that the defendant, who had been charged with burglary and sexual assault while on a foreign-flagged cruise ship located 100 miles off the coast of Florida, could be prosecuted under Fla. Stat. § 910.006(3)(d). This law gives Florida courts criminal jurisdiction over acts that occur on a voyage on which more than half the paying passengers embark and disembark from a Florida port. In enacting it, the Florida Legislature specifically directed that it be applied in accordance with federal and international law. *See* Fla. Stat. § 910.006(5)(a). When applicable, the statute is strictly construed. *See Batiz v. State*, 2019 WL 5485560 (Fla. 5th Dist. Ct. App. 2019).

C.   LANGUAGE

Art. II, § 9 designates English as Florida's official language. It was adopted in 1988 during a period when many states, alarmed by rising immigration, took similar steps.

To date, 32 states (including Florida) have made English their official language. Because English-only requirements are highly perniciousness, state and local governments have tended to ignore them. When challenged in court, such provisions have been struck down on either equal protection or free speech grounds. *See, e.g., Ruiz v. Hull*, 957 P.2d 984 (Ariz. 1998), *cert. denied sub nom. Arizonans for Official English v. Arizona*, 525 U.S. 1093 (1999).

D. SYMBOLS

Art. II, § 4 requires the state to have both a flag and a seal, but does not prescribe the design of either. Previous constitutions had done so, making changes difficult. The Florida Department of State is the custodian of both the flag and the seal. *See* Fla. Stat. §§ 15.02 and 15.03(2)(a).

Fla. Stat. ch. 15 designates many other state symbols, including a state animal (panther), beverage (orange juice), pie (key lime), reptile (alligator), and song (Stephen Foster's 1851 "Old Folks at Home," edited in recent years to omit its racist lyrics). Additionally, H.C.R. 5514 (1970) makes "Sunshine State" Florida's official nickname.

1. FLAG

Fla. Stat. § 15.012 specifies that the state flag shall consist of a white field supporting a diagonal red cross ("saltire") and the state seal. Rules for displaying the flag appear in Fla. Stat. ch. 256.

Five different national flags have flown over Florida: Confederate States of America ("CSA"), France, Great Britain, Spain, and the United States. Other flags popularly associated with Florida include those of the Miccosukee and Seminole Indian tribes; the Prisoner of War-Missing in Action flag (see Fla. Stat. §§ 256.12–256.14); the tongue-in-cheek "Conch Republic" flag of Key West; and the "diver down" scuba flag (see Fla. Stat. § 327.331(1)(c)).

Throughout Spain's second occupation of Florida, various groups seeking independence had their own flags. The best known was the "Bonnie Blue Flag," which was popular in west Florida.

From 1821 to 1861, Florida did not have an official flag and therefore typically displayed the U.S. flag. From 1861 to 1865, the state used a modified version of the CSA's national flag (although how often it flew is subject to debate).

The end of the Civil War caused Floridians to view the U.S. flag as a "conqueror's" flag. As a result, Florida's 1868 constitution adopted the current flag, but without the saltire. In 1900, a constitutional amendment added the saltire.

The suggestion to add the saltire arose because on windless days, the flag would hang limp, making it look like a flag of surrender. Some believe that a red saltire was chosen because at one time, Spain's flag had been the Cross of Burgundy, which consisted of a white field and a serrated red saltire. Others, however, believe that the saltire was meant to subtly recall the blue saltire on the CSA's battle flag. As a result, there have been periodic calls to redesign Florida's flag. Another reason for such calls is that Florida's flag is virtually indistinguishable from Alabama's, which consists of a red saltire on a white field.

2.   SEAL

Fla. Stat. § 15.03(1) provides that the state seal shall include: a Seminole woman scattering flowers, two sabal palmetto palm trees (the state's official tree since 1953, see Fla. Stat. § 15.031), a steamboat, and sun rays. Encircling the seal are the words "Great Seal of the State of Florida" and "In God We Trust." The latter is the state's official motto, having been adopted in 2006. *See* Fla. Stat. § 15.0301. (In 1956, Congress adopted "In God We Trust" as the official motto of the United States. *See* 36 U.S.C. § 302.)

The seal was approved in 1868. Thereafter, it was revised repeatedly to correct various errors. The background, for example, included mountains, even though Florida is flat. The clothing worn by the woman was that of a Great Plains Indian, while her headdress was that of a male. Both the vegetation and the vessel were non-indigenous. These mistakes have given rise to the claim, probably apocryphal, that the original seal was designed for a Western state and, after being rejected by it, was purchased by Florida because the seal maker was willing to sell it at a bargain price.

The seal assumed its present appearance in 1985. Misuse of it is a misdemeanor. *See* Fla. Stat. 15.03(3).

E. OPERATIONS

1.   BRANCHES

Art. II, § 3 divides Florida's government into three branches: legislative, executive, and judicial. The Florida Supreme Court has explained that this arrangement is intended to prevent the excessive concentration of power, see *In re Advisory Opinion to Governor*, 276 So. 2d 25 (Fla. 1973), and promote careful policy deliberation. *See Petition of Florida*

Bar, 61 So. 2d 646 (Fla. 1952). It also, of course, mirrors the U.S. Constitution.

Each branch plays a specific role: the legislature makes the laws, the executive carries out the laws, and the judiciary interprets the laws. As a result, "[n]o person belonging to one branch" is permitted to "exercise any powers appertaining to either of the other branches" except when expressly permitted to do so by the constitution. *See Abdool v. Bondi*, 141 So. 3d 529 (Fla. 2014); *Florida Motor Lines v. Railroad Commissioners*, 129 So. 876 (Fla. 1930) (en banc).

The courts have recognized, however, that not every power falls within the purview of a single branch. *See Sullivan v. Askew*, 348 So. 2d 312 (Fla.), *cert. denied*, 434 U.S. 878 (1977). Thus, for example, in *Simms v. State, Department of Health & Rehabilitative Services*, 641 So. 2d 957 (Fla. 3d Dist. Ct. App.), *review denied*, 649 So. 2d 870 (Fla. 1994), the power to protect children was held to be a shared one.

All of Florida's constitutions have included similar language, although the 1868 constitution was the first to combine the principles of separation and exclusivity into a single section. The 1968 constitution is the first to use the word "branches" (rather than "departments").

Because each branch has its own area of responsibility, it is not permitted to "encroach" on another branch. However, in appropriate circumstances, a branch can "delegate" to another branch.

Encroachment occurs when one branch usurps the power of another branch. Prominent examples include: *Florida House of Representatives v. Crist*, 999 So. 2d 601 (Fla. 2008), *cert. denied sub nom. Seminole Tribe of Florida v. Florida House of Representatives*, 555 U.S. 1212 (2009) (governor's negotiation of tribal gambling compact encroached legislature's power to set gambling policy); *Bush v. Schiavo*, 885 So. 2d 321 (Fla. 2004), *cert. denied*, 543 U.S. 1121 (2005) (law authorizing governor to resolve intra-family dispute over comatose patient encroached judiciary's power to decide lawsuits); *Chiles v. Children A, B, C, D, E, and F*, 589 So. 2d 260 (Fla. 1991) (governor's attempt to balance budget encroached legislature's power to establish spending priorities). *See also In re Florida Board of Bar Examiners*, 353 So. 2d 98 (Fla. 1977) (legislature could not make testing accommodation rules for bar examinations); *In re Advisory Opinion to the Governor*, 213 So. 2d 716 (Fla. 1968) (governor had no power to remove a judge).

Delegation, on the other hands, occurs when one branch attempts to give its power to another branch. Normally, this is not permitted. *See Sims v. State*, 444 So. 2d 922 (Fla. 1983), *cert. denied*, 467 U.S. 1246 (1984). However, a proper delegation will be upheld. To be proper, a delegation must be limited and contain clear guidelines. *See, e.g., Warner Cable Communications, Inc. v. City of Niceville*, 911 F.2d 634 (11th Cir.), *reh'g denied*, 920 F.2d 13 (11th Cir. 1990), *cert. denied*, 501 U.S. 1222 (1991); *Southern Alliance for Clean Energy v. Graham*, 113 So. 3d 742 (Fla. 2013).

In certain instances, the constitution expressly authorizes one branch to perform acts normally reserved to a different branch. Thus, for example, the legislature, not the judiciary, admits and expels representatives and senators (Art. III, §§ 2 and 4(d)); the legislature, not the judiciary, brings and tries impeachments (Art. III, § 17); the legislature, not the executive, decides whether to grant clemency in treason cases (Art. IV, § 8(b)); and in the event of a "revenue shortfall," the executive and the judiciary, not the legislature, decide what to cut from their respective budgets (Art. IV, § 13).

Likewise, the governor can call the legislature into a special session (Art. III, § 3(c)(1)); the governor can adjourn the legislature in the event of a deadlock (Art. III, § 3(f)); the governor can veto the legislature's enactments and budget appropriations (Art. III, § 8); the judiciary can reapportion the state if the legislature fails to do so, or does so improperly (Art. III, § 16(f)); the governor presides over impeachment trials when the defendant is the chief justice (Art. III, § 17(c)); and the legislature can repeal rules adopted by the judiciary (Art. V, § 2(a)).

In addition to the three branches, the constitution creates six independent commissions: Florida Commission on Ethics (Art. II, § 8(f)); Florida Fish and Wildlife Conservation Commission (Art. IV, § 9); Judicial Nominating Commission (Art. V, § 11(d)); Judicial Qualifications Commission (Art. V, § 12(a)); Constitution Revision Commission (Art. XI, § 2(a)); and the Taxation and Budget Reform Commission (Art. XI, § 6(a)). It also authorizes, but does not mandate, creation of a seventh commission dealing with parole and probation (Art. IV, § 8(c)). As explained in Ch. 7 of this book, since 2014 this entity has been known as the Florida Commission on Offender Review.

2. CAPITAL

Art. II, § 2 directs:

> The seat of government shall be the City of Tallahassee, in Leon County, where the offices of the governor, lieutenant governor, cabinet members and the supreme court shall be maintained and the sessions of the legislature shall be held; provided that, in time of invasion or grave emergency, the governor by proclamation may for the period of the emergency transfer the seat of government to another place.

Under both the British and the Spanish, Florida had two capitals: St. Augustine (in East Florida) and Pensacola (in West Florida). When Florida became a single U.S. territory in 1821, the impracticality of this arrangement became obvious. As a result, Gov. William DuVal appointed Dr. William Simmons of St. Augustine and John Williams of Pensacola to select a new site.

In 1823, the pair chose Tallahassee, a former Indian village located roughly halfway between the two cities. In the 1838 constitution, it was agreed that Tallahassee would serve as Florida's capital during the first five years of statehood (1845–50).

Thereafter, the legislature would be permitted to move the capital but had to make a final decision within 10 years of statehood (*i.e.*, by 1855). Prior to this deadline, a referendum (discussed below) was held in which the public voted to keep the capital in Tallahassee.

The 1861 constitution did not mention Tallahassee, referring only to "the seat of government." The 1865 constitution again expressly made Tallahassee the capital "until otherwise provided for by the action of a Convention of the people of the State." The 1868 constitution recognized Tallahassee as the capital "until otherwise located by a majority vote of the Legislature, and by a majority vote of the people." The 1885 constitution declared Tallahassee to be the capital and said nothing about moving it.

The requirement that the governor, cabinet, and supreme court have their offices in the capital first appeared in the 1868 constitution. The legislature always has been required to hold its sessions in the capital.

The governor's power to temporarily transfer the capital—to date never used—has been a part of every constitution, although the triggers have changed from "enemy or disease" (1838, 1861, 1865) to "invasion or violent epidemics" (1868, 1885) to "invasion or grave emergency" (1968). The governor's power to temporarily transfer the capital is further spelled out in Fla. Stat. § 22.15(1).

As Florida's population has grown, Tallahassee has become increasingly inaccessible. It now takes 86% of Florida's citizens more than three hours to drive to Tallahassee. A car ride from Miami, where 25% of the state's population lives, requires seven hours.

Because of the state's changing demographics, efforts periodically have been made to move the capital to a more central location. Voters have twice rejected the idea: in 1854 (46%–54%) and 1900 (47%–53%) (the 1854 ballot simply asked if the capital should be moved; the 1900 ballot gave voters three alternatives: Jacksonville, Ocala, and St. Augustine). Failed legislative attempts include: 1870 (proposing Jacksonville), 1881 (Gainesville) (passed but vetoed by Gov. William Bloxham), 1883 (Palatka), 1921 (Orlando), 1967 (Orlando), and 2018–19 (Orlando). Since 1900, the major stumbling block has been the cost of relocation (currently estimated to be at least $5 billion).

The 1967 effort to move the capital to Orlando was led by Sen. Lee Weissenborn (D-Miami). Alarmed that it might succeed, north Florida legislators authorized the building of a new capitol building that would be so massive, and so expensive, that no one ever again would propose relocating the capital. The result was the "New Capitol," a 22-story tower that opened in 1977 and cost $43 million to build (see https://www.floridacapitol.myflorida.com/). In its shadow sits the "Old Capitol," which now serves as a museum (see http://www.flhistoriccapitol.gov/). Inside the New Capitol is a bronze marker that reads:

"This plaque is dedicated to Senator Lee Weissenborn, whose valiant effort to move the Capitol to Orlando was the prime motivation for construction of this building."

Due to Tallahassee's inconvenient location, the Florida Legislature in 2019 included in the state budget a provision allowing Lt. Gov. Jeanette Núñez to have a personal office in Miami (her home district), receive "subsistence pay" when in Tallahassee, and be reimbursed for the cost of travelling to and from capital. *See* Fla. Stat. § 112.061(4)(d). It also passed a law allowing supreme court justices to work remotely. *See* Fla. Stat. § 25.025.

A common law principle known as the "home venue privilege" allows the state, its agencies, and its subdivisions to require that they be sued where they have their principal office, which almost always is Tallahassee. In *Smith v. Williams*, 35 So. 2d 844 (Fla. 1948) (Div. A), the Florida Supreme Court set out the reasons for the privilege:

[I]n order to promote orderly, efficient, and economical government, controversies involving the proper interpretation to be given rules and regulations promulgated by state agencies ought to be concentrated at the seat of state government where such state agencies are located, where such rules and regulations are promulgated, and where such suits can be defended at a minimum expenditure of effort and public funds. Such concentration of litigation manifestly makes for uniformity of interpretation of rules and regulations promulgated by such state instrumentalities and prevents conflicting judicial rulings in different jurisdictions[.]

Id. at 847.

In *Bush v. Florida*, 945 So. 2d 1207, 1212 (Fla. 2006), the court further observed: "Absent waiver or application of an identified exception, the home venue privilege appears to be an absolute right." As a result, the bulk of Florida's constitutional litigation is heard by the Second Judicial Circuit Court and the First District Court of Appeal, both of which are in Tallahassee.

3.   PERSONNEL

(a) Assumption of Office

Art. II, § 5(b) requires state and county officers to take the following oath before assuming office:

I do solemnly swear (or affirm) that I will support, protect, and defend the Constitution and Government of the United States and of the State of Florida; that I am duly qualified to hold office under the Constitution of the state; and that I will well and faithfully perform the duties of (title of office) on which I am now about to enter. So help me God.

Every one of Florida's constitutions has contained an oath requirement. Because of the "de facto officer" doctrine, however, a failure to take the oath will not invalidate an officer's acts. *See, e.g., The Florida Bar v. Sibley*, 995 So. 2d 346 (Fla. 2008), *cert. denied*, 555 U.S. 1188, *reh'g denied*, 556 U.S. 1204 (2009).

Art. II, § 5(b) also requires state and county officers to be bonded. Such bonds protect the government in case the officer fails to faithfully discharge his or her duties. The premiums for such bonds are paid by the government. *See* Fla. Stat. § 113.07(3).

Once an officer has taken the oath and provided the necessary bond, he or she "continue[s] in office until a successor qualifies." *See Gray v. Bryant*, 125 So. 2d 846 (Fla. 1960); *Tappy v. State ex rel. Byington*, 82 So. 2d 161 (Fla. 1955) (en banc).

(b) Dual Office-Holding

Art. II, § 5(a) bars an individual from holding two government offices at the same time. This puts into practice the adage that "a person cannot serve two masters." *See Gryzik v. State*, 380 So. 2d 1102 (Fla. 1st Dist. Ct. App.), *review denied*, 388 So. 2d 1113 (Fla. 1980). Such language has appeared in all of Florida's constitutions.

The prohibition on dual office-holding is broad. It applies to all "offices of emolument" created by foreign governments, the federal government, and other states. In addition, a state official cannot simultaneously hold a county or municipal office (and vice-versa).

The word "emolument" means anything of value, including fees, rewards, and stipends. In *Vinales v. State*, 394 So. 2d 993 (Fla. 1981), the Florida

Supreme Court found no violation where two city police officers were hired as temporary state investigators because they did not receive any additional compensation for their services.

Despite its general ban on dual office-holding, § 5(a) permits a government official to also be "a notary public or military officer . . . [or] a member of a constitution revision commission, taxation and budget reform commission, constitutional convention, or statutory body having only advisory powers." The Taxation and Budget Reform Commission exception was added in 1988.

For a further look at the rules regarding dual office-holding in Florida, see http://myfloridalegal. com/webfiles.nsf/WF/MNOS-AYKKHJ/$file/Dual OfficeHoldingPamphlet.pdf (informational pamphlet prepared by the Florida attorney general's office).

Other states have their own dual office-holding rules. *See* http://www.ncsl.org/research/ethics/ restrictions-on-holding-concurrent-office.aspx. The U.S. Constitution also has a dual office-holding provision. *See* Art. I, § 9, cl. 8.

Under Fla. Stat. § 99.012(3)(a), popularly known as the "Resign-to-Run Law," an official cannot "qualify as a candidate for another state, district, county, or municipal public office if the terms or any part thereof run concurrently with each other without resigning from the office he or she presently holds." The law is inapplicable to federal officeholders as well as to state officeholders running for federal office "if the term of the office that he or she presently holds is scheduled to expire and be filled by election in the same primary and general election period as the federal office he or she is seeking." Fla. Stat. § 99.012(8). Nationally, only five states (including Florida) have resign-to-run laws, which are designed to keep politicians from dividing their time between their official duties and their personal advancement. *See Holley v. Adams*, 238 So. 2d 401 (Fla. 1970).

(c) Incidents of Office

i. *Duties*

Art. II, § 5(c) provides in part: "The powers [and] duties . . . of state and county officers shall be fixed by law." While this provision gives the legislature considerable latitude, there are some limits: "[T]he legislature may impose additional powers and duties on both constitutional and statutory officers so long as such duties are not inconsistent with their duties imposed by the Constitution." *State ex rel. Watson v. Caldwell*, 23 So. 2d 855, 856 (Fla. 1945) (en banc).

When the legislature directs a state or county officer to do something, it also implicitly grants him or her any powers needed to accomplish the task. *See, e.g., Knight v. Chief Judge of Florida's Twelfth Judicial Circuit*, 235 So. 3d 996 (Fla. 2d Dist. Ct. App. 2017); *Brock v. Board of County Commissioners of Collier County*, 21 So. 3d 844 (Fla. 2d Dist. Ct. App. 2009), *review granted*, 26 So. 3d 581 (Fla.), *review dismissed*, 48 So. 3d 810 (Fla. 2010).

ii. Salaries

Art. II, § 5(c) further provides that the "compensation and method of payment of state and county officers shall be fixed by law." In *Askew v. Green, Simmons, Green and Hightower, P.A.*, 348 So. 2d 1245 (Fla. 1st Dist. Ct. App. 1977), *cert. denied*, 366 So. 2d 879 (Fla. 1978), the court held that this language did not prohibit a county from covering its officers' legal expenses.

(d) Ethics

Art. II, § 8 declares: "A public office is a public trust. The people shall have the right to secure and sustain that trust against abuse." While all states have "clean government" laws, Florida is the only one that has put the subject into its constitution.

Sec. 8 was added in 1976 after Gov. Reubin Askew led the state's first successful citizens' initiative petition drive. Askew acted after he repeatedly failed to convince the legislature to strengthen Florida's anti-corruption laws. *See Weber v. Smathers*, 338 So. 2d 819 (Fla. 1976).

Sec. 8 has been amended twice. In 1998, Art. III, § 18 was repealed. As a result, its requirement that the legislature promulgate a code of ethics for all state employees and non-judicial officers was moved to Art. II, § 8(g). In 2018, the lobbying rules for former officials were toughened. *See* Art. II, § 8(e).

Sec. 8 can be summarized as follows:

1) Paragraph (a) requires all elected constitutional officers and candidates to publicly disclose their financial interests. The legislature is authorized to extend this requirement to other public officers, candidates, and employees. Whether the use of a blind trust violates this provision remains an open question. *See Apthorp v. Detzner*, 162 So. 3d 236 (Fla. 1st Dist. Ct. App.), *review denied*, 171 So. 3d 113 (Fla. 2015).

2) Paragraph (b) requires all elected constitutional officers and candidates to publicly disclose their campaign finances. The legislature is permitted to extend this requirement to other public officers, candidates, and employees.

3) Paragraph (c) requires all public officers and employees to disgorge the "financial benefits" they receive by breaching the public's trust. The person or entity who induces the breach also is liable. It has been held that this paragraph does not create a private cause of action. *See St. John Medical Plans, Inc. v. Gutman*, 721 So. 2d 717 (Fla. 1998).

4) Paragraph (d) forfeits the pension of any public officer or employee who is convicted of a felony involving the public's trust. No distinction is made between state

convictions and federal convictions. *See Jenne v. State, Department of Management Services, Division of Retirement*, 36 So. 3d 738 (Fla. 1st Dist. Ct. App.), *review denied*, 46 So. 3d 566 (Fla. 2010). A plea of "no contest" is treated the same as a conviction. *See Brock v. Department of Management Services, Division of Retirement*, 98 So. 3d 771 (Fla. 4th Dist. Ct. App. 2012).

5) As explained above, paragraph (e) places lobbying restrictions on legislators and statewide elected officials. The legislature can extend these restrictions to public officers and employees not specifically covered by these paragraphs. Appearing before a court is not considered lobbying. *See Myers v. Hawkins*, 362 So. 2d 926 (Fla. 1978).

6) Paragraph (f) creates an independent commission "to conduct investigations and make public reports on all complaints concerning breach of public trust by public officers or employees not within the jurisdiction of the judicial qualifications commission." Pursuant to paragraph (i)(3), the commission's formal name is the Florida Commission on Ethics ("FCE") (http://www.ethics.state.fl.us/).

7) As explained above, paragraph (g) requires the legislature to promulgate a code of ethics "for all state employees and nonjudicial officers prohibiting conflict[s]

between public duty and private interests."
The legislature has complied with this
directive. *See* Fla. Stat. §§ 112.311–
112.3261.

8)   Paragraph (h) allows the legislature to
     require additional public disclosures and
     impose additional prohibitions.

9)   Lastly, paragraph (i) makes July 1 the
     annual deadline for submitting net worth
     statements to the FCE. Such statements
     must include a copy of the filer's most
     recent federal tax return or a "sworn
     statement which identifies each separate
     source and amount of income which exceeds
     $1,000." The July 1 deadline applies to both
     office holders and office seekers. *See Plante
     v. Smathers*, 372 So. 2d 933 (Fla. 1979). A
     failure to file is not grounds for keeping a
     candidate off the ballot. *See Norman v.
     Ambler*, 46 So. 3d 178 (Fla. 1st Dist. Ct.
     App. 2010).

In 2018, nearly 39,000 persons were required to
file reports with the FCE. In addition to tracking
these reports and levying late fines on those who
missed the July 1 deadline, the FCE received 211
complaints of improper behavior. Municipal officers
and employees accounted for 45.9% of the complaints,
followed by county officers and employees (15.2%),
state officers and employees (14.2%), district officers
and employees (13.8%), and candidates (10.9%).
Ninety-six of the complaints were ordered to
investigation, with the most common allegations

being misuse of position (47) and disclosure violations (39). *See* http://www.ethics.state.fl.us/Documents/Publications/2018%20Annual%20Report.pdf?cp=2019125 (FCE 2018 annual report).

Since its adoption, § 8 has been the subject of various court challenges:

1) In *Plante v. Gonzalez*, 575 F.2d 1119 (5th Cir.), *reh'g denied*, 580 F.2d 1052 (5th Cir. 1978), *cert. denied*, 439 U.S. 1129 (1979), for example, five state senators argued that the duty to file disclosure reports violated their privacy rights. In rejecting this contention, the Fifth Circuit held that the public's "right to know" outweighed the senators' "right not to be known."

2) In *Florida Commission on Ethics v. Plante*, 369 So. 2d 332 (Fla. 1979), the Florida Supreme Court held that the FCE can investigate legislators, notwithstanding the fact that Art. III, § 4(d) gives the legislature the sole power to punish its members.

3) In *Childers v. State, Department of Management Services, Division of Retirement*, 989 So. 2d 716 (Fla. 4th Dist. Ct. App. 2008), a county commissioner was stripped of his pension benefits after being found guilty of taking bribes. To get them back, he claimed that § 8(d) violated the U.S. Constitution's provisions on double jeopardy, excessive fines, and ex post facto

laws. The court rejected these arguments as baseless.

4)   In *Bollone v. Department of Management Services, Division of Retirement*, 100 So. 3d 1276 (Fla. 1st Dist. Ct. App. 2012), a community college professor was fired after child pornography was discovered on his work computer. He also lost his pension. Although admitting that his actions had been wrong, the professor insisted he had not abused the public's trust. The court disagreed: "Appellant committed the felony of possession of child pornography willfully and with intent to defraud the public of the right to receive the faithful performance of his duties as a professor[.]" *Id.* at 1281.

Despite § 8, Florida has not fared well in national clean government surveys. In 2012, for example, the Center for Public Integrity gave the state a "C-" and ranked it 18th. In 2015, it gave the state a "D-" and ranked it 30th. Contributing to Florida's low standing in both surveys was its failure to aggressively police lobbyists and the FCE's limited powers.

As explained above, in 2018 the lobbying restrictions in § 8 were toughened. As a result, starting in 2023: 1) current officials will be prohibited from lobbying while in office; 2) former legislators and statewide elected officers will have to wait six years before lobbying any state entity; and, 3) other retired officials will have to wait six years before lobbying their former employers. In addition, starting in 2021 public officers and employees will be prohibited from attempting to obtain a "disproportionate benefit" for themselves or their families, employers, or business interests. To accommodate these changes, a new paragraph (f) will be added (covering the enhanced lobbying rules); the section's subsequent paragraphs will be re-lettered; and current paragraph (g), which will become paragraph (h), will receive a new sub-paragraph (2) implementing the "disproportionate benefit" ban.

(e) Civil Service System

Art. III, § 14 requires the legislature to create a civil service system for all "non-exempt" state employees. It also permits the legislature to create such systems for "county, district or municipal employees and for such offices thereof as are not elected or appointed by the governor."

This provision was added to the constitution in 1956. As originally written, it allowed, but did not require, the legislature to create civil service systems. The 1968 constitution made creation of the state system mandatory.

Civil service systems protect government employees in two ways. First, they require that hiring and promotion be based on merit. Second, they prohibit firings except "for cause." This means that the government must prove to a neutral factfinder that the employee has failed to meet the minimum requirements of his or her job. *See Ison v. Zimmerman*, 372 So. 2d 431 (Fla. 1979). These protections are in addition to an employee's other legal rights. *See, e.g., Morris v. Crow*, 817 F. Supp. 102 (M.D. Fla. 1993) (fired deputy sheriff could sue under 42 U.S.C. § 1983).

The federal government began a civil service system in 1871; by 1909, nearly two-thirds of federal employees were covered by it. In 1884, New York became the first state to have a civil service system. Florida's system began in 1936 and grew piecemeal until 1967, when the legislature abolished the Florida Merit System Council and replaced it with the Career Service Council.

The details of Florida's state civil service system are set out in Fla. Stat. §§ 110.201–110.235. As permitted by the constitution, certain government employees are not covered by it. "Exempt" employees include elected officials as well as managerial-level employees. *See* Fla. Stat. § 110.205. *See also Delong v. Florida Fish & Wildlife Conservation Commission*, 145 So. 3d 123 (Fla. 3d Dist. Ct. App. 2014) (probationary employee was not protected by state's civil service system).

In 2018, Florida had 163,000 state employees. Of these, 97,000 were part of the State Personnel System ("SPS"). Of this number, 81,000 were covered while 16,000 were exempt. The 66,000 state employees not in the SPS were distributed among the state's five other personnel systems, the largest of which is the State University System (49,000 employees). Each of these systems has its own merit protection procedures.

The Florida Legislature has authorized counties to create civil service systems. *See* Fla. Stat. § 125.01(1)(u). Pursuant to their general powers, municipalities also can create civil service systems. *See* Fla. Stat. § 166.021(4). A local civil service system is subject to, and can be preempted by, state law. *See City of Casselberry v. Orange County Police Benevolent Association*, 482 So. 2d 336 (Fla. 1986); *Davis v. Gronemeyer*, 251 So. 2d 1 (Fla. 1971).

(f) Continuity of Government

Because of the importance of keeping the government running, the Florida Constitution contains detailed instructions regarding the filling of vacancies.

i. *Individual Vacancies*

Art. X, § 3 provides that a vacancy in office occurs upon the happening of any of the following events:

> [T]he creation of an office, upon the death, removal from office, or resignation of the incumbent or the incumbent's succession to another office, unexplained absence for sixty consecutive days, or failure to maintain the residence required when elected or appointed, and upon failure of one elected or appointed to office to qualify within thirty days from the commencement of the term.

When a vacancy occurs, the following provisions control how the position is filled:

Art. III, § 15(d) addresses legislative vacancies. *See* Ch. 13 of this book.

Art. IV, § 3 addresses gubernatorial vacancies. *See* Ch. 14 of this book.

Art. IV, § 7 addresses state, county, and municipal vacancies. *See* Ch. 14 of this book.

Art. V, § 11 addresses judicial vacancies. *See* Ch. 15 of this book.

Except for legislative vacancies (which can be filled only by election) and gubernatorial vacancies (which are filled first by the lieutenant governor and then according to the gubernatorial succession law—see Fla. Stat. § 14.055), vacancies are filled by gubernatorial appointment. *See Hoy v. Firestone*, 453 So. 2d 814 (Fla. 1984).

Although Florida's constitutions always have indicated *how* vacancies are to be filled, the 1968 constitution is the first to include a section explaining *when* a vacancy occurs. *See Spector v. Glisson*, 305 So. 2d 777 (Fla. 1974).

ii. Mass Vacancies

A different section of the constitution deals with mass vacancies. Art. II, § 6 states:

In periods of emergency resulting from enemy attack the legislature shall have power to provide for prompt and temporary succession to the powers and duties of all public offices the incumbents of which may become unavailable to execute the functions of their offices, and to adopt such other measures as may be necessary and appropriate to insure the continuity of governmental operations during the emergency. In exercising these powers, the legislature may depart from other requirements of this constitution, but only to the extent necessary to meet the emergency.

This provision, which was added in 1968, is modeled after a 1959 law that was enacted to protect the state in the event of an attack by the Soviet Union. *See* Fla. Stat. § 22.02.

The U.S. Constitution does not have a mass vacancy provision. In the wake of 9/11, calls were made to add one but nothing came of the idea.

4. SOVEREIGN IMMUNITY

Art. X, § 13 reads: "Provision may be made by general law for bringing suit against the state as to all liabilities now existing or hereafter originating." This language first appeared in the 1868 constitution and has remained unchanged.

The government's immunity from lawsuits is premised on the ancient maxim, "The king can do no wrong." Today, sovereign immunity serves three purposes: 1) it gives effect to the principle of separation of powers; 2) it protects the public treasury; and, 3) it allows government officials to carry out their duties without having to constantly look over their shoulders. *See American Home Assurance Co. v. National Railroad Passenger Corp.*, 908 So. 2d 459 (Fla. 2005).

Sec. 13 applies only to lawsuits in Florida state courts. In federal court, states are protected by the 11th Amendment (ratified 1795). *See Tuveson v. Florida Governor's Council on Indian Affairs, Inc.*, 734 F.2d 730 (11th Cir. 1984). By its own terms, the 11th Amendment only prohibits suits filed "by Citizens of another State, or by Citizens or Subjects of any Foreign State." However, in *Hans v. Louisiana*, 134 U.S. 1 (1890), the U.S. Supreme Court held that federal courts cannot hear suits brought against a state by its own citizens. This holding sometimes is referred to as the "11½ Amendment."

The U.S. Constitution is silent as to whether an unwilling state can be sued in another state's courts. In *Nevada v. Hall*, 440 U.S. 410, *reh'g denied*, 441 U.S. 917 (1979), the U.S. Supreme Court held that such suits are permissible. However, in *Franchise Tax Board of California v. Hyatt*, 139 S. Ct. 1485 (2019), the Court reversed itself and held that such suits are barred by the common law.

Sec. 13 does not confer sovereign immunity upon the State of Florida—the state has such immunity because it is sovereign. *See Southern Drainage District v. State*, 112 So. 561 (Fla. 1927) (en banc); *Klonis v. State, Department of Revenue*, 766 So. 2d 1186 (Fla. 1st Dist. Ct. App. 2000). What § 13 does do is authorize the state to waive its immunity. *See Florida Livestock Board v. Gladden*, 86 So. 2d 812 (Fla. 1956) (Spec. Div. A). Presumably, however, it could do so even in the absence of such a grant.

Due to the constitution's wording, the state can waive its sovereign immunity only through a general law (*i.e.*, a local or special law is insufficient). *See State v. Love*, 126 So. 374 (Fla. 1930) (en banc). Because they represent a departure from the common law, waivers are strictly construed. *See Joynt v. Star Insurance Co.*, 314 F. Supp. 3d 1233 (M.D. Fla.), *appeal dismissed sub nom. Joynt v. Volusia County*, 2018 WL 6978390 (11th Cir. 2018); *City of Key West v. Florida Keys Community College*, 81 So. 3d 494 (Fla. 3d Dist. Ct. App.), *review denied*, 105 So. 3d 518 (Fla. 2012).

In 1969, Florida enacted a broad waiver statute, but this law was repealed in 1970. In 1973, a much more modest statute was passed. *See* Fla. Stat. § 768.28. It waives the state's sovereign immunity in tort cases but limits the government's financial exposure:

Neither the state nor its agencies or subdivisions shall be liable to pay a claim or a judgment by any one person which exceeds the sum of $200,000 or any claim or judgment, or portions thereof, which, when totaled with all other claims or judgments paid by the state or its agencies or subdivisions arising out of the same incident or occurrence, exceeds the sum of $300,000. However, a judgment or judgments may be claimed and rendered in excess of these amounts and may be settled and paid pursuant to this act up to $200,000 or $300,000, as the case may be; and that portion of the judgment that exceeds these amounts may be reported to the Legislature, but may be paid in part or in whole only by further act of the Legislature.

Id. § 768.28(5). These amounts, which were last raised in 2011 (when they were increased from $100,000/$200,000), remain among the country's lowest.

In two cases currently pending before the Florida Supreme Court, the appellants are challenging lower court rulings that a mass shooting that results in multiple deaths is a "single incident" subject to the overall cap of $300,000. *See Barnett v. State of Florida, Department of Financial Services*, 2019 WL 1123751 (Fla. 2019), and *Guttenberg v. School Board of Broward County*, 2019 WL 1578798 (Fla. 2019).

As noted above, a judgment that exceeds the statutory caps will not be paid absent approval by the Florida Legislature. This requires passage of a private claims bill (also known as a relief act). *See Zamora v. Florida Atlantic University Board of Trustees*, 969 So. 2d 1108 (Fla. 4th Dist. Ct. App. 2007). For a discussion of such bills, see Ch. 13 of this book.

The statutory caps are applicable even when the government has insurance that exceeds them. *See* Fla. Stat. § 768.28(5). *See also Wagner v. Orange County*, 960 So. 2d 785 (Fla. 5th Dist. Ct. App. 2007) (explaining that governments often purchase excess insurance to guard against the possibility of a successful private claims bill).

To further protect the government, the statute prohibits plaintiffs from recovering either pre-judgment interest or punitive damages. *See* Fla. Stat. § 768.28(5). The government also benefits from two court-created exceptions. Under the first, the government can be sued only for "operational acts," as opposed to "discretionary functions." *See Smith v. Rainey*, 747 F. Supp. 2d 1327 (M.D. Fla. 2010). To distinguish between them, courts have developed a four-part test:

An act is discretionary where all of the following conditions have been met: (1) the challenged act, omission, or decision necessarily involves a basic governmental policy, program, or objective; (2) the questioned act, omission, or decision is essential to the realization or accomplishment of that policy, program, or objective as opposed to one which would not change the course or direction of the policy, program, or objective; (3) the act, omission, or decision requires the exercise of basic policy evaluation, judgment, and expertise on the part of the governmental agency involved; and (4) the governmental agency involved possesses the requisite constitutional, statutory, or lawful authority and duty to do or make the challenged act, omission, or decision.

Ermini v. Scott, 249 F. Supp. 3d 1253, 1281 (M.D. Fla. 2017) (homeowner accidentally shot by a deputy sheriff could not sue the sheriff's department for inadequate training because deciding what training deputies should receive is a discretionary function).

The second court-created exception is known as the "public duty doctrine." Under it, the government cannot be held liable for uniquely government acts. Such acts include law enforcement, lawmaking, licensing, and permitting. *See Anderson v. Snyder*, 389 F. Supp. 3d 1082 (S.D. Fla. 2019).

Sec. 768.28 contains strict filing deadlines, imposes special pre-suit notice requirements, and specifies how service is to be made. *See* Fla. Stat. § 768.28(6)–(7) and (14). Failure to pay close attention to these details ordinarily will result in the dismissal of the plaintiff's claim. *See, e.g., Rumler v. Department of Corrections, Florida*, 546 F. Supp. 2d 1334 (M.D. Fla. 2008).

In addition to § 768.28, the Florida Legislature has enacted several other laws waiving the state's tort immunity. The 2008 Victims of Wrongful Incarceration Compensation Act, for example, authorizes $50,000 to be paid for each year an exonerated prisoner was wrongfully incarcerated, up to a maximum of $2 million. *See* Fla. Stat. §§ 961.01–961.07.

At one time, the state also enjoyed absolute immunity in contract cases. In *Pan-Am Tobacco Corp. v. State Department of Corrections*, 471 So. 2d 4 (Fla. 1984), however, the Florida Supreme Court decided that the principle of mutuality required this rule to be jettisoned:

Respondent contends that the requirement of mutuality of remedy is satisfied by petitioner's opportunity to bring a claims bill before the legislature. . . . We cannot now, in good conscience, hold that the chance to seek an act of grace from the legislature is sufficient remedy to create mutuality. . . . We therefore hold that where the state has entered into a contract fairly authorized by the powers granted by general law, the defense of sovereign immunity will not protect the state from action arising from the state's breach of that contract.

Id. at 5.

Sec. 13 mentions only the state. Numerous cases, however, make it clear that counties, municipalities, school districts, and special districts also are protected. *See, e.g., Geidel v. City of Bradenton Beach,* 56 F. Supp. 2d 1359 (M.D. Fla. 1999); *Southwest Florida Water Management District v. Nanz,* 642 So. 2d 1084 (Fla. 1994); *Town of Gulf Stream v. Palm Beach County,* 206 So. 3d 721 (Fla. 4th Dist. Ct. App. 2016); *Duyser by Duyser v. School Board of Broward County,* 573 So. 2d 130 (Fla. 4th Dist. Ct. App. 1991).

The same is true of private individuals and companies that "step into the shoes" of the government. *See, e.g., Stoll v. Noel,* 694 So. 2d 701 (Fla. 1997); *Skoblow v. Ameri-Manage, Inc.,* 483 So. 2d 809 (Fla. 3d Dist. Ct. App. 1986), *decision approved by Spooner v. Department of Corrections,* 514 So. 2d 1077 (Fla. 1987), *cert. denied,* 491 U.S. 904 (1989). *See also* Fla. Stat. § 768.28(10)–(12). *But see Dixon v. Whitfield,* 654 So. 2d 1230 (Fla. 1st Dist. Ct. App. 1995) (school board's sovereign immunity did not extend to school bus company, lessee, or driver because they were independent contractors).

As "domestic dependent nations," Florida's Indian tribes have sovereign immunity as a matter of federal law. Such immunity can be waived only by Congress or the tribe. *See Contour Spa at the Hard Rock, Inc. v. Seminole Tribe of Florida*, 692 F.3d 1200 (11th Cir. 2012), *cert. denied*, 568 U.S. 1086 (2013).

F.   CENSUS

Throughout history, governments have conducted censuses, or counts, of their populations. The birth of Jesus, for example, has been linked to the census of Judea.

The word "census" is derived from the Latin word *censere* ("to estimate"). Although censuses serve many purposes, they traditionally have been used to determine a citizen's military and tax obligations. In more recent times, censuses have become a key means of detecting and predicting demographic shifts. In the United States, the census's best-known function is reapportioning Congress (while every state has two senate seats, house seats are determined by population). In addition, the census is used annually to distribute $1.5 trillion in federal funds to state and local governments.

During the Spanish occupation of Florida, government officials regularly conducted censuses. Although most of these enumerations have been lost, those that still exist are surprisingly detailed. Particularly notable are the 1786 census of East Florida and the 1820 census of West Florida.

The British did not take any official censuses during their short time in Florida. However, in 1765 John De Brahm, King George III's royal surveyor, conducted a census while mapping East Florida.

The first American census of Florida occurred in 1825. A second territorial census was completed in 1837. Only fragments of these censuses survive.

Florida's 1838 constitution required the state to conduct a census once every 10 years. This requirement was repeated in each of the next four constitutions. Thus, from 1845 to 1945 such censuses were taken every 10 years, although the Civil War pushed back the 1865 census to 1867. Due to a lack of proper recordkeeping, most of the data collected by these censuses no longer exists. *See* Karen Packard Rhodes, *Non-Federal Censuses of Florida, 1784–1945: A Guide to Sources* (McFarland & Co., 2010).

In 1950, the requirement that the state conduct its own census was dropped from the constitution. As a result, Art. X, § 8(a) now provides: "Each decennial census of the state taken by the United States shall be an official census of the state."

Art. I, § 2, cl. 3 of the U.S. Constitution requires a federal census to be taken once every 10 years. The first such census was taken in 1790. Since 1930, the census has been taken on April 1 ("Census Day"). Pursuant to 13 U.S.C. § 141(b), the U.S. Census Bureau (https://www.census.gov/) must report its findings to the president within nine months (*i.e.*, by December 31).

The 2010 census found that Florida had 18.8 million residents. The 2020 census is likely to boost this number to 21.3 million. As a result, Florida is expected to gain two additional house seats (27 to 29) and two additional Electoral College votes (29 to 31).

Art. X, § 8(b) directs: "Each decennial census, for the purpose of classifications based upon population, shall become effective on the thirtieth day after the final adjournment of the regular session of the legislature convened next after certification of the census." Thus, in *State ex rel. Pettigrew v. Kirk*, 243 So. 2d 147 (Fla. 1970), the Florida Supreme Court held: "[T]he Board of Business Regulation [is] prohibit[ed] from issuing new alcoholic beverage licenses based upon population increases reflected by the 1970 Federal Census until 30 days after adjournment of the 1971 regular session of the Florida Legislature."

The use of the census is discussed further in Ch. 13 of this book.

G. MILITARY FORCES

Given that Florida was founded at a time when there was no standing federal army, invasion by a foreign country remained a serious threat, and Indian-settler relations were marked by continuing unrest, it is not surprising that the constitution contains multiple sections dealing with military matters. Such provisions have appeared in every one of Florida's constitutions.

Art. I, § 7 provides: "The military power shall be subordinate to the civil." All democracies have such a rule, which is designed to prevent the military from seizing control of the government (as has happened repeatedly in Africa and Latin America).

Art. X, § 2(a) makes "all able[-]bodied inhabitants of the state who are or have declared their intention to become citizens of the United States" members of the state militia. This broad directive is put into effect by Fla. Stat. § 250.02, which divides the state's armed forces into the "organized militia" and the "unorganized militia." Both Art. X, § 2(a) and Fla. Stat. § 250.02(4) provide exemptions for conscientious objectors.

The organized militia consists of Florida's Army and Air Force National Guard units. At present, the former has 9,000 members and the latter has 2,000 members.

Neither the U.S. Navy nor the U.S. Marine Corps has a National Guard component. Accordingly, federal law permits states to form their own units. In line with this authority, Fla. Stat. § 250.04 provides: "The Governor may organize a naval militia and a marine corps in accordance with federal law[.]" Florida last had a naval militia in 1941. To date, it has not had a marine corps.

In contrast, the "unorganized militia" includes all Floridians who are subject to military service but are not part of the organized militia.

Art. X, § 2(b) authorizes the Florida Legislature to pass laws for "the organizing, equipping, housing, maintaining, and disciplining of the militia." *See State v. Dickenson*, 33 So. 514 (Fla. 1902). On a day-to-day basis, these details are overseen by the Florida Department of Military Affairs ("FDMA") (http://dma.myflorida.com/). The FDMA is headquartered in the historic St. Francis Barracks in St. Augustine and is the oldest continuous fighting force in the United States.

The head of the FDMA is the state's adjutant general, a gubernatorial appointee subject to senate confirmation. *See* Art. X, § 2(c). Pursuant to Art. X, § 2(d), the qualifications, disciplining, and removal of FDMA members follows federal military regulations. Military trials (known as "courts-martial") are discussed in Ch. 15 of this book.

Art. IV, § 1(a) makes the governor the "commander-in-chief of all military forces of the state not in active service of the United States." This wording recognizes that a presidential order "calling up" a state's National Guard units transfers authority over them to the federal government. *See Perpich v. Department of Defense*, 496 U.S. 334 (1990) (governor could not block overseas deployment of federalized National Guard units). *See also In re Advisory Opinion to the Governor*, 9 So. 2d 172 (Fla. 1942) (recognizing president's wartime authority over state troops). Since 9/11, the federal government has called up 20,000 Florida guardsmen and sent them on more than 100 overseas missions.

Under Art. IV, § 1(d), the governor can "call out the militia to preserve the public peace, execute the laws of the state, suppress insurrection, or repel invasion." In exercising this power, the governor can direct any soldier to any part of the state. *See In re Advisory Opinion to Governor*, 77 So. 87 (Fla. 1917).

In recent times, Florida's governors usually have called on the National Guard to deal with natural disasters. In 2019, for example, Gov. Ron DeSantis activated 4,400 guardsmen in advance of Hurricane Dorian. In 1968, however, Gov. Claude Kirk used 800 guardsmen to put down a riot in Miami's Liberty City. In 1980, Gov. Bob Graham used 3,500 guardsmen to stop an even larger riot in the same area.

In 2018, the constitution was amended to require the state to pay death benefits to the survivors of active duty military members and Florida National Guardsmen killed in the line of duty. *See* Art. X, § 31. The survivors of first responders and law enforcement officers also are covered.

CHAPTER 3
ELECTORAL PROCESS

A. OVERVIEW

Art. VI deals with voting. In 2019, Florida had 13.4 million registered voters: five million Democrats, 4.7 million Republicans, and 3.6 million Independents. An assortment of "minor" parties accounted for the state's remaining 100,000 voters.

Elections in Florida are overseen by the Division of Elections (https://dos.myflorida.com/elections/). The division is part of the Florida Department of State. *See* Fla. Stat. § 20.10(2)(a). By law, the secretary of state is the state's chief election official. *See* Fla. Stat. § 97.012. However, each county has its own elected supervisor of elections. *See* Art. VIII, § 1(d); Fla. Stat. § 98.015(1). On a day-to-day basis, it is the supervisors who make sure that elections run smoothly. A list of the state's 67 supervisors can be found at https://dos.myflorida.com/elections/contacts/supervisor-of-elections/. See also the web site of the Florida State Association of Supervisors of Elections (https://www.myfloridaelections.com/).

Although Florida's elections are conducted by local officials, the entire nation depends on them. The disputed 2000 U.S. presidential election, for example, largely turned on the results in a few Florida counties. *See Palm Beach County Canvassing Board v. Harris*, 772 So. 2d 1220 (Fla.), *cert. granted in part sub nom. Bush v. Palm Beach County Canvassing*

Board, 531 U.S. 1004, *vacated*, *Bush v. Gore*, 531 U.S. 70 (2000).

During the 2016 U.S. presidential election, Russian hackers breached the servers of several still-unidentified Florida counties (speculation has centered on Broward, Sumter, and Washington). In 2019, Gov. Ron DeSantis ordered a review of Florida's election practices and subsequently announced the state would spend $5.1 million to bolster the cybersecurity of county election boards and voter registration files.

B. ELECTIONS

1. TIMING

Art. VI, § 5(a) requires a statewide general election to "be held in each county on the first Tuesday after the first Monday in November of each even-numbered year." This provision originated with the 1885 constitution (earlier constitutions had left it to the legislature to set the date) and follows U.S. practice. (Since 1845, Congress has required federal elections to take place on the first Tuesday after the first Monday of November. *See* 5 Stat. 721. This date was chosen to accommodate farmers, who could not leave their homes until after the fall harvest. In 1845, 64% of Americans lived on farms.)

A 1992 amendment to the Florida Constitution allows a general election to "be suspended or delayed due to a state of emergency or impending emergency." *See* Art. VI, § 5(a); Fla. Stat. §§ 101.731–101.74. (Contrary to popular belief, this amendment was *not* proposed due to Hurricane Andrew, which hit South Florida in Aug. 1992—at the request of Secretary of State Jim Smith, it had been placed on the ballot by the legislature in Feb. 1992.) To date, this provision has not been used. In 2018, however, Gov. Rick Scott relaxed the election rules in eight western counties following Hurricane Michael. *See* Executive Order 18–283, available at https://www.fl gov.com/wp-content/uploads/orders/2018/EO_18-28 3.pdf.

The constitution does not set the dates of special elections and referenda. Instead, it leaves their timing to the legislature. *See* Art. VI, § 5(a). The same is true for district and municipal elections. *See* Art. VI, § 6.

2. REGULATIONS

Art. VI, § 1 makes the legislature responsible for both elections and political parties. As a result, most of Florida's election rules are contained in Fla. Stat. chs. 97–107. *See, e.g., Jacobson v. Lee*, 411 F. Supp. 3d 1249 (N.D. Fla. 2019), *appeal filed*, 19–14621 (11th Cir.) (striking down Fla. Stat. § 101.151(3)(a), which requires the governor's party to be listed first on all ballots). Nevertheless, the constitution does set out a few basic principles.

First, § 1 requires all elections to be "by direct and secret vote." It is a first-degree misdemeanor for a voter to show his or her ballot to anyone. *See* Fla. Stat. § 104.20.

Second, § 1 stipulates: "[T]he requirements for a candidate with no party affiliation or for a candidate of a minor party for placement of the candidate's name on the ballot shall be no greater than the requirements for a candidate of the party having the largest number of registered voters." This provision, which was added in 1998, has been liberally interpreted by the courts to enhance voter choice. *See Reform Party of Florida v. Black*, 885 So. 2d 303 (Fla. 2004).

Third, Art. VI, § 5(b), also added in 1998, directs that when all primary candidates are from the same political party, "and the winner will have no opposition in the general election, all qualified electors, regardless of party affiliation, may vote in the primary elections for that office." This change represents a loosening of Florida's "closed primary" rule, which limits primary voting to party members. Only nine states (including Florida) have such a rule.

Soon after it was added, however, § 5(b) was sabotaged by the Division of Elections, which ruled that the existence of a "write-in" candidate closes a primary. Thus, since 2000 political parties have arranged for such candidates to appear on the ballot (after filing the necessary paperwork, such candidates simply disappear). In 2016, write-in candidates closed the primaries in six senate districts and 14 house districts. In 2018, they closed the primaries in two senate districts and three house districts.

In 2018, both the Constitution Revision Commission and the legislature rejected efforts to end the write-in loophole. As a result, a group called All Voters Vote has proposed a 2020 constitutional amendment that would require the holding of a single primary involving all candidates (regardless of party affiliation) followed by a runoff between the two highest vote getters. *See Advisory Opinion to the Attorney General re Voting in Primary Elections*, SC19–1267 and SC19–1505 (Fla.). To date, Alaska, California, Louisiana, and Washington have experimented with this type of system (often called a "jungle" primary or "top-two" primary). *See, e.g., Washington State Grange v. Washington State Republican Party*, 552 U.S. 442 (2008).

3. RESULTS

Pursuant to Art. VI, § 1, the winner of any general election is the candidate who receives the most votes, even if his or her total is less than a majority. *See also* Art. X, § 12(d). This is known as plurality voting, also called "winner-take-all" voting. The advantage of this system is that it avoids run-offs and produces a clear winner. The disadvantage is that the winner may be an unpopular candidate who happens to have a loyal (but narrow) base. Additionally, in a close race, the second-place finisher may be almost as popular as the first-place finisher, yet his or her supporters are entirely shut out.

C. VOTERS

1. QUALIFICATIONS

Florida's 1838 constitution enfranchised all "free white male[s]" who were at least 21 years old, had lived in the state for two years and in the county for six months, and either were in the military or exempt from military service.

The 1861 constitution reduced the state residency period to one year, omitted the military service requirement, and added two new conditions: Confederate States of America citizenship and payment of all taxes. The 1865 constitution changed the former requirement to "United States citizenship" and dropped the latter requirement.

Like its predecessors, the 1865 constitution limited voting to white men. As explained in Ch. 1 of this book, this caused Congress to: 1) reject the 1865 constitution; 2) place Florida under military rule; and, 3) order the state to draft a new constitution.

The 1868 constitution extended the vote to "[e]very male person of the age of twenty-one years . . . of whatever race, color, nationality, or previous condition, who [is] a citizen of the United States . . . and [has] resided . . . in Florida for one year, and in the county for six months. . . ." It also directed the legislature to adopt minimum education standards for all new voters registering after 1880. The 1885 constitution annulled this change.

Several 20th century amendments to the U.S. Constitution expanded the pool of eligible voters: the

19th Amendment (1920) gave women the right to vote; the 24th Amendment (1964) outlawed "poll taxes" (used to disenfranchise African-Americans—see Ch. 21 of this book); and the 26th Amendment (1971) lowered the voting age from 21 to 18.

As a result, Art. VI, § 2 of the Florida Constitution now reads: "Every citizen of the United States who is at least eighteen years of age and who is a permanent resident of the state, if registered as provided by law, shall be an elector of the county where registered."

A group called Florida Citizen Voters has proposed a 2020 constitutional amendment that would change § 2's opening words from "Every citizen" to "Only a citizen." *See Advisory Opinion to the Attorney General re Citizenship Requirement to Vote*, SC19–1165 and SC19–1503 (Fla.). The goal of this amendment (which will not change any voter's eligibility) is to increase Republican voter turnout in the 2020 presidential election.

2. DISQUALIFICATIONS

Florida's first three constitutions gave the legislature the "power to exclude . . . from the right of suffrage . . . all persons convicted of bribery, perjury, or other infamous crime [*i.e.*, felony]."

The 1868 constitution changed this language to read: "No person under guardianship, *non compos mentis*, or insane, shall be qualified to vote at any election, nor shall any person convicted of felony be qualified to vote at any election unless restored to civil rights." It also barred from voting duelists and those who bet on elections. The 1885 constitution retained these provisions with only minor tweaking.

The 1968 constitution streamlined the 1885 constitution's language: "No person convicted of a felony, or adjudicated in this or any other state to be mentally incompetent, shall be qualified to vote or hold office until restoration of civil rights or removal of disability."

In 2018, a citizens' initiative known as Amendment 4, see *Advisory Opinion to the Attorney General re Voting Restoration Amendment*, 215 So. 3d 1202 (Fla. 2017), made significant changes to Art. VI, § 4(a), which now reads as follows:

(a) No person convicted of a felony, or adjudicated in this or any other state to be mentally incompetent, shall be qualified to vote or hold office until restoration of civil rights or removal of disability. Except as provided in subsection (b) of this section, any disqualification from voting arising from a felony conviction shall terminate and voting rights shall be restored upon completion of all terms of sentence including parole or probation.

(b) No person convicted of murder or a felony sexual offense shall be qualified to vote until restoration of civil rights.

At the time of Amendment 4, Florida was one of only 11 states that did not automatically restore the voting rights of former felons. *See Johnson v. Bush*, 405 F.3d 1214 (11th Cir.) (en banc), *cert. denied*, 546

U.S. 1015 (2005). As a result, such persons were forced to petition the government for restoration. Believing most leaned Democratic, Republican officials made restoration as difficult as possible. *See Hand v. Scott*, 315 F. Supp. 3d 1244 (N.D. Fla.), *stay granted*, 888 F.3d 1206 (11th Cir. 2018).

Amendment 4 is expected to add up to 1.4 million persons to Florida's voting rolls. Alarmed by the effect this influx could have on the state's politics, in 2019 Republican lawmakers passed S.B. 7066 (Fla. Laws ch. 2019–162). It makes restoration contingent upon a person completing his or her sentence *and* paying all court-ordered fees, fines, and restitution orders (known as "legal financial obligations"). It is estimated this requirement will prevent 80% of Florida's former felons, who collectively owe $3 billion, from obtaining restoration.

Critics believe S.B. 7066 is a modern-day poll tax. As a result, they have filed multiple federal lawsuits (now consolidated) seeking to strike it down under the 24th Amendment. *See Jones v. DeSantis*, 410 F. Supp. 3d 1284 (N.D. Fla. 2019) (granting a partial temporary restraining order), *appeal filed*, 19–14551 (11th Cir.). In the meantime, Gov. Ron DeSantis has asked the Florida Supreme Court to weigh in. *See Advisory Opinion to the Governor re: Implementation of Amendment 4*, SC 19–1341 (Fla.).

As paragraph (b) makes clear, former felons convicted of murder or a felony sexual offense must still petition for restoration. This provision, which is being challenged in the *Hand* litigation, was included to make Amendment 4 more palatable to the public.

It has been criticized, however, for driving a wedge into the ex-offender community.

The requirement that a person adjudicated mentally incompetent cannot vote until a judge issues an order finding them to be mentally competent has proven uncontroversial. *See, e.g.,* Fla. Att'y Gen. Op. 74–15 (*voluntary* admission to a mental health facility does not forfeit the right to vote).

3. OATH

Before being allowed to vote, a qualified individual must register with his or her county's supervisor of elections. Florida's voter registration laws appear in Fla. Stat. ch. 97. In 2019, 3.6 million eligible Floridians were not registered to vote.

In 1994, Florida implemented the federal "motor-voter" law, which allows an individual to register to vote while applying for, or renewing, a driver's license. *See* Fla. Stat. § 97.057. Since 2017, Florida also has offered on-line voter registration. *See* Fla. Stat. § 97.0525. Florida does not have "automatic registration," which exists in 13 states. Florida also does not have "same day registration," which exists in 11 states. Instead, in Florida an individual must register to vote at least 29 days before an election. *See* Fla. Stat. § 97.055.

Florida does not allow voting by fax or internet. It does, however, permit both early voting, see Fla. Stat. § 101.657, and voting by mail. *See* Fla. Stat. § 101.62.

As part of the registration process, a person must take the "elector's oath," which is set out in Art. VI, § 3: "I do solemnly swear (or affirm) that I will protect and defend the Constitution of the United States and the Constitution of the State of Florida, and that I am qualified to register as an elector under the Constitution and laws of the State of Florida." In *Fields v. Askew*, 279 So. 2d 822 (Fla. 1973), *appeal dismissed*, 414 U.S. 1148 (1974), the court rejected the plaintiff's claim that the elector's oath is an impermissible loyalty oath.

D.   PUBLIC CAMPAIGN FINANCING

In 1986, the Florida Legislature passed the Florida Election Campaign Financing Act ("FECFA"). In doing so, it hoped to level the playing field between poor and rich candidates, reduce the influence of wealthy donors, and put the brakes on rising campaign costs.

In 1998, the system was constitutionalized. As a result, Art. VI, § 7 requires the legislature to provide "[a] method of public financing for campaigns for state-wide office" that is "at least as protective of effective competition by a candidate who uses public funds as the general law in effect on January 1, 1998." For the current version of FECFA, see Fla. Stat. §§ 106.30–106.36.

Florida is one of 14 states that has a public financing option. While Florida provides funding only for gubernatorial and cabinet races, five states provide funding for legislative races and two states provide funding for supreme court races. In 1974,

Congress created a public financing procedure for presidential races. *See* 88 Stat. 1263.

To be eligible for FECFA funding, gubernatorial candidates must raise $150,000 and cabinet candidates must raise $100,000. *See* Fla. Stat. § 106.33. Once the applicable threshold is met, FECFA matches individual contributions of $250 or less. *See* Fla. Stat. § 106.35. In exchange, recipients must limit their overall campaign expenditures to either $2 per registered Florida voter (gubernatorial candidates) or $1 per registered Florida voter (cabinet candidates). *See* Fla. Stat. § 106.34. In 2018, this worked out to $27 million for gubernatorial candidates and $13.5 million for cabinet candidates. Money raised by political action committees do not count against these limits.

There is no requirement that a candidate accept FECFA funds, and those who decline are not subject to FECFA's limits. Opponents of such candidates are "released from [the] expenditure limit to the extent the nonparticipating candidate exceed[s] the limit." Fla. Stat. § 106.355.

For a further discussion of FECFA's mechanics, see *Scott v. Roberts*, 612 F.3d 1279 (11th Cir. 2010); *Thurston v. State Florida Elections Commission*, 210 So. 3d 684 (Fla. 4th Dist. Ct. App. 2017); and the Division of Elections' *2018 Public Campaign Financing Handbook*, available at https://dos.my florida.com/media/698987/public-campaign-financing-2018.pdf.

Since 2006, $31.4 million in FECFA funds have been distributed to 35 candidates: $11.1 million in 2006 (10 candidates); $6.1 million in 2010 (10 candidates); $4.3 million in 2014 (six candidates); and $9.9 million in 2018 (nine candidates). The bulk of the 2018 funds went to gubernatorial candidates Ron DeSantis (R) ($3.2 million) and Andrew Gillum (D) ($2.6 million). Although both men honored the $27 million cap, they each raised millions more in donations that did not count for FECFA purposes ($26.5 million by DeSantis and $25.5 million by Gillum).

During their respective 2018 races, Jeremy Ring, the Democratic candidate for chief financial officer, and Matt Caldwell, the Republican candidate for commissioner of agriculture, refused to take FECFA funds. When their opponents—Jimmy Patronis ($335,000) and Nikki Fried ($159,000)—accepted such money, Ring and Caldwell tried to make their decisions into campaign issues. On election day, however, both Patronis and Fried won.

Despite its good intentions, FECFA has failed to achieve its goals (critics have labelled it "welfare for politicians"). As a result, in 2010 the Florida Legislature proposed a constitutional amendment repealing § 7. Although supported by 52.5% of the voters, the amendment failed to pass because it did not reach the constitution's 60% cut-off. *See* Art. XI, § 5(e).

CHAPTER 4
ENVIRONMENT

A. OVERVIEW

Florida is a vast state (65,758 square miles). Its coastline, second only to Alaska's, extends 8,436 miles, while its beaches cover 663 miles. It also is home to an astonishing array of animals (nearly 500 native species) and plants (more than 2,800 native species).

Florida's economy relies heavily on the state's natural resources. Besides grapefruits, oranges, and sugar cane, the state is an important source of cotton, seafood, and timber. In addition, its six active phosphate mines produce 25% of the world's annual output. Florida also attracts more than 110 million visitors a year, many of whom are lured by its recreational opportunities, scenic beauty, and temperate climate.

Given the foregoing, it is not surprising that Florida's constitution contains multiple sections dealing with the environment, most of which appear in either Art. II or Art. X.

B. GENERAL PROVISIONS

Art. II, § 7(a), added in 1968, declares, "It shall be the policy of the state to conserve and protect its natural resources and scenic beauty." This section also requires the legislature to pass laws to abate air, noise, and water pollution. In 1998, laws conserving and protecting natural resources were added to the list.

The state's power to enact environmental laws was recognized in *Askew v. Game and Fresh Water Fish Commission*, 336 So. 2d 556 (Fla. 1976). Since 1993, the Florida Department of Environmental Protection ("FDEP") (https://floridadep.gov/) has been chiefly responsible for the state's environmental laws.

Very few cases exist interpreting § 7(a). However, in *Seadade Industries, Inc. v. Florida Power & Light Co.*, 245 So. 2d 209 (Fla. 1971), the Florida Supreme Court held that the trial court could take it into account while reviewing plans for a new drainage canal. A similar result was reached in *Florida Power & Light Co. v. Berman*, 429 So. 2d 79 (Fla. 4th Dist. Ct. App.), *petition for review denied*, 436 So. 2d 98 (Fla. 1983) (proposed power line).

C. LAND RESOURCES

1. EVERGLADES

The Everglades, three million acres of tropical wetlands, are one of Florida's most important environmental resources. Until recently, however, their ecological importance was poorly understood. As a result, government officials, believing they were a nuisance, spent decades trying to drain them.

One side effect of these efforts was the development of commercial sugar fields in the Everglades. When the United States banned the importation of Cuban sugar in 1960, sugar production in the Everglades soared. To boost their yields, farmers used large amounts of phosphate-rich fertilizer. The resulting run-off choked the Everglades, which in turn reduced their bird populations and allowed non-native plants (*e.g.*, cattails) to crowd out naturally-occurring ones (*e.g.*, sawgrass).

In 1993, a political action committee called Save Our Everglades ("SOE") proposed a constitutional amendment to reverse the damage. The proposal had three parts. First, it required polluters to help cover the clean-up costs. Second, it established a trust fund that could be used to pay for such projects. Third, for a period of 25 years, it imposed a one cent tax on every pound of raw sugar grown in the Everglades. To account for inflation, the tax included an escalator clause.

In *In re Advisory Opinion to the Attorney General— Save Our Everglades*, 636 So. 2d 1336 (Fla. 1994), the Florida Supreme Court held that the proposal violated the single-subject requirement of Art. XI, § 3. As a result, it did not appear on the 1994 ballot.

To overcome this ruling, in 1996 SOE submitted three separate petitions. After the Florida Supreme Court validated each of them, see *Advisory Opinion to the Attorney General—Fee on the Everglades Sugar Production*, 681 So. 2d 1124 (Fla. 1996), they appeared on the ballot as, respectively, Amendments 4 ("sugar tax"), 5 ("polluter pays"), and 6 ("trust fund").

Amendments 5 and 6 generated relatively little opposition, as the sugar industry focused its attention on defeating Amendment 4. To do so, it spent $22.7 million blanketing the state's airwaves with ads claiming that if Amendment 4 passed, consumers would see a sharp increase in food prices. In response, SOE and its allies spent $7.3 million defending Amendment 4, arguing that it would raise $875 million for the Everglades. In the end, Amendment 4 was defeated while Amendments 5 (now Art. II, § 7(b)) and 6 (now Art. X, § 17) passed. *See Advisory Opinion to Governor—1996 Amendment 5 (Everglades)*, 706 So. 2d 278 (Fla. 1997).

Both amendments mention the "Everglades Agricultural Area" and the "Everglades Protection Area." The former refers to the northern part of the Everglades (one million acres) in which farming takes place. The latter refers to the southern part of the Everglades (1.5 million acres) that, since 1947, has been a national park. The Everglades' remaining 500,000 acres are a water conservation area.

Following Amendment 4's defeat, Florida turned to Congress for help. In 2000, it approved a $16.4 billion plan to clean up the Everglades. *See* 114 Stat. 2572. To date, however, only six of its 68 projects have been started. At this rate, the Everglades will not be remediated until 2100.

2. SOVEREIGNTY LANDS

"Sovereignty lands" are lands located under the state's navigable waters. As their name suggests, they are an incident of sovereignty. During the

British and Spanish occupations, they were owned by those countries. After the United States acquired Florida, they became the property of the federal government. *See Ex parte Powell*, 70 So. 392 (Fla. 1915). When Congress admitted Florida to the Union, they passed to the state. *See Martin v. Busch*, 112 So. 274 (Fla. 1927) (Div. B). Pursuant to the U.S. Constitution, the federal government continues to have considerable control over such waterways, particularly when it comes to navigation. *See, e.g., Freed v. Miami Beach Pier Corp.*, 112 So. 841 (Fla. 1927) (Div. B).

The duty of the state to administer sovereignty lands for the benefit of the people (known as "the public trust doctrine") existed at common law. *See Pembroke v. Peninsular Terminal Co.*, 146 So. 249 (Fla. 1933) (en banc). In 1968, this duty was enshrined in the constitution as Art. X, § 11. This change did not impose any new obligations on the government. *See Coastal Petroleum Co. v. American Cyanamid Co.*, 492 So. 2d 339 (Fla. 1986), *cert. denied sub nom. Mobil Oil Corp. v. Board of Trustees of Internal Improvement Trust Fund of Florida*, 479 U.S. 1065 (1987).

Florida's sovereignty lands are overseen by the Board of Trustees of the Internal Improvement Trust Fund (*i.e.*, the governor and the cabinet). *See 5F, LLC v. Dresing*, 142 So. 3d 936 (Fla. 2d Dist. Ct. App. 2014). Because they are state property, sovereignty lands are exempt from the Marketable Record Title Act, see Fla. Stat. § 712.03(7), and are not subject to adverse possession. *See Board of Trustees of the*

Internal Improvement Trust Fund v. Sand Key Associates, Ltd., 512 So. 2d 934 (Fla. 1987).

Sovereignty lands cannot be sold by the state unless the sale is in the public's interest. *See River Place Condominium Association at Ellenton, Inc. v. Benzing*, 890 So. 2d 386 (Fla. 2d Dist. Ct. App. 2004). A donation by the state is treated the same as a sale. *See Weller v. Askew*, 363 So. 2d 1091 (Fla. 1978) (approving Florida's gifting of land under the Turner River to facilitate a federal conservation project).

The private use of sovereignty lands also is disfavored, although a lower standard is used in assessing such applications (*i.e.*, the use must not be contrary to the public's interest). *See Mariner Properties Development, Inc. v. Board of Trustees of Internal Improvement Trust*, 743 So. 2d 1121 (Fla. 1st Dist. Ct. App. 1999).

Prior to 1970, both sales and uses were judged by this lower standard. A 1970 amendment raised the burden of proof for sales. If a proper sale takes place, however, it extinguishes the land's sovereign character. *See Herbits v. Board of Trustees of Internal Improvement Trust Fund*, 195 So. 3d 1149 (Fla. 1st Dist. Ct. App. 2016).

Lands not covered by navigable waters do not qualify as sovereignty lands. The term "navigable waters" refers to a body of water that can be used by the public for commercial or recreational navigation. *See Brevard County v. Blasky*, 875 So. 2d 6 (Fla. 5th Dist. Ct. App.), *review denied*, 889 So. 2d 71 (Fla. 2004). Whether a given body of water is capable of such use is a factual question. *See, e.g., Florida Board of Trustees of Internal Improvement Trust Fund v. Wakulla Silver Springs Co.*, 362 So. 2d 706 (Fla. 3d Dist. Ct. App. 1978), *cert. denied*, 368 So. 2d 1366 (Fla. 1979) (finding that Rock Harbor inlet and basin were not navigable because they were only 6–12 inches deep).

While Art. X, § 11 mentions only "beaches below mean high water lines," it also applies to the land under bays, harbors, lakes, rivers, and streams, so long as they are navigable. In contrast, lowlands, mud flats, and shallow inlets generally are excluded. *See Lee v. Williams*, 711 So. 2d 57 (Fla. 5th Dist. Ct. App.), *review denied*, 722 So. 2d 193 (Fla. 1998).

In applying § 11, courts sometimes consider Art. II, § 7(a), which, as explained above, requires the government to protect the state's environment. *See, e.g., Walton County v. Stop Beach Renourishment, Inc.*, 998 So. 2d 1102 (Fla. 2008), *cert. granted sub nom. Stop Beach Renourishment, Inc. v. Florida Dept. of Environmental Protection*, 557 U.S. 903 (2009), *aff'd*, 560 U.S. 702 (2010).

3.   CONSERVATION LANDS

Art. X, § 18, adopted in 1998, prohibits the disposal of "conservation lands" except when no longer needed for conservation purposes. This idea was copied from the "Florida Preservation 2000" bond program. *See* Fla. Stat. § 259.101.

Sec. 18 does not define the phrase "conservation lands." However, Art. X, § 28, adopted in 2014 and discussed below, provides examples of such lands.

Prior to 1998, the rules applicable to conservation lands depended on which state entity administered them. In addition, the rules could be modified at the discretion of the legislature. Sec. 18 replaced this confusing, and often inconsistent, patchwork with a single uniform standard that cannot be changed by lawmakers.

4. LAND ACQUISITION TRUST FUND

At one time, Florida was a leader in setting aside money to purchase land to be put in trust for the public. These efforts began in 1963 and originally were paid for by a 5% tax on outdoor clothing, with the proceeds deposited in the state's Land Acquisition Trust Fund ("LATF"). In 1968, the tax was dropped in favor of bonds funded by an excise tax on certain types of legal documents (primarily real estate mortgages). In 2009, however, the legislature began using the money in the LATF to pay for other programs.

In 2012, Florida's Water and Land Legacy ("FWLL"), a coalition representing more than 50 conservation and environmental groups, called for the LATF to have a dedicated revenue source. After making the ballot, see *Advisory Opinion to the Attorney General re Water and Land Conservation*, 123 So. 3d 47 (Fla. 2013), FWLL's proposal was approved by the voters in 2014. *See* Art. X, § 28.

Sec. 28(a) requires, for a period of 20 years, that the LATF receive at least 1/3 of the net revenues derived from the state's document excise tax. It is estimated that $20 billion will be raised by the time the amendment sunsets on July 1, 2035.

Sec. 28(b)(1) specifies that the money can be used to acquire, improve, or restore the state's "land, water areas, and related property interests," including beaches and shores, fish and wildlife habitats, forests, geologic and historic sites, outdoor recreation lands, rural landscapes, urban open space, wetlands, wildlife management areas, and working farms and ranches. Sec. 28(b)(2) additionally permits the money to be used to pay the debt service on any bonds issued for these purposes.

To ensure that the funds generated by the amendment are not diverted, § 28(c) provides: "The moneys deposited into the Land Acquisition Trust Fund . . . shall not be or become commingled with the general revenue fund of the state." *See also* Fla. Stat. § 375.041. Nevertheless, a pending lawsuit accuses the legislature of diverting LATF funds. *See Oliva v. Florida Wildlife Federation, Inc.*, 281 So. 3d 531 (Fla. 1st Dist. Ct. App. 2019), *appeal filed*, SC19–1935 (Fla.).

D.   LIVING RESOURCES

1.   FLORIDA FISH AND WILDLIFE CONSERVATION COMMISSION

In 1942, Florida's voters approved a constitutional amendment designed to improve the "management, restoration, conservation, and regulation . . . of the [state's] birds, game, fur bearing animals, and fresh water fish." The result was an independent constitutional agency known as the Game and Fresh Water Fish Commission ("GFWFC"), the members of which were to be chosen by the governor. A 1974 amendment required the governor's appointees to be confirmed by the senate and took away the GFWFC's appropriation powers (as a result, fishing and hunting license fees are set by the legislature).

A 1998 amendment merged the GFWFC and the Marine Fisheries Commission, resulting in the creation of the Florida Fish and Wildlife Conservation Commission ("FFWCC") (http://myfwc.com/). *See* Art. IV, § 9. This amendment was proposed by the Constitutional Revision Commission after a similar citizen petition was invalidated due to a defective ballot summary. *See Advisory Opinion to the Attorney General re Fish and Wildlife Conservation Commission*, 705 So. 2d 1351 (Fla. 1998). The FFWCC works closely with the FDEP, particularly when it comes to protecting threatened and endangered animal and fish species.

The FFWCC is unique in that its regulations cannot be overridden by the legislature. *See Florida Fish and Wildlife Conservation Commission v. Daws*, 256 So. 3d 907 (Fla. 1st Dist. Ct. App.), *review denied*, 2018 WL 6605838 (Fla. 2018); *Airboat Association of Florida, Inc. v. Florida Game and Fresh Water Fish Commission*, 498 So. 2d 629 (Fla. 3d Dist. Ct. App. 1986). This is because Art. IV, § 9 provides: "The legislature may enact laws in aid of the commission, not inconsistent with this section[.]" Thus, while the legislature can pass laws if the FFWCC has not acted, it may not enact legislation that is contrary to the FFWCC's regulations. Likewise, a law in conflict with a later-passed FFWCC regulation is invalid.

Because of the power wielded by the FFWCC, § 9 requires the "commission [to] establish procedures to ensure adequate due process in the exercise of its regulatory and executive functions." Sec. 9 also makes it clear that the FFWCC cannot regulate air or water pollution except as authorized by the legislature.

Sec. 9 prohibits the FFWCC from being made a part of any other state agency and guarantees that it will "have its own staff, which includes management, research, and enforcement." At present, the FFWCC has 2,100 full-time employees. For a further look at the FFWCC, see Fla. Stat. § 20.331.

2.   GILL NET FISHING

In 1994, Florida's voters passed a citizens' initiative petition outlawing the use of certain types of fishing nets. This measure, championed by the group Save Our Sealife ("SOS"), followed years of contentious, but inconclusive, legislative debate. *See Advisory Opinion to Attorney General—Limited Marine Net Fishing*, 620 So. 2d 997 (Fla. 1993).

According to SOS, Florida's fishing stocks were being imperiled by the large nets used by commercial fishermen. In addition, SOS contended that the nets often trapped and killed birds, dolphins, and sea turtles. Fishermen, marine supply dealers, and seafood retailers and wholesalers insisted that their livelihoods would be destroyed if the amendment passed. They also accused SOS of exaggerating the harm caused by net fishing.

Under the amendment, gill and other entangling nets are banned in all Florida waters, while nets larger than 500 square feet in mesh area are banned in Florida's near-shore and in-shore waters. *See* Art. X, § 16(a)–(c). Exceptions exist for governmental and scientific ships. *See* Art. X, § 16(d). Violators are subject to fines and imprisonment. *See* Art. X, § 16(e); Fla. Stat. § 379.407.

Following its adoption, Art. X, § 16 was challenged by commercial fishermen. In *Lane v. Chiles*, 698 So. 2d 260 (Fla. 1997), the Florida Supreme Court found that the measure was rationally related to its goals and did not violate the plaintiffs' due process or equal protection rights. In subsequent rulings, the First District Court of Appeal has rejected the industry's efforts to have the amendment and its implementing rules declared unenforceable. *See, e.g., Florida Fish and Wildlife Conservation Commission v. Wakulla Fishermen's Association, Inc.*, 141 So. 3d 723 (Fla. 1st Dist. Ct. App. 2014), *review denied*, 163 So. 3d 516 (Fla. 2015); *State v. Kirvin*, 718 So. 2d 893 (Fla. 1st Dist. Ct. App, 1998), *review denied sub nom. Taylor v. State*, 729 So. 2d 918 (Fla. 1999).

Although there is a great deal of disagreement over whether the amendment is achieving its goals, in *Wakulla Commercial Fishermen's Association, Inc. v. Florida Fish and Wildlife Conservation Commission*,

951 So. 2d 8 (Fla. 1st Dist. Ct. App.), *review denied*, 965 So. 2d 123 (Fla. 2007), unrebutted expert testimony demonstrated that the ban on entangling nets had led to an increase in the state's mullet population.

3.   PREGNANT PIGS

Art. X, § 21, an initiative petition sponsored by Floridians for Humane Farms, bans the cruel and inhumane treatment of pregnant pigs. Specifically, it makes it a first-degree misdemeanor to confine or tether such animals in a way that prevents them from freely turning around. Violators also can be fined up to $5,000. *See* Art. X, § 21(a) and (d).

The foregoing provisions are suspended when the animal is undergoing a veterinary procedure or is in the pre-birthing period. *See* Art. X, § 21(b). The pre-birthing period is defined as "the seven[-]day period prior to a pig's expected date of giving birth." *See* Art. X, § 21(c)(6).

After making the ballot, see *Advisory Opinion to Attorney General ex rel. Limiting Cruel and Inhumane Confinement of Pigs During Pregnancy*, 815 So. 2d 597 (Fla. 2002), the amendment passed by a margin of 54.75%–42.25%. However, because it contained a six-year waiting period, see Art. X, § 21(g), it did not become effective until 2008.

Due to its subject matter, the amendment caused the state to endure a great deal of mocking (despite several other states having similar legislation). As a result, in 2006 the minimum percentage required to pass a citizens' initiative petition was increased from a simple majority to 60%. *See* Art. XI, § 5(e). Other restrictions also were implemented. *See* Ch. 23 of this book.

In 2002, Florida had only two pig farms (most pig farms are in Iowa). Both went out of business shortly after the amendment passed. Subsequently, one of the owners filed an inverse condemnation claim, alleging that the amendment had resulted in a "taking" of his property, and was awarded $505,000. *See State v. Basford*, 119 So. 3d 478 (Fla. 1st Dist. Ct. App. 2013). Inverse condemnation claims are discussed in Ch. 12 of this book.

E.   OCEAN RESOURCES

In 2018, the Florida Constitution was amended to include a ban on offshore drilling. As a result, a new paragraph (c) was added to Art. II, § 7:

> To protect the people of Florida and their environment, drilling for exploration or extraction of oil or natural gas is prohibited on lands beneath all state waters which have not been alienated and that lie between the mean high water line and the outermost boundaries of the state's territorial seas. This prohibition does not apply to the transportation of oil and gas products produced outside of such waters. This subsection is self-executing.

The impact of this provision is quite limited. As explained in Ch. 2 of this book, Florida's territorial waters extend only three miles on the east coast and

10.4 miles on the west coast. Further out, drilling is controlled by the federal government. In 2019, a federal court struck down Pres. Donald Trump's plan to permit drilling in the Atlantic Ocean. *See League of Conservation Voters v. Trump*, 363 F. Supp. 3d 1013 (D. Alaska 2019), *appeal filed*, 19–35461 (9th Cir.). Subsequently, the U.S. House of Representatives voted to permanently ban drilling in both the Atlantic Ocean and the Pacific Ocean, see H.R. 1941 (Coastal and Marine Economies Protection Act), as well as off Florida's west coast. *See* H.R. 205 (Protecting and Securing Florida's Coastline Act of 2019). Neither bill is expected to pass the U.S. Senate.

PART II
INDIVIDUAL RIGHTS

CHAPTER 5
ACCESS TO INFORMATION

A. OVERVIEW

The Florida Constitution contains three sections that affect the government's power to obtain and withhold information. One of these is Art. I, § 12, which determines when and how the government can gather information for law enforcement purposes. It is discussed in Ch. 7 of this book.

In addition, the constitution recognizes a general right of privacy. *See* Art. I, § 23. This means, for example, that citizens have the right to limit the amount and type of information the government collects about them.

Sec. 23 is closely related to Art. I, § 24. This latter provision requires the government to operate transparently. Thus, the government must: 1) notify the public whenever it plans to hold a meeting (and let interested citizens attend); and, 2) make its records available to any citizen who asks for them.

B. PERSONAL PRIVACY

The first sentence of Art. I, § 23 stipulates: "Every natural person has the right to be let alone and free from governmental intrusion into the person's private life except as otherwise provided herein." This provision has an interesting history.

In 1890, Boston lawyer Samuel Warren and future U.S. Supreme Court Justice Louis Brandeis called for judicial recognition of a right to privacy, which they defined as the "right to be let alone." *See* Samuel D. Warren & Louis D. Brandeis, *The Right to Privacy*, 4 Harv. L. Rev. 193 (1890). In 1883, Warren had married Mabel Bayard, the daughter of a U.S. senator. Due to the Bayard family's prominence, it was the subject of unrelenting—and often sensational—press coverage. When Warren began appearing in these stories, he turned to his close friend Brandeis, who wrote the article hoping it would persuade courts to gag reporters.

In *Katz v. United States*, 389 U.S. 347 (1967), the U.S. Supreme Court held that a person's privacy rights largely depend on state law. Subsequently, the Florida Supreme Court ruled that there was no general right of privacy under Florida law. *See Laird v. State*, 342 So. 2d 962 (Fla. 1977). As a result, the 1978 Constitution Revision Commission ("CRC") proposed that a right of privacy be added to the Florida Constitution.

The CRC bundled this proposal with a host of other reforms. On election day, the entire package was soundly defeated (voters found it overwhelming). Two years later, when the legislature resubmitted the idea as a stand-alone amendment, it passed easily.

The existence of § 23 means that the Florida Constitution contains an explicit right of privacy, a feature not found in the U.S. Constitution. And while the U.S. Supreme Court has fashioned a federal right of privacy out of various provisions of the Bill of Rights, see, e.g., *Griswold v. Connecticut*, 381 U.S.

479 (1965), the Florida Supreme Court has made it clear that § 23 goes further than federal law. *See, e.g., D.M.T. v. T.M.H.*, 129 So. 3d 320 (Fla. 2013). Nevertheless, § 23 is subject to three important limitations.

First, it applies only to "natural" persons, meaning that it does not protect "juridical" persons (*i.e.*, businesses). *See Alterra Healthcare Corp. v. Estate of Shelley*, 827 So. 2d 936 (Fla. 2002).

Second, it applies only to a person's "private life," meaning that public behavior is not covered. *See, e.g., University Books and Videos, Inc. v. Metropolitan Dade County*, 78 F. Supp. 2d 1327 (S.D. Fla. 1999) (right to view sexually explicit material applies only in one's home).

Third, the inclusion of the phrase "except as otherwise provided herein" means that whenever there is a conflict between § 23 and another constitutional provision, the latter prevails. *See Winfield v. Division of Pari-Mutuel Wagering, Department of Business Regulation*, 477 So. 2d 544 (Fla. 1985) (taxpayers could not keep their business records secret).

Although conflicts normally are *implicit*, Art. X, § 22 creates an *explicit* conflict: "Notwithstanding a minor's right of privacy provided in Sec. 23 of Article I, the Legislature is authorized to require by general law for notification to a parent or guardian of a minor before the termination of the minor's pregnancy." Sec. 22 is discussed in Ch. 9 of this book.

To make out a colorable claim under § 23, a plaintiff must establish that the government has interfered with a legitimate expectation of privacy. *See, e.g., McFall v. Welsh*, 2019 WL 5485550, at *1 (Fla. 5th Dist. Ct. App. 2019) ("Article I, section 23 . . . protects the disclosure of financial information of private persons . . . because 'personal finances are among those private matters kept secret by most people.' ").

It is not enough for the plaintiff to show that a single government employee, acting beyond his or her authority, has interfered with the plaintiff's privacy. *See Resha v. Tucker*, 670 So. 2d 56 (Fla. 1996). Similarly, interference by a private party is insufficient. *See Gilbert v. Sears, Roebuck and Co.*, 899 F. Supp. 597 (M.D. Fla. 1995).

Once the plaintiff has made out a prima facie case, the government must prove that the challenged act or regulation serves a compelling state interest and is the least intrusive means available. *See Pottinger v. City of Miami*, 810 F. Supp. 1551 (S.D. Fla. 1992). *See also North Florida Women's Health and Counseling Services, Inc. v. State*, 866 So. 2d 612 (Fla. 2003).

Although many § 23 cases involve disputes over information, not all do. In a series of decisions, for example, the Florida Supreme Court has held that because of § 23, the government cannot force parents to allow grandparents to visit their grandchildren. *See Saul v. Brunetti*, 753 So. 2d 26 (Fla. 2000); *Von Eiff v. Azicri*, 720 So. 2d 510 (Fla. 1998); *Beagle v. Beagle*, 678 So. 2d 1271 (Fla. 1996). As a result, such visits now are statutorily authorized only when both parents are dead, missing, or in a persistent vegetative state or one parent meets these criteria and the other parent "has been convicted of a felony or an offense of violence evincing behavior that poses a substantial threat of harm to the minor child's health or welfare." *See* Fla. Stat. § 752.011.

Similarly, the Florida Supreme Court has held that § 23 prohibits government interference in medical decision-making. *See In re Guardianship of Browning*, 568 So. 2d 4 (Fla. 1990) (upholding a patient's right to refuse treatment). This includes a woman's right to have an abortion. *See Gainesville Woman Care, LLC v. State*, 210 So. 3d 1243 (Fla. 2017). In *Krischer v. McIver*, 697 So. 2d 97 (Fla. 1997), however, the court determined that Florida's ban on assisted suicide (see Fla. Stat. § 782.08) does not violate § 23 due to the government's interest in preserving life, preventing death, and maintaining the integrity of the medical profession.

The second sentence of § 23 reads: "This section shall not be construed to limit the public's right of access to public records and meetings as provided by law." At the time that § 23 was adopted (1980), the public's rights regarding these matters were not yet constitutionally protected. Now that they are, see Art. I, § 24 (discussed below), this language largely is surplusage.

C.   PUBLIC MEETINGS AND RECORDS

In 1905, Florida passed a law requiring all government meetings to be open to the public (the first such law in the country). In *Turk v. Richard*, 47 So. 2d 543 (Fla. 1950) (Div. B), however, the Florida Supreme Court severely undercut the law by limiting it to municipalities. In 1967, the Florida Legislature replaced the law with a new one that made it clear that all government meetings are open to the public.

In 1909, Florida passed a law requiring all government records to be available for inspection and copying by the public. In *State ex rel. Davidson v. Couch*, 155 So. 153 (Fla. 1934) (en banc), the Florida Supreme Court upheld the law.

Today, these requirements are found, respectively, in Fla. Stat. ch. 119 (open records) and Fla. Stat. ch. 286 (open meetings). Technically, Chapter 119 is known as the "Public Records Act" while Chapter 286 is called the "Sunshine Law." In every day conversation, however, it is common to refer to both as the "sunshine law." All states, as well as the federal government, now have their own sunshine laws. (The term "sunshine law" comes from another Brandeis article. *See* Louis D. Brandeis, *What Publicity Can Do*, Harper's Weekly, Dec. 20, 1913, at 10. In it, Brandeis famously said that sunlight is the best disinfectant for public corruption.)

In 1978, the CRC proposed constitutionalizing both requirements but its suggestion was rejected (as explained above, its entire package of government reforms was defeated). In 1992, the legislature revived the CRC's idea after the Florida Supreme Court held that Chapter 119 did not apply to the legislature. *See Locke v. Hawkes*, 595 So. 2d 32 (Fla.

1992). The result is Art. I, § 24, which has four paragraphs.

Paragraph (a), governing open records, applies to "the legislative, executive, and judicial branches of government and each agency or department created thereunder; counties, municipalities, and districts; and each constitutional officer, board, and commission, or entity created pursuant to law or [the] Constitution."

Paragraph (b), governing open meetings, applies to "the executive branch of state government [as well as] any collegial public body of a county, municipality, school district, or special district." Paragraph (b) does not apply to meetings of the legislature because, as explained below, such meetings are "open and noticed as provided in Article III, Section 4(e)." Paragraph (b) also does not apply (for obvious reasons) to the courts. *See, e.g., The Florida Bar v. Committe*, 916 So. 2d 741 (Fla. 2005), *cert. denied*, 547 U.S. 1098 (2006).

Paragraph (c) allows the legislature to enact "exemptions" to both paragraph (a) and paragraph (b). To be effective, an exemption must: 1) pass by a 2/3 vote; 2) "state with specificity the public necessity" for it; and, 3) "be no broader than necessary to accomplish [its] stated purpose." *See Halifax Hospital Medical Center v. News-Journal Corp.*, 724 So. 2d 567 (Fla. 1999) (exemption for public hospitals' "strategic plans" was both too broad and too vague to be enforceable).

Lastly, paragraph (d) retains all exemptions that existed on July 1, 1993 until they are repealed.

By the time § 24 was added, two sections of the constitution already required the legislature to have open meetings (hence the reason for the legislature's omission from § 24(b)). First, Art. III, § 4(b) (whose roots go back to the 1838 constitution) requires legislative sessions to be open. Second, Art. III, § 4(e) states:

> The rules of procedure of each house shall provide that all legislative committee and subcommittee meetings of each house, and joint conference committee meetings, shall be open and noticed to the public. The rules of procedure of each house shall further provide that all prearranged gatherings, between more than two members of the legislature, or between the governor, the president of the senate, or the speaker of the house of representatives, the purpose of which is to agree upon formal legislative action that will be taken at a subsequent time, or at which formal legislative action is taken, regarding pending legislation or amendments, shall be reasonably open to the public.

Art. III, § 4(e) was added in 1990. This step followed a 1989 change to the senate's rules that required senators to more closely adhere to Chapter 286, a reaction to the public's growing dissatisfaction with the legislature's penchant for making deals behind closed doors.

Both the house and the senate have adopted rules implementing their constitutional obligations. *See* House Rules 3.4 (Open Meetings) and 14.1 (Open Records) and Senate Rules 1.44 (Open Meetings) and 1.48 (Legislative Records). These rules can be found, respectively, on www.myfloridahouse.gov and www. flsenate.gov.

There is a substantial body of case law, as well as numerous advisory opinions, interpreting Florida's sunshine law. As these precedents make clear, there is no practical difference between the constitutional provisions and the statutory provisions. *See, e.g., Monroe County v. Pigeon Key Historical Park, Inc.*, 647 So. 2d 857 (Fla. 3d Dist. Ct. App. 1994). And like all state enactments, both yield in the face of a conflicting federal law. *See, e.g., Rios v. Direct Mail Express, Inc.*, 435 F. Supp. 2d 1199 (S.D. Fla. 2006) (Art. I, § 24 held not to apply in a case subject to the federal Driver's Privacy Protection Act, 18 U.S.C. §§ 2721–2725).

Annually, Florida's attorney general publishes a detailed "sunshine manual" that collects and summarizes the relevant precedents. The 2019 version can be found at http://myfloridalegal.com/ webfiles.nsf/WF/MNOS-B9QQ79/$file/Sunshine Manual.pdf.

Certain issues recur so frequently, however, that they merit a quick word here. First, with respect to meetings:

(a) Meetings involving government officials are not supposed to be held "accidentally," or at a place or time when the public is unable to attend. *See Rhea v. School Board of Alachua County*, 636 So. 2d 1383 (Fla. 1st Dist. Ct. App. 1994). *See also Town of Palm Beach v. Gradison*, 296 So. 2d 473 (Fla. 1974).

In Apr. 2019, House Democrats held a secret meeting in Tallahassee. After reporters from the *Miami Herald* and the *Orlando Sentinel*, who were listening through a wall, tweeted what was happening, the lawmakers let them in. Rep. Shevrin Jones (D-West Park) later claimed there had been a "miscommunication."

In May 2019, Gov. Ron DeSantis (R) and the cabinet announced, shortly before leaving for a trip to Israel, that they would meet in Jerusalem. Various organizations sued, citing § 24. *See* https://floridafaf.org/wp-content/uploads/2019/06/Complaint-Tel-Aviv-Cabinet-Meeting.pdf. Because the plaintiffs were unable to make timely service, the lawsuit was dismissed and the meeting (which officials by now were calling "ceremonial") was held as planned.

(b) A private "middle man" cannot be used to evade the requirements of the open meetings law. Whether there has been evasion depends on whether the liaison had any decision-making authority. *See, e.g., Sarasota Citizens for Responsible Government v. City of Sarasota*, 48 So. 3d

755 (Fla. 2010) (no violation where private individuals merely gave advice to county official negotiating spring training contract with major league baseball team).

(c) Meetings between the government and its lawyers to discuss litigation strategy can be closed to the public. However, such sessions, which are known as "shade meetings," cannot be used as subterfuges to discuss other matters. *See Anderson v. City of St. Pete Beach*, 161 So. 3d 548 (Fla. 2d Dist. Ct. App. 2014).

(d) A private company performing a government function is subject to the open meetings law. *See Memorial Hospital-West Volusia, Inc. v. News-Journal Corp.*, 729 So. 2d 373 (Fla. 1999).

Second, with respect to records:

(a) The term "public records" is construed liberally, while exemptions are construed narrowly. *See Board of Trustees, Jacksonville Police & Fire Pension Fund v. Lee*, 189 So. 3d 120 (Fla. 2016).

(b) The government cannot impose conditions that make it unreasonably burdensome for members of the public to exercise their inspection and copying rights. *Id. See also Grapski v. City of Alachua*, 31 So. 3d 193 (Fla. 1st Dist. Ct. App.), *review denied*, 47 So. 3d 1288 (Fla. 2010).

(c)   If a public official uses his or her private computer or phone to conduct government business, any records generated by such activity will be deemed public records and must be turned over when requested. *See Media General Operation, Inc. v. Feeney*, 849 So. 2d 3 (Fla. 1st Dist. Ct. App.), *review denied*, 857 So. 2d 196 (Fla. 2003). In contrast, communications dealing only with non-work matters do not become public records simply because they are stored on a government-owned computer. *See State v. City of Clearwater*, 863 So. 2d 149 (Fla. 2003).

(d)   A private company performing a government function is subject to the open records law. *See Prison Health Services, Inc. v. Lakeland Ledger Publishing Co.*, 718 So. 2d 204 (Fla. 2d Dist. Ct. App. 1998), *review denied by The Florida Bar v. Bassie*, 727 So. 2d 912 (Fla. 1999).

Since 1995, the Florida Legislature has become increasingly hostile to the sunshine law. As a result, it has passed 280 bills creating new exemptions. (The total number of exemptions now stands at 1,122.) In response, the Florida Society of News Editors has begun publishing an annual "Sunshine Scorecard" that evaluates each legislator's commitment to open government. In 2019, the average grade was a "C-." *See* https://fsne.org/resources/. The highest grade ("B") was earned by Sen. Joe Gruters (R-Sarasota).

The 2018 mass shooting at Marjory Stoneman Douglas high school in Parkland has given rise to two notable sunshine law decisions. First, in *State Attorney's Office of Seventeenth Judicial Circuit v. Cable News Network, Inc.*, 251 So. 3d 205 (Fla. 4th Dist. Ct. App.), *review denied*, 2018 WL 4049131 (Fla. 2018), the Broward County School Board was ordered to release its video surveillance tapes. Second, in *Cruz v. State of Florida*, 279 So. 3d 154 (Fla. 4th Dist. Ct. App. 2019), *appeal filed*, SC19–1784 (Fla.), an effort by the gunman to keep out of the public's hands jail logs indicating which mental health experts he was meeting with was denied.

CHAPTER 6
COURT PROCEEDINGS

A. OVERVIEW

Art. V regulates the establishment, jurisdiction, and operation of the courts. *See* Ch. 15 of this book. Other parts of the constitution, however, also affect how the courts go about their business. This chapter examines three of them: Art. I, § 2 (equal protection); Art. I, § 21 (access to courts); and Art. I, § 22 (jury trials). *See also* Ch. 7 of this book (criminal prosecutions).

B. EQUAL PROTECTION

Art. I, § 2 provides: "All natural persons, female and male alike, are equal before the law . . . [and] [n]o person shall be deprived of any right because of race, religion, national origin, or physical disability." A version of this provision has appeared in every one of Florida's constitutions, although the 1838, 1861, and 1865 constitutions assured equality only for "freemen." This limitation was dropped beginning with the 1868 constitution.

In 1974, "physical handicap" was added to the list. This amendment was proposed by the Florida Legislature. Although the house wanted to include "mental handicap," the senate rejected the idea.

In 1998, at the suggestion of the Constitution Revision Commission ("CRC"), the phrase "physical handicap" was changed to "physical disability."

Florida is one of only three states that has a disability provision in its constitution (Louisiana and Rhode Island are the others).

The 1998 CRC also persuaded voters to add the words "female and male alike" to § 2. In lobbying for this change, the CRC stressed it was neither recognizing gay rights nor sanctioning same-sex marriages. Florida is one of 26 states with a constitutional provision banning gender discrimination.

In nearly all respects, Florida's courts interpret § 2 the same as the 14th Amendment. Thus, the government ordinarily can treat similarly-situated persons differently if a rational basis exists for doing so. Its actions are subject to intermediate ("heightened") scrutiny when it indirectly burdens a fundamental right or affects a quasi-suspect class (*e.g.*, illegitimates). Strict scrutiny applies if a fundamental right is infringed or a suspect class (*e.g.*, aliens) is involved. It should be noted that each of the rights in the Declaration of Rights (*i.e.*, Art. I) is considered fundamental. As such, they all are subject to strict scrutiny.

Under the rational basis test, a statute will be upheld if it serves a legitimate public purpose and it is neither arbitrary nor capricious. *See Department of Corrections v. Florida Nurses Association*, 508 So. 2d 317 (Fla. 1987). To survive intermediate scrutiny, a statute must be substantially related to an important governmental objective and there must be a reasonably close fit between the ends and the means. *See Norman v. State*, 215 So. 3d 18 (Fla.), *reh'g denied*, 2017 WL 1365211 (Fla.), *cert. denied*, 138 S. Ct. 469 (2017).

Statutes subject to strict scrutiny almost always are struck down:

> The strict scrutiny analysis requires careful examination of the governmental interest claimed to justify the classification in order to determine whether that interest is substantial and compelling and requires inquiry as to whether the means adopted to achieve the legislative goal are necessarily and precisely drawn. *Examining Board v. Flores De Otero*, 426 U.S. 572, 96 S.Ct. 2264, 49 L.Ed.2d 65 (1976). This test, which is almost always fatal in its application, imposes a heavy burden of justification upon the state and applies only when the statute operates to the disadvantage of some suspect class such as race, nationality, or alienage or impinges upon a fundamental right explicitly or implicitly protected by the constitution.

In re Greenberg's Estate, 390 So. 2d 40, 42–43 (Fla. 1980), *appeal dismissed sub nom. Pincus v. Estate of Greenberg*, 450 U.S. 961 (1981).

Considering Florida's demographics, it is odd that § 2 does not include either age or sexual orientation in its list of suspect classes. More understandable is the omission of the economically disadvantaged, given that the U.S. Supreme Court has held that wealth is not a suspect class. *See San Antonio*

Independent School District v. Rodriguez, 411 U.S. 1, *reh'g denied*, 411 U.S. 959 (1973).

Because of its use of the phrase "natural persons," § 2 does not apply to corporations and other artificial persons. They are protected, however, by the 14th Amendment. *See Faircloth v. Mr. Boston Distiller Corp.*, 245 So. 2d 240, 249–50 (Fla. 1970) (Drew, J., concurring specially). Sec. 2 also does not apply to discrimination by private persons. *See Schreiner v. McKenzie Tank Lines, Inc.*, 432 So. 2d 567 (Fla. 1983).

C. ACCESS TO COURTS

Art. I, § 21 directs: "The courts shall be open to every person for redress of any injury, and justice shall be administered without sale, denial or delay." A version of this provision has appeared in every Florida constitution except the 1868 constitution.

Read literally, the first half of § 21 would allow anyone to sue for anything, even if the claim was stale, trivial, or did not concern them. Unsurprisingly, the courts have rejected such an interpretation. *See, e.g., Damiano v. McDaniel*, 689 So. 2d 1059 (Fla. 1997) (four-year statute of repose barred plaintiffs' medical malpractice claim); *McCarty v. Myers*, 125 So. 3d 333 (Fla. 1st Dist. Ct. App. 2013), *review denied*, 143 So. 3d 921 (Fla. 2014) (action dismissed because plaintiffs lacked standing).

Thus, § 21 permits only *colorable* claims that are *justiciable. See, e.g., Tananta v. Cruise Ships Catering and Services International, N.V.*, 909 So. 2d

874, 888 (Fla. 3d Dist. Ct. App. 2004), *review denied*, 917 So. 2d 195 (Fla. 2005) ("While 'the Florida Constitution guarantees . . . access to our courts for redress of injuries, . . . that right has never been understood as a limitless warrant[.]' "). Moreover, access can be denied to a party that abuses the right. *See, e.g., Smith v. Fisher*, 965 So. 2d 205 (Fla. 4th Dist. Ct. App. 2007), *review denied*, 980 So. 2d 490 (Fla. 2008) (upholding Florida's Vexatious Litigant Law). *See also Pinder v. State*, 217 So. 3d 130 (Fla 3d Dist. Ct. App.), *review denied*, 2017 WL 1179490 (Fla. 2017) (inmate could be barred from repeatedly appealing his sentence).

The second half of § 21 is equally unremarkable. It requires the courts to dispense justice as fairly and quickly as possible, while ignoring all improper influences and temptations. The sentence's archaic wording ("without sale, denial or delay") is borrowed from the early constitutions of other states. They, in turn, picked it up from various colonial charters.

Most of the litigation that has arisen under § 21 has concerned the elimination of causes of action by the legislature. As a result, the following rule has emerged: the legislature cannot abolish a cause of action that existed on either of two different dates without providing a substantially equivalent substitute unless no alternative can be provided. *See Full Circle Dairy, LLC v. McKinney*, 467 F. Supp. 2d 1343 (M.D. Fla. 2006).

The foregoing is most easily grasped by examining the history of Florida's "heart balm" statute. *See* Fla. Stat. § 771.01. At one time, Florida, like other jurisdictions, allowed parties to sue for the torts of alienation of affection, criminal conversation (*i.e.*, adultery), seduction, and breach of the promise to marry. The money collected through these lawsuits was meant to act as a balm for the plaintiff's broken heart.

In 1945, the Florida Legislature abolished all four actions by enacting § 771.01. It took this step because defendants (especially publicity-shy ones) were being shaken down by unscrupulous plaintiffs and their lawyers. When the statute was challenged, the Florida Supreme Court had no trouble upholding it:

> The causes of action proscribed by the act under review were a part of the common law and have long been a part of the law of the country. They have no doubt served a good purpose, but when they become an instrument of extortion and blackmail, the legislature has the power to, and may, limit or abolish them.

Rotwein v. Gersten, 36 So. 2d 419, 421 (Fla. 1948) (en banc).

In determining whether the legislature can abolish a cause of action, two questions must be answered: 1) did the cause of action exist at common law?; and, 2) if not, did it exist by statute prior to the adoption of the 1968 Florida Constitution?

The term "common law" refers to July 4, 1776. *See* Fla. Stat. § 2.01. The relevant statutory date is November 5, 1968. *See Kluger v. White*, 281 So. 2d 1 (Fla. 1973).

As *Kluger* makes clear, if the cause of action did not exist on either of these dates, the legislature can abolish it. Otherwise, the legislature must provide an adequate alternative remedy unless no alternative is available or every alternative would be worse. *See University of Miami v. Echarte*, 618 So. 2d 189 (Fla.), *cert. denied*, 510 U.S. 915 (1993); *Lasky v. State Farm Insurance Co.*, 296 So. 2d 9 (Fla. 1974).

If the legislature fails to provide an alternative remedy (when a suitable alternative exists), or gives one that is not equivalent, the courts normally revive the prior remedy. *See, e.g., Westphal v. City of St. Petersburg*, 194 So. 3d 311 (Fla. 2016) (reinstating prior statute that provided 260 weeks of temporary total disability benefits after finding that the new statute, which granted 104 weeks of benefits, was unconstitutional).

Eliminating a cause of action is not the only way the legislature can violate § 21. For example, a statute that makes it unnecessarily difficult for a party to access the courts violates § 21. *See, e.g., Weaver v. Myers*, 229 So. 3d 1118 (Fla. 2017) (statute that required medical malpractice plaintiffs to give up their privacy rights in exchange for being allowed to sue was invalid); *Mitchell v. Moore*, 786 So. 2d 521 (Fla. 2001) (statute that forced prisoners to procure various records before being able to proceed as indigent litigants was invalid). *But see Partnership for Community Health, Inc. v. Department of Children and Families*, 93 So. 3d 1191 (Fla. 1st Dist. Ct. App. 2012) (statute that required bond to be posted to challenge administrative agency's decision was valid).

A mistake by a court that prejudices a party can, under certain circumstances, also give rise to a § 21 violation. In *Merian v. Merhige*, 641 So. 2d 475 (Fla. 3d Dist. Ct. App. 1994), for example, a trial court in a post-divorce action violated the husband's right of access by striking his objections to the general master's report for untimeliness. Due to a clerical error, the general master had failed to send out his report on schedule, resulting in the husband receiving it late.

The rule that prohibits lawyers from communicating with jurors after they have rendered their verdict has been challenged repeatedly under § 21. The Florida Supreme Court, however, has upheld it as necessary to protect the judicial process. *See Power v. State*, 886 So. 2d 952 (Fla. 2004); *Johnson v. State*, 804 So. 2d 1218 (Fla. 2001); *Rose v. State*, 774 So. 2d 629 (Fla. 2000).

D. JURY TRIALS

Art. I, § 22 states: "The right of trial by jury shall be secure to all and remain inviolate. The qualifications and the number of jurors, not fewer than six, shall be fixed by law." The right to a jury trial has been included in every version of the Florida Constitution. Because of its fundamental nature, the right to a jury trial is broadly construed. *See Wiggins v. Williams*, 18 So. 859 (Fla. 1896).

Civil cases are heard by six jurors. *See* Fla. Stat. § 69.071. Criminal capital cases are heard by 12 jurors. *See* Fla. Stat. § 913.10. All other criminal cases are heard by six jurors. *Id.* Where a defendant is charged with a capital crime, but does not face the death penalty, a jury of six is permissible. *See Jimenez v. State*, 167 So. 3d 497 (Fla. 3d Dist. Ct. App.), *review denied*, 192 So. 3d 38 (Fla. 2015).

A defendant can waive his or her jury rights, but the waiver must be knowing and informed. *See, e.g., Blair v. State*, 698 So. 2d 1210 (Fla. 1997); *Westberry v. State*, 239 So. 3d 186 (Fla. 3d Dist. Ct. App.), *review denied*, 2018 WL 1737054 (Fla. 2018); *Flanning v. State*, 597 So. 2d 864 (Fla. 3d Dist. Ct. App.), *review denied*, 605 So. 2d 1266 (Fla. 1992).

A suit for money damages ordinarily gives rise to a right to a jury trial. *See 381651 Alberta, Ltd. v. 279298 Alberta, Ltd.*, 675 So. 2d 1385 (Fla. 4th Dist. Ct. App. 1996). *But see Cerrito v. Kovitch*, 457 So. 2d 1021 (Fla. 1984) (statute requiring forfeiture of usurious interest did not create a cause of action triable by a jury).

In contrast, a demand for equitable or injunctive relief ordinarily does not give rise to a right to a jury trial. *See Boyce v. Hort*, 666 So. 2d 972 (Fla. 5th Dist. Ct. App. 1996). In cases seeking multiple forms of relief, only the claims for money damages are entitled to a jury trial, unless the non-money claims are so intertwined that the court orders the entire case to be submitted to the jury. *See Yer Girl Tera Mia v. Wimberly*, 962 So. 2d 993 (Fla. 5th Dist. Ct. App. 2007).

The right to a jury trial also does not apply to attorney disbarments, see *State v. McRae*, 38 So. 605 (Fla. 1905); eminent domain proceedings, see *Carter v. State Road Department*, 189 So. 2d 793 (Fla. 1966); inverse condemnation claims, see *Department of Agriculture and Consumer Services v. Bonanno*, 568 So. 2d 24 (Fla. 1990); mortgage foreclosures, see *Nerbonne, N.V. v. Lake Bryan International Properties*, 689 So. 2d 322 (Fla. 5th Dist. Ct. App. 1997); or tax appraisals, see *Section 3 Property Corp. v. Robbins*, 632 So. 2d 596 (Fla. 1993). Workers' compensation claimants also have no right to a jury trial. *See De Ayala v. Florida Farm Bureau Casualty Insurance Co.*, 543 So. 2d 204 (Fla. 1989).

The fact that a case includes complicated issues is not a proper basis for refusing a party's request for a jury trial. *See Martell & Sons, Inc. v. Friedman*, 461 So. 2d 1023 (Fla. 3d Dist. Ct. App.), *review denied sub nom. Bravo Electric Co. v. Martell & Sons, Inc.*, 469 So. 2d 748 (Fla. 1985); *Cheek v. McGowan Electric Supply Co.*, 404 So. 2d 834 (Fla. 1st Dist. Ct. App. 1981).

CHAPTER 7
CRIMINAL PROSECUTIONS

A. OVERVIEW

The Florida Constitution contains numerous provisions affecting the criminal justice system. These can be divided into four categories: pre-trial rights, trial rights, post-trial rights, and victims' rights.

B. CODIFICATION

1. COMMON LAW CRIMES

Nearly all crimes in Florida appear in the Florida Criminal Code. *See* Fla. Stat. chs. 775–896. A small number of crimes, however, have not been codified. Such crimes are known as "common law crimes." *See* Fla. Stat. § 775.01. An example of a common law crime is criminal contempt. *See Gems v. State*, 188 So. 3d 42 (Fla. 3d Dist. Ct. App. 2016).

At one time, every state recognized common law crimes, but today most (36) do not for due process reasons. Florida remains one of the few that does. *See State v. Egan*, 287 So. 2d 1 (Fla. 1973) (rejecting a "void for vagueness" challenge to Fla. Stat. § 775.01 in a case involving the common law crime of nonfeasance). All federal crimes must be authorized by statute. *See United States v. Hudson and Goodwin*, 11 U.S. (7 Cranch) 32 (1812).

2.   REPEAL OF CRIMINAL STATUTES

Until 2018, Art. X, § 9, better known as the constitution's "savings clause," read: "Repeal or amendment of a criminal statute shall not affect prosecution or punishment for any crime previously committed." In 2018, this language was changed to: "Repeal of a criminal statute shall not affect prosecution for any crime committed before such repeal." *See Jimenez v. Secretary, Florida Department of Corrections*, 758 F. App'x 682 (11th Cir.), *cert. denied*, 139 S. Ct. 659 (2018).

The proposal to modify § 9 came from the Constitution Revision Commission. Following an unsuccessful court challenge, see *Detzner v. Anstead*, 256 So. 3d 820 (Fla. 2018), it appeared on the ballot as Amendment 11.

Sec. 9 was added to the constitution in 1885 to prevent criminal defendants from taking advantage of subsequent legislative changes (hence its nickname). A good example is *Castle v. State*, 330 So. 2d 10 (Fla. 1976).

In 1970, Darion Castle attempted to burn down his sailboat to collect on a $15,000 insurance policy. At the time, the maximum penalty for arson was 10 years. In 1972, Castle was found guilty and sentenced to 10 years. In 1973, the maximum penalty for arson was reduced to five years. When Castle sought a reduction in his sentence, the Florida Supreme Court rejected his request: "[A]ppellant was not entitled to the benefit of the later-enacted lower maximum sentence, and to the extent that Section

775.12 suggests otherwise it would have been unconstitutional. See Florida Constitution Article X, § 9." *Id*. at 11 (footnote omitted).

The passage of Amendment 11 does not change § 9 when it comes to criminal prosecutions (as opposed to criminal punishments). Thus, even if a statute is repealed, a person who violated it while it was in effect remains subject to prosecution.

Amendment 11's supporters had hoped that it would lead to a reduction in Florida's prison population. Shortly before the election, the ACLU calculated that Florida could cut its prison population by 47%, and save $1.6 billion a year, if it made its criminal penalties less draconian and applied the changes to those already incarcerated. Instead, in 2019 the Florida Legislature adopted a statutory savings clause that reads much like the one the voters repealed. *See* Fla. Laws ch. 2019–63 (codified as Fla. Stat. § 775.022). *See also Stapleton v. State*, 2019 WL 5485556 (Fla. 5th Dist. Ct. App. 2019).

At the time of the 2018 election, only Florida, New Mexico, and Oklahoma had savings clauses in their constitutions. Florida's clause has a particularly interesting history.

In 1880, Christopher Higginbotham tried to kill a man in Marion County. After being found guilty, he was sentenced to 10 years under an 1868 law that made the maximum penalty for assault 20 years. In 1881, the legislature repealed the 1868 law and replaced it with a new law that made the maximum penalty seven years.

When Higginbotham's appeal reached the Florida Supreme Court, it held that because of the way the 1881 law was written, he could not be tried under either it or the 1868 law. As a result, it ordered him freed. *See Higginbotham v. State*, 19 Fla. 557 (1882). This outcome so enraged the public that inclusion of a savings clause in the 1885 constitution became a top priority. *See State v. Watts*, 558 So. 2d 994 (Fla. 1990).

C. DEFINITIONS

1. FELONIES, MISDEMEANORS, AND VIOLATIONS

Art. X, § 10 states: "The term 'felony' as used herein and in the laws of this state shall mean any criminal offense that is punishable under the laws of this state, or that would be punishable if committed in this state, by death or by imprisonment in the state penitentiary." This provision was added during the constitution's 1968 revision.

Fla. Stat. § 775.08 provides the following additional definitions:

(1) The term "felony" shall mean any criminal offense that is punishable under the laws of this state, or that would be punishable if committed in this state, by death or imprisonment in a state penitentiary. . . .

(2) The term "misdemeanor" shall mean any criminal offense that is punishable under the laws of this state, or that would be punishable if committed in this state, by a term of imprisonment in a county correctional facility, except an extended term, not in excess of 1 year. . . .

(3) The term "noncriminal violation" shall mean any offense that is punishable under the laws of this state, or that would be punishable if committed in this state, by no other penalty than a fine, forfeiture, or other civil penalty. A noncriminal violation does not constitute a crime, and conviction for a noncriminal violation shall not give rise to any legal disability based on a criminal offense. . . .

(4) The term "crime" shall mean a felony or misdemeanor.

Thus, the difference between a felony and a misdemeanor is the amount of time to which a defendant can be sentenced, with the dividing line being one year.

Most states use the same definitions as Florida. Massachusetts, however, defines a misdemeanor as any crime that is punishable by up to 30 months in jail. New Jersey has replaced the words "felony" and "misdemeanor" with "crime" and "disorderly person offense." The federal government uses the terms "felony," "misdemeanor," and "infraction." *See* 18 U.S.C. § 3559.

2. BILLS OF ATTAINDER

A bill of attainder is a law that declares a person, or a group of persons, guilty of a crime without the benefit of a judicial trial. Art. I, § 10 prohibits the legislature from passing such laws. For a further discussion, see Ch. 13 of this book.

3. EX POST FACTO LAWS

An ex post facto law is a law that retroactively criminalizes previously legal behavior. Art. I, § 10 prohibits the legislature from passing such laws. For a further discussion, see Ch. 13 of this book.

4. TREASON

Art. I, § 20 explains: "Treason against the state shall consist only in levying war against it, adhering to its enemies, or giving them aid and comfort, and no person shall be convicted of treason except on the testimony of two witnesses to the same overt act or on confession in open court." This provision was added by the 1868 constitution and has been retained in each succeeding constitution. Treason is the only crime defined in the constitution. Fla. Stat. § 876.32 makes treason a felony.

Treason is a rare crime, and there have been no prosecutions for it in Florida's history. Outside Florida, fewer than 50 people have been tried for treason. Despite now being popularly associated with the word "treason," Benedict Arnold escaped to England before he could be charged.

Treason requires the government to prove that the defendant was "disloyal." Except in wartime, this is a very difficult standard to meet. As a result, prosecutors typically charge defendants under other laws. The principal statute used is the Espionage Act of 1917, 18 U.S.C. §§ 792–799, which makes it a crime to reveal classified information.

D. PRE-TRIAL RIGHTS

1. SEARCHES AND SEIZURES

Art. I, § 12 protects citizens "against unreasonable searches and seizures, and against the unreasonable interception of private communications by any means." As a result, except in exigent circumstances, a law enforcement officer must obtain a warrant from a judge before conducting a search or seizure. In applying for the warrant, the officer must submit an "affidavit, particularly describing the place or places to be searched, the person or persons, thing or things to be seized, the communication to be intercepted, and the nature of evidence to be obtained." *Id*.

Sec. 12 first appeared in Florida's 1861 constitution. It remained largely the same for the next 120 years, the only significant change being the addition (in 1968) of the words "private communications," a reference to electronic wiretaps.

In the 1970s, federal courts interpreting the Fourth Amendment began recognizing a "good faith" exception to the exclusionary rule. This allowed otherwise tainted evidence to be used by prosecutors so long as it had been gathered in good faith. The

Florida Supreme Court refused to read this exception into § 12. *See State v. Sarmiento*, 397 So. 2d 643 (Fla. 1981).

To overturn *Sarmiento*, the Florida Legislature in 1982 proposed "linking" § 12 to the Fourth Amendment. As a result, the following two sentences now appear at the end of § 12:

This right shall be construed in conformity with the 4th Amendment to the United States Constitution, as interpreted by the United States Supreme Court. Articles or information obtained in violation of this right shall not be admissible in evidence if such articles or information would be inadmissible under decisions of the United States Supreme Court construing the 4th Amendment to the United States Constitution.

No other state's constitution has such a provision (known as a "conformity clause"), and the 1982 amendment has been roundly criticized as an inappropriate delegation of state power.

Even if a law enforcement officer complies with the Fourth Amendment (and, thus, with § 12), evidence will be suppressed if its collection violates another Florida law. *See, e.g., State v. Slaney*, 653 So. 2d 422 (Fla. 3d Dist. Ct. App. 1995) (involuntary drawing of a motorist's blood in a DUI case did not violate the Fourth Amendment but did violate the procedures prescribed by Florida's implied consent statute).

2.   INDICTMENTS

Art. I, § 15(a) provides:

> No person shall be tried for capital crime without presentment or indictment by a grand jury, or for other felony without such presentment or indictment or an information under oath filed by the prosecuting officer of the court, except persons on active duty in the militia when tried by courts martial.

This provision first appeared in the 1838 constitution. Although its wording has been changed repeatedly since the 1865 constitution, its basic principles have remained the same. Thus, a person can be charged with a capital crime (*i.e.*, a crime for which the maximum penalty is death) only when a grand jury issues an indictment (known as a "true bill"). For all other felonies, the state attorney's office is permitted to file an information.

Florida currently has only two capital crimes: murder and high-level drug trafficking. *See* Fla. Stat. §§ 782.04 and 893.135. As a result, grand juries rarely are used in Florida. When they are, they must have between 15 and 21 members. *See* Fla. Stat. § 905.01(1). For an example of a grand jury indictment, see https://www.foxnews.com/projects/pdf/Anthony_Indictment.PDF (2008 indictment of Casey Anthony).

Since 1973, the governor has been authorized to request that a statewide grand jury be empaneled to investigate crime occurring in two more judicial circuits. Such requests are made to the Florida

Supreme Court. *See* Fla. Stat. §§ 905.31–905.40. To date, governors have used this power 20 times. In 2019, for example, the court granted Gov. Ron DeSantis's request for a statewide grand jury "to examine the crimes and wrongs that precipitated the [2018] Marjory Stoneman Douglas [high] school shooting." *See Statewide Grand Jury #20*, 2019 WL 908518 (Fla. 2019). For a further discussion, see https://www.floridasupremecourt.org/News-Media/ Statewide-Grand-Jury.

Other than Liberia, the United States is the only common law country that still has grand juries. The Fifth Amendment obligates the federal government to use grand juries in all felony cases. This requirement does not apply to the states. *See Hurtado v. California*, 110 U.S. 516 (1884). As a result, two states (Connecticut and Pennsylvania) have abolished grand juries, 25 have made them optional, and the remaining 23 (including Florida) require their use only in certain types of cases.

Florida also has civil grand juries. These are used to examine the operation of public entities. At the end of such an investigation, the grand jury normally issues a report, known as a "presentment," in which it recommends changes. *See, e.g.,* http://www.miami sao.com/publications/grandjuryreports.htm (collection of Miami-Dade County civil grand jury reports).

For a further look at grand juries in Florida, see Fla. Stat. §§ 905.01–905.28.

3. BAIL

When a person is arrested, he or she typically is given the opportunity to "make" bail. To do so, a defendant must put up a specified amount of money, which is held in the court's registry.

A defendant who makes bail is released until his or her trial. Thus, bail takes the place of the defendant. A defendant who shows up for trial (as well as all ancillary proceedings) gets his or her money back (without interest). Conversely, a defendant who "skips" forfeits his or her money.

The amount of bail that a defendant must post is determined by a judge. In setting bail, the judge takes various factors into account, including the seriousness of the crime and the defendant's financial condition. The goal is to set a bail high enough that the defendant is likely to show up for trial, without setting it so high that the defendant has no realistic chance of making bail.

It is in society's interest to have as many defendants as possible make bail. This is so for four reasons. First, all defendants are presumed innocent—thus, holding a defendant who has yet to be found guilty of any crime is unjust. Second, it costs the government money to keep a defendant locked up prior to trial. Third, it is much easier for a released defendant to participate in his or her defense. Fourth, a defendant who is not in jail is able to work, support his or her family, and pay taxes.

Given the foregoing, the right to bail has appeared in every one of Florida's constitutions. In 1982, however, the Florida Legislature persuaded voters to make it more difficult to obtain bail. It also recommended that the word "bail" be replaced by the words "pretrial release." As a result, Art. I, § 14 now reads:

> Unless charged with a capital offense or an offense punishable by life imprisonment and the proof of guilt is evident or the presumption is great, every person charged with a crime or violation of municipal or county ordinance shall be entitled to pretrial release on reasonable conditions. If no conditions of release can reasonably protect the community from risk of physical harm to persons, assure the presence of the accused at trial, or assure the integrity of the judicial process, the accused may be detained.

As can be seen, bail *may* be denied if the government can demonstrate either of the following:

1) The defendant is charged with a crime that could result in the death penalty or life imprisonment *and* the proof of guilt is "evident."

2) The defendant is charged with a crime that could result in the death penalty or life imprisonment *and* the presumption of guilt is "great."

Although bail normally is denied in capital cases, a capital defendant must be given a chance to argue that it should be granted. *See Reeves v. Nocco*, 141 So. 3d 775 (Fla. 2d Dist. Ct. App. 2014).

Bail also *may* be denied if the government can demonstrate:

1) Granting bail likely would result in the defendant committing new crimes involving physical injury; *or*,

2) Granting bail likely would result in the defendant fleeing the jurisdiction; *or*,

3) Granting bail likely would result in the defendant intimidating witnesses or tampering with evidence.

In the absence of the foregoing, the defendant must be granted "pretrial release on reasonable conditions." Although it is up to the judge to determine what constitutes reasonable conditions, Fla. Stat. § 903.046 offers the following guidance:

(1) The purpose of a bail determination in criminal proceedings is to ensure the appearance of the criminal defendant at subsequent proceedings and to protect the community against unreasonable danger from the criminal defendant.

(2) When determining whether to release a defendant on bail or other conditions, and what that bail or those conditions may be, the court shall consider:

(a) The nature and circumstances of the offense charged.

(b) The weight of the evidence against the defendant.

(c) The defendant's family ties, length of residence in the community, employment history, financial resources, and mental condition.

(d) The defendant's past and present conduct, including any record of convictions, previous flight to avoid prosecution, or failure to appear at court proceedings. . . .

(e) The nature and probability of danger which the defendant's release poses to the community.

(f) The source of funds used to post bail or procure an appearance bond, particularly whether the proffered funds, real property, property, or any proposed collateral or bond premium may be linked to or derived from the crime alleged to have been committed or from any other criminal or illicit activities. . . .

(g) Whether the defendant is already on release pending resolution of another criminal proceeding or on probation, parole, or other release pending completion of a sentence.

(h) The street value of any drug or controlled substance connected to or involved in the criminal charge. . . .

(i) The nature and probability of intimidation and danger to victims.

(j) Whether there is probable cause to believe that the defendant committed a new crime while on pretrial release.

(k) Any other facts that the court considers relevant. . . .

In addition to setting a bail amount, a judge may impose specific conditions that the defendant must follow, such as: avoiding specific places or people (including the victim); maintaining or seeking employment; obeying all laws; observing a curfew; refraining from alcohol or drug use; surrendering all passports; and wearing a tracking device. *See* Fla. Stat. § 903.047.

If the defendant fails to make bail, he or she remains incarcerated until trial. Likewise, if the defendant makes bail but fails to follow the conditions set by the judge, bail can be revoked. In such cases, the defendant is returned to jail until trial.

Some defendants are released on their own recognizance ("ROR"). First-time offenders who are charged with non-serious crimes typically receive ROR. In such instances, the defendant does not put up any money but simply signs an agreement promising to appear for all future court dates.

Defendants who do not have enough money to post bail often turn to a "bail bond agent" (known, in everyday speech, as a "bail bondsman"). In Florida, bail bondsmen are licensed by the state. *See* Fla. Stat. §§ 648.24–648.58.

A bail bondsman is required to charge 10% for his or her services. *See* Fla. Stat. § 648.33. This payment is called the "premium" and is non-refundable. *See Holton v. State*, 311 So. 2d 711 (Fla. 3d Dist. Ct. App. 1975). Thus, if a defendant's bail is $20,000, the defendant must pay the bail bondsman $2,000.

If the amount of the bond is very large, the bail bondsman may require, in addition to the premium, collateral equal to the value of the bond. *See* Fla. Stat. § 648.442. Thus, for example, if the defendant's bond is $200,000, the bail bondsman may insist that the defendant pledge assets worth this amount. Typically, bail bondsmen prefer real estate as collateral because it is easy to value and keep tabs on.

If the defendant makes all court appearances, the bail bondsman simply keeps the premium. If the defendant skips, however, the bail bondsman forfeits his or her bond to the court. In such instances, Florida law allows the bail bondsman to go after the defendant. *See* Fla. Stat. § 648.30(3) (granting bail bondsmen arrest powers). If the bail bondsman brings the defendant back to court in a timely fashion, the bond is reinstated. *See* Fla. Stat. §§ 903.20–903.29. For a further look at bail bondsmen, see the web site of the American Bail Coalition (http://ambailcoalition.org/), the industry's trade group.

For-profit bail bondsmen exist in only two countries: the Philippines and the United States. Many observers are highly critical of U.S. bail bondsmen, claiming that they prey on the poor. *See, e.g.,* https://d11gn0ip9m46ig.cloudfront.net/images/059_Bail_Report.pdf (ACLU report describing the bail bond industry).

In 2006, bail bondsmen convinced the Florida Legislature to require judges to set a separate amount for each offense charged, rather than just the highest offense. *See* Fla. Stat. § 903.02(4). This has greatly increased the industry's profits because a defendant charged with multiple offenses now must obtain multiple bonds.

The greatest failing of the bail system, however, is that even with it many defendants are unable to "bond out." Indeed, studies have found that 1/3 of the inmates in Florida's jails are there because they lack the money needed to make bail. This problem has become increasingly acute over the past 20 years.

Because of the disproportionate impact on minorities and other marginalized groups, multiple lawsuits have been filed contending that the current bail system is unconstitutional. To date, these actions have not been successful. *See, e.g., Knight v. Sheriff of Leon County*, 369 F. Supp. 3d 1214 (N.D. Fla. 2019).

4.   HABEAS CORPUS

Art. I, § 13 states: "The writ of habeas corpus shall be grantable of right, freely and without cost. It shall be returnable without delay, and shall never be suspended unless, in case of rebellion or invasion, suspension is essential to the public safety." Such a provision has appeared in every one of Florida's constitutions.

The writ (*i.e.*, order) of habeas corpus (Latin for "bring forth the body") is known as the "Great Writ" and is considered, along with the right to trial by jury, to be one of the cornerstones of Anglo-American jurisprudence. Because of its importance, the Florida Constitution permits any justice, as well as most lower court judges, to grant it. *See* Art. V, § 3(b)(9) (supreme court justices); Art. V, § 4(b)(3) (district court of appeal judges); Art. V, § 5(b) (circuit court judges).

When granted, the writ requires the person holding the prisoner to come forward and explain the legal basis for the detention. *See Allison v. Baker*, 11 So. 2d 578 (Fla. 1943) (Div. B). If the court is not satisfied with the explanation, it must free the prisoner. *See* Fla. Stat. § 79.01. Conversely, if the detention is lawful, the court must remand the prisoner to custody. *See* Fla. Stat. § 79.08.

Except in unusual circumstances, the writ is filed and heard in the circuit where the prisoner is being detained. *See Richardson v. State*, 918 So. 2d 999 (Fla. 5th Dist. Ct. App. 2006). The writ is not available if the petitioner is not currently in custody. *See Lambertson v. State*, 479 So. 2d 773 (Fla. 5th Dist. Ct. App. 1985).

In modern practice, the writ most often is used when a convicted defendant, having exhausted his or her direct appeal rights, claims that his or her trial was constitutionally defective. In *Banks v. Jones*, 232 So. 3d 963 (Fla. 2017), however, the Florida Supreme Court allowed it to be used by an inmate who objected to being moved from a prison's "general population" to a restricted housing unit as punishment for spitting in a prison psychiatrist's face.

The writ has never been suspended in Florida. As a result, it is unclear who can suspend it. In England, only parliament can suspend the writ.

While the writ normally is considered a criminal tool, it is available in civil cases. Thus, for example, a person who has been involuntarily confined to a mental health facility can use it to try to gain his or her freedom. *See* Fla. Stat. § 394.459(8). *See also Ex parte Hansen*, 162 So. 715 (Fla. 1935) (en banc).

E.   TRIAL RIGHTS

1.   ADULTS

Art. I, § 9 states: "No person shall be deprived of life, liberty or property without due process of law, or be twice put in jeopardy for the same offense, or be compelled in any criminal matter to be a witness against oneself." Art. I, § 16(a) further directs:

In all criminal prosecutions the accused shall, upon demand, be informed of the nature and cause of the accusation, and shall be furnished a copy of the charges, and shall have the right to have compulsory process for witnesses, to confront at trial adverse witnesses, to be heard in person, by counsel or both, and to have a speedy and public trial by impartial jury in the county where the crime was committed. If the county is not known, the indictment or information may charge venue in two or more counties conjunctively and proof that the crime was committed in that area shall be sufficient; but before pleading the accused may elect in which of those counties the trial will take place. Venue for prosecution of crimes committed beyond the boundaries of the state shall be fixed by law.

The rights contained in these sections can be summarized as follows:

1) The defendant must be given a list of the charges he or she will face at trial.

2) The defendant must be allowed to retain an attorney.

3) The defendant must be given a speedy and public trial.

4) The defendant's case must be heard by an impartial jury.

5) The defendant must be tried in the county where the crime took place.

6) The defendant must be allowed to present favorable witnesses.

7) The defendant must be allowed to cross-examine unfavorable witnesses.

8) The defendant must be allowed to remain silent at the trial.

9) The defendant cannot be tried for the same offense twice.

10) The process used to try the defendant must be fair.

Rights 1–9 first appeared in the 1838 constitution and have been retained in every subsequent constitution. Right 10 was added by the 1865 constitution. Each of these rights has a counterpart in the U.S. Constitution, either in the Fifth Amendment (rights 8–10) or the Sixth Amendment (rights 1–7).

2. CHILDREN

Art. I, § 15(b) states:

When authorized by law, a child as therein defined may be charged with a violation of law as an act of delinquency instead of crime and tried without a jury or other requirements applicable to criminal cases. Any child so charged shall, upon demand made as provided by law before a trial in a juvenile proceeding, be tried in an appropriate court as an adult. A child found delinquent shall be disciplined as provided by law.

At one time, children routinely were tried as juvenile delinquents to spare them from the harshness of the adult criminal justice system. In 2001, however, Lionel Tate was found guilty of murder and sentenced to life imprisonment without the possibility of parole for killing a six-year-old girl that his mother was babysitting (the pair had been wrestling). At the time of the murder, Tate was 12, making him the youngest person in modern times to receive such a sentence.

Although Tate's sentence later was reduced after questions were raised about his mental competency, see *Tate v. State*, 864 So. 2d 44 (Fla. 4th Dist. Ct. App. 2003), his conviction marked a turning point in Florida's approach to crimes committed by minors. Specifically, prosecutors, using a process known as "direct file," began to increasingly charge children as adults. By 2018, 900 Florida children were being tried in adult courts each year, more than any other state.

The willingness of Florida prosecutors to try children as adults, often to help their re-election chances, provoked a great deal of criticism. As a result, numerous changes were made to the system in 2019, including the elimination of mandatory direct filing. *See* Fla. Laws ch. 2019–167 (amending Fla. Stat. § 985.557).

F. POST-TRIAL RIGHTS

1. EXCESSIVE PUNISHMENTS

Art. I, § 17 provides:

Excessive fines, cruel and unusual punishment, attainder, forfeiture of estate, indefinite imprisonment, and unreasonable detention of witnesses are forbidden. The death penalty is an authorized punishment for capital crimes designated by the legislature. The prohibition against cruel or unusual punishment, and the prohibition against cruel and unusual punishment, shall be construed in conformity with decisions of the United States Supreme Court which interpret the prohibition against cruel and unusual punishment provided in the Eighth Amendment to the United States Constitution. Any method of execution shall be allowed, unless prohibited by the United States Constitution. Methods of execution may be designated by the legislature, and a change in any method of execution may be applied retroactively. A sentence of death shall not be reduced on the basis that a method of execution is invalid. In any case in which an execution method is declared invalid, the death sentence shall remain in force until the sentence can be lawfully executed by any valid method. This section shall apply retroactively.

A prohibition on excessive punishments has been included in every one of Florida's constitutions. In 1998, the Florida Legislature proposed that this section be "linked" to the Eighth Amendment. Although the proposal passed easily, the Florida Supreme Court nullified it in 2000 because its ballot title and summary were defective. *See Armstrong v. Harris*, 773 So. 2d 7 (Fla. 2000), *cert. denied*, 532 U.S. 958 (2001). After fixing these problems, the legislature re-submitted the amendment to the voters in 2002, who again passed it (but by a narrower margin).

It is helpful to divide § 17 into its two parts. The first sentence—"Excessive fines, cruel and unusual punishment, attainder, forfeiture of estate, indefinite imprisonment, and unreasonable detention of witnesses are forbidden."—is what appeared in the 1968 constitution. The only difference is that the 1968 constitution used the word "or," which the 2002 amendment changed to "and." This was done to conform § 17 to the Eighth Amendment, which reads: "Excessive bail shall not be required, nor excessive fines imposed, nor cruel and unusual punishments inflicted." As a result, a § 17 petitioner now must show that a punishment is both cruel *and* unusual.

The first sentence of § 17 is both self-explanatory and exceedingly vague. As a result, the courts have had to fill in the gaps on a case-by-case basis. *See, e.g., Ferguson v. State*, 101 So. 3d 362 (Fla.), *cert. denied*, 568 U.S. 973 (2012) (being on death row for more than three decades does not constitute cruel and unusual punishment); *State v. Cotton*, 198 So. 3d 737 (Fla. 2d Dist. Ct. App.), *review denied*, 2016 WL 3272991 (Fla. 2016) ($5,000 fine for soliciting prostitution is not excessive).

The remainder of § 17 was added by the 2002 amendment. Its purpose and effect have been described as follows:

This amendment was proposed in the wake of challenges to the use of electrocution as the method of execution in Florida. After Florida's electric chair malfunctioned for a second time, causing burns to the condemned, a claim was made that this method of execution constitutes cruel or unusual punishment. *Jones v. State*, 701 So. 2d 76 (Fla. 1997). The *Jones* sentence was upheld in a 4–3 decision. The Legislature wished to ensure that should electrocution be held unconstitutional sometime in the future, death sentences would not be commuted to life sentences, as happened in 1972. *See, e.g., Furman v. Georgia*, 408 U. S. 238 (1972); *Anderson v. State*, 267 So. 2d 8 (Fla. 1972).

William A. Buzzett & Deborah K. Kearney, "Commentary to 1998 Amendment," 25B *West's Florida Statutes Annotated* 180 (2004).

Florida carried out its first execution in 1827, when it hung a Pensacola soldier named Benjamin Donica for killing his commanding officer. To date, a total of 447 individuals have been executed in Florida.

At the end of 2019, Florida had 341 prisoners (including three women) on death row. Contrary to popular belief, the majority—59.8%—were white. *See* http://www.dc.state.fl.us/OffenderSearch/deathrow roster.aspx.

Florida is one of 29 states that still has the death penalty. Since 1976 (when the U.S. Supreme Court lifted its moratorium on the death penalty), Florida has executed more persons (99) than any other state except Oklahoma (113), Texas (568), and Virginia (113). *See* https://deathpenaltyinfo.org/state-and-federal-info/state-by-state. Florida also has had more exonerations from death row (29) than any other state.

The U.S. government also has the death penalty, but it voluntarily stopped executing prisoners in 2003. In July 2019, the Trump administration announced plans to resume federal executions. *See Matter of Federal Bureau of Prisons' Execution Protocol Cases*, 2019 WL 6691814 (D.D.C.), *stay denied sub nom. Barr v. Roane*, 140 S. Ct. 353 (2019).

2.   IMPRISONMENT FOR DEBT

Although Florida outlawed imprisonment for debt in 1828, such language was not added to the constitution until 1868. Today, Art. I, § 11 stipulates: "No person shall be imprisoned for debt, except in cases of fraud."

England began imprisoning debtors in the Middle Ages. By the 1800s, as many as 10,000 debtors were being incarcerated annually. In addition to being inhumane, this policy was self-defeating, for once in prison a debtor had no way to make money to pay back his or her creditors. As a result, England abolished its debtors' prisons in 1869.

In colonial times, the United States had its own debtors' prisons, and two of the signers of the Declaration of Independence (Robert Morris and James Wilson) spent time in them. In 1821, Kentucky became the first state to outlaw debtors' prisons. Today, 41 states (including Florida) ban imprisonment for debt by constitutional provision; the remaining nine do so by statute.

Florida does not consider court-ordered alimony to be debt. *See Bronk v. State*, 31 So. 248 (Fla. 1901). As a result, a party who has the means to pay support *and* refuses to do so can be held in contempt of court and imprisoned. *See Fishman v. Fishman*, 656 So. 2d 1250 (Fla. 1995). The courts have refused to extend this exception to other types of financial obligations. *See, e.g., Al Ghurair v. Zaczac*, 255 So. 3d 485 (Fla. 3d Dist. Ct. App. 2018) (unpaid legal bills).

As noted earlier in this chapter, criminal defendants often are unable to make bail and therefore are forced to sit in jail until their trial comes up. Critics have denounced this policy as a modern form of debtors' prison. Similarly, releasees who cannot pay court-ordered fees, fines, or restitution orders often are sent back to jail, even though doing so is illegal. *See Bearden v. Georgia*, 461 U.S. 660 (1983); *Del Valle v. State*, 80 So. 3d 999, 1002 (Fla. 2011) ("[B]efore a trial court may properly revoke probation and incarcerate a probationer for failure to pay, it must inquire into the probationer's ability to pay and determine whether the probationer had the ability to pay but willfully refused to do so.").

3.   COSTS

Art. I, § 19 directs: "No person charged with [a] crime shall be compelled to pay costs before a judgment of conviction has become final." This provision first appeared in the 1885 constitution.

Defendants who are convicted of a crime are required to pay a variety of court costs. *See* Fla. Stat. §§ 938.01–938.35. These range from $3 for violation of a municipal or county ordinance to $225 for felonies. Many crimes carry multiple mandatory and discretionary costs. According to one study, "Since 1996, Florida [has] added more than 20 new categories of financial obligations for criminal defendants and . . . eliminated most exemptions for those who cannot pay." *See* https://www.brennan center.org/sites/default/files/legacy/Justice/Florida F&F.pdf.

Fla. Stat. § 322.245(5)(a) requires the Florida Department of Highway Safety and Motor Vehicles to suspend the driver's license of any criminal defendant who fails to pay court costs. Pursuant to this law, 1.99 million Floridians (nearly 10% of all drivers) have had their licenses suspended. As many observers have pointed out, this often results in poor defendants losing their only reliable means of getting to work, causing them to sink even deeper into poverty. For a further discussion, see https://finesand feesjusticecenter.org/content/uploads/2019/11/ florida-fines-fees-drivers-license-suspension-driving-on-empty.pdf (report of the Fines and Fees Justice Center).

4.   CLEMENCY

Art. IV, § 8 provides:

(a)   Except in cases of treason and in cases where impeachment results in conviction, the governor may, by executive order filed with the custodian of state records, suspend collection of fines and forfeitures, grant reprieves not exceeding sixty days and, with the approval of two members of the cabinet, grant full or conditional pardons, restore civil rights, commute punishment, and remit fines and forfeitures for offenses.

(b)   In cases of treason the governor may grant reprieves until adjournment of the regular session of the legislature convening next after the conviction, at which session the legislature may grant a pardon or further reprieve; otherwise the sentence shall be executed.

(c)   There may be created by law a parole and probation commission with power to supervise persons on probation and to grant paroles or conditional releases to persons under sentences for crime. The qualifications, method of selection and terms, not to exceed six years, of members of the commission shall be prescribed by law.

All of Florida's constitutions have provided some form of clemency, although the exact details have varied over time. The 1885 constitution, for example, provided that clemency decisions were to be made by the "Governor, Justices of the Supreme Court, and

Attorney General, or a major part of them, of whom the Governor shall be one. . . ."

In contrast, the 1968 constitution called for clemency decisions to be made by the governor "with the approval of three members of the cabinet." In 1998, this number was changed to two (due to the reduction in the cabinet's size).

Florida's governor and cabinet collectively act as the state's Executive Clemency Board ("ECB"). *See* Fla. Stat. §§ 940.01–940.061. Since 1975, clemency petitions have been processed by the Office of Executive Clemency, part of the Florida Commission on Offender Review ("FCOR") (https://www.fcor. state.fl.us/).

Florida grants clemency sparingly—in a typical year, it receives 1,500 pardon requests but approves just 25–40. More shockingly, it has not spared a death row prisoner since 1983. Florida's clemency rules can be found at https://www.fcor.state.fl.us/ docs/clemency/clemency_rules.pdf. For a detailed description of them, see https://ccresourcecenter.org/ state-restoration-profiles/florida-restoration-of- rights-pardon-expungement-sealing/.

Although clemency procedures exist in all 50 states, there are great variations in who makes clemency decisions and how often clemency is granted. *See* https://ccresourcecenter.org/state- restoration-profiles/50-state-comparison characteristics-of-pardon-authorities/. In the federal system, the president has sole control of the clemency process. *See* U.S. Const. Art. II, § 2, cl. 1.

As indicated above, Art. IV, § 8(c) takes up the closely-related subjects of parole (*i.e.*, conditional release before the end of a prisoner's sentence) and probation (*i.e.*, supervision in lieu of incarceration). Parole in Florida is overseen by the FCOR (created in 1941 as the Florida Parole Commission but renamed in 2014). Between 1983 and 1995, Florida eliminated parole for all newly-committed crimes. As a result, only 4,500 inmates (out of 95,000) remain eligible for parole. *See* https://www.fcor.state.fl.us/release-types. shtml. Florida is one of 16 states that no longer has parole. In 1987, the federal government also eliminated parole.

Probation is the responsibility of the Florida Department of Corrections' Office of Community Control. In 2018, 166,000 Floridians (*i.e.*, one out of every 75 adults) were on probation. *See* http://www. dc.state.fl.us/cc/index.html. Nationally, the figure is one out of every 55 adults, with Georgia having the highest number (one out of every 18 adults) and New Hampshire having the lowest number (one out of every 168 adults).

G.   VICTIMS' RIGHTS

Art. I, § 16(b)–(e) gives crime victims specific rights. Initially added in 1988 at the suggestion of the legislature, the Constitution Revision Commission substantially rewrote this provision in 2018.

The 1988 amendment consisted of a now-deleted paragraph (b). It modestly provided crime victims with the right "to be informed, to be present, and to be heard when relevant, at all crucial stages of criminal proceedings, to the extent that these rights do not interfere with the constitutional rights of the accused."

The 2018 amendment replaced paragraph (b) with a new paragraph (b) and added paragraphs (c)–(e). After surviving a ballot challenge, see *Department of State v. Hollander*, 256 So. 3d 1300 (Fla. 2018), it was handily approved.

New paragraph (b) provides crime victims, their families, and their lawful representatives with specific and detailed rights, including a right to due process; a right to be treated with fairness and respect; a right to be free from intimidation, harassment, and abuse; a right to have the victim's welfare considered when setting bail; a right to proceedings free from unreasonable delay; and a right to restitution from each convicted defendant. As paragraph (b) explains, its goal is to "ensure that crime victims' rights and interests are respected and protected by law in a manner no less vigorous than protections afforded to criminal defendants and juvenile delinquents[.]"

Paragraph (c) gives victims standing to enforce their rights. Paragraph (d) makes the amendment self-executing; "saves" any rights the victim may have under other laws; and immunizes the government from victim lawsuits. Paragraph (e) provides an expansive definition of the word "victim."

The 2018 amendment is modeled after the California Victims' Bill of Rights Act of 2008, better known as "Marsy's Law." In 1983, Marsy Nicholas, a senior at the University of California-Santa Barbara, was murdered by her former boyfriend. In 2007, Marsy's brother Henry pushed California to adopt a crime victims' law. When this effort proved successful, he launched a national campaign. To date, 11 states (including Florida) have adopted a Marsy's Law. During Florida's campaign, actor Kelsey Grammer (*Cheers*, *Frasier*) was one of the amendment's leading advocates.

While proponents insist that the amendment simply "levels" the playing field, critics contend that it contravenes the Sixth Amendment, gives prosecutors undue leverage, and is likely to result in innocent defendants being found guilty. Because of its detailed language, the amendment also is expected to force courts to reevaluate many well-settled principles. *See*, *e.g.*, *Toole v. State*, 270 So. 3d 371 (Fla. 4th Dist. Ct. App.), *review dismissed*, 2019 WL 2275025 (Fla. 2019) (questioning whether the current method used to determine victim restitution satisfies the amendment's requirements).

CHAPTER 8
GUNS

A. OVERVIEW

The Florida Constitution grants citizens the right to own guns. It also allows the government to regulate gun ownership. This power is tempered by the Second Amendment: "A well regulated Militia, being necessary to the security of a free State, the right of the people to keep and bear Arms, shall not be infringed." In *McDonald v. City of Chicago*, 561 U.S. 742 (2010), the U.S. Supreme Court held that the Second Amendment applies to states. Previously, it had been understood as limiting only the federal government.

B. RIGHT TO BEAR ARMS

Art. I, § 8(a) provides: "The right of the people to keep and bear arms in defense of themselves and of the lawful authority of the state shall not be infringed, except that the manner of bearing arms may be regulated by law."

A provision guaranteeing "free white men" the right to bear arms was included in Florida's first two constitutions (1838, 1861). The 1865 constitution omitted this provision to avoid giving newly-freed black men the right to possess guns. The 1868 constitution reinstated the right to bear arms in race-neutral terms. This language was carried over to the 1885 constitution, which added that the government could regulate gun ownership. *See Watson v. Stone*, 4

So. 2d 700 (Fla. 1941) (en banc). The 1968 wording is nearly identical to the 1885 wording.

The Florida Legislature has promulgated numerous guns laws. *See* Fla. Stat. ch. 790 (particularly § 790.064—possession and § 790.065— sales). The Florida Supreme Court repeatedly has recognized its right to do so. *See, e.g., Norman v. State*, 215 So. 3d 18, *reh'g denied*, 2017 WL 1365211 (Fla.), *cert. denied*, 138 S. Ct. 469 (2017) (upholding Florida's "Open Carry" law, which prohibits displaying a gun in public); *Rinzler v. Carson*, 262 So. 2d 661 (Fla. 1972) (endorsing a ban on machine guns, short-barreled rifles, and short-barreled shotguns); *Davis v. State*, 146 So. 2d 892 (Fla. 1962) (approving a statute requiring a license to own pistols and repeating rifles). *See also Robarge v. State*, 432 So. 2d 669 (Fla. 5th Dist. Ct. App. 1983), *review denied*, 450 So. 2d 855 (Fla. 1984) (state has substantial discretion when it comes to regulating gun ownership).

In 1987, the legislature adopted the Joe Carlucci Uniform Firearms Act. As a result, Fla. Stat. § 790.33(1) declares:

Except as expressly provided by the State Constitution or general law, the Legislature hereby declares that it is occupying the whole field of regulation of firearms and ammunition, including the purchase, sale, transfer, taxation, manufacture, ownership, possession, storage, and transportation thereof, to the exclusion of all existing and future county, city, town, or municipal ordinances or any administrative regulations or rules adopted by local or state government relating thereto. Any such existing ordinances, rules, or regulations are hereby declared null and void.

The courts have ruled that § 790.33 is a valid exercise of the legislature's power. *See, e.g., Florida Carry, Inc. v. University of Florida*, 180 So. 3d 137 (Fla. 1st Dist. Ct. App. 2015), *review denied*, 2016 WL 1427725 (Fla. 2016) (university regulation governing firearms was invalid because legislature has preempted the entire field); *National Rifle Association of America, Inc. v. City of South Miami*, 812 So. 2d 504 (Fla. 3d Dist. Ct. App. 2002) (nullifying city's gun safety ordinance).

As originally enacted, a violation of § 790.33 carried no penalties. In 2011, however, it was amended to make local officials who fail to comply with it subject to civil fines and removal from office. These penalties were ruled unconstitutional in *City of Weston v. Scott*, 2019 WL 4806195 (Fla. 2d Cir. Ct. 2019), *appeal filed*, 1D19–2819 (Fla. 1st Dist. Ct. App.).

In *Bruley v. LBK, LP*, 333 F. App'x 491 (11th Cir. 2009), the Eleventh Circuit held that § 8(a) does not prevent a private employer from firing an employee who brings a gun to work.

Because of Florida's large number of mass shooting incidents (152 since 2013, surpassed only by California and Illinois—see https://www.vox.com/a/mass-shootings-america-sandy-hook-gun-violence), a citizens group called Ban Assault Weapons Now has proposed a 2020 constitutional amendment that, if successful, will add a new paragraph (e) to § 8 banning assault weapons. *See Advisory Opinion to the Attorney General re Prohibits Assault Weapons*, SC19–1266 and SC19–1601 (Fla.).

C. WAITING PERIODS

In 1990, a three-day waiting period on handgun purchases was approved by the voters. As a result, Art. I, § 8 was restructured, with the right to bear arms becoming new paragraph (a) and the waiting period provision becoming new paragraphs (b)–(d).

In pertinent part, paragraph (b) provides: "There shall be a mandatory period of three days, excluding weekends and legal holidays, between the purchase and delivery at retail of any handgun." Paragraph (c) requires the legislature to implement this provision by December 31, 1991, with the further stipulation that any violation of paragraph (b) be made a felony. The legislature has complied with these directives. *See* Fla. Stat. § 790.0655.

Paragraph (b) is quite limited. First, it applies only to retail purchases, which are defined as transactions in which "money or other valuable consideration [is paid] to the retailer." Second, it applies only to handguns, which are defined as "a firearm capable of being carried and used by one hand, such as a pistol or revolver." Third, it does not apply to holders of a concealed weapons permit (because such persons already have passed a state background check).

Paragraph (d) creates an exception for handgun trades (even if the guns are of different calibers).

The term "retailer" is not defined in paragraph (b). However, Fla. Stat. § 790.0655(1)(a) provides: " 'Retailer' means and includes a licensed importer, licensed manufacturer, or licensed dealer engaged in the business of making firearm sales at retail or for distribution, or use, or consumption, or storage to be used or consumed in this state, as defined in § 212.02(13)."

In 1998, a second waiting period was added to the constitution to close the so-called "gun show loophole." As a result, Art. VIII, § 5(b) provides:

Each county shall have the authority to require a criminal history records check and a 3 to 5-day waiting period, excluding weekends and legal holidays, in connection with the sale of any firearm occurring within such county. For purposes of this subsection, the term "sale" means the transfer of money or other valuable consideration for any firearm when any part of the transaction is conducted on property to which the public has the right of access. Holders of a concealed weapons permit as prescribed by general law shall not be subject to the provisions of this subsection when purchasing a firearm.

The primary purpose of the section is to rein in sales by collectors and other non-retailers at gun shows held in government-owned buildings. It represents an exception to Fla. Stat. § 790.33, which, as explained above, makes the subject of gun regulation exclusively a legislative prerogative.

The term "firearm" is not defined in paragraph (b). However, Fla. Stat. § 790.001(6) explains:

> "Firearm" means any weapon (including a starter gun) which will, is designed to, or may readily be converted to expel a projectile by the action of an explosive; the frame or receiver of any such weapon; any firearm muffler or firearm silencer; any destructive device; or any machine gun. The term "firearm" does not include an antique firearm unless the antique firearm is used in the commission of a crime.

Ten counties currently have gun show ordinances. Five have three-day waiting periods (Leon, Orange, Pinellas, Sarasota, and Volusia), while five have five-day waiting periods (Alachua, Broward, Hillsborough, Miami-Dade, and Palm Beach). Three counties that once had such ordinances have repealed them (Charlotte, Citrus, and Hernando).

CHAPTER 9
HEALTH AND MEDICINE

A. OVERVIEW

The Florida Constitution addresses three distinct health issues: abortions for minors, medical marijuana, and smoking (including vaping). It also tackles the subject of medical malpractice.

The group Florida Decides Healthcare has proposed a 2020 constitutional amendment requiring the state to provide Medicaid to low-income adults (defined as persons at or below 138% of the federal poverty level). *See Advisory Opinion to the Attorney General re Provide Medicaid Coverage to Eligible Low-Income Adults*, SC19–1070 (Fla.). If passed, the amendment could affect up to 1.1 million Floridians and cost as much as $4.7 billion (90% of which would be borne by the federal government).

B. ABORTIONS FOR MINORS

Art. X, § 22 states in relevant part: "[T]he Legislature is authorized to require by general law for notification to a parent or guardian of a minor before the termination of the minor's pregnancy. The Legislature shall provide exceptions to such requirement for notification and shall create a process for judicial waiver of the notification." This provision was added in 2004. Florida is one of 11 states that requires parental notification before a minor can have an abortion. In 2018, Florida recorded 70,239 abortions, of which 1,398 were performed on minors.

To implement § 22, in 2005 the Florida Legislature passed the "Parental Notice of Abortion Act." *See* Fla. Stat. § 390.01114. It requires either the attending or referring physician to give "actual notice" to the minor's parent at least 48 hours before the operation. Such notice can be given in person or by telephone. If actual notice cannot be given, the physician can give "constructive notice" by mailing a letter to the parent at least 72 hours before the operation.

No notice is required if a "medical emergency" makes it necessary to immediately terminate the pregnancy; the parent has waived his or her right to notification (such waivers must in writing, notarized, and dated within 30 days of the operation); the minor is married or emancipated; or a judge has ruled that parental notice is not necessary ("judicial bypass").

In *Womancare of Orlando, Inc. v. Agwunobi*, 448 F. Supp. 2d 1309 (N.D. Fla. 2006), the foregoing requirements were found to be constitutional.

A Florida minor who wants an abortion and petitions for judicial bypass must prove that: 1) she is mature enough to make the decision herself; and, 2) informing her parents is not in her best interest. *See In re Doe*, 153 So. 3d 925 (Fla. 2d Dist. Ct. App. 2014). It is improper for a court to deny a bypass petition simply because it disagrees with the minor's decision to have an abortion. *See In re Doe*, 113 So. 3d 882 (Fla. 2d Dist. Ct. App. 2012).

In *In re Doe*, 204 So. 3d 175 (Fla. 1st Dist. Ct. App. 2016), a minor's request for judicial bypass was denied for lack of maturity. The appellate court affirmed, but also pointed out that most requests are granted: "For the past three years, the statewide approval rate for judicial grants of petitions has grown from about 89.5% in 2013, to 90.5% in 2014, to 94.7% in 2015." *Id.* at 177 n.1 (Makar, J., concurring). In 2018, Florida minors filed 193 petitions, of which 182 were granted (94.3%).

In 2020, the Florida Legislature is expected to consider H.B. 265/S.B. 404, which require minors to obtain their parents' permission before receiving an abortion (both bills contain a judicial bypass procedure). Currently, 26 states have such laws. In *Planned Parenthood of Kansas City, Missouri, Inc. v. Ashcroft*, 462 U.S. 476 (1983), the U.S. Supreme Court held that parental consent laws are constitutional if they include a judicial bypass procedure. However, in *In re T.W.*, 551 So. 2d 1186 (Fla. 1989), the Florida Supreme Court struck down Florida's 1988 parental consent law (which had a judicial bypass procedure) on privacy grounds. H.B. 265/S.B. 404's supporters are hoping the court's recent rightward tilt (discussed in Ch. 15 of this book) will lead it to overrule *T.W.*

In Aug. 2019, Sen. Lauren Book (D-Plantation) proposed a 2020 constitutional amendment that would prohibit the Florida Legislature from voting on any bill that limits access to abortions unless at least half of Florida's lawmakers are women. *See* S.J.R. 60. At the time Book filed her bill, both the house (84 out of 120 members) and the senate (28/40) were 70% male.

C. MEDICAL MARIJUANA

Art. X, § 29 prohibits the Florida Legislature from criminalizing or otherwise penalizing the medical use of marijuana. This section was proposed in 2016 by People United for Medical Marijuana ("PUMM"), a group whose principal backer was Orlando trial attorney John Morgan.

In 2014, PUMM had placed a similar proposal on the ballot. *See Advisory Opinion to the Attorney General re Use of Marijuana for Certain Medical Conditions*, 132 So. 3d 786 (Fla. 2014). It failed to pass because many voters were troubled by its "open-ended" nature—in addition to a specific list of diseases, it authorized doctors to prescribe medical marijuana for any condition "for which a physician believes that the medical use of marijuana would likely outweigh the potential health risks for a patient."

PUMM's 2016 proposal was rewritten to address these concerns. *See Advisory Opinion to the Attorney General re Use of Marijuana for Debilitating Medical Conditions*, 181 So. 3d 471 (Fla. 2015). Thus, medical marijuana can be ordered only for

cancer, epilepsy, glaucoma, positive status for human immunodeficiency virus (HIV), acquired immune deficiency syndrome (AIDS), post-traumatic stress disorder (PTSD), amyotrophic lateral sclerosis (ALS), Crohn's disease,

Parkinson's disease, multiple sclerosis, or other debilitating medical conditions of the same kind or class as or comparable to those enumerated, and for which a physician believes that the medical use of marijuana would likely outweigh the potential health risks for a patient.

Art. X, § 29(b)(1).

Sec. 29 does not permit the non-medical use of marijuana. This is made clear by paragraph (c)(2): "Nothing in this section shall affect or repeal laws relating to non-medical use, possession, production, or sale of marijuana." *See also Forest v. State*, 257 So. 3d 603 (Fla. 1st Dist. Ct. App. 2018).

Growing, possessing, distributing, or using marijuana for any purpose is a crime under federal law, see *Gonzales v. Raich*, 545 U.S. 1 (2005), and § 29 provides no protection from federal prosecution. This is made clear by paragraph (c)(5): "Nothing in this section . . . purports to give immunity under federal law." (In Nov. 2019, the Judiciary Committee of the U.S. House of Representatives voted 24–10 to decriminalize marijuana, a first step in changing federal law.)

The Florida Legislature has dragged its feet on implementing § 29, despite the very detailed directions contained in paragraphs (d)–(f). It also has placed various roadblocks in the way of providers, known as medical marijuana treatment centers ("MMTCs"). As a result, its actions are being challenged in court. *See Florida Department of Health v. Florigrown, LLC*, 2019 WL 2943329 (Fla.

1st Dist. Ct. App.), *reh'g en banc denied*, 2019 WL 4019919 (Fla. 1st Dist. Ct. App.), *review granted*, 2019 WL 5208142 (Fla. 2019).

The group Sensible Florida has proposed a 2020 constitutional amendment that, if passed, would authorize the recreational use of marijuana and allow the public to grow its own plants. *See Advisory Opinion to the Attorney General re Regulate Marijuana Similar to Alcohol*, SC19–1536 (Fla.). Another group—Make It Legal Florida—has proposed a separate 2020 constitutional amendment that also would authorize the recreational use of marijuana but would require sales to be handled by MMTCs. *See Advisory Opinion to the Attorney General re Adult Use of Marijuana*, SC19–2116 (Fla.). Both proposals acknowledge that they do not provide immunity from federal prosecution.

At present, marijuana is fully legal in 11 states, is partially legal in 28 (including Florida), and remains fully illegal in 11.

D. SMOKING

Two different sections of the Florida Constitution address smoking. First, Art. X, § 20 prohibits smoking (including vaping) in the workplace. Second, Art. X, § 27 requires the government to operate a comprehensive anti-smoking program.

1. WORKPLACES

In 1985, the Florida Legislature enacted the Florida Clean Indoor Air Act ("FCIAA"). *See* Fla.

Stat. §§ 386.201–386.2125. The FCIAA was supported by the tobacco industry because it prohibited local governments from passing more robust smoking bans. *See* Fla. Stat. § 386.209. *See also* Fla. Att'y Gen. Ops. 92–89 (counties preempted); 2005–63 (municipalities preempted); 2010–53 (school districts preempted); 2011–15 (water management districts preempted).

To address some of the FCIAA's weaknesses, Art. X, § 20 was added to the constitution in 2002 following a petition drive by the group Smoke-Free for Health. *See Advisory Opinion to Attorney General re Protect People from the Health Hazards of Second-Hand Smoke by Prohibiting Workplace Smoking*, 814 So. 2d 415 (Fla. 2002).

In 2003, the Florida Legislature amended the FCIAA to incorporate the changes mandated by § 20. Thus, smoking now is banned in nearly all indoor workplaces. *See* Fla. Stat. § 386.204. Exempted, however, are: 1) airport lounges; 2) designated hotel guest rooms; 3) smoking-related research facilities; 4) retail tobacco shops; 5) smoking cessation programs; and, 6) stand-alone bars. *See* Fla. Stat. § 386.2045. Smoking is permitted in private residences except when they are being used to provide adult, child, or health care services. *Id.*

At present, 38 states ban indoor smoking. Twenty-six have complete bans while 12 (including Florida) have partial bans.

Outdoor areas are not covered by the FCIAA. Accordingly, local governments cannot ban smoking at public beaches or parks. *See City of Sarasota v. Bonilla* (Fla. Sarasota Cnty. Ct. 2012) (No. 2012 MO 12197 NC) (unreported; available at https://secure. sarasotaclerk.com/). A 2019 bill (S.B. 218) that would have banned smoking on public beaches died in committee.

The FCIAA does not apply to Native American reservations. As a result, smoking is permitted in all of Florida's tribal casinos. Part XVIII(D) of the 2010 gambling compact between the Seminoles and Florida, however, requires the tribe to designate non-smoking areas in its facilities and include state-of-the-art ventilation systems in any new construction projects. *See* http://www.myfloridalicense.com/dbpr/ pmw/documents/2010_Compact-Signed1.pdf.

In 2018, § 20 was amended to include vaping.

2.   ANTI-SMOKING PROGRAM

In 1994, Mississippi sued the tobacco industry to recover the health care costs it was incurring due to smoking. Other states soon followed, including Florida. *See State of Florida v. American Tobacco Co.*, No. 95–1466AH (Fla. 15th Cir. Ct.).

In 1997, the industry sought a master settlement. When this effort bogged down, the industry negotiated individual agreements with four states, including Florida. *See State v. American Tobacco Co.*, 723 So. 2d 263 (Fla. 1998).

Florida's settlement calls for the defendants to pay $11.3 billion over 25 years. It also places various advertising and promotion restrictions on the defendants; limits their ability to engage in political lobbying; and requires them to combat underage smoking. *See State of Florida v. R.J. Reynolds Tobacco Co.*, No. 95–1466AH (Fla. 15th Cir. Ct. Dec. 27, 2017) (unpublished order reaffirming settlement), *appeal filed*, 4D18–2616 (Fla. 4th Dist. Ct. App.). By the end of 2018, Florida had collected $9.4 billion.

In 2006, a group called Floridians for Youth Tobacco Education persuaded voters to pass a constitutional amendment requiring a portion of the settlement's yearly proceeds to be used to fund "a comprehensive statewide tobacco education and prevention program consistent with recommendations of the U.S. Centers for Disease Control and Prevention (CDC)." *See* Art. X, § 27. *See also Advisory Opinion to the Attorney General re Protect People, Especially Youth, from Addiction, Disease, and Other Health Hazards of Using Tobacco*, 926 So. 2d 1186 (Fla. 2006).

Paragraph (a) sets out the program's minimum requirements. Paragraph (b) obligates the state to annually spend 15% of the amount it received from the settlement in 2005 ($380 million), adjusted for inflation. Paragraph (c) defines the terms "tobacco" and "tobacco settlement." Paragraph (d) makes the amendment effective upon passage.

The amendment's implementing legislation can be found in Fla. Stat. § 381.84. It places the Florida Department of Health in charge of the program, creates a "Tobacco Education and Use Prevention Advisory Council," and permits no more than 5% of the annual appropriated amount to be spent on administrative expenses. *See* http://www.florida health.gov/programs-and-services/prevention/ tobacco-free-florida/index.html.

Pursuant to § 27, $68.6 million in settlement proceeds were directed to the state's anti-smoking program in 2018. This represents just a fraction (35.3%) of the amount recommended by the CDC's guidelines. Moreover, in 2018 the tobacco industry spent $605 million on advertising in Florida. Nevertheless, the amendment has been credited with helping to reduce Florida's adult smoking rate from 21% to 15.8% and its youth smoking rate from 10.6% to 3.0%.

E.   MEDICAL MALPRACTICE

1.   ATTORNEY FEE CAPS

In 2004, a doctors group called Citizens for a Fair Share ("CFS") proposed that medical malpractice lawyers be limited to 30% of any damages collected up to $250,000, and 10% of any damages collected above $250,000, exclusive of costs.

CFS's proposal was bitterly opposed by Floridians for Patient Protection ("FPP"), a group funded by medical malpractice lawyers. FPP argued that CFS's real motivation was not to put more money in the pockets of medical malpractice victims but to keep such suits from being filed in the first place. (On the plaintiff's side, nearly all medical malpractice cases are handled on contingency, with the customary fee being 1/3 of any recovery.)

CFS's proposal appeared on the 2004 ballot as Amendment 3, see *Advisory Opinion to the Attorney General re Medical Liability Claimant's Compensation Amendment*, 880 So. 2d 675 (Fla. 2004), but quickly became known as the "Stop Greedy Lawyers" amendment. After passing easily, it was added to the constitution as Art. I, § 26.

As matters turned out, CFS's victory proved short-lived. To get around the new limits, the plaintiffs' bar began having prospective clients sign agreements letting them charge their normal rates. In 2006, the Florida Supreme Court expressly approved this approach. *See In re Amendment to the Rules Regulating the Florida Bar—Rule 4–1.5(f)(4)(B) of the Rules of Professional Conduct*, 939 So. 2d 1032 (Fla. 2006).

A particularly notable aspect of the court's decision is its discussion of when constitutional rights can be waived:

> The comments in opposition to the Bar's proposal center around two main issues: first, whether the right granted in the constitution may be waived; and, second, whether the courts must approve any waiver. The first contention is that the personal right granted to medical liability claimants by article I, section 26 may never be waived because it embraces certain policies that are beyond the control of the claimants themselves. We note, however, that on its face, article I, section 26 unquestionably creates a personal right, one for the direct benefit of a medical malpractice claimant. It is

entitled "Claimant's right to fair compensation" and provides that "the claimant is entitled to receive" the stated percentages of the damages. Art. I, § 26(a), Fla. Const. Further, the Bar and other commentators point out that most personal constitutional rights may be waived. . . . Numerous instances of judicial recognition of the right to waive constitutional rights have been cited to the Court. For example, even the most basic fundamental constitutional rights, such as the Fifth Amendment right to remain silent and the Sixth Amendment right to counsel may be knowingly and voluntarily waived. . . . Additionally, Florida's highly valued constitutional homestead protection is subject to waiver. . . . We also note that nothing in the plain language of article I, section 26 prohibits a waiver of the rights granted.

Id. at 1038.

Rule 4–1.5(f)(4)(B)(iii) of the Florida Rules of Professional Conduct now includes a form that clients must sign to waive their § 26 rights.

2.   ADVERSE MEDICAL INCIDENTS

In response to CFS's proposal to limit medical malpractice fees, FPP successfully proposed two amendments of its own. The first, designated Amendment 7, see *Advisory Opinion to the Attorney General re Patients' Right to Know About Adverse Medical Incidents*, 880 So. 2d 617 (Fla. 2004), appears in the constitution as Art. X, § 25.

Paragraph (a) states that "patients have a right to have access to any records made or received in the course of business by a health care facility or provider relating to any adverse medical incident."

Paragraph (b) directs: "In providing such access, the identity of patients involved in the incidents shall not be disclosed, and any privacy restrictions imposed by federal law shall be maintained." This sentence is a nod to both Art. I, § 23 and the Health Insurance Portability and Accountability Act of 1996 ("HIPAA"), a federal law that specifically protects personal medical records. *See* 42 U.S.C. § 1320d–6.

Paragraph (c) explains that an adverse medical incident includes "medical negligence, intentional misconduct, and any other act, neglect, or default of a health care facility or health care provider that caused or could have caused injury to or death of a patient." Paragraph (c) also defines the terms "access," "health care facility," "health care provider," and "patient."

In 2005, the Florida Legislature passed implementing legislation. *See* Fla. Stat. § 381.028. In *Florida Hospital Waterman, Inc. v. Buster*, 984 So. 2d 478 (Fla. 2008), the Florida Supreme Court partially invalidated the statute because it limited how much information defendants had to disclose. It also held that the amendment applies retroactively.

Other attempts to withhold information from plaintiffs have been similarly rebuffed. *See, e.g., Edwards v. Thomas*, 229 So. 3d 277 (Fla. 2017) (§ 25 removes all limitations on the discovery of medical records, including the attorney-client privilege and work-product doctrine); *Charles v. Southern Baptist Hospital of Florida, Inc.*, 209 So. 3d 1199 (Fla.), *cert. denied*, 138 S. Ct. 129 (2017) (§ 25 is not preempted by the Federal Patient Safety and Quality Improvement Act, 42 U.S.C. § 299b–22, which makes patient safety reports confidential); *West Florida Regional Medical Center, Inc. v. See*, 79 So. 3d 1 (Fla. 2012) (§ 25 requires disclosure of credentialing and peer review materials).

3.   REPEATED MEDICAL MALPRACTICE

FPP's second amendment appears in the constitution as Art. X, § 26. Although officially labeled Amendment 8, see *Advisory Opinion to the Attorney General re Public Protection from Repeated Medical Malpractice*, 880 So. 2d 667 (Fla. 2004), it quickly became known as the "Stop Bad Doctors" amendment, a retort to CSF's "Stop Greedy Lawyers" slogan. Today, however, it usually is referred to as the "Three Strikes Law."

Paragraph (a) states: "No person who has been found to have committed three or more incidents of medical malpractice shall be licensed or continue to be licensed by the State of Florida to provide health care services as a medical doctor."

Paragraph (b)(1) makes it clear that it does not matter where an incident occurs. Thus, incidents count if they take place in Florida, another U.S. state, or a foreign country.

Paragraph (b)(2) explains that mere allegations, as well as out-of-court settlements, are insufficient: "[M]alpractice has [to have] been found [in] a final judgment of a court of law, final administrative agency decision, or decision of binding arbitration."

The Florida Legislature has enacted legislation implementing § 26. *See* Fla. Stat. § 456.50. In *In re Farkas*, 343 B.R. 336 (Bankr. S.D. Fla. 2006), a neurosurgeon defending two unrelated malpractice lawsuits filed for bankruptcy. Convinced that the doctor's real goal was to avoid § 26, the patients moved for dismissal. In denying their motion, the bankruptcy court wrote:

> Were this Court to agree with the [patients'] position, a physician faced with pending medical malpractice claims could never file for bankruptcy protection. There does not appear to be any case authority to support the position that a Florida physician with pending malpractice claims is precluded from filing a bankruptcy proceeding.

Id. at 338.

CHAPTER 10
LABOR AND EMPLOYMENT

A. OVERVIEW

Two provisions of the Florida Constitution directly address the subjects of labor and employment. First, Art. X, § 24 sets a state minimum wage that is higher than the federal minimum wage. Second, Art. I, § 6 prohibits employers from hiring or firing a person based on their membership (or non-membership) in a union.

Several other provisions of the constitution also bear on work matters:

Art. I, § 8(b)–(d) and Art. VIII, § 5(b), discussed in Ch. 8 of this book, regulate gun sellers.

Art. II, § 8(e), discussed in Ch. 2 of this book, imposes lobbying restrictions on former government employees.

Art. III, § 14, discussed in Ch. 13 of this book, mandates creation of a civil service system to protect public employees.

Art. V, § 8, discussed in Ch. 15 of this book, requires state justices and judges to retire at age 75.

Art. V, § 15, discussed in Ch. 15 of this book, places the admission, disciplining, and disbarment of attorneys in the hands of the Florida Supreme Court.

Art. VIII, § 5(a), discussed in Ch. 16 of this book, allows counties to prohibit the commercial dispensing of alcohol.

Art. X, § 14, discussed in Ch. 20 of this book, limits public employee pensions.

Art. X, § 16, discussed in Ch. 4 of this book, prevents fishermen from using certain types of nets.

Art. X, § 20, discussed in Ch. 9 of this book, bans smoking in indoor workplaces.

Art. X, § 21, discussed in Ch. 4 of this book, specifies how farmers must treat pregnant pigs.

Art. X, § 25, discussed in Ch. 9 of this book, forces health care providers to make public their "adverse incident" records.

Art. X, § 26, discussed in Ch. 9 of this book, strips doctors of their licenses if they commit repeated acts of malpractice.

Art. X, § 29, discussed in Ch. 9 of this book, authorizes medical marijuana treatment centers.

Lastly, Art. X, § 32, discussed in Ch. 13 of this book, outlaws dog tracks (after 2020).

B. MINIMUM WAGE

Since 1938, the Fair Labor Standards Act ("FLSA"), 29 U.S.C. §§ 201–219, has required employers to pay employees a minimum hourly wage. States can set a higher rate but cannot set a lower rate. At present, 29 states exceed the federal rate.

In 2004, a union-backed political action committee called Floridians for All ("FFA") proposed adding a minimum wage provision to the Florida Constitution. *See Advisory Opinion to the Attorney General re*

Florida Minimum Wage Amendment, 880 So. 2d 636 (Fla. 2004).

Floridians to Save Florida Jobs ("FSFJ"), whose major donors included Burger King, Disney, and Walgreens, opposed the idea. Although FSFJ ($4.1 million) spent almost twice as much as FFA ($2.1 million), the amendment passed easily. As a result, Art. X, § 24(a) declares:

All working Floridians are entitled to be paid a minimum wage that is sufficient to provide a decent and healthy life for them and their families, that protects their employers from unfair low-wage competition, and that does not force them to rely on taxpayer-funded public services in order to avoid economic hardship.

Paragraph (b) defines the terms "employer," "employee," and "wage," using the definitions contained in the FLSA. *See* 29 U.S.C. § 203. Paragraph (c) sets Florida's minimum wage at $6.15 per hour and requires it to be adjusted annually for inflation using the U.S. Department of Labor's Consumer Price Index for Urban Wage Earners and Clerical Workers. Paragraph (d) prohibits retaliation against anyone who reports a violation or otherwise asserts their rights. Paragraphs (e)–(g) focus, respectively, on enforcement, implementation, and severability.

Paragraph (c) requires the Agency for Workforce Innovation, now known as the Florida Department of Economic Opportunity (http://www.floridajobs.org/), to recalculate the state's minimum wage each

September 30. The new rate then goes into effect on January 1.

Under the FLSA, special rules exist for "tipped" employees, such as restaurant waiters. These rules are preserved by paragraph (c). *See Shaw v. Set Enterprises, Inc.*, 241 F. Supp. 3d 1318 (S.D. Fla. 2017).

Sec. 24 is implemented by the Florida Minimum Wage Act. *See* Fla. Stat. § 448.110. In 2019, Florida's minimum wage was $8.46; in Oct. 2019, an increase to $8.56 was announced for 2020. In contrast, the federal minimum wage, which was last raised in 2009, is $7.25. Even at $8.56, Florida's minimum wage comes out to just $17,804.80 a year (assuming 52 weeks of work at 40 hours per week). This is only slightly above the 2019 one-person federal poverty level of $12,490.

To spur higher wages, § 24(f) states:

This amendment provides for payment of a minimum wage and shall not be construed to preempt or otherwise limit the authority of the state legislature or any other public body to adopt or enforce any other law, regulation, requirement, policy or standard that provides for payment of higher or supplemental wages or benefits, or that extends such protections to employers or employees not covered by this amendment.

Relying on this language, in 2016 the City of Miami Beach passed an ordinance setting a local minimum wage of $13.31. In *City of Miami Beach v.*

Florida Retail Federation, Inc., 233 So. 3d 1236 (Fla. 3d Dist. Ct. App. 2017), *review granted*, 2018 WL 4607913 (Fla. 2018), *review dismissed*, 2019 WL 446549 (Fla. 2019), the ordinance was struck down because of Fla. Stat. § 218.077. This statute prohibits a local government from exceeding the state rate except when: 1) paying its own employees; or, 2) hiring, or providing tax assistance to, private companies. *See Calderon v. Baker Concrete Construction, Inc.*, 771 F.3d 807 (11th Cir. 2014) (firm that helped build Miami Marlins' publicly-funded baseball stadium had to pay city-approved wages).

A group known as Florida for a Fair Wage has proposed a 2020 constitutional amendment that would raise Florida's minimum wage to $15 (generally recognized as "a living wage") by 2026 (§ 24 would be suspended in the interim). *See Advisory Opinion to the Attorney General re: Raising Florida's Minimum Wage*, 2019 WL 6906963 (Fla. 2019). Several states already have passed laws that will raise their minimum wage to $15 prior to 2026 (*e.g.*, California (2022), Massachusetts (2023), and New Jersey (2024)).

C. UNION MEMBERSHIP

Art. I, § 6 states:

The right of persons to work shall not be denied or abridged on account of membership or non-membership in any labor union or labor organization. The right of employees, by and through a labor organization, to bargain collectively shall not be denied or abridged. Public employees shall not have the right to strike.

This provision was added in 1944 and was carried over, with one important modification, to the 1968 constitution. In its present form, it does three things: 1) makes Florida a "right to work" state; 2) elevates collective bargaining to a fundamental right; and, 3) prohibits public employees from striking.

1. RIGHT TO WORK

As a right to work state, Florida prohibits employers from hiring or firing employees because they either do, or do not, belong to a union. Twenty-eight states currently have right to work laws, although Florida is one of only nine to include such a provision in its constitution.

Some history is needed to understand § 6. In 1935, Congress passed the National Labor Relations Act ("NLRA"), 29 U.S.C. §§ 151–169. It permitted businesses to operate as "closed shops," "union shops," "agency shops," or "open shops."

A closed shop is one that requires employees to be union members when they are hired and to remain members for as long as they are employed. Thus, an employee who is expelled from the union for any reason must be fired.

A union shop is one that does not require employees to be union members when they are hired, but does require them to join the union once they are hired.

An agency shop is one that does not require employees to be union members, but does require them to help defray the union's operating costs. The amount paid by such workers usually is less than the dues paid by union members.

Lastly, an open shop does not require employees to be, or become, union members and does not require them to financially support the union. By the same token, it does not penalize employees who decide to join the union.

In 1947, Congress repealed parts of the NLRA by passing the Labor Management Relations Act ("LMRA"), 29 U.S.C. §§ 141–197, better known as the Taft-Hartley Act. It outlawed closed shops and authorized states to prohibit union and agency shops. The LMRA's enactment mooted a union challenge to Florida's 1944 constitutional amendment. *See American Federation of Labor v. Watson*, 60 F. Supp. 1010 (S.D. Fla. 1945), *rev'd*, 327 U.S. 582 (1946).

Although Florida is a right to work state, whether a specific contract provision violates § 6 requires a careful parsing of its language. In *Trowel Trades Employees Health and Welfare Trust Fund of Dade County v. Edward L. Nezelek, Inc.*, 645 F.2d 322 (5th Cir. 1981) (Unit B), for example, the Fifth Circuit held that a collective bargaining agreement that required a general contractor to use certain sub-contractors was not a "union-security" rule and therefore did not violate § 6.

In proposing § 6's predecessor, the Florida Legislature hoped to weaken Florida's existing unions and prevent new ones from forming. Its hostility towards unions was (and is) largely economic—unionized workplaces tend to pay employees better than non-unionized workplaces (on average, salaries are 18.2% higher in unionized workplaces). In 1944, the Florida Legislature also viewed unions as communist-dominated organizations that promoted "race-mixing."

The legislature's goals largely have been met. In 2018, Florida had 8.7 million workers, of whom only 484,000 belonged to a union. An additional 104,000 workers were represented by a union but did not belong to it. Thus, the total percentage of Floridians covered by unions was just 6.8%. There is a particularly sharp difference in participation rates between private workers and public workers. While just 5% of private workers in Florida belong to a union, 35% of public workers in Florida are union members.

Nationally, 10.5% of all workers belong to a union. This is down from 20.1% in 1983 and reflects the fact that union membership in the United States has been falling since the end of World War II (when roughly one out of every three workers belonged to a union). Many factors account for the shrinking role of unions: automation, the emergence of the "gig economy," international competition, public hostility to union pensions and pay scales (often stoked by anti-union politicians), and, of course, the passage of right to work laws.

Right to work laws have given rise to a phenomenon that economists call the "free rider effect." Because workers cannot be forced to join unions, they do not. At the same time, they hope others will join, thereby allowing them to reap the benefits of union membership without having to pay for it. Because many people think this way, there often are more free riders than payers. *See Florida Education Association/United v. Public Employees Relations Commission*, 346 So. 2d 551 (Fla. 1st Dist. Ct. App. 1977) (rejecting union's attempt to get non-members to pay their "fair share"). *See also United Teachers of Dade v. School District of Miami-Dade County*, 68 So. 3d 1003 (Fla. 3d Dist. Ct. App. 2011) (union could not negotiate benefits just for its members).

2.   RIGHT TO BARGAIN COLLECTIVELY

Although Florida is a right to work state, § 6 protects the right of employees to bargain together. This is because the NLRA says that employees must be allowed "to bargain collectively through representatives of their own choosing." *See* 29 U.S.C. § 157.

In collective bargaining, employees negotiate with their employer as a group rather than individually. Of course, the existence of a union is an essential pre-requisite to collective bargaining. In addition to wages, a collective bargaining agreement usually addresses a host of other subjects, including grievance procedures, health and safety rules, overtime pay, retirement benefits, training methods, and working hours. Whether a given subject must be submitted to collective bargaining depends on whether it directly impacts "wages, hours, or working conditions." *See Fraternal Order of Police, Miami Lodge 20 v. City of Miami*, 609 So. 2d 31 (Fla. 1992).

The right to bargain collectively is considered a fundamental right. As such, any attempt by the government to interfere with it triggers strict scrutiny, meaning that the government must have a compelling reason. Even then, the government must use the narrowest means available to achieve its goals. *See Coastal Florida Police Benevolent Association, Inc. v. Williams*, 838 So. 2d 543 (Fla. 2003); *City of Tallahassee v. Public Employees Relations Commission*, 410 So. 2d 487 (Fla. 1981); *Amalgamated Transit Local 1593 v. Hillsborough Area Rapid Transit*, 139 So. 3d 345 (Fla. 2d Dist. Ct. App. 2014).

In 2018, the Florida Legislature made it more difficult for teachers to engage in collective bargaining. *See* Fla. Stat. § 1012.2315(4). This provision requires a teachers' union to prove that at least half of all eligible employees belong to it and pay dues. If this threshold is not met, the union can be decertified. If this happens, collective bargaining cannot take place (because there is no one to represent the employees), leaving the school board largely free to make whatever workplace rules it wants. Although the Florida Education Association filed a lawsuit challenging the change, it dismissed it after the trial court, in an unpublished opinion, rejected its main arguments. *See Florida Education Association v. Poole* (Fla. 2d Cir. Ct. Aug. 9, 2019)

(No. 2018–CA–1446) (available at https://cvweb. clerk.leon.fl.us/).

3. PUBLIC EMPLOYEE STRIKES

The 1944 version of § 6 neither included nor excluded public workers. Instead, it simply referred to "employees."

In Feb. 1968, the Florida Education Association called a strike that crippled Florida's school system. *See Pinellas County Classroom Teachers Association, Inc. v. Board of Public Instruction of Pinellas County*, 214 So. 2d 34 (Fla. 1968). In response, the Florida Legislature in June 1968 added the following sentence to § 6: "Public employees shall not have the right to strike." In *School Board of Escambia County v. Public Employees Relations Commission*, 350 So. 2d 819 (Fla. 1st Dist. Ct. App. 1974), the court explained:

We do not believe that the constitutional and legislative prohibitions against strikes by public employees were ever intended to give public employers a power advantage over their employees in contract negotiations. Strikes are prohibited to protect the public, not to circumvent the rights of public employees to meaningful collective bargaining with their employer.

Id. at 821.

In *Local 532 of the American Federation of State, County and Municipal Employees, AFL-CIO v. City of Fort Lauderdale, Broward County, Florida*, 273 So.

2d 441 (Fla. 4th Dist. Ct. App. 1973), a union convinced the city's garbage collectors to "walk off" their jobs for 10 days. Although not technically labelled a strike, the court treated it as such and held that it was illegal. A similar tactic, known as the "blue flu," involves public workers calling in sick when they are not, thereby leaving their employer short-handed. The term gets its name from the color of police uniforms.

By including the "no public strikes" language in § 6, the legislature has made it clear that, except for strikes, public workers have the same rights as private employees. *See Dade County Classroom Teachers Association, Inc. v. Legislature of the State Florida*, 269 So. 2d 684 (Fla. 1972). *See also Chiles v. State Employees Attorneys Guild*, 734 So. 2d 1030 (Fla. 1999).

CHAPTER 11
PERSONAL EXPRESSION

A. OVERVIEW

The Florida Constitution protects personal expression in three areas: politics (Art. I, § 5), religion (Art. I, § 3), and speech (Art. I, § 4). The provision on speech also recognizes the importance of a free press.

In contrast, Art. I, § 27 restricts personal expression by prohibiting an individual from marrying a person of the same sex. However, as explained in Ch. 23 of this book, this provision is inoperative due to *Obergefell v. Hodges*, 135 S. Ct. 2584 (2015).

B. POLITICS

Art. I, § 5 states: "The people shall have the right peaceably to assemble, to instruct their representatives, and to petition for redress of grievances." Some version of this language has been included in every one of Florida's constitutions.

1. ASSEMBLY

The right to assemble means that a person is free to associate with whomever he or she wishes. *See Wyche v. State*, 619 So. 2d 231 (Fla. 1993). It also means that he or she has the right *not* to associate with others. *See Boy Scouts of America v. Dale*, 530 U.S. 640 (2000).

A private organization enjoys substantial discretion in choosing its members. *See Nelson v. Dean*, 528 F. Supp. 2d 1271 (N.D. Fla. 2007). The same is true regarding expulsions. *See Everglades Protective Syndicate, Inc. v. Makinney*, 391 So. 2d 262 (Fla. 4th Dist. Ct. App. 1980). Whether an entity is a private organization depends on its formation, funding, and goals. *See Satan Fraternity v. Board of Public Instruction for Dade County*, 22 So. 2d 892 (Fla. 1945) (en banc).

The right to assemble becomes particularly important when a group of like-minded individuals wants to stage a public demonstration. In such instances, the government is permitted to impose reasonable "time, place, and manner" restrictions. Such restrictions may be adopted to: 1) ensure the public's safety; 2) minimize disruption of the event; and, 3) limit the inconvenience to non-participants (such as surrounding homes and businesses).

Whether a restriction is reasonable depends on a careful review of the facts. *See, e.g., Wood v. State*, 2003 WL 1955433 (Fla. 14th Cir. Ct. 2003). Clearly, however, any restriction must be "content-neutral." Thus, the government cannot stifle a speaker simply because it disagrees with his or her message. However, the government *can* ban a speaker who advocates violence. *See Lieberman v. Marshall*, 236 So. 2d 120 (Fla. 1970) (finding that the speaker's message created a "clear and present danger" to the public's safety).

The right to assemble extends to minors. Thus, juvenile curfews are subject to challenge if they prevent minors from exercising their assembly rights. In *State v. J.P.*, 907 So. 2d 1101, 1106 (Fla. 2004), the Florida Supreme Court upheld a municipal curfew because it contained a specific exception for juveniles "attending or traveling to or from an activity that involves the exercise of rights protected under the First Amendment to the United States Constitution (e.g., religious services, government meetings, political party meetings)."

2. INSTRUCTION

The right of instruction means that a citizen has the right to make his or her views known to his or her legislator. The legislator, however, has no duty to follow or implement the citizen's views. This is because in a representative democracy, legislators are expected to vote their consciences.

In *In re Apportionment Law Appearing as Senate Joint Resolution No. 1305, 1972 Regular Session*, 263 So. 2d 797 (Fla. 1972), the Florida Supreme Court held that the right of instruction is not limited to a person's own legislator, but instead extends to all legislators.

3. PETITION

In *Krivanek v. Take Back Tampa Political Committee*, 625 So. 2d 840, 843 (Fla. 1993), *cert. denied sub nom. Clewis v. Krivanek*, 511 U.S. 1030 (1994), the Florida Supreme Court explained that "the right to petition is inherent and absolute. This does not mean, however, that such a right is not subject to reasonable regulation." Based on this standard, the court held that individuals whose names had been purged from the voting rolls were not authorized to sign a petition calling for the repeal of a municipal ordinance.

In *Larson v. State*, 572 So. 2d 1368 (Fla. 1991), a criminal defendant was ordered to stay away from Tallahassee for five years after pleading nolo contendere to a charge of witness tampering. This unusual condition was imposed because the witness lived in Tallahassee. When the defendant later claimed the condition was unconstitutional, the Florida Supreme Court rejected his argument:

> We also do not agree that this restriction is illegal on grounds it prohibits his right to petition state government; it in no sense deters him from communicating by mail or by telephone, or by contacting state officers when they are outside Tallahassee. Moreover, if Larson had some legitimate grievance or concern that required him to visit state officials in Tallahassee, he could petition—and the trial court would be required to grant—a motion to modify the terms of his probation to permit the visit.

Id. at 1371–72.

Those who petition the government for redress are protected from retaliation by government officials. *See Nodar v. Galbreath*, 462 So. 2d 803 (Fla. 1984) (high school teacher could not sue parent who complained about her at a school board meeting); *Cate v. Oldham*, 450 So. 2d 224 (Fla. 1984) (state attorney could not sue citizen who filed unsuccessful wrongful death suit against him).

The foregoing rule does not apply to suits by private parties. In *Florida Fern Growers Association, Inc. v. Concerned Citizens of Putnam County*, 616 So. 2d 562 (Fla. 5th Dist. Ct. App. 1993), for example, a group of citizens complained to the St. Johns River Water Management District after it granted hundreds of permits to commercial fern growers. The growers later sued the citizens, accusing them of injuring their businesses. When the citizens raised § 5 as a defense, contending that it granted them absolute immunity, the court disagreed and permitted the suit to go forward. In *Hurchalla v. Lake Point Phase I, LLC*, 278 So. 3d 58 (Fla. 4th Dist. Ct. App. 2019), *appeal filed*, SC19–1729 (Fla.), the same result was reached under the First Amendment.

C. RELIGION

Art. I, § 3 contains three directives. First, it bars laws "respecting the establishment" of religion. Second, it forbids the government from interfering with the "free exercise" of a person's religious beliefs or practices, except to the extent that the latter are "inconsistent with public morals, peace or safety." Third, it prohibits the government from using public money to directly or indirectly "aid . . . any church, sect, or religious denomination or . . . sectarian institution."

The first and second directives are interpreted in the same manner as the First Amendment. *See*

Williamson v. Brevard County, 928 F.3d 1296 (11th Cir. 2019) (establishment); *Toca v. State*, 834 So. 2d 204 (Fla. 2d Dist. Ct. App. 2002), *review denied*, 846 So. 2d 1150 (Fla. 2003) (free exercise). The third directive has no First Amendment counterpart.

Every version of the Florida constitution has contained the first two directives. The third directive first appeared in the 1885 constitution.

1.   ESTABLISHMENT

Under the Florida Constitution, the government is barred from promoting religion. This applies both in a "macro" sense (*i.e.*, promoting religion generally) and in a "micro" sense (*i.e.*, promoting a specific religion). *See Nohrr v. Brevard County Educational Facilities Authority*, 247 So. 2d 304 (Fla. 1971). By the same token, the government cannot hinder or inhibit religion. *See Koerner v. Borck*, 100 So. 2d 398 (Fla. 1958).

In *State ex rel. Singleton v. Woodruff*, 13 So. 2d 704 (Fla. 1954) (en banc), the Florida Supreme Court struck down a municipal ordinance that required peddlers of religious pamphlets to pay a licensing fee. But in *Brown v. Orange County Board of Public Instruction*, 128 So. 2d 181 (Fla. 2d Dist. Ct. App. 1960), *cert. denied*, 129 So. 2d 141 (Fla. 1961), *judgment aff'd*, 155 So. 2d 371 (Fla. 1963), a school board's decision to distribute free copies of the King James version of the Bible was ruled unconstitutional. As these two cases make clear, a citizen can promote his or her religion but the government must remain neutral.

Whether a given law promotes religion is determined by its primary purpose or effect. For example, a law prohibiting betting on Sundays was held valid because its primary purpose was to give the public a respite from gambling. *See Division of Pari-Mutuel Wagering, Department of Business Regulation v. Florida Horse Council, Inc.*, 464 So. 2d 128 (Fla.), *appeal dismissed sub nom. Calder Race Course, Inc. v. Division of Pari-Mutuel Wagering, Department of Business Regulation*, 474 U.S. 802 (1985).

Similarly, a law providing enhanced penalties for defacing religious property or objects was held to be primarily a crime prevention measure. *See Todd v. State*, 643 So. 2d 625 (Fla. 1st Dist. Ct. App. 1994), *review denied*, 651 So. 2d 1197 (Fla.), *cert. denied*, 515 U.S. 1143 (1995). *See also Rice v. State*, 754 So. 2d 881 (Fla. 5th Dist. Ct. App.), *review denied*, 779 So. 2d 272 (Fla. 2000) (upholding a statute that authorized enhanced penalties for drug sales within 1,000 feet of a place of worship).

In *Silver Rose Entertainment, Inc. v. Clay County*, 646 So. 2d 246 (Fla. 1st Dist. Ct. App. 1994), *review denied*, 658 So. 2d 992 (Fla.), *cert. denied*, 516 U.S. 932 (1995), the plaintiff challenged a county ordinance that banned alcohol sales on Christmas. The court held that the ordinance did not promote religion because Christmas has become a secular holiday. For similar reasons, Florida's use of the motto "In God We Trust" (discussed in Ch. 2 of this book) also is permissible. *Cf. O'Hair v. Blumenthal*, 588 F.2d 1144 (5th Cir.), *cert. denied*, 442 U.S. 930

(1979) (finding that the motto's use by the United States does not violate the First Amendment).

Numerous cases exist challenging the common practice of starting government meetings with a religious blessing. The courts have made it clear that such invocations are permissible so long as they do not associate the government with a specific religion and all religions are given an equal opportunity to participate in such ceremonies. *See Williamson v. Brevard County*, 928 F.3d 1296 (11th Cir. 2019).

Another contentious issue concerns religious displays on government-owned land. In *Calvary Chapel Church, Inc. v. Broward County, Florida*, 299 F. Supp. 2d 1295 (S.D. Fla. 2003), the court, after deciding that the government had to allow such a display, ordered the church to modify it so that viewers would not think the government was endorsing its message.

Because of the establishment clause, Florida's courts are not permitted to decide disputes involving religious bodies. *See, e.g., House of God Which is the Church of the Living God, the Pillar and Ground of the Truth Without Controversy, Inc. v. White*, 792 So. 2d 491 (Fla. 4th Dist. Ct. App. 2001) (dismissing congregant's slander suit against pastor). This rule is designed to prevent the courts from becoming "excessively entangled" in religious matters. As a result, many religions in Florida have their own courts. *See* Ch. 15 of this book.

Despite the foregoing, a Florida state court can hear a case governed by "neutral principles." *See Doe v. Evans*, 814 So. 2d 370 (Fla. 2002) (permitting parishioner to sue church for its pastor's sexual misconduct); *Guinan v. State*, 65 So. 3d 589 (Fla. 4th Dist. Ct. App. 2011) (authorizing criminal prosecution of a pastor accused of stealing church funds).

2.   FREE EXERCISE

The Florida Constitution forbids the government from interfering with a person's religious beliefs. Thus, for example, a patient can reject medical treatment if it conflicts with his or her religious beliefs, even if doing so increases the likelihood of death. *See Matter of Dubreuil*, 629 So. 2d 819 (Fla. 1993). However, a parent who refuses such treatment for his or her child may be subject to prosecution for child abuse. *See Hermanson v. State*, 604 So. 2d 775 (Fla. 1992).

The constitution allows the government to prohibit religious practices that threaten the public welfare. The courts, however, have held that officials may only act when the danger is clear. Even then, they must employ the least restrictive means available to achieve their goals. *See Church of the Lukumi Babalu Aye, Inc. v. City of Hialeah*, 508 U.S. 520 (1993) (invalidating city ordinances prohibiting Santeria animal sacrifice rituals). In 1998, the Florida Legislature codified these requirements in the Religious Freedom Restoration Act ("RFRA"). *See* Fla. Stat. §§ 761.01–761.061. *See also Warner v. City of Boca Raton*, 887 So. 2d 1023 (Fla. 2004) (explaining that due to the RFRA, Florida law provides more protection for religious practices than federal law).

In *Freeman v. Department of Highway Safety and Motor Vehicles*, 924 So. 2d 48 (Fla. 5th Dist. Ct. App.), *review denied*, 940 So. 2d 1124 (Fla. 2006), the plaintiff, a Muslim, refused for religious reasons to have her picture taken without her niqab (a veil that covered all but her eyes). As a result, her driver's license was cancelled because it lacked a full-face photograph. When she sued, the government argued that full-face photographs allow police officers to quickly identify drivers, thereby protecting the public from criminal activity and security threats. It also argued that forcing the plaintiff to briefly remove her niqab for a photograph constituted only a minor burden. Agreeing with these points, the court ruled for the government.

In *Austin v. Crosby*, 866 So. 2d 742 (Fla. 5th Dist. Ct. App. 2004), an inmate challenged a regulation that prevented him from practicing his religion (Wicca). Because the regulation had been adopted for safety reasons, the court upheld it as a valid penological measure.

In *Pacchiana v. State*, 240 So. 3d 803 (Fla. 4th Dist. Ct. App.), *review granted*, 2018 WL 6617941 (Fla. 2018), a woman was prevented by the government from serving on a jury because of her religion (Jehovah's Witness). On appeal, this decision was held to have unconstitutionally interfered with her right to practice her religion.

3.   PUBLIC AID

In *Lemon v. Kurtzman*, 403 U.S. 602 (1971), the U.S. Supreme Court held that public funds cannot be spent on religious schools. But in *Trinity Lutheran Church of Columbia, Inc. v. Comer*, 137 S. Ct. 2012 (2017), the Court ruled that Missouri had wrongfully excluded a religious school from a state program that provides money to make playgrounds safer.

The battle over whether the government should be allowed to provide financial assistance to religious entities is an old one. In 1875, Rep. James Blaine (R-Me.) proposed an amendment to the U.S. Constitution that, had it passed, would have prohibited states from providing either land or money to religious bodies. Blaine's motivation was to ensure that Catholic schools did not receive public funds (at the time, public sentiment was strongly anti-Catholic due to an influx of Catholic immigrants).

Despite the amendment's defeat, 38 states added such language to their own constitutions. Such provisions are known as Little Blaine Amendments ("LBA"), to distinguish them from Blaine's actual proposal. When Florida drafted its 1885 constitution, it included a LBA.

Thus, while the federal constitution is silent as to whether public money can be spent on religious institutions, the Florida Constitution quite clearly prohibits such expenditures. *See, e.g., Council for Secular Humanism, Inc. v. McNeil*, 44 So. 3d 112 (Fla. 1st Dist. Ct. App.), *review denied*, 41 So. 3d 215

(Fla. 2010) (faith-based prison program ineligible for public funds).

Trinity Lutheran has upended the foregoing analysis. This is because the U.S. Supreme Court held that Missouri's LBA violated the First Amendment. In a footnote, however, Chief Justice Roberts expressly limited his ruling to the facts before him: "This case involves express discrimination based on religious identity with respect to playground resurfacing. We do not address religious uses of funding or other forms of discrimination." 137 S. Ct. at 2024 n.3. Accordingly, it currently is unclear to what extent any state's LBA remains operational. In Jan. 2020, however, the Court is scheduled to hear *Espinoza v. Montana Department of Revenue*, 435 P.3d 603 (Mont. 2018), *cert. granted*, 139 S. Ct. 2777 (2019), a case involving a challenge to Montana's LBA. It is expected to clarify matters.

D.   SPEECH

Art. I, § 4 gives every person to right to "speak, write and publish sentiments on all subjects," but makes him or her "responsible for [any] abuse of [this] right." In both libel and slander actions, "if the matter charged as defamatory is true and was published with good motives," the defendant must be "acquitted or exonerated."

Sec. 4 also prohibits the government from passing any law that "abridge[s] the liberty of speech or of the press." These rights have been included in every one of Florida's constitutions.

The right to speak is a fundamental one. As such, the burden of proof is on the party seeking to restrict it. *See Americas Homes, Inc. v. Esler*, 668 So. 2d 239 (Fla. 5th Dist. Ct. App. 2006) (homeowners permitted to post a sign on their property warning about local flooding, even though doing so affected the plaintiff's ability to sell other homes in the neighborhood).

The right to speak is not limited to words. Instead, it encompasses any expressive activity that is designed to communicate with others. *See, e.g., Occupy Fort Myers v. City of Fort Myers*, 882 F. Supp. 2d 1320 (M.D. Fla. 2011).

Florida's courts interpret § 4 in essentially the same manner as the First Amendment. *See, e.g., University Books and Videos, Inc. v. Metropolitan Dade County*, 78 F. Supp. 2d 1327 (S.D. Fla. 1999); *Cafe Erotica v. Florida Department of Transportation*, 830 So. 2d 181 (Fla. 1st Dist. Ct. App. 2002), *review denied*, 845 So. 2d 888 (Fla. 2003). This is not surprising given their similar wording and purpose.

1.   DEFAMATION

Defamation occurs when a person makes a false statement about another person. If the statement is oral, the speaker has committed slander. If the statement is written, the author has committed libel. A false statement that is not defamatory may still be actionable as a "false light" tort. *See Gannett Co., Inc. v. Anderson*, 947 So. 2d 1 (Fla. 1st Dist. Ct. App. 2006), *review granted*, 954 So. 2d 1155 (Fla. 2007), *aff'd on other grounds*, 994 So. 2d 1048 (Fla. 2008).

Opinions are not actionable as defamation. To support a claim for defamation, a statement must have been presented, or reasonably understood, as a fact. *See LRX, Inc. v. Horizon Associates Joint Venture*, 842 So. 2d 881 (Fla. 4th Dist. Ct. App.), *review denied*, 859 So. 2d 514 (Fla. 2003). *See also Lampkin-Asam v. Miami Daily News, Inc.*, 408 So. 2d 666 (Fla. 3d Dist. Ct. App. 1981), *review denied*, 417 So. 2d 329 (Fla.), *cert. denied*, 459 U.S. 806 (1982), *reh'g denied*, 459 U.S. 1189 (1983).

Similarly, a statement that is protected by a privilege normally will not give rise to a defamation action even if it is false. *See Nodar v. Galbreath*, 462 So. 2d 803 (Fla. 1984). In *Jarzynka v. St. Thomas University School of Law*, 310 F. Supp. 2d 1256 (S.D. Fla. 2004), for example, a counselor reported to the law school's dean that a student was dangerous. The court held this statement was privileged and therefore protected, even if it was false.

A court normally will not act to prevent a possible future defamatory act. Such "prior restraints" are disfavored because of their chilling effect. *See Fox v. Hamptons at Metrowest Condominium Association, Inc.*, 223 So. 3d 453 (Fla. 5th Dist. Ct. App. 2017) (condominium resident could not be prohibited from commenting about his condominium association). Instead, a party must wait until the act occurs and then bring a suit for defamation. *See Vrasic v. Leibel*, 106 So. 3d 485 (Fla. 4th Dist. Ct. App. 2013) (former boyfriend could not prevent former girlfriend from using his name in her book, but could sue once the book was published if it contained defamatory language).

The "good motives" language in § 4 is outdated. It refers to lawsuits brought by public figures or officials against the media. At one time, the defendant in such a lawsuit had to prove the statement was both true *and* published with good motives. *See Florida Publishing Co. v. Lee*, 80 So. 245 (Fla. 1918). In *New York Times v. Sullivan*, 376 U.S. 254 (1964), the U.S. Supreme Court held that the burden of proof in such cases is on the plaintiff, who must show that the defendant acted with "actual malice." Florida courts now follow this standard.

In cases involving private figures, negligence is the applicable standard. *See Miami Herald Publishing Co. v. Ane*, 458 So. 2d 239 (Fla. 1984) (newspaper failed to use reasonable care in reporting, incorrectly, that plaintiff was the owner of a truck that had been seized for carrying three tons of marijuana).

Fla. Stat. § 770.02 limits plaintiffs who have been defamed by broadcasters or publishers to "actual damages" if the defendant issues a timely retraction upon being informed of its mistake.

2.   CENSORSHIP

Art. I, § 4 prohibits the government from engaging in censorship. Thus, whenever the government seeks to regulate speech because of its content, it bears a heavy burden. *See State v. T.B.D.*, 656 So. 2d 479 (Fla. 1995), *cert. denied*, 516 U.S. 1145 (1996) (observing that such restrictions are presumptively invalid). *See also State v. Hanna*, 901 So. 2d 201 (5th Dist. Ct. App. 2005).

In *Simmons v. State*, 944 So. 2d 317 (Fla. 2006), a statute that prohibited adults from sending sexually-explicit material to minors was deemed constitutional because of the government's duty to protect children. In reaching this conclusion, the court explained that the strict scrutiny standard was applicable, the government's interest had to be compelling, and the means chosen had to be the least restrictive ones available.

If, however, a regulation is "content-neutral," the government has more leeway to act. *See Public Citizen, Inc. v. Pinellas County*, 321 F. Supp. 2d 1275 (M.D. Fla. 2004). Accordingly, if the regulation is designed to achieve a legitimate goal, the government does not need to prove that it used the least intrusive means available. *See Frandsen v. Department of Environmental Protection*, 829 So. 2d 267 (Fla. 1st Dist. Ct. App. 2002), *review denied*, 845 So. 2d 889 (Fla.), *cert. denied*, 540 U.S. 948 (2003).

In *State v. Catalano*, 104 So. 3d 1069 (Fla. 2012), a state statute regulated how loud motorists could play their car radios but exempted business and political vehicles. Because of these exemptions, the court held that the statute was content-based. As such, it was subject to strict scrutiny and was struck down because it was not narrowly tailored to the government's goal of improving traffic safety and sparing citizens from excessive noise.

A court order requiring buffer zones to be erected around abortion clinics in central Florida was held to be content-neutral. The zones were found to be larger than necessary, however, thereby improperly burdening the speech rights of the protesters. *See Madsen v. Women's Health Center, Inc.*, 512 U.S. 753 (1994).

Four types of speech receive no constitutional protection. Thus, the government can punish language that is defamatory, obscene, poses a "clear and present danger," or constitutes "fighting words." *See Rodriguez v. State*, 906 So. 2d 1082 (Fla. 3d Dist. Ct. App.), *stayed*, 868 So. 2d 530 (Fla. 3d Dist. Ct. App. 2004), *aff'd*, 920 So. 2d 624 (Fla. 2005). The classic example, famously given by Justice Holmes, is that a person may not falsely yell fire in a crowded theater. *See Schenck v. United States*, 249 U.S. 47 (1919). *See also* 18 U.S.C. § 35 (prohibiting, for example, jokes about bombs while in airports).

As a practical matter, however, courts rarely uphold such statutes. *See, e.g., Brown v. State*, 358 So. 2d 16 (Fla. 1978) (striking down a statute that made it a misdemeanor to use profane language in public); *McCall v. State*, 354 So. 2d 869 (Fla. 1978) (striking down a statute that made it a crime to insult a teacher on school property). *See also Weisbrod v. Florida Career Service Commission*, 375 So. 2d 1102 (Fla. 1st Dist. Ct. App. 1979) (explaining that the line between protected speech and unprotected speech is a thin one).

3. FREEDOM OF THE PRESS

Art. I, § 4 recognizes that a free press is essential to a functioning democracy. Thus, it prohibits the government from attempting to restrain or "muzzle" the press. The Florida Supreme Court has indicated that this provision is not designed to protect the private property interests of the media but to ensure the public is able to learn about current events in a timely fashion. *See State ex rel. Miami Herald Publishing Co. v. McIntosh*, 340 So. 2d 904 (Fla. 1976).

During jury selection in a murder case, the trial court issued an order sharply restricting what the press could report. This order was struck down because it interfered with the public's ability to follow the case. *See Times Publishing Co. v. State*, 632 So. 2d 1072 (Fla. 4th Dist. Ct. App. 1994).

In *Palm Beach Newspapers, Inc. v. Nourse*, 413 So. 2d 467 (Fla. 4th Dist. Ct. App. 1982), a trial court agreed to close the courtroom during the sentencing of a defendant who was pleading guilty to performing a lewd and lascivious act on a minor. The newspaper reporters who were present asked to stay to be able to cover the story. The trial court rejected their request and later ordered the case file to be sealed. The appellate court deemed these rulings to be unconstitutional.

In *Sarasota Herald-Tribune v. State*, 916 So. 2d 904 (Fla. 2d Dist. Ct. App. 2005), a trial court order prohibiting the press from having any contact with jurors hearing a high-profile murder case was struck down as overly broad.

CHAPTER 12
PROPERTY

A. OVERVIEW

The Florida Constitution includes four provisions that directly affect property. Art. I, § 2 recognizes a basic right to own property. Art. X then modifies this right in three specific instances: 1) when a homestead is involved (§ 4); 2) when spousal property is at issue (§ 5); and, 3) when the government takes private property (§ 6).

In 2018, Art. I, § 2 was amended by repealing its ban on alien land ownership. This provision had been added in 1926 to discourage California's Japanese farmers from moving to Florida. A short time earlier, California had stripped such farmers of their land rights. *See Porterfield v. Webb*, 263 U.S. 225 (1923).

Many other parts of the constitution also have an impact on property. The most important is Art. VII, which authorizes property taxes. *See* Ch. 21 of this book.

The group Citizens for Energy Choices has proposed a 2020 constitutional amendment that would give citizens the right to: 1) choose their electric provider; and, 2) generate their own electricity. *See Advisory Opinion to the Attorney General re Competitive Energy Market*, SC19–328 and SC19–479 (Fla.).

B.   RIGHT TO OWN PROPERTY

Art. I, § 2 recognizes that all human beings "have inalienable rights, among which are the right to enjoy and defend life and liberty, to pursue happiness, to be rewarded for industry, and to acquire, possess and protect property."

The first three of these rights have no practical meaning. The right "to acquire, possess, and protect property" stands on a different footing. It has been included, in one form or another, in every one of Florida's constitutions, although it was restricted to "freemen" in the 1838, 1861, and 1865 constitutions.

In *Shriners Hospitals for Crippled Children v. Zrillic*, 563 So. 2d 64 (Fla. 1990), the Florida Supreme Court relied on § 2 to strike down the state's mortmain statute, which prohibited dying persons from making gifts to charitable institutions: "[A] common sense reading of the language in article I, section 2, leads to the conclusion that the right to devise property is a property right protected by the Florida Constitution." *Id.* at 67.

Zrillic was distinguished in *Lee v. Estate of Payne*, 148 So. 3d 776 (Fla. 2d Dist. Ct. App.), *review denied*, 132 So. 3d 221 (Fla. 2013). In *Lee*, the decedent's fiancée tried to have a Colorado holographic (*i.e.*, handwritten) will accepted for probate. Florida, however, does not recognize such wills. *See* Fla. Stat. § 732.502.

To get around the law, the fiancée argued that it was an unconstitutional restraint on the decedent's right to dispose of his Florida-based property. The court disagreed: "[The statute] focuses not on the testator's choices in making a devise; rather it operates to assure authenticity and reliability. It promotes fulfillment of the testator's intent." 148 So. 3d at 780.

The right to use one's property as one wishes lies at the heart of § 2. In *Duvall v. Fair Lane Acres, Inc.*, 50 So. 3d 668 (Fla. 2d Dist. Ct. App. 2010), for example, a homeowners' association sought to convert a mobile home park into a "55-and-older" community. The plaintiffs objected to the plan and refused to give their consent. The trial court entered judgment for the association, but on appeal its decision was reversed:

> To impose a limitation on who can use and enjoy property is a direct restriction on the Homeowners' ownership rights in their properties. . . . Similarly, to restrict the ability to transfer property by imposing an obligation to seek the approval of the Association is an improper infringement on the Homeowners' property rights. These property rights are constitutionally protected, and the trial court erred in ordering the Homeowners to sign the Agreement by which they would be required to surrender these rights.

Id. at 671.

In *Smith v. Wiker*, 192 So. 3d 603 (Fla. 2d Dist. Ct. App. 2016), the plaintiff and the defendant were neighbors. The plaintiff obtained a protection order against the defendant due to stalking. Among other things, the order prohibited the defendant from "lingering" on his own driveway. On appeal, this provision was deemed overbroad:

> Here, the prohibition that Smith not linger on his driveway is overbroad because it encompasses conduct that could constitute stalking by harassing the neighbor but could also encompass activity that is perfectly legal. For instance, Smith asserts that he is required to maintain his yard and his driveway and control plant growth. Or he could simply choose to sit on his driveway and read a book. Because the challenged language broadly prohibits Smith from engaging in legal activity on his property, we reverse the portion of the injunction prohibiting Smith from lingering on his driveway and remand with directions for the trial court to more narrowly tailor the provision to prevent harassment of the neighbor.

Id. at 604–05.

As *Smith* makes clear, an infringement on property rights normally triggers strict scrutiny (meaning that the government must have a compelling reason and use the narrowest means that will achieve its objectives). If the infringement is minor, however, the rational basis test is used. *See Ricketts v. Village of Miami Shores*, 232 So. 3d 1095 (Fla. 3d Dist. Ct. App. 2017), *review denied*, 2018 WL 794717 (Fla. 2018). (In 2019, the result in *Ricketts* was overturned by S.B. 82, codified as Fla. Stat. § 604.71.)

C. HOMESTEADS

Florida's homestead laws are extremely complicated, and the discussion below does not attempt to address their finer points. For a comprehensive examination, see Charles Rubin, *Rubin on Florida Homestead* (2018) (https://www.rubinonfloridahomestead.com/).

1. BASICS

A homestead is a dwelling that is: 1) located in Florida; 2) owned by a natural person; and, 3) being used by the owner as his or her actual principal residence. *See Wechsler v. Carrington*, 214 F. Supp. 2d 1348 (S.D. Fla. 2002) (because the owner was not yet living in his condominium full-time, it was not his homestead); *In re Wiley*, 570 B.R. 661 (Bankr. N.D. Fla. 2016) (beach house used just for vacations did not qualify as a homestead); *In re Wilson*, 393 B.R. 778 (Bankr. S.D. Fla. 2008) (only portion of building serving as the debtor's home qualified as a homestead). At present, there are 4.3 million homesteads in Florida.

Art. X, § 4(a)(1) draws distinctions based on a homestead's location. Homesteads within cities cannot exceed 0.5 acres, while homesteads outside cities cannot exceed 160 acres. *See In re Kellogg*, 197 F.3d 1116 (11th Cir. 1999). *See also Navellier v. Florida*, 672 F. App'x 925 (11th Cir. 2016) (dismissing equal protection claim filed by homeowners whose in-city property consisted of 1.2 acres). Additionally, only contiguous land is included. *See In re Jackson*, 169 B.R. 742 (Bankr. N.D. Fla.

1994) (because public roadway intersected debtor's land, debtor could claim homestead in only one of the two parcels). The subsequent inclusion of a homestead in a city does not reduce the amount of land that can be claimed as homestead, except with the owner's consent. *See In re Burns*, 395 B.R. 756 (Bankr. M.D. Fla. 2008).

Corporate entities cannot have Florida homesteads because only natural persons are protected. *See Buchman v. Canard*, 926 So. 2d 390 (Fla. 3d Dist. Ct. App. 2005), *review denied*, 929 So. 2d 1051 (Fla. 2006). Out-of-staters cannot have Florida homesteads because only Floridians can have a Florida homestead. *See Stuart v. Ryan*, 232 So. 3d 418 (Fla. 4th Dist. Ct. App. 2017), *review denied*, 2018 WL 1721767 (Fla.), *cert. denied*, 139 S. Ct. 244 (2018). Married couples are allowed only one homestead, unless they are separated and living apart. *See In re Colwell*, 196 F.3d 1225 (11th Cir. 1999), *reh'g and reh'g en banc denied*, 209 F.3d 726 (11th Cir. 2000).

Condominiums can be homesteads. *See Geraci v. Sunstar EMS*, 93 So. 3d 384 (Fla. 2d Dist. Ct. App. 2012), *review granted*, 123 So. 3d 559 (Fla.), *review dismissed*, 129 So. 3d 1069 (Fla. 2013). Because of their unique legal structure, cooperative apartments are homesteads for some purposes (*e.g.*, forced sale) but not for others (*e.g.*, devise). *See Phillips v. Hirshon*, 958 So. 2d 425 (Fla. 3d Dist. Ct. App.), *review granted*, 963 So. 2d 227 (Fla. 2007), *review dismissed sub nom. Levine v. Hirshon*, 980 So. 2d 1053 (Fla. 2008).

Fla. Stat. § 222.05 allows mobile homes to be claimed as homesteads, even if the owner does not have title to the underlying land. At least one court has found that this statute also applies to vessels. *See In re Mead*, 255 B.R. 80 (Bankr. S.D. Fla. 2000). In summing up matters, another court has opined: "[S]o long as a debtor actually lived on real property being claimed as exempt, a non-exempt tree house or tent would establish the requisite degree of permanency." *In re McClain*, 281 B.R. 769, 773 (Bankr. M.D. Fla. 2002).

Once a property becomes a homestead, it continues as such until one of three things happens: 1) the owner stops being a Florida resident; 2) the owner stops using the property as his or her principal residence; or, 3) it is sold. *See Beltran v. Kalb*, 63 So. 3d 783 (Fla. 3d Dist. Ct. App. 2011). Of course, after a sale the new owner may be able to establish his or her own homestead. However, the new owner cannot "piggyback" on the former owner's homestead.

Determining that a homestead has been sold usually is an easy matter. In contrast, it may be difficult to know whether the owner has stopped being a Florida resident or has stopped using the property as his or her homestead. Much depends on the owner's intention, see *In re Herr*, 197 B.R. 939 (Bankr. S.D. Fla. 1996), although other factors (such as whether the owner has removed the furniture, gotten a new driver's license, or changed where he or she receives mail) also are probative. *See In re Minton*, 402 B.R. 380 (Bankr. M.D. Fla. 2008); *In re Lloyd*, 394 B.R. 605 (Bankr. S.D. Fla. 2008); *Novoa v.*

Amerisource Corp., 860 So. 2d 506 (Fla. 3d Dist. Ct. App. 2003).

Homesteads receive special treatment under several different sections of the Florida Constitution. First, they qualify for tax breaks that are unavailable to non-homestead property. *See* Ch. 21 of this book. Second, as discussed below, they are protected from most, but not all, of the owner's creditors. *See* Art. X, § 4(a). At death, these protections pass to the owner's spouse or heirs. *See* Art. X, § 4(b). In exchange for these protections, the constitution significantly restricts the alienation (*i.e.*, transfer) of homesteads. *See* Art. X, § 4(c). For a further discussion of these sections, see *Baldwin v. Henriquez*, 279 So. 3d 328 (Fla. 2d Dist. Ct. App. 2019).

2.   CREDITOR CLAIMS

Under Art. X, § 4(a), a homestead is "exempt from forced sale under process of any court, and no judgment, decree or execution shall be a lien thereon." This provision became a part of the constitution in 1868. In 1984, the phrase "head of household" was changed to "natural person" to make it clear that § 4(a) protects all homesteads.

Thus, a court cannot order a homestead to be sold to pay a person's creditors and a creditor cannot "cloud" (*i.e.*, encumber) a homestead's title. *See Sepulveda v. Westport Recovery Corp.*, 145 So. 3d 162 (Fla. 3d Dist. Ct. App. 2014). Homesteads similarly are protected from civil and criminal forfeitures. *See Butterworth v. Caggiano*, 605 So. 2d 56 (Fla. 1992).

As explained in *Miskin v. City of Fort Lauderdale*, 661 So. 2d 415 (Fla. 4th Dist. Ct. App. 1995), § 4(a) does not invalidate a debt. Instead, it simply makes it unenforceable against the homestead. Liens that arise before homestead, however, can be enforced against the property. *See Moorhead v. Yongue*, 183 So. 804 (Fla. 1938) (en banc).

The goal of § 4(a) is to keep a roof over families, even when economic misfortune befalls them. This is considered important for two reasons: 1) it promotes family stability; and, 2) it keeps the family from becoming a burden on society. *See In re Englander*, 95 F.3d 1028 (11th Cir. 1996), *cert. denied sub nom. Englander v. Mills*, 520 U.S. 1186 (1997).

Sec. 4(a) shields 100% of a homestead's value. This makes Florida one of just seven states with unlimited homestead protection. Most states cap their homestead protection, often at very low amounts. *See, e.g.,* Illinois ($15,000), Tennessee ($5,000), and Virginia ($5,000). Two states (New Jersey and Pennsylvania) do not grant any protection to homeowners.

Sec. 4(a) makes its forced sale protection inapplicable to three types of creditors, who colloquially are known as "super creditors": 1) the government, to satisfy unpaid taxes or assessments; 2) mortgagees, if they lent the debtor money to buy or improve the homestead; and, 3) laborers and materialmen, if they were hired to work on the homestead (*e.g.*, gardeners, painters, roofers). *See In re Adell*, 321 B.R. 562 (Bankr. M.D. Fla. 2005).

The exception for taxes includes federal taxes. *See Weitzner v. United States*, 309 F.2d 45 (5th Cir. 1962), *cert. denied*, 372 U.S. 913 (1963). It also applies to assessments. In contrast to a tax, which is imposed on all homes for general government services, an assessment is imposed only on certain homes to pay for a specific benefit. Thus, for example, homes located on a given block might be assessed for the cost of hooking them up to the city's sewer system.

The exception for mortgagees protects lenders whose borrowers default. *See In re Arnold*, 166 F. App'x 424 (11th Cir. 2006); *Spikes v. One West Bank FSB*, 106 So. 3d 475 (Fla. 4th Dist. Ct. App. 2012), *review denied*, 119 So. 3d 444 (Fla. 2013). It includes both institutional lenders (*e.g.*, banks, insurance companies, and pension funds) and non-institutional lenders (*e.g.*, friends and relatives). Likewise, it applies to both purchase-money mortgages and home improvement loans.

The exception for laborers and materialmen covers anyone who maintains or improves the homestead. It does not, however, include attorneys. *See Law v. Law*, 163 So. 3d 553 (Fla. 3d Dist. Ct. App. 2015). This is true even when they are hired to defend the owner's interest in the house, see *Bakst, Cloyd & Bakst, P.A. v. Cole*, 750 So. 2d 676 (Fla. 4th Dist. Ct. App. 1999), or recover insurance proceeds to repair the house. *See Quiroga v. Citizens Property Insurance Corp.*, 34 So. 3d 101 (Fla. 3d Dist. Ct. App.), *review denied sub nom. Katzman Garfinkel and Berger v. Citizens Property Insurance Corp.*, 46 So. 3d 566 (Fla. 2010). As part of an attorney's retainer agreement, however, a client can agree to waive his or her homestead rights. *See Trontz v. Winig*, 905 So. 2d 1026 (Fla. 4th Dist. Ct. App. 2005).

Because Florida has unlimited homestead protection, while most states do not, Florida attracts many out-of-state debtors. In 1989, for example, as their Manhattan law firm was collapsing due to fraud, Bowie Kuhn, the former commissioner of Major League Baseball, and Harvey Myerson flew to Florida and purchased homesteads in, respectively, Ponte Vedra Beach and Key West. Their goal was to shield their assets from the firm's creditors. *See United States v. Myerson*, 18 F.3d 153 (2d Cir.), *cert. denied*, 513 U.S. 855 (1994).

Such subterfuges have given Florida a reputation as a "debtor's haven." As a result, creditors have asked Florida's courts to recognize fraud as a fourth exception to the prohibition on forced sales. Such requests have been rejected. *See, e.g., Havoco of America, Ltd. v. Hill*, 790 So. 2d 1018, 1030 (Fla. 2001) ("[A] homestead acquired by a debtor with the specific intent to hinder, delay, or defraud creditors is not excepted from the protection of article X, section 4.").

Havoco does permit a court to impose an equitable lien on a homestead "where funds obtained through fraud or egregious conduct were used to invest in, purchase, or improve the homestead." *Id.* at 1028. Thus, in *In re Lee*, 574 B.R. 286 (Bankr. M.D. Fla. 2017), *aff'd sub nom. Lee v. Wiand*, 603 B.R. 161 (M.D. Fla. 2018), a house that had been purchased with funds derived from a Ponzi scheme was held not to be protected from creditors.

An owner who sells his or her homestead often plans to use the proceeds to buy a new homestead. In such instances, the proceeds will be protected from creditor claims for a "reasonable amount of time," assuming the owner acts in good faith to find a new homestead and does not commingle the proceeds with other monies. *See Zivitz v. Zivitz*, 16 So. 3d 841 (Fla. 2d Dist. Ct. App.), *review denied*, 23 So. 3d 1182 (Fla. 2009); *Myers v. Lehrer*, 671 So. 2d 864 (Fla. 4th Dist. Ct. App.), *review denied*, 678 So. 2d 1287 (Fla. 1996). What constitutes a reasonable amount of time depends on the facts but ordinarily means two years. *See In re Kalynych*, 284 B.R. 149 (Bankr. M.D. Fla. 2002). If any of the proceeds are not used to purchase a new homestead, they become "surplus" and lose their exempt status. *See JBK Associates, Inc. v. Sill Bros., Inc.*, 191 So. 3d 879 (Fla. 2016).

If a debtor claims that his or her property is a homestead, and a creditor wishes to dispute this claim, the creditor must show by convincing evidence that the property is not the debtor's homestead. *See In re Minton*, 402 B.R. 380 (Bankr. M.D. Fla. 2008).

Sec. 4(a)(2) provides further protection from creditors. Under it, personal property worth up to $1,000 is exempt. This figure was significant when it was added to the constitution in 1868 but has been badly eroded by inflation. As a result, many debtors instead opt for the $4,000 "enhanced" or "wildcard" exemption authorized by Fla. Stat. § 222.25(4). This exemption is only available "if the debtor does not claim or receive the benefits of a homestead exemption under § 4, Art. X of the State Constitution." *Id. See also In re Rodale*, 452 B.R. 290 (Bankr. M.D. Fla. 2011).

As explained above, § 4(b) passes the exemptions contained in paragraph (a) to the owner's surviving spouse or heirs. In *Estate of Shefner v. Shefner-Holden*, 2 So. 3d 1076 (Fla. 3d Dist. Ct. App. 2009), the decedent committed suicide. As a result, one of his adult sons inherited his homestead. Claims subsequently were made against it. In rejecting them, the court wrote:

> Here, Frank is a qualified heir, and the decedent's will directed that Frank not be forced to sell the house. Therefore, the homestead property passed directly to Frank, and never became a part of decedent's probate estate. Because the property was not a part of decedent's probate estate, the trial court properly concluded that the proceeds from the subsequent sale of the property could not be used to pay creditors' claims or administrative expenses of the estate

Id. at 1079.

3. ALIENATION

To ensure that spouses and minor children do not become homeless, Art. X, § 4(c) places restrictions on homestead transfers:

> The homestead shall not be subject to devise if the owner is survived by spouse or minor child,

except the homestead may be devised to the owner's spouse if there be no minor child. The owner of homestead real estate, joined by the spouse if married, may alienate the homestead by mortgage, sale or gift and, if married, may by deed transfer the title to an estate by the entirety with the spouse. If the owner or spouse is incompetent, the method of alienation or encumbrance shall be as provided by law.

The first sentence means that homesteads cannot be transferred by will, except when there is no minor child and the transfer is to the testator's spouse. *See Lyons v. Lyons*, 155 So. 3d 1179 (Fla. 4th Dist. Ct. App. 2014), *review denied*, 177 So. 3d 1268 (Fla. 2015). This exception was added in 1972.

The second sentence prohibits an owner from mortgaging, selling, or giving away a homestead unless his or her spouse joins in the conveyance. *See Vera v. Wells Fargo Bank, N.A.*, 178 So. 3d 517 (Fla. 4th Dist. Ct. App. 2015) (mortgage); *Steadly v. Weinberg*, 979 So. 2d 445 (Fla. 4th Dist. Ct. App. 2008) (sale); *Clemons v. Thornton*, 993 So. 2d 1054 (Fla. 1st Dist. Ct. App. 2008) (gift). This sentence also allows couples to title homestead property as "tenants by the entirety." When held in this way, property passes to the survivor outside of probate. *See Bendl v. Bendl*, 246 So. 2d 574 (Fla. 3d Dist. Ct. App. 1971).

The final sentence recognizes that an owner, or his or her spouse, may become incompetent and thus unable to join in a transfer. It therefore authorizes the legislature to make provisions for such situations, which it has done. *See* Fla. Stat. § 744.441(12). *See also In re Guardianship of Tanner,* 564 So. 2d 180 (Fla. 3d Dist. Ct. App. 1990). Under the 1885 constitution, the Florida Supreme Court had held that homestead property could not be conveyed without the consent of both spouses, even if one of them was institutionalized and unable to give consent. *See Stokes v. Whidden,* 122 So. 566 (Fla. 1929) (Div. B).

If an owner is survived by both a spouse and a minor child, the spouse receives a life estate in the homestead and the child receives the remainder. *See* Fla. Stat. § 732.401(1). As an alternative, a spouse can take a 50% interest in the homestead, but this decision must be made within six months of the other spouse's death. *See* Fla. Stat. § 732.401(2). Such an election then allows the surviving spouse to sell his or her half of the property (after partition by a court).

Sec. 4(c) has no application where a homestead owner is survived by neither a spouse nor a minor child. *See Webb v. Blue,* 243 So. 3d 1054 (Fla. 1st Dist. Ct. App.), *review denied,* 2018 WL 6304830 (Fla. 2018). Similarly, a spouse can waive his or her homestead rights (*e.g.,* in a pre- or post-nuptial agreement). *See* Fla. Stat. §§ 732.702 and 732.7025. *See also Stone v. Stone,* 157 So. 3d 295 (Fla. 4th Dist. Ct. App. 2014). In contrast, a minor child's homestead rights can never be waived. *See Friscia v. Friscia,* 161 So. 3d 513 (Fla. 2d Dist. Ct. App. 2014).

D. SPOUSAL PROPERTY

Art. X, § 5 states: "There shall be no distinction between married women and married men in the holding, control, disposition, or encumbering of their property, both real and personal; except that dower or curtesy may be established and regulated by law." As explained below, this provision both retains and abolishes important historical concepts.

1. MARRIED WOMEN

At common law, a single woman (*"feme sole"*) could own property and enter into contracts. Once she married, however, she became a *"feme covert"* and lost these powers because of the doctrine of "coverture." This doctrine rested on two legal fictions: 1) a wedded couple is one person; and, 2) a husband is his wife's protector. *See Merchant's Hostess Service of Florida v. Cain*, 9 So. 2d 373 (Fla. 1942) (en banc).

Florida began to chip away at coverture in the 1868 constitution: "All property, both real and personal, of the wife, owned by her before marriage, or acquired afterward by gift, devise, descent, or purchase, shall be her separate property, and not liable for the debts of her husband." The 1885 constitution modified this language to make it clear that wives could pledge their separate property to pay for their husband's debts.

In 1943, Florida further chipped away at coverture by adopting a "Married Women's Property Act." *See* Fla. Stat. §§ 708.05–708.10. Prior to its enactment, a wife could not sell or otherwise dispose of her separate property without her husband joining in the conveyance. *See Bogle v. Perkins*, 240 So. 2d 801 (Fla. 1970).

In *Hallman v. Hospital and Welfare Board of Hillsborough County*, 262 So. 2d 669 (Fla. 1972), the Florida Supreme Court held that § 5 eliminates all distinctions between married men and married women. Nevertheless, in *Connor v. Southwest Florida Regional Medical Center, Inc.*, 668 So. 2d 175 (Fla. 1995), the court relied on the 14th Amendment, rather than § 5, to abrogate the common law rule that husbands are responsible for their wives' necessaries but wives are not responsible for their husbands' necessaries.

2.   DOWER AND CURTESY

"Dower" refers to the life estate that, by law, a widow is entitled to in her husband's estate. "Curtesy" refers to the life estate that, by law, a widower is entitled to in his wife's estate. Historically, both were set at one-third of the decedent's estate.

Dower and curtesy arose during the Middle Ages. They were (and are) designed to ensure that the surviving spouse continues to receive support from the decedent. As such, a will provision that purports to deprive a surviving spouse of his or her dower or curtesy rights is void.

Florida, like 43 other states, has abolished dower and curtesy. *See* Fla. Stat. § 732.111. In their place, it has adopted the "elective share." *See* Fla. Stat.

§ 732.201. The elective share is 30% of the decedent's "elective estate." *See* Fla. Stat. § 732.2065. Generally, a decedent's elective estate consists of all the property he or she owned at death. *See* Fla. Stat. § 732.2035. Since 2017, this has included the decedent's interest in any homestead property, regardless of how it is titled. *Id.*

A surviving spouse must exercise his or her elective share rights in writing within the shorter of: 1) two years of the decedent's death; or, 2) six months after service of the notice of administration. *See* Fla. Stat. § 732.2135. These periods are subject to extension. *Id.*

Normally, there is no need for an elective share election because the decedent has provided adequate support for the survivor. Where this is not true, serious problems can arise. In 1990, for example, Miami Dolphins owner Joe Robbie died. Although he had an elaborate estate plan, his wife Elizabeth decided to exercise her elective share rights. This resulted in a $47 million estate tax bill. To pay it, the Robbie family was forced to sell both the team and the stadium at fire sale prices. *See* https://trust counsel.com/2015/04/remember-the-joe-robbie-stadium/.

E.   TAKINGS

Art. X, § 6 limits the government's ability to divest owners of their property. Paragraph (a) states that a taking is lawful only when it is for a "public purpose" and the owner receives "full compensation." Paragraph (b) allows the government to impose drainage easements on private land. Lastly, paragraph (c) prohibits the government from transferring private property to another "natural person or private entity" unless 60% of the legislature approves.

Paragraphs (a) and (b) first appeared in the 1885 constitution. Paragraph (c) was added in 2006.

1. EMINENT DOMAIN: GENERAL PRINCIPLES

Using the power of eminent domain, the government can take ("condemn") such private property as it needs. This includes both real property and personal property. *See Palm Beach County v. Cove Club Investors Ltd.*, 734 So. 2d 379 (Fla. 1999). A taking can be either permanent or temporary. *See Rubano v. Department of Transportation*, 656 So. 2d 1264 (Fla. 1995).

Eminent domain is an inherent attribute of sovereignty. *See Spafford v. Brevard County*, 110 So. 451 (Fla. 1926) (en banc). As such, § 6(a) does not create the power of eminent domain but rather puts limits on its use. *See System Components Corp. v. Florida Department of Transportation*, 14 So. 3d 967 (Fla. 2009).

The Fifth Amendment directs that private property shall not be "taken for public use . . . without just compensation." Because the Florida Constitution uses the word "full" rather than the word "just," an owner whose property is taken by the government can recover greater damages under

Florida law than under federal law. *See Joseph B. Doerr Trust v. Central Florida Expressway Authority*, 177 So. 3d 1209 (Fla. 2015). In all other respects, Florida takings law and federal takings law are nearly identical. *See Chmielewski v. City of St. Pete Beach*, 890 F.3d 942 (11th Cir. 2018).

Eminent domain proceedings are controlled by Fla. Stat. ch. 73. As it makes clear, the power of eminent domain can be exercised by the state as well as by counties, municipalities, school districts, special districts, and water management districts. In *Lost Tree Village Corp. v. City of Vero Beach*, 838 So. 2d 561 (Fla. 4th Dist. Ct. App. 2002), the court observed: "Both Constitutional provisions [state and federal] emphasize the taking of the property, not the governmental unit responsible for the taking."

The government can delegate its eminent domain powers to private entities. *See Clark v. Gulf Power Co.*, 198 So. 2d 368 (Fla. 1st Dist. Ct. App. 1967). Such delegations, however, are strictly construed. *Id.*

To be valid, a taking must serve a public purpose. In wartime, this means the government can take private property to support combat operations. *See Yulee v. Canova*, 11 Fla. 9 (1864) (food for troops). In peacetime, this means the government can take private property to improve daily life. *See Demeter Land Co. v. Florida Public Service Co.*, 128 So. 402 (Fla. 1930) (en banc) (land for power lines).

Whether a public purpose exists is a question of law. However, a decision made in good faith is unlikely to be set aside by the courts. In *Wilton v. St.*

Johns County, 123 So. 527 (Fla. 1929) (en banc), the Florida Supreme Court stressed that the government

> is vested with a considerable discretionary power, and may determine the location of the land required to be appropriated in order to accomplish the public purpose in view; and such determination will not be interfered with by the courts if it is made in good faith and is not capricious or wantonly injurious. . . . The landowner cannot object merely because some other location might have been made or some other property obtained which would have been suitable for the purpose. . . . It may be said to be a general rule that, unless [the government] acts in bad faith or is guilty of oppression, its discretion in the selection of land will not be interfered with.

Id. at 535. *See also Shavers v. Duval County*, 73 So. 2d 684 (Fla. 1954) (en banc); *Test v. Broward County*, 616 So. 2d 111 (Fla. 4th Dist. Ct. App. 1993).

In exercising its eminent domain powers, the government is only allowed to take as much property as it reasonably needs to achieve its objectives. *See Trailer Ranch, Inc. v. City of Pompano Beach*, 500 So. 2d 503 (Fla. 1986). *But see Department of Transportation v. Fortune Federal Savings and Loan Association*, 532 So. 2d 1267 (Fla. 1988) (allowing state agency to take more land than it needed to save money).

The government must pay the owner for the property it takes. *See* Fla. Stat. § 73.071(3)(a). How much it must pay is a question of fact to be decided by a jury. *See* Fla. Stat. § 73.071(1) (requiring 12 jurors to hear such cases). As such, a statute that sets the level of compensation to be paid will not be enforced. *See Florida Department of Agriculture and Consumer Services v. Lopez-Brignoni*, 114 So. 3d 1138 (Fla. 3d Dist. Ct. App. 2012), *reh'g denied*, 114 So. 3d 1135 (Fla. 3d Dist. Ct. App. 2013), *review denied*, 133 So. 3d 526 (Fla. 2014).

If the government does not take the owner's entire property, it also must pay "severance damages," which are any "damages to the remainder caused by the taking." *See* Fla. Stat. § 73.071(3)(b).

The property owner is entitled to both costs, see Fla. Stat. § 73.091, and attorneys' fees, see Fla. Stat. § 73.092. Pre-judgment interest also is recoverable. *See Atlantic Coast Line Railway Co. v. United States*, 132 F.2d 959 (5th Cir. 1943). Business damages (*e.g.*, loss of goodwill, lost opportunities, lost profits, and relocation costs) normally are not compensable. *See Sabal Trail Transmission, LLC v. +/- 18.27 Acres of Land in Levy County, Florida*, 280 F. Supp. 3d 1331 (N.D. Fla. 2017).

All parties having an interest in the property are entitled to compensation. *See Winn-Dixie Stores, Inc. v. Department of Transportation*, 839 So. 2d 727 (Fla. 2d Dist. Ct. App. 2003). The determination of their respective rights occurs in two steps:

> Florida follows the "unity rule" or "undivided fee rule." [citations omitted] The rule requires the jury in an eminent domain proceeding to value

the property as a whole, irrespective of the interests held in the parcel. The trial court then determines in a summary, supplemental proceeding the portion to be awarded to all interested parties, including lessees.

Orlando/Orange County Expressway Authority v. Tuscan Ridge, LLC, 84 So. 3d 410, 415 (Fla. 5th Dist. Ct. App. 2012).

It sometimes is necessary for the government to take private property before a final judgment can be entered. This is permitted by Fla. Stat. ch. 74, which is known as the "take-quick" statute (to distinguish it from ch. 73, the "take-slow" statute). When the government uses ch. 74, it must deposit into the court's registry "such sum of money as [the court believes] will fully secure and fully compensate the persons entitled to compensation as ultimately determined by the final judgment." *See* Fla. Stat. § 74.051(2). *See also Division of Administration, State of Florida Department of Transportation v. Dade County*, 388 So. 2d 326 (Fla. 3d Dist. Ct. App. 1980).

Although most eminent domain claims involve land, any type of property that is taken by the government will support such proceedings. *See, e.g., Central Waterworks, Inc. v. Town of Century*, 754 So. 2d 814 (Fla. 1st Dist. Ct. App. 2000) (government's agreement to supply water to new correctional facility violated plaintiff's franchise rights). *But see City of Hollywood v. Bien*, 209 So. 3d 1 (Fla. 4th Dist. Ct. App. 2016) (city's prospective change to its pension plan did not constitute a taking of plaintiffs' rights).

2.   EMINENT DOMAIN AND PRIVATE DEVELOPERS

Art. X, § 6(c) was added in 2006 to nullify *Kelo v. City of New London*, 545 U.S. 469, *reh'g denied*, 545 U.S. 1158 (2005). In that case, the U.S. Supreme Court ruled that local governments could use eminent domain to aid private developers.

At the time, it was common for local governments to increase their tax bases by taking private land that was not producing much tax revenue and turning it over to a private developer. Such takings relied on the fiction that the land in question was "blighted" and needed "rehabilitation." *See, e.g., City of Hollywood Community Redevelopment Agency v. 1843, LLC*, 980 So. 2d 1138 (Fla. 4th Dist. Ct. App), *review denied*, 994 So. 2d 307 (Fla. 2008) (upholding 2004 agreement under which city agreed to take defendant's low-rise building, which housed a hair salon and several other small businesses, and turn it over to a private developer who planned to replace it with a 19-story condominium and retail tower).

In its first session after *Kelo*, the Florida Legislature passed H.B. 1567, a law prohibiting nearly all such deals. *See* Fla. Stat. § 73.014(2). It then convinced voters to constitutionalize the law.

Sec. 6(c) still allows such takings when a "general law [is] passed by a three-fifths vote of the membership of each house of the Legislature." To date, no such law has been enacted.

Along with Florida, 43 other states have taken steps to limit *Kelo* (Florida is one of 11 to do so by a constitutional amendment). In a ranking of these efforts, the Castle Coalition gave Florida an "A":

> Florida has gone from being among the worst eminent domain abuse offenders to offering some of the best protection in the nation for homes, businesses, and houses of worship that formerly could have been condemned for private development. HB 1567 and Florida's new constitutional amendment should be models for other state legislatures. They prohibit takings for private benefit while still allowing the government to condemn property for traditional public uses such as roads, bridges, and government buildings.

50 State Report Card (2007), at http://castlecoalition. org/florida.

Critics, on the other hand, believe that § 6(c) is causing much greater problems than it is solving:

> Proponents . . . believed the government's right to authorize condemnation for properties it termed slums, nuisances, and blighted was problematic. Such power gave the government a blank check to acquire any property it sought by a mere declaration of the property as blighted or as meeting slum conditions. [However], the success of H.B. 1567 and [§ 6] . . . has been even more problematic. The limit of these powers has

largely removed the government's ability to engage in the process of advantageous takings. [The] restrictions [have] limited the government's ability to exercise effective authority when it comes to issues concerning historic preservation, the environment, health and safety issues, and climate change response.

Jared Kelly, "Condemning Condemnation: The Ramifications of Tallahassee's Eminent Domain Reform," 2 *N.Y.U. Undergrad. L. Rev.* 32, 36 (2019).

3. EMINENT DOMAIN AND THE GOVERNMENT'S OTHER POWERS

(a) Police Powers

When the government properly exercises its police powers, no compensation is due for any taking that occurs. *See Pondella Hall for Hire, Inc. v. Lamar*, 866 So. 2d 719 (Fla. 5th Dist. Ct. App.), *review denied*, 879 So. 2d 623 (Fla. 2004) (operator of illegal bingo games shut down by the government lacked colorable claim for compensation); *Strickland v. Department of Agriculture and Consumer Services*, 922 So. 2d 1022 (Fla. 5th Dist. Ct. App. 2006) (no taking occurred where state's firefighters damaged plaintiff's dike, fencing, and trees while trying to control blaze).

In *Keshbro, Inc. v. City of Miami*, 801 So. 2d 864 (Fla. 2001), the city's nuisance abatement board ordered a motel to close for six months, and an apartment building to close for 12 months, after concluding that criminal activity was taking place at both locations. On appeal, the Florida Supreme Court found that the motel owner had not suffered a taking because its property had become "inextricably intertwined" with drugs and prostitution. In contrast, it held that the apartment building owner had suffered a taking because the board had acted based on just two cocaine sales.

In *Department of Agriculture & Consumer Services v. Bogorff*, 35 So. 3d 84 (Fla. 4th Dist. Ct. App.), *review denied*, 48 So. 3d 835 (Fla. 2010), *cert. denied*, 563 U.S. 974 (2011), the government destroyed 100,000 healthy citrus trees in Broward County. It took this action because the trees were within 1,900 feet of trees suffering from "citrus canker." A class action was brought by the healthy trees' 50,000 owners, and a jury ended up awarding them $11.5 million (later reduced to $8 million). The government appealed, arguing that no money was due because the healthy trees represented a threat and cutting them down was the only way to stop the disease from spreading. In upholding the jury's verdict, the court wrote:

> There is substantial competent evidence that healthy, privately owned citrus trees are not harmful or destructive, even though found within 1,900 feet of a tree having citrus canker. . . . There was expert testimony that no study using an acceptable scientific method supports a conclusion that healthy trees so situated will necessarily develop citrus canker or bring trouble or damage to anybody.

Id. at 88.

(b) Taxing Powers

As a general proposition, taxes are not takings. However, a tax that is "purely confiscatory" will support an eminent domain action. To qualify, a tax must bear no relationship to the taxpayer and provide him or her with no benefit whatsoever. *See Koontz v. St. Johns River Water Management District*, 570 U.S. 595 (2013).

4. INVERSE CONDEMNATION

The term "inverse condemnation" refers to situations in which the government unintentionally takes private property. *See Sarasota Welfare Home, Inc. v. City of Sarasota*, 666 So. 2d 171 (Fla. 2d Dist. Ct. App. 1995). Thus, an "inverse condemnation" is the opposite of a "direct condemnation" (*i.e.*, eminent domain). When the government is found to have taken private property through inverse condemnation, it must pay the owner full compensation. *See Stewart v. City of Key West*, 429 So. 2d 784 (Fla. 3d Dist. Ct. App. 1983).

To make out a claim for inverse condemnation, a party must show that the government has: 1) caused a temporary or permanent physical occupation of the party's land; or, 2) enacted a regulation, or imposed a condition, that has deprived the party of all economically beneficially use of the land. *See Florida Fish and Wildlife Conservation Commission v. Daws*, 256 So. 3d 907 (Fla. 1st Dist. Ct. App.), *review denied*, 2018 WL 6605838 (Fla. 2018). The latter type of claim is known as a "regulatory taking."

A good example of the first type of claim is *City of North Miami Beach v. Reed*, 749 So. 2d 1275 (Fla. 3d Dist. Ct. App. 2000). The court held that by erecting a concrete curb in front of their property, the government had taken the plaintiffs' parking spaces by making them inaccessible.

In *Foster v. City of Gainesville*, 579 So. 2d 774 (Fla. 1st Dist. Ct. App. 1991), the court ruled that an extension of a municipal airport's runway was a taking because its noise, vibration, and residue had caused a drop in the value of the plaintiffs' homes.

In *In re Forfeiture of 1976 Kenworth Tractor Trailer Truck, Altered VIN 243340M*, 576 So. 2d 261 (Fla. 1990), the government seized the plaintiff's truck, believing it was stolen. When the trial court ordered the truck returned to the plaintiff, the government dragged its feet for two years. The Florida Supreme Court found this to be an unlawful taking and permitted the plaintiff to file an inverse condemnation claim.

A regulatory taking case, on the other hand, requires a court to consider: 1) the regulation's economic impact; and, 2) the extent to which it interferes with the plaintiff's investment-backed expectations. *See Reahard v. Lee County*, 968 F.2d 1131 (11th Cir. 1992). In other words, the court must decide if the regulation is the functional equivalent of a taking. *See Teitelbaum v. South Florida Water Management District*, 176 So. 3d 998 (Fla. 3d Dist. Ct. App. 2015), *review denied*, 2016 WL 1065552 (Fla. 2016). *See also Alachua Land Investors, LLC v. City of Gainesville*, 107 So. 3d 1154 (Fla. 1st Dist. Ct. App.

2013) ("The general rule . . . is that while property may be regulated to a certain extent, if regulation goes too far it will be recognized as a taking. . . . Whether the government has gone too far depends on the particular facts.").

In *Lucas v. South Carolina Coastal Council*, 505 U.S. 1003 (1992), the plaintiff purchased two vacant beachfront lots for $975,000. He planned to build homes on both, keep one, and sell the other. Before he could execute his plan, the state prohibited further beach construction.

The trial court found a regulatory taking and awarded Lucas $1.2 million. The South Carolina Supreme Court reversed, holding that the state's action was a proper exercise of its police power. On appeal, the U.S. Supreme Court further reversed. It held that the trial court had been correct when it found that the state had deprived Lucas of all economically beneficial use of his land, thereby thwarting his investment-backed expectations.

In *Shands v. City of Marathon*, 999 So. 2d 718 (Fla. 3d Dist. Ct. App. 2008), the court relied on *Lucas* in rejecting the plaintiffs' inverse condemnation claim. The plaintiffs had sought a permit to add a boat dock to their property. This request was denied due to recent zoning changes that severely restricted building on conservation offshore islands.

The court first explained that "the ordinances at issue [do] not eliminate all economically beneficial use of the property" because "at least six acres of the upland portion [can still be partially developed, meaning] that some, perhaps not insignificant, economic value remains." *Id.* at 724–25.

The court next found that the regulations did not thwart the plaintiffs' investment-backed expectations:

> Although R.E. Shands bought the property in 1956 with the idea to eventually build a family home on it, the Shands family's "investment-backed expectations" were minimal at best. The Shands had no specific development plan and only recently sought a dock permit. To be sure, they had not pursued any development of the property since it was purchased in 1956. . . . Indeed, the Shands inherited the property, and have not shown any substantial personal financial investment in Shands Key. [These facts] emphasize the Shands' difficulty in demonstrating that they had any *reasonable* expectation of selling Shands Key for residential development, or that they have suffered any substantial loss as a result of the regulations.

Id. (emphasis in original).

5. DRAINAGE EASEMENTS

Because of Florida's topography, proper drainage is critical. Without it, water can "pool up" and damage surrounding structures. It also can act as a breeding ground for mosquitos and other pests. As a result, Art. X, § 6(b) states: "Provision may be made by law for the taking of easements, by like proceedings, for the drainage of the land of one person over or through the land of another."

Drainage easements allow the government to build canals, ditches, pipelines, sewers, and trenches on, over, or under a person's land. They also prohibit the property owner from blocking access to, or interfering with, these systems. Thus, for example, a homeowner cannot pave over a drainage easement to create a driveway.

Although drainage easements are authorized by the Florida Constitution, the government can be held responsible if their use causes harm. *See, e.g., Drake v. Walton County*, 6 So. 3d 717 (Fla. 1st Dist. Ct. App.), *review denied*, 19 So. 3d 312 (Fla. 2009) (plaintiff was entitled to compensation after county flooded his property to protect his neighbors' homes); *Blankenship v. Department of Transportation*, 890 So. 2d 1130 (Fla. 5th Dist. Ct. App. 2004) (plaintiff's suit against state agency for flooding expected to be caused by planned underground pipeline allowed to proceed).

Although not included in the constitution, many other types of easements exist. The most common ones are access easements and utility easements. *See* Fla. Stat. §§ 704.01–704.08.

PART III
STATE GOVERNMENT

CHAPTER 13
LEGISLATURE

A. OVERVIEW

Art. III describes Florida's legislature. The job of the legislature is to make the state's laws. Pursuant to Art. II, § 3, the legislature is one of the three branches of Florida's state government.

B. BASICS

Art. III, § 1 explains: "The legislative power of the state shall be vested in a legislature of the State of Florida, consisting of a senate composed of one senator elected from each senatorial district and a house of representatives composed of one member elected from each representative district."

Art. III, § 16(a) requires there to be "not less than thirty nor more than forty consecutively numbered senatorial districts . . . and . . . not less than eighty nor more than one hundred twenty consecutively numbered representative districts. . . ." Multi-member districts are permitted. *See In re Apportionment Law Appearing as Senate Joint Resolution Number 1305, 1972 Regular Session*, 263 So. 2d 797 (Fla. 1972). To date, however, all districts have been single-member.

The legislature's web site is http://www.leg.state. fl.us. The house's web site is https://www.myflorida house.gov/. The senate's web site is https://www. flsenate.gov/.

1. POWERS

The Florida Legislature has the power to: 1) prohibit conduct, see *L. Maxcy, Inc., v. Mayo*, 139 So. 121 (Fla. 1931) (en banc); 2) regulate conduct, see *Hopkins v. Special Road & Bridge District No. 4, in Brevard County*, 74 So. 310 (Fla. 1917); and, 3) tax conduct. *See Jerome H. Sheip Co. v. Amos*, 130 So. 699 (Fla. 1930) (en banc). In exercising these powers, it has a "broad range of discretion in its choice of means and methods." *Horsemen's Benevolent and Protective Association, Florida Division v. Division of Pari-Mutuel Wagering[,] Department of Business Regulation[ ]*, 397 So. 2d 692, 695 (Fla. 1981).

In *B.H. v. State*, 645 So. 2d 987, 992 (Fla. 1994), *cert. denied*, 515 U.S. 1132 (1995), the court explained that the legislature has the power "to declare what the law shall be" and "to enact laws." This suggests its power is absolute. In practice, three significant limitations exist:

1) It cannot pass a law that contravenes federal law. *See State v. Atlantic Coast Line Railway Co.*, 87 So. 773, 776–77 (Fla. 1921) ("[W]here a power is exclusive in the national government it cannot be exercised by the states, but [if] it is a concurrent power of the federal and state governments, it may be exercised by the states until the same field is covered by Congress, and when that is done state legislation on the subject becomes inoperative and ineffective.").

2) <u>It cannot pass a law prohibited by the Florida Constitution</u>. *See State v. Board of Public Instruction for Dade County*, 170 So. 602, 606 (Fla. 1936) (Div. B) ("The power of the Legislature is inherent, though it may be limited by the Constitution. The Legislature, therefore, looks to the Constitution for limitations on its power, and if not found to exist, its discretion reasonably exercised is the sole brake on the enactment of legislation.").

3) <u>It cannot pass a law that binds future legislatures</u>. *See Kirklands v. Town of Bradley*, 139 So. 144, 144–45 (Fla. 1932) (Div. A) ("The act . . . contained the following provisions: 'That the territorial boundaries of the town of Bradley hereby created shall not be changed. . . .' The language 'shall not be changed' can have no preventive force or effect.").

As noted above, the legislature's power is "inherent." Two important consequences flow from this fact:

1) <u>The Florida Constitution does not grant lawmaking power to the legislature</u>. Instead, it acts as a check on such power. *See State ex rel. Collier Land Investment Corp. v. Dickinson*, 188 So. 2d 781 (Fla. 1966); *Sparkman v. State ex rel. Scott*, 58 So. 2d 431 (Fla. 1952) (en banc); *City of Miami Beach v. Crandon*, 35 So. 2d 285 (Fla. 1948) (en banc).

2) The legislature cannot delegate its
    lawmaking power. *See Mahon v. County of
    Sarasota*, 177 So. 2d 665 (Fla. 1965).
    However, it can authorize designated
    officials to promulgate rules and
    regulations to carry out the laws it has
    made. *See State v. Florida State Turnpike
    Authority*, 80 So. 2d 337 (Fla. 1955) (en
    banc). *See also* Ch. 2 of this book.

2.   STRUCTURE

Florida did not have a legislature during either the
first or second Spanish occupations. In the British
period, provincial councils existed in both East
Florida and West Florida.

In 1822, shortly after Florida became part of the
United States, a territorial council with 13 members
appointed by the president was established. In 1826,
it became elective. In 1838, Congress divided the
council into a house of representatives (29 members)
and a senate (11 members).

When Florida became a state in 1845, the council
was replaced by the general assembly. Like its
predecessor, the general assembly had a house of
representatives and a senate. The 1868 constitution
renamed both the general assembly (to "legislature")
and the house of representatives (to "assembly"). The
1885 constitution changed the assembly's name back
to the house of representatives. The 1968
constitution retained the 1885 constitution's
nomenclature and structure. Confusingly, however,
it often refers to the legislature's "houses," as in "each

house of the legislature." *See*, *e.g.*, Art. I, § 24(c). (A better approach is to refer to the legislature's "chambers.")

Every state except Nebraska has a bicameral legislature. Between 1967 and 1977, several bills were introduced proposing that Florida switch back to a unicameral legislature. In addition, Sen. William Gunter (D-Orlando) led an unsuccessful effort to place the issue on the 1970 ballot. *See Adams v. Gunter*, 238 So. 2d 824 (Fla. 1970). In 2015, Sen. Donald Gaetz (R-Niceville) briefly pushed for a unicameral legislature after the house derailed that year's legislative session.

C. MEMBERS

1. QUALIFICATIONS

To serve in either the house or the senate, a person must meet the qualifications contained in Art. III, § 15(c): "Each legislator shall be at least twenty-one years of age, an elector and resident of the district from which elected and shall have resided in the state for a period of two years prior to election." All of Florida's constitutions have had similar requirements.

Sec. 15(c)'s list is exclusive. As such, the legislature cannot change it. *See Matthews v. Steinberg*, 153 So. 3d 295 (Fla. 1st Dist. Ct. App. 2014), *aff'd*, 2016 WL 3419207 (Fla. 2016); *Norman v. Ambler*, 46 So. 3d 178 (Fla. 1st Dist. Ct. App. 2010).

Compared to other states, Florida's age requirement is typical. Although some states have no minimum age requirement, most require legislators to be at least 18. Many states impose a lower age for representatives and a higher age for senators. In North Carolina, for example, there is no minimum age to be a representative but senators must be at least 25.

A Florida legislator must meet the district requirement at the time of his or her election. *See James v. County of Volusia*, 683 So. 2d 555 (Fla. 5th Dist. Ct. App. 1996). This is quite generous—most states have district requirements ranging from 30 days (*e.g.*, Nevada) to two years (*e.g.*, Illinois).

Although a few states have no state residency requirements, most, like Florida, have a one-year, two-year, or three-year requirement. In Kentucky, a house seat requires two years of state residency while a senate seat requires six years. Split requirements can be found in several other states.

The U.S. Constitution sets three requirements for members of Congress: age (25 for representatives, 30 for senators); U.S. citizenship (seven years for representatives, nine years for senators); and state residency. *See* Art. I, § 2, cl. 2 (representatives); Art. I, § 3, cl. 3 (senators). These provisions are exclusive and cannot be changed except by amending the constitution. *See Cook v. Gralike*, 531 U.S. 510 (2001).

2. DISQUALIFICATIONS

Art. VI, § 4(c)(1) term limits representatives to eight years. Likewise, Art. VI, § 4(c)(2) terms limits senators to eight years. These provisions, which were added in 1992, are discussed later in this chapter.

Florida's constitution also contains two general disqualification provisions:

1) Art. III, § 17(c) permits the senate, in an impeachment trial that results in conviction, to bar the defendant from holding future public office.

2) Art. VI, § 4(a) bars from public office felons who have not had their civil rights restored and persons who have been adjudicated mentally incompetent (until "removal of disability"). Previous Florida constitutions barred from office bankers, duelists, ministers, and those who bet on elections.

Most state constitutions include disqualification provisions of one sort or another. In *Silverman v. Campbell*, 486 S.E.2d 1 (S.C. 1997), for example, South Carolina's requirement that office seekers believe in a supreme being was struck down due to the First Amendment.

The U.S. Constitution does not term limit U.S. representatives or U.S. senators. It does, however, contain two general disqualification provisions:

1) Art. I, § 3, cl. 7 permits the senate, in an impeachment trial that results in

conviction, to bar the defendant from future office.

2) Sec. 3 of the 14th Amendment bars anyone who engages in insurrection or rebellion against the United States, or gives aid or comfort to its enemies, from holding public office. This disqualification can be lifted by Congress by a 2/3 vote.

3. SEATING DISPUTES

Art. III, § 2 provides in part: "Each house shall be the sole judge of the qualifications, elections, and returns of its members[.]" Accordingly, candidacy disputes that occur before election day are heard by the courts. After election day, they become non-justiciable "seating disputes."

Florida's first three constitutions directed: "[A] contested election . . . shall be determined in such manner . . . as shall be directed by law." This language was omitted from the 1868 and 1885 constitutions. By using the word "sole," the 1968 constitution makes it clear that courts cannot hear seating disputes. *See Harden v. Garrett*, 483 So. 2d 409 (Fla. 1985); *McPherson v. Flynn*, 397 So. 2d 665 (Fla. 1981).

Art. I, § 5 of the U.S. Constitution lacks the word "sole." As a result, the U.S. Supreme Court has held that federal courts can hear federal seating disputes. *See Powell v. McCormack*, 395 U.S. 486 (1969).

4.   ASSUMPTION OF OFFICE

Art. III, § 15(d) states: "Members of the legislature shall take office upon election." *See also* Fla. Stat. § 100.041(1). All prior constitutions have contained similar language.

In *Davis v. Crawford*, 116 So. 41, 44 (Fla. 1928) (en banc), the court explained: "[T]erms shall begin on the election day and shall end on the election day." This same conclusion was reached in *In re Advisory Opinions to the Governor*, 79 So. 874 (Fla. 1918), and *Ruiz v. Farias*, 43 So. 3d 124 (Fla. 3d Dist. Ct. App. 2010).

5.   LENGTH OF TERMS

Pursuant to Art. III, § 15(a)–(b), a representative's term lasts two years while a senator's term lasts four years. A senator's term can be reduced to two years following reapportionment, if doing so is needed to maintain the senate's staggered terms or is required for geographical reasons. *See* Art. III, § 15(a). *See also In re Apportionment Law Appearing as Senate Joint Resolution 1 E, 1982 Special Apportionment Session*, 414 So. 2d 1040 (Fla. 1982).

Florida's legislative terms have changed over time. In the 1838 constitution, senators served two years and representatives served one year. In the 1861 constitution, senators served four years and representatives served two years. In the 1865 constitution, senators and representatives both served two years. In the 1868 constitution, senate terms went back to four years while representative terms stayed at two years.

Due to a 1992 citizens' initiative nicknamed "Eight is Enough," representatives and senators are term-limited. *See Advisory Opinion to the Attorney General—Limited Political Terms in Certain Elective Offices*, 592 So. 2d 225 (Fla. 1991). Specifically, Art. VI, § 4(c) provides that legislators cannot serve for more than "eight consecutive years." *See Ray v. Mortham*, 742 So. 2d 1276 (Fla. 1999).

Including Florida, 15 states currently impose term limits on legislators (six other states previously did but no longer do). Nine states have "consecutive limits," while six have "lifetime limits." Because Florida is a consecutive limits state, a legislator who sits out one election cycle (*i.e.*, two years) is eligible for a new eight-year period.

Periodically, efforts have been made to either repeal § 4(c) or lengthen its limits. Proponents typically make three arguments: 1) the constant turnover caused by term limits deprives the public of experienced leadership; 2) term limits are undemocratic, because they deny citizens the right to vote for their preferred candidates; and, 3) term limits increase the power of "the unelected" (*i.e.*, lobbyists and legislative staffers). In 2005, the Florida Legislature voted to put a constitutional amendment on the 2006 ballot changing § 4(c) to 12 years. Public reaction was so negative that the proposal had to be withdrawn. A similar bill in 2015 died even more quickly.

Although § 4(c)(5)–(6) includes Florida's U.S. representatives and senators, the U.S. Supreme Court has held that states cannot term limit members of Congress. *See U.S. Term Limits, Inc. v. Thornton*, 514 U.S. 779 (1995). As such, these two provisions are inoperative.

6. SALARIES

The constitution permits legislators to set their own salaries. *See* Art. II, § 5, discussed in Ch. 2 of this book. Florida legislators currently earn $29,697 a year. They also receive a daily per diem of $152 while in Tallahassee. These amounts are roughly in line with other states.

The 1838 constitution provided: "Each member of the General Assembly shall receive from the public Treasury such compensation for his services as may be fixed by law, but no increase of compensation shall take effect during the term for which the Representatives were elected when such law passed." The 1861 and 1865 constitutions repeated this language. The 1868 constitution introduced a fixed rate ($500 a year) and a travel allowance (10 cents a mile). The 1885 constitution changed the rate to $6 for every day the legislature was in session.

In 2019, 70 of Florida's 160 legislators were millionaires (up from 51 in 2013). While Florida's representatives had an average net worth of $1.7 million, Florida's senators had an average net worth of $5.9 million. The presence of so many millionaires in the legislature is a direct result of the legislature's low salaries, which keeps most working people from running.

7.   PUNISHMENTS AND EXPULSIONS

Art. III, § 4(d) provides: "Each house may punish a member for contempt or disorderly conduct and, by a two-thirds vote of its membership, may expel a member." Such language, in nearly identical form, has appeared in every one of Florida's constitutions.

To date, only two legislators have been expelled. In 1872, the senate ousted Charles Pearce (R-Tallahassee) after he was convicted of bribery. In 1961, the house ousted Rep. Bert Riddle (D-DeFuniak Springs) for sending an obscene note to a female page.

In 1947, a resolution was introduced calling for the expulsion of Rep. Bernie Papy, Sr. (D-Key West). After it was read on the House floor, Papy resigned. One day earlier, Papy had been indicted for trying to bribe other legislators to oppose a bill cutting off telephone service to bookmakers.

In 2017, the Florida Legislative Black Caucus filed a complaint calling for the expulsion of Sen. Frank Artiles (R-Miami). Two days earlier, Artiles had used racial and sexual slurs to describe other legislators. Two days after apologizing, Artiles resigned.

8.   VACANCIES

Art. III, § 15(d) declares: "Vacancies in legislative office shall be filled only by election as provided by law." All of Florida's prior constitutions have included similar language.

Fla. Stat. § 100.101(2) authorizes the holding of a special election whenever "a vacancy occurs in the office of state senator or member of the state house of representatives." In 2018, there were five special elections: two in the house and three in the senate. All were caused by resignations. In 2019, there were three special elections, all in the house due to resignations.

In addition to an incumbent's resignation, a legislative office can become vacant for any of the reasons listed in Art. X, § 3. *See* Ch. 2 of this book.

D. OFFICERS

Under Art. III, § 2, the legislature's presiding officers are the president of the senate and the speaker of the house. Both are elected biennially from the membership.

Sec. 2 also requires the house to appoint a clerk; the senate to appoint a secretary; and the legislature to appoint an auditor. All serve at the pleasure of their appointing bodies.

Every one of Florida's prior constitutions required the house to have a speaker and the senate to have a president. Under both the 1865 and 1868 constitutions, the lieutenant governor served as the senate's president.

The 1968 constitution was the first to mention the other three officers. However, the house has had a clerk since 1840; the senate has had a secretary since 1839; and the state has had an auditor since 1903.

The president and the speaker are responsible for supervising their respective bodies. This includes presiding over them when they are in session; setting their calendars (*i.e.*, agendas); appointing their committees and committee chairs; and managing the flow of bills (*i.e.*, proposed legislation).

The clerk and the secretary take care of the legislature's day-to-day operations. This includes publishing the daily journals and calendars; providing bill drafting services; conducting training for new members and their staffs; authenticating documents; creating, maintaining, and making available records; interfacing with the press and public; and working with other government units. In contrast, the auditor, who must be a certified public accountant, see Fla. Stat. § 11.42(2), oversees the government's financial accounts and is responsible for improving the efficiency of public programs. *See* https://flauditor.gov/.

E. SESSIONS

1. LOCATION

Art. II, § 2 states: "The seat of government shall be the City of Tallahassee, in Leon County, where . . . the sessions of the legislature shall be held. . . ." *See further* Ch. 2 of this book.

2. TYPES

State legislatures are classified as full-time, part-time, or hybrid. In a full-time legislature, legislators typically spend 84% of their time on legislative matters (*e.g.*, attending hearings, drafting bills, and meeting with constituents). This number falls to 74% in hybrid legislatures and 57% in part-time legislatures. Ten states currently have full-time legislatures; 26 have hybrid legislatures; and 14 have part-time legislatures.

Most large states, including California and New York, have full-time legislatures. Florida's legislature, on the other hand, is a hybrid legislature. One consequence of this fact is that it meets only periodically.

The constitution authorizes three types of legislative sessions: organizational, regular, and special. Until the 1968 constitution, special sessions were called extraordinary sessions.

(a) Organizational Sessions

Art. III, § 3(a) provides: "On the fourteenth day following each general election the legislature shall convene for the exclusive purpose of organization and selection of officers." As explained in Ch. 3 of this book, general elections are held in even-numbered years in November.

The 1838, 1861, and 1865 constitutions required the legislature to select its officers at its first meeting. The 1868 constitution left the timing to the legislature. The 1885 constitution revived the previous practice.

In 1966, the constitution was amended to require that a separate organizational meeting be held "on the first Tuesday in November after the general election for the purpose of organization, swearing in new members and selecting officers. No other business shall be transacted." The 1968 constitution retained this provision but changed its wording.

(b) Regular Sessions

Art. III, § 3(b) directs: "A regular session of the legislature shall convene on the first Tuesday after the first Monday in March of each odd-numbered year, and on the second Tuesday after the first Monday in January of each even-numbered year."

The 1838 constitution required the legislature to meet beginning "on the fourth Monday in November in each year, or at such other time, as may be prescribed by law." In 1847, the constitution was amended to provide for biennial sessions. An 1860 amendment reinstated annual meetings and changed the starting date to "the 3d Monday of November in each year, or at such other times as may be prescribed by law."

The 1861 constitution retained the 1860 changes.

The 1865 constitution changed the starting date to "the second Wednesday in November in each year."

The 1868 constitution changed the starting date to the "first Tuesday after the first Monday of January."

In 1875, a constitutional amendment reinstated biennial sessions.

The 1885 constitution changed the starting date to "the first Tuesday after the first Monday in April."

The 1968 constitution returned to annual sessions and changed the starting date to "the first Tuesday after the first Monday in April of each odd-numbered year, and . . . the first Tuesday after the first Monday in April, or such other date as may be fixed by law, of each even-numbered year."

In 1990, the constitution was amended to make the starting date "the first Tuesday after the first Monday in February of each odd-numbered year, and . . . the first Tuesday after the first Monday in February, or such other date as may be fixed by law, of each even-numbered year."

In 1994, the constitution was amended to change the starting date to "the first Tuesday after the first Monday in March of each odd-numbered year, and . . . the first Tuesday after the first Monday in March, or such other date as may be fixed by law, of each even-numbered year."

In 2018, the constitution was changed to its present language.

Although biennial legislative sessions once were the norm, today only four states (Montana, Nevada, North Dakota, and Texas) still have them.

(c) Special Sessions

i. *Called by the Governor*

Art. III, § 3(c)(1) authorizes the "governor, by proclamation stating the purpose, [to] convene the legislature in special session during which only such legislative business may be transacted as is within the purview of the proclamation, or of a communication from the governor, or is introduced by consent of two-thirds of the membership of each house."

The 1838, 1861, and 1865 constitutions permitted the governor "by proclamation, on extraordinary occasions, [to] convene the General Assembly at the seat of Government." The 1868 constitution required the governor to "state to both houses, when organized, the purpose for which they have been convened" and also prohibited them from transacting any other "legislative business . . . except by the unanimous consent of both houses." The 1885 constitution reduced the requirement of "unanimous consent" to "a two-thirds vote of each House."

In *Lasseter v. State*, 64 So. 847 (Fla. 1914), the Florida Supreme Court held that the governor may call special sessions as he or she sees fit. In *Martinez v. Martinez*, 545 So. 2d 1338 (Fla. 1989), the court likewise held there is no limit on the number of special sessions a governor may call or how many subjects he or she may designate for discussion.

ii. *Called by the Legislature*

Art. III, § 3(c)(2) provides that a special session "may be convened as provided by law." This is in line with modern practices: only 15 states still make calling a special session an exclusively gubernatorial prerogative.

Florida's first four constitutions did not permit the legislature to call a special session. The 1885 constitution continued this practice until 1956, when it was amended to allow the legislature to call such a session "upon the affirmative vote of three-fifths (3/5) of the members of both houses."

Because it permits the legislature to call itself into session, Art. III, § 3(c)(2) often is referred to as the "self-starter provision." It can be activated in two different ways, both of which are found in Fla. Stat. § 11.011:

(1) The President of the Senate and the Speaker of the House of Representatives, by joint proclamation duly filed with the Department of State, may convene the Legislature in special session pursuant to the authority of § 3, Art. III of the State Constitution.

(2) The Legislature may also be convened in special session in the following manner: When 20 percent of the members of the Legislature shall execute in writing and file with the Department of State their certificates that conditions warrant the convening of the Legislature into special

session, the Department of State shall, within 7 days after receiving the requisite number of such certificates, poll the members of the Legislature, and upon the affirmative vote of three-fifths of the members of both houses, shall forthwith fix the day and hour for the convening of such special session.

Between 1977 and 2018, 27 special sessions were called under the first method. A special session has never been called under the second method. Although several proposals have garnered the necessary 20% to trigger a poll, none have come close to the 60% needed to hold a special session.

In 2019, following mass shootings in El Paso, Texas, and Dayton, Ohio, Democratic lawmakers called for a special session on gun rights. After being turned down by House Speaker José Oliva (R-Miami Lakes) and Senate President Bill Galvano (R-Bradenton), the Democrats gathered enough support to force a poll but failed to garner 60% in either the house (38 Yes—68 No—14 Did Not Vote) or the senate (14–20–6).

iii. Frequency

Special sessions are relatively rare occurrences in Florida. Typically, they are used to deal with an issue that requires immediate action. In the wake of 9/11, for example, a special session was held on terrorism. Between 2000 and 2019, 27 special sessions were held.

It is estimated that special sessions cost taxpayers, on average, $50,000 a day. As a result, legislators try to get through them quickly, so as not to be accused of wasting the public's money. A second reason is that special sessions take time away from a legislator's district activities, such as campaigning and constituent services.

3.   LENGTH

Art. III, § 3(d) states: "A regular session of the legislature shall not exceed sixty consecutive days, and a special session shall not exceed twenty consecutive days, unless extended beyond such limit by a three-fifths vote of each house. During such an extension no new business may be taken up in either house without the consent of two-thirds of its membership."

The 1838 constitution did not place a time limit on legislative sessions. In 1860, a constitutional amendment limited them to 30 days:

[T]he sessions of the General Assembly shall not extend over thirty days in duration, unless a constitutional majority of the members shall deem it expedient. No member shall receive pay from the State for his services after the expiration of thirty days continuously from the commencement of the session.

The 1861 constitution tweaked this language:

The sessions of the General Assembly shall not extend in duration over thirty days, unless it be deemed expedient by a concurrent majority of two-thirds of the members of each House, and no member shall receive pay from the State for his services after the expiration of sixty days continuously from the commencement of the session.

The 1865 constitution retained this language. The 1868 constitution changed the provision to read: "Regular sessions of the Legislature may extend to sixty days, but any special session convened by the Governor shall not exceed twenty days." The 1885 constitution tweaked this language.

While regular sessions always run the full 60 days, special sessions normally are quite short (often less than a day).

4.   ADJOURNMENTS

(a) By the Legislature

Art. III, § 3(e) states: "Neither house shall adjourn for more than seventy-two consecutive hours except pursuant to concurrent resolution." This language originated with the 1838 constitution. Every subsequent constitution has had similar language.

Sec. 3(e) is poorly-worded, for it confuses two different matters: adjournments (which permanently end a session) and recesses (which temporarily pause them). *See State ex rel. Landis v. Thompson*, 170 So. 464 (Fla. 1936) (en banc). While there is only one adjournment during a session, there are frequent recesses.

Adjournments are said to occur "sine die." The term sine die is Latin for "with no appointed date for resumption." Since 1923, sine die has been marked by the dropping of white handkerchiefs (a ritual now performed jointly by the sergeants-at-arms of the house and senate).

As § 3(e) makes clear, the house and the senate must jointly agree on an adjournment date. This requirement recognizes an obvious fact: unless both are in session, no legislation can get passed. In 2015, however, the house unilaterally adjourned three days before the scheduled end of the regular 60-day session (according to its leaders, it had no more work to do). Incensed, the senate sued. In *Joyner v. Florida House of Representatives*, 163 So. 3d 503, 503 (Fla. 2015), the court, without reaching the merits, declined to issue a writ of mandamus because, "The petitioners, who filed their petition at approximately 3:20 p.m. on April 30, 2015, have failed to show that in the circumstances presented here, the issuance of a writ of mandamus would produce any beneficial result."

For a list of Florida's legislative sessions (1845–2019), including their adjournment dates, see https://www.flsenate.gov/PublishedContent/OFFICES/SECRETARY/SessionsoftheFloridaSenateFrom Statehood.pdf.

(b) By the Governor

Art. III, § 3(f) states:

> If, during any regular or special session, the two houses cannot agree upon a time for adjournment, the governor may adjourn the session sine die or to any date within the period authorized for such session; provided that, at least twenty-four hours before adjourning the session, and while neither house is in recess, each house shall be given formal written notice of the governor's intention to do so, and agreement reached within that period by both houses on a time for adjournment shall prevail.

The 1838 constitution provided: "[I]n case of disagreement between the two Houses with respect to the time of adjournment, [the Governor] may adjourn them to such time as he shall think proper, not beyond the day of the next meeting designated by this Constitution." A similar provision has appeared in every one of Florida's constitutions.

The legislature has been gubernatorially adjourned only once. In 1956, Gov. LeRoy Collins dissolved the legislature to prevent it from passing an anti-integration bill.

5.   PROCEDURES

(a) Quorum

The first sentence of Art. III, § 4(a) states: "A majority of the membership of each house shall constitute a quorum, but a smaller number may adjourn from day to day and compel the presence of absent members in such manner and under such penalties as it may prescribe."

This language originated with the 1838 constitution, which provided: "A majority of each House shall constitute a quorum to do business, but a smaller number may adjourn from day to day, and may compel the attendance of absent members in such manner and under such penalties as each House may prescribe." With slight modification, every subsequent constitution has carried this language forward.

In *In the Matter of the Executive Communication of the 9th of November, A. D. 1868*, 12 Fla. 653 (1868), the court held that a quorum means a majority of the *authorized* number of legislators, not the *actual* number of legislators. Thus, it currently takes 61 representatives (out of 120), or 21 senators (out of 40), to have a quorum. *See also* Art. X, § 12(e).

Legislators who oppose a proposed course of action, but do not have the votes needed to defeat it, sometimes attempt to bring matters to a halt by depriving the legislature of a quorum. This can be done in two ways: by refusing to vote ("disappearing quorum") or by being physically absent ("quorum-busting").

The Florida Legislature has solved the disappearing quorum problem by treating as "present" all legislators who have made an appearance. *See* House Rule 3.3(b)(2) and Senate Rule 1.23.

Art. III, § 4(a) deals with the quorum-busting problem by allowing legislators to use whatever means are necessary to force the quorum-busters back to work. The best-known example of quorum-busting in Florida occurred in 1891, when 17 senators fled to Georgia to prevent the re-election of Wilkinson Call as Florida's U.S. senator. *See State ex rel. Fleming, Governor v. Crawford, Secretary of State*, 10 So. 118 (Fla. 1891). Despite this maneuver, the U.S. Senate seated Call.

(b) Rules

The second sentence of Art. III, § 4(a) provides: "Each house shall determine its rules of procedure." Similar language has appeared in all of Florida's constitutions.

The Florida Supreme Court has held that so long as a legislative rule does not violate the constitution, it is valid. *See State ex rel. Lane Drug Stores, Inc. v. Simpson*, 166 So. 262 (Fla.) (en banc), *reh'g denied sub nom. State ex rel. X-Cel Stores v. Lee*, 166 So. 574 (Fla. 1936) (en banc). Likewise, the legislature can change its rules as its sees fit. *See Crawford v. Gilchrist*, 59 So. 963 (Fla. 1912). The legislature's failure to follow its own rules constitutes a breach of "parliamentary law" but is not actionable. *See State ex rel. Landis v. Thompson*, 163 So. 270 (Fla. 1935) (en banc).

The rules of the house and senate can be found on the respective web sites.

(c) Journals

Art. III, § 4(c) states:

Each house shall keep and publish a journal of its proceedings; and upon the request of five members present, the vote of each member voting on any question shall be entered on the journal. In any legislative committee or subcommittee, the vote of each member voting on the final passage of any legislation pending before the committee, and upon the request of any two members of the committee or subcommittee, the vote of each member on any other question, shall be recorded.

In 1990, the second sentence (recording committee and sub-committee votes) was added as part of a broader effort to increase the legislature's transparency. *See* Ch. 5 of this book.

The requirement that the legislature keep journals of its proceedings first appeared in the 1838 constitution. Similar language has appeared in each of the succeeding constitutions.

Except as specifically required by the constitution, the legislature is free to determine both the form and the content of its journals. *See Advisory Opinion to the Governor*, 12 So. 2d 583 (Fla. 1943).

The house's journals (since 1998) can be found at https://www.myfloridahouse.gov/Sections/ Documents/publications.aspx. Journals before this date can be found at http://ufdc.ufl.edu/fhrp.

The senate's journals (since 2010) can be found at https://www.flsenate.gov/Session/Journals/2019. Journals before this date can be found at http:// archive.flsenate.gov.

(d) Transparency

Art. III, § 4(b) directs: "Sessions of each house shall be public; except sessions of the senate when considering appointment to or removal from public office may be closed." Similar language has appeared in every one of Florida's constitutions.

In 1990, because of the public's growing dissatisfaction with how much legislative business was being conducted behind closed doors, § 4(b) was augmented by a new paragraph. *See* Art. III, § 4(e). It requires all committee, sub-committee, and joint conference committee meetings, as well as certain pre-arranged gatherings between legislators or between legislative leaders and the governor, to be open to the public. *See* Ch. 5 of this book.

Although the public has the right to attend legislative sessions, Art. III, § 5 gives the legislature the power to punish "any person not a member who has been guilty of disorderly or contemptuous conduct in its presence." Such punishment can consist of a "fine not exceeding one thousand dollars or imprisonment not exceeding ninety days, or both." *Id.* Every one of Florida's constitutions has authorized the legislature to punish non-members.

F. LAWMAKING DUTIES

1. RECEPTION STATUTE

As noted at the outset of this chapter, the legislature's primary function is to pass laws for the public's benefit. However, until it does so, the laws of England as they existed on July 4, 1776 remain in force in Florida. *See* Fla. Stat. § 2.01. *See also Florida House of Representatives v. Expedia, Inc.*, 85 So. 3d 517 (Fla. 1st Dist. Ct. App. 2012) (concluding that England's 16th century "parliamentary privilege," having been neither repealed nor replaced, is still the law of Florida).

Sec. 2.01 is known as a "reception statute." All states either have such a statute or have adopted the English common law by constitutional provision or judicial decision (except for Louisiana, which has retained parts of the Code Napoléon). For a further discussion of § 2.01, see Michael Cavendish & Blake J. Hood, "Florida Common Law Jurisprudence," 81 *Fla. B.J.* 9 (Jan. 2007).

2. LIMITATIONS

In exercising its lawmaking powers, the Florida Legislature is limited by both federal law and the Florida Constitution. *See Taylor v. Dorsey*, 19 So. 2d 876 (Fla. 1944) (en banc).

The Florida Constitution imposes numerous limitations on the legislature's lawmaking powers (see below). In addition, the public has the power to add new ones. This is made clear by Art. I, § 1: "All political power is inherent in the people. . . ."

(a) Prohibited Laws

Art. I, § 10 states: "No bill of attainder, ex post facto law or law impairing the obligation of contracts shall be passed." Every one of Florida's constitutions has had such language, although the 1868 constitution was the first to combine them into a single section. The U.S. Constitution contains the same prohibitions. *See* Art. I, § 10, cl. 1.

i. *Bills of Attainder*

A bill of attainder is a law that deprives a person of life, liberty, or property without the benefit of judicial process. Depending on its wording, a bill of attainder might be directed at an individual, a group, or an entire class of people.

In *In re Adoption of Doe*, 2008 WL 5070056 (Fla. 16th Cir. Ct. 2008), a law that prohibited gays and lesbians from adopting children was held to be a bill of attainder:

The facts and circumstances surrounding enactment of section 63.042(3) demonstrate that its singular purpose was to repress gay Floridians as a group, without any consideration being given to allowing even one gay Floridian an opportunity to establish his actual ability to parent. There were no legislative hearings at which any evidence was presented supporting the sweep of the ban. . . . Overwhelmingly less burdensome alternatives existed by which the legislature could have achieved the non[-]punitive objective of ensuring that only persons be allowed to adopt who are able to parent. Instead, every Floridian who is gay or lesbian was found guilty by the legislature of being unfit to parent an adopted child without the benefit and protection of a judicial trial. . . .

Based on a careful consideration of the history surrounding the gay adoption ban and applicable case law, there can be no doubt that section 63.042(3) is a constitutionally prohibited bill of attainder.

Id. at *24, *27 (footnotes omitted).

A law will not be deemed a bill of attainder simply because it treats some groups less favorably than others. In *Houston v. Williams*, 547 F.3d 1357 (11th Cir. 2008), for example, sex offenders and convicted felons were barred from participating in a county's weatherization assistance program. In deciding that this policy did not constitute a bill of attainder, the court wrote:

Houston argues that the Policy singles out ascertainable members of a group who alone are subject to its provisions and inflicts punishment on them without judicial action, and thus, the Policy is an unlawful bill of attainder under the U.S. and Florida Constitutions. We hold that the district court correctly determined that the Policy neither determined guilt nor inflicted punishment on Houston and was therefore not a bill of attainder. . . . [T]he Policy furthers the non-punitive goal of allocating resources, and no intent to punish can be established from the record.

Id. at 1364

The lack of judicial process is the telltale sign of a bill of attainder. In *Jones v. Slick*, 56 So. 2d 459 (Fla. 1952) (en banc), for example, a city ordinance authorized the city council to punish "disobedient" city officials. In striking it down, the court explained:

This brings us to ordinance No. 233, enacted 8 May 1951. . . . Passed as an emergency measure it contained the provision that all ordinances, resolutions and orders of the council should be obeyed by all city officials and that any official who should be found guilty of disobedience "by a two thirds vote of the City Council" should be fined or imprisoned, or both, and removed from office. . . . The measure providing for the imposition of fine, imprisonment or both by a majority vote of the city council strongly resembles an attainder and its operation would constitute deprivation without due process of law. . . . Even if the council had the power to discipline all "officers" this manner of exercising it would be improper.

Id. at 459–60.

ii.   *Ex Post Facto Laws*

An ex post facto law is a law that retroactively changes the criminal law to the defendant's detriment. *See Doe #1 v. Miami-Dade County, Florida*, 846 F.3d 1180, 1183 (11th Cir. 2017) ("An ex post facto law is a law that 'appl[ies] to events occurring before its enactment' and that 'disadvantage[s] the offender affected by it, by altering the definition of criminal conduct or increasing the punishment for the crime.' "); *State v. Hootman*, 709 So. 2d 1357, 1359 (Fla. 1998) ("[A] law is 'retrospective' for purposes of ex post facto prohibition if it changes the legal consequences of acts completed before its effective date."); *Turbeville v. Department of Financial Services*, 248 So. 3d 194, 199 (Fla. 1st Dist. Ct. App. 2018) ("A law violates the prohibition against ex post facto laws if two conditions are met: (a) it is retrospective in effect, and (b) it alters the definition of criminal conduct or increases the penalty by which a crime or civil infraction is punishable.").

Whether a law is meant to apply to past acts is determined by looking at the legislature's intent. *See Love v. State,* 2019 WL 6906479 (Fla. 2019); *Environmental Confederation of Southwest Florida, Inc. v. State*, 886 So. 2d 1013, 1017 (Fla. 1st Dist. Ct. App. 2004) ("In the absence of clear legislative intent that a law apply retroactively, the general rule is that procedural statutes apply retroactively and substantive statutes apply prospectively.").

iii. *Impairment of Contracts*

A law that invalidates, significantly changes, or unreasonably interferes with an existing contract is invalid. *See Citrus County Hospital Board v. Citrus*

Memorial Health Foundation, Inc., 150 So. 3d 1102 (Fla. 2014) (state law that restructured relationship between private company and public hospital was invalid); *Sears, Roebuck & Co. v. Forbes/Cohen Florida Properties, L.P.*, 223 So. 3d 292 (Fla. 4th Dist. Ct. App. 2017) (county ordinance that restricted mall tenant's sub-leasing rights was invalid). Despite this clear command, the 2019 Florida Legislature passed a bill (CS/HB 843—see Fla. Laws ch. 2019–138, codified as Fla. Stat. § 542.336) allowing four Fort Myers physicians to break their non-compete covenants with their former employer (21st Century Oncology).

Where the government acts to protect the public, impairment may be allowed. *See, e.g., Yellow Cab Company of Dade County v. Dade County, Florida*, 412 So. 2d 395 (Fla. 3d Dist. Ct. App. 1982), *review denied*, 424 So. 2d 764 (Fla. 1983) (county ordinance that terminated taxi cab company's hotel pick-up monopoly was valid). The level of impairment that is permissible depends on the interests involved:

> To determine how much impairment is tolerable, we must weigh the degree to which a party's contract rights are statutorily impaired against both the source of authority under which the state purports to alter the contractual relationship and the evil which it seeks to remedy. Obviously, this becomes a balancing process to determine whether the nature and extent of the impairment is constitutionally tolerable in light of the importance of the state's objective, or whether it unreasonably intrudes

into the parties' bargain to a degree greater than is necessary to achieve that objective.

Pomponio v. Claridge of Pompano Condominium, Inc., 378 So. 2d 774, 780 (Fla. 1979).

Future contracts are not protected from impairment. *See Blaesser v. State Board of Administration*, 134 So. 3d 1013 (Fla. 1st Dist. Ct. App. 2012), *review denied*, 110 So. 3d 440 (Fla. 2013). Likewise, quasi-contracts are not protected. *See Anders v. Nicholson*, 150 So. 639 (Fla. 1933) (Div. B). Where the plaintiff fails to prove that a contract existed, there can be no impairment. *See Abele v. Hernando County*, 161 F. App'x 809 (11th Cir. 2005).

Statutory changes will be given effect if the contract so provides. Otherwise, the law in effect at the time the contract was made governs. *See Cohn v. Grand Condominium Association, Inc.*, 62 So. 3d 1120 (Fla. 2011); *Hassen v. State Farm Mutual Automobile Insurance Co.*, 674 So. 2d 106 (Fla. 1996). *But see Herrick v. Florida Department of Business Regulation, Division of Florida Land Sales, Condominiums and Mobile Homes*, 595 So. 2d 148 (Fla. 1st Dist. Ct. App. 1992) (1986 version of mobile home statute, rather than 1985 version, would be used where changes did not abrogate landlord's rights).

(b) Other Limitations

i. *Religious Aid*

As explained in Ch. 11 of this book, Art. I, § 3 prohibits the legislature from providing, either directly or indirectly, aid to religious entities.

ii. *Special Laws*

Art. III, § 11(a) prohibits the legislature from regulating certain subjects by means of a special law, local law, or general law of local application. As a result, only a general law will do. As discussed later in this chapter, the list of prohibited subjects is lengthy.

iii. *Term of Office*

Art. III, § 13 directs: "No office shall be created the term of which shall exceed four years except as provided herein." The 1868 constitution was the first to have such a provision. The 1885 constitution retained this language. The 1968 constitution added the words "except as provided herein."

Because of the change made by the 1968 constitution, terms exceeding four years are permissible when they are expressly authorized by the constitution. *See* Art. X, § 12(a). The current exceptions are scattered throughout the constitution:

1) "[A]n officer or board appointed by and serving at the pleasure of the governor" may serve more than four years. *See* Art. IV, § 6. This provision includes officers and

boards subject to either cabinet approval or senate confirmation, or who are "authorized to grant and revoke licenses to engage in regulated occupations." *Id. See In re Advisory Opinion of Governor, Term of Appointments for Governor*, 306 So. 2d 509 (Fla. 1975); *State ex rel. Investment Corporation of South Florida v. Harrison*, 247 So. 2d 713 (Fla. 1971).

2) Members of the Parole and Probation Commission, known since 2014 as the Florida Commission on Offender Review, serve legislatively-prescribed terms. Such terms can last up to six years. *See* Art. IV, § 8(c).

3) Members of the Florida Fish and Wildlife Conservation Commission serve five-year terms. *See* Art. IV, § 9.

4) Justices and judges serve six-year terms. *See* Art. V, § 10.

5) Members of the Judicial Qualifications Commission serve legislatively-prescribed terms. Such terms can last up to six years. *See* Art. V, § 12(a)(2).

6) Members of appointive bodies dealing with education serve legislatively-prescribed terms. There is no limit on the length of such terms. *See* Art. IX, § 3; *Nohrr v. Brevard County Educational Facilities Authority*, 247 So. 2d 304 (Fla. 1971).

7) State university trustees serve five-year terms. *See* Art. IX, § 7(c).

8) State university governors serve seven-year terms. *See* Art. IX, § 7(d).

iv. *Florida Fish and Wildlife Conservation Commission*

Art. IV, § 9 creates the Florida Fish and Wildlife Conservation Commission. It also provides: "The legislature may enact laws in aid of the commission, not inconsistent with this section." Thus, the legislature is prohibited from passing laws that conflict with the commission's regulations. *See* Ch. 4 of this book.

v. *Gambling*

The Florida Constitution contains six provisions that limit the legislature's ability to regulate gambling. Two of them appeared in earlier constitutions and were carried over to the 1968 constitution. *See* Art. VII, § 7 (pari-mutuel taxes) and Art. X, § 7 (lotteries). The others were added, respectively, in 1986 (Art. X, § 15) (state lottery); 2004 (Art. X, § 23) (slot machines); and 2018 (Art. X, § 30 and Art. X, § 32) (casinos and dog racing). Of course, gambling that is policed by the federal government (*i.e.*, internet, shipboard, and tribal) falls outside the legislature's purview.

[a] *Pari-Mutuel Taxes*

Art. VII, § 7 provides: "Taxes upon the operation of pari-mutuel pools may be preempted to the state or allocated in whole or in part to the counties. When allocated to the counties, the distribution shall be in equal amounts to the several counties." This provision was added in 1940. The 1968 constitution retained it with a slight change in wording. Thus, while the state does not have to share pari-mutuel taxes, if it decides to do so it must give each county an equal share.

Pari-mutuel betting originated in France and is the type that takes place at dog tracks, jai-alai frontons, and horse tracks. At the time of the 1940 amendment, counties were receiving annual payouts worth $27,000. By 1968, this figure had grown to nearly $300,000. This represented nearly the entire budget of some small counties.

The decline of the pari-mutuel industry in Florida has left little to allocate. In 1968, the industry generated $41.8 million in taxes. Since reaching $130 million in 1988, it has dropped steadily due to the emergence of more attractive gambling options, including the state lottery (1988) and tribal casinos (2004). In 2018, pari-mutuel taxes amounted to just $25.8 million.

At the time of the 1940 amendment, pari-mutuel taxes were split 90%–10% in favor of the counties. By 1968, this figure had changed to 53%–47%. In 1971, when pari-mutuel taxes hit $55.9 million (and were on an upward trajectory), the state capped each county's share at $446,500 (a total of $29.9 million). Because this amount now exceeds the taxes generated by the pari-mutuel industry, the state pays the rest from sales taxes. *See* Fla. Stat. § 212.20(6)(d)6.a.

[b] Lotteries

Art. X, § 7 provides: "Lotteries, other than the types of pari-mutuel pools authorized by law as of the effective date of this constitution, are hereby prohibited in this state." This provision first appeared in the 1868 constitution and was carried over to the 1885 and 1968 constitutions. As a result, the legislature cannot authorize either public or private lotteries.

Although lotteries had been a popular way to fund buildings, roads, and schools in colonial America, states began to ban them in the 19th century on moral and religious grounds. By 1894, lotteries were illegal in every state. In 1895, to stop Americans from turning to lotteries in other countries, Congress made it a crime to ship lottery tickets through the mail. *See The Lottery Cases*, 188 U.S. 321 (1903).

[c] State Lottery

In 1964, New Hampshire became the first state to reintroduce a lottery. Other states soon followed. To gain voter approval, many promised that a portion of the proceeds would go to education. This idea originated with the New York lottery.

By 1985, 21 states had lotteries. Thus, in 1986 a citizens' initiative petition proposed that Florida start a lottery, with all its profits going to education. After surviving a ballot challenge, see *Carroll v.*

Firestone, 497 So. 2d 1204 (Fla. 1986), the idea passed easily. As a result, Art. X, § 15 was added to the constitution. For a further discussion, see Ch. 18 of this book.

[d]   Slot Machines

In 1996, the Florida Legislature granted the state's pari-mutuels the exclusive right to have poker rooms. In 2002, in a bid for more revenue, the pari-mutuels proposed a constitutional amendment giving them the right to add slot machines. Deciding that the amendment violated the constitution's "single subject" rule, see Art. XI, § 3, the Florida Supreme Court struck it from the ballot. *See Advisory Opinion to the Attorney General re Authorization for County Voters to Approve or Disapprove Slot Machines Within Existing Pari-Mutuel Facilities*, 813 So. 2d 98 (Fla. 2002).

In 2004, the pari-mutuels in Broward and Miami-Dade Counties returned with a new proposal allowing slot machines only in their facilities. This time, the court gave its approval. *See Advisory Opinion to the Attorney General re Authorizes Miami-Dade and Broward County Voters to Approve Slot Machines in Parimutuel Facilities*, 880 So. 2d 522 (Fla. 2004). On election day, the amendment squeaked by with the narrowest margin of victory in Florida history (see Ch. 23 of this book). As a result, Art. X, § 23 was added to the constitution.

To become effective, the amendment required both counties to hold post-election referendums. *See* Art. X, § 23(a). This "second level" of approval was achieved on the first try in Broward (2005) and on the second try in Miami-Dade (2008).

The amendment requires slot taxes to "supplement public education funding statewide." *See* Art. X, § 23(b). In 2018, such taxes amounted to $199.2 million. For a further discussion, see Ch. 18 of this book.

It remains something of a mystery why Palm Beach County (South Florida's third county) did not join the 2004 amendment. Many, however, believe that Art Rooney, the owner of Palm Beach County's only pari-mutuel, is the reason. In 2003, Rooney, who also owned the NFL's Pittsburgh Steelers, had helped stop a planned casino in downtown Pittsburgh.

[e]   Casinos

In 2018, a citizens' initiative dubbed "Voters in Control" called for transferring the power to authorize casinos from the legislature to the public. After making the ballot, see *Advisory Opinion to the Attorney General re: Voter Control of Gambling in Florida*, 215 So. 3d 1209 (Fla. 2017), it passed easily. As a result, Art. X, § 30 was added to the constitution. Its paragraph (a) provides in pertinent part: "This amendment ensures that Florida voters shall have the exclusive right to decide whether to authorize casino gambling in the State of Florida. This amendment requires a vote by citizens' initiative pursuant to Article XI, section 3, in order for casino gambling to be authorized under Florida law."

Although populist in tone, the amendment is the handiwork of two large enterprises: Disney and the Seminole Indian tribe. Both feared that after years of rejecting the idea, the legislature was getting close to allowing Las Vegas-style casinos in Florida. Such a development would cut deeply into the bottom lines of Disney's theme parks and the Seminoles' own casinos (which exist pursuant to federal law). Thus, by making the cumbersome citizens' initiative petition process (described in Ch. 23 of this book) the exclusive means for authorizing new casinos, Disney and the Seminoles have removed a serious threat to their bottom lines.

[f]   Dog Racing

Also on the 2018 ballot was Amendment 13, a Constitution Revision Commission proposal calling for the end of dog racing in Florida. After surviving a ballot summary challenge, see *Department of State v. Florida Greyhound Association, Inc.*, 253 So. 3d 513 (Fla. 2018), it passed easily. As a result, Art. X, § 32 has been added to the constitution. In pertinent part, it states:

The humane treatment of animals is a fundamental value of the people of the State of Florida. After December 31, 2020, a person authorized to conduct gaming or pari-mutuel operations may not race greyhounds or any member of the *Canis Familiaris* subspecies in connection with any wager for money or any other thing of value in this state, and persons in this state may not wager money or any other thing of value on the outcome of a live dog race occurring in this state.

At its peak in 1989, dog racing was legal in 19 states, but by 2018 only six still had tracks. Collectively, these states had 17 tracks, with the bulk (11) in Florida.

Despite forcing them to close their businesses, Florida's dog tracks supported Amendment 13. This is because it allows them to keep their poker room licenses and, in Broward and Miami-Dade Counties, their slot machine licenses. *See* Art. X, § 32 (third sentence).

Over the years, "decoupling" had become an urgent goal for Florida's dog tracks, as patrons increasingly preferred poker and slots to betting on dogs (making the latter a financial drain). Thus, Amendment 13 has improved the financial outlook of Florida's dog tracks. It also is likely to cause horse tracks and jai-alai frontons, who have seen a similar shift in patron preferences, to step up their own decoupling efforts.

A federal lawsuit challenging Amendment 13 currently is pending. *See Support Working Animals, Inc. v. DeSantis*, 2019 WL 4958070 (S.D. Fla.) (filed Oct. 4, 2019) (now being heard in the Northern District of Florida as 4:19-cv-00570-mw-cas). It claims that the amendment deprives dog racing workers of their livelihoods without due process.

vi. *Unfunded Mandates*

An "unfunded mandate" is a state law that requires a local government to undertake a specific task but does not allocate any money to pay for it. At one time, the Florida Legislature routinely passed such laws, thereby playing havoc with county and municipal budgets. When these entities protested, the legislature in 1978 promised to rein itself in. During the next decade, however, it passed more than 300 new unfunded mandates. As a result, in 1990 the Florida League of Cities convinced voters to add Art. VII, § 18.

Paragraph (a) prohibits the legislature from passing new laws that require counties or municipalities to spend money unless the law "fulfills an important state interest" and:

[1] funds have been appropriated that have been estimated at the time of enactment to be sufficient to fund such expenditure; [2] the legislature authorizes or has authorized a county or municipality to enact a funding source not available for such county or municipality on February 1, 1989, that can be used to generate the amount of funds estimated to be sufficient to fund such expenditure by a simple majority vote of the governing body of such county or municipality; [3] the law requiring such expenditure is approved by two-thirds of the membership in each house of the legislature; [4] the expenditure is required to comply with a law that applies to all persons similarly situated, including the state and local governments; or [5] the law is either required to comply with a federal requirement or required for eligibility for a federal entitlement, which federal

requirement specifically contemplates actions by counties or municipalities for compliance.

Paragraphs (b) and (c) further prohibit the legislature, except upon a 2/3 vote, from enacting, amending, or repealing any general law if doing so would reduce the taxing powers of counties and municipalities or their share of state taxes (subject to certain exceptions). Both paragraphs are pegged to February 1, 1989.

Paragraph (d) makes the foregoing inapplicable to:

Laws adopted to require funding of pension benefits existing on the effective date of this section, criminal laws, election laws, the general appropriations act, special appropriations acts, laws reauthorizing but not expanding then-existing statutory authority, laws having insignificant fiscal impact, and laws creating, modifying, or repealing noncriminal infractions. . . .

Lastly, paragraph (e) authorizes the legislature to "enact laws to assist in the implementation and enforcement of this section."

In *Lewis v. Leon County*, 15 So. 3d 777 (Fla. 1st Dist. Ct. App. 2009), *aff'd*, 73 So. 3d 151 (Fla. 2011), the court cited § 18 in striking down a law requiring counties to contribute to the legal costs of indigent defendants.

vii. New or Increased State Fees and Taxes

Art. VII, § 19, added in 2018, requires that new or increased state fees or taxes be approved by 2/3 of the legislature. Previously, only a simple majority was needed. *See* Ch. 21 of this book for a further discussion.

viii. Medical Marijuana

In 2016, the voters ratified Art. X, § 29. As explained in Ch. 9 of this book, this provision prohibits the legislature from criminalizing or otherwise penalizing the medical use of marijuana.

3.   BILLS

(a) Terminology

Every law passed by the Florida Legislature begins as a "bill." (A helpful glossary of legislative acronyms and words can be found at https://www.flsenate.gov/Reference/Glossary.) Every bill must be introduced ("sponsored") by a legislator.

Under the rules of the house, representatives are limited to six bills, although this limit can be waived by a 2/3 vote. There is no limit on the number of bills that a senator can introduce.

In 2019, a total of 1,861 bills were introduced, but just 194 were passed. These numbers are typical, and indicate just how difficult it is to get a bill passed.

If a legislator decides to sponsor a bill, he or she works with the legislature's bill drafting service to put it in proper form. Next, the bill is given a number and its title is published in the appropriate journal. This counts as the bill's "first reading"—all bills must be read three times before a final vote can be held. Each reading must occur on a separate day, although this requirement can be waived by a 2/3 vote.

The bill then proceeds to the relevant committees. In 2018, for example, S.B. 928, dealing with theft, was referred to the senate's criminal justice, judiciary, and rules and calendar committees.

When a bill reaches a committee, the chair normally schedules a hearing. This gives interested persons an opportunity to express their views. Such input, in turn, helps the committee's members decide how to vote and identifies any changes that are needed.

Much of the input that legislators receive comes from lobbyists. In 2019, 2,035 lobbyists, representing 4,290 principals, were paid $150 million to lobby the Florida Legislature. Lobbyists must register with the Lobbyist Registration Office (https://www.florida lobbyist.gov/). As part of the registration process, they must indicate who hired them. *See* Fla. Stat. §§ 11.044–11.062. Unsurprisingly, many Florida lobbyists are lawyers. For a further discussion, see the web site of the Florida Association of Professional Lobbyists (https://www.fapl.us/). The association's current chair is Jeffrey Kottkamp, a lawyer who served as Gov. Charlie Crist's lieutenant governor (2007–11).

When it is ready to vote, a committee can take the following actions:

(a) Report favorably on the bill (*i.e.*, suggest no changes). If the entire committee supports the bill, it is reported "unanimously favorable."

(b) Report favorably on the bill with amendments (*i.e.*, suggest some changes).

(c) Report favorably on the bill with a "committee substitute" (*i.e.*, suggest many changes).

(d) Report unfavorably on the bill.

Each of these actions moves a bill forward. The committee also can decide to take no action. This leaves the bill in limbo and causes it to "die in committee."

The committee's chair decides when to hold a hearing and when to take a vote. Thus, the chair can "kill" a bill by refusing to place it on the committee's agenda. When a bill is unable to move out of a committee for any reason, it is said to be "bottled up" or "pigeonholed." A bill also can die if the committee runs out of time.

Once a bill clears its committees, it moves to the "special order" calendar, where it is read a second time. After being read a third time, it is debated and then voted on by the entire house or senate (this is done by a roll call vote, so that each legislator's vote can be officially recorded). If the bill is passed (in most instances, a simple majority is sufficient), it is sent to the other chamber, where the same process is repeated.

Bills that are passed by both the house and the senate often contain differences (usually due to amendments made during the committee process). In such instances, the bill is submitted to a conference committee which, despite its name, is composed of separate house and senate committees that cast votes as needed. The conference reconciles the two bills and sends the reconciled bill to the legislature for an "up-or-down" vote (meaning no amendments are permitted). Especially important bills often begin in conference.

If the house and senate approve the conference's report, the bill is "engrossed" (*i.e.*, checked one last time to make sure that all amendments have been properly added) and then "enrolled." Once enrolled, it is presented to the governor for signing. *See* Fla. Stat. § 11.07. Unless the governor vetoes the bill, it becomes operational on its effective date (the constitution provides a "fall back" date if no date is specified). Vetoed bills are returned to the legislature, which can override the governor's veto by a 2/3 vote.

Normally, it is not possible for bills to navigate the entire legislative process in the limited time that the Florida Legislature is in session. As a result, several techniques have been developed to expedite matters. One, discussed above, is limiting how many bills a representative can introduce. Others include committee, companion, pre-filed, and short-form ("skeleton") bills.

The most important time-saving method is having committees meet before the legislature convenes.

Following the Nov. 6, 2018 general election, for example, the legislature held its constitutionally-mandated "organizational session" two weeks later (Nov. 20). Subsequently, committees met during the weeks of Dec. 11, Jan. 7, Jan. 22, Feb. 4, Feb. 11, and Feb. 18. This gave them a head-start prior to the opening of the 2019 legislative session on Mar. 5.

Despite such short cuts, Florida's legislative sessions always are marked by a "mad dash" at the end. Commenting on the 2019 session, for example, one veteran observer wrote:

> Every year, Florida lawmakers wrap up their regular session after 60 days, and Capitol reporters write about all the bills they rushed through in the final week or hours, even as others died on the vine. . . .

> Critics ask why Florida's Legislature operates the way it does. It has one of the nation's shortest sessions despite being the third-largest state. . . .

> The last few days in April [2019] saw amendments added to bills that made it more difficult to get citizen initiatives on the ballot and to allow former felons . . . to vote. Another bill created three new controversial toll roads.

> The [toll] bill came as lawmakers faced the ticking clock of "sine die," the term for the day the Legislature adjourns. There is no requirement that they meet again for the rest of the year.

Special sessions are generally rare, and the result is what [Rep. Carlos Smith (D-Orlando)] calls "a mad dash to sine die, with bills rushed through without being read and vetted by the public."

Steven Lemongello, "Is a More Efficient Legislature Possible?," *Orlando Sentinel*, Aug. 18, 2019, at A1.

(b) Legislator's Privileges

The Florida Constitution does not include either of the two "legislator's privileges." Forty-eight state constitutions provide that a lawmaker cannot be sued or prosecuted for anything he or she says in the legislature. Similarly, 43 state constitutions prohibit a lawmaker from being arrested while the legislature is in session. The first privilege promotes robust debate on bills; the second ensures that a lawmaker can represent his or her constituents.

The "Speech or Debate Clause" of the U.S. Constitution includes both privileges. *See* Art. I, § 6, cl. 1. Florida's first three constitutions contained similar language.

The 1868 constitution eliminated both privileges, and these omissions were carried over to the 1885 and 1968 constitutions. *See Girardeau v. State*, 403 So. 2d 513 (Fla. Dist. Ct. App.), *petition for review dismissed*, 408 So. 2d 1093 (Fla. 1981). In 1984, the legislature recommended that a speech and debate privilege be added to the constitution, but this proposal was rejected by the voters.

Despite the foregoing, the Florida Supreme Court has recognized a speech and debate privilege but has made it clear that it will not be applied "where another compelling, competing interest is at stake." *See League of Women Voters v. Florida House of Representatives*, 132 So. 3d 135, 146 (Fla. 2013). *See also Hauser v. Urchisin*, 231 So. 2d 6 (Fla. 1970).

(c) Investigations

Art. III, § 5 provides in pertinent part:

Each house, when in session, may compel attendance of witnesses and production of documents and other evidence upon any matter under investigation before it or any of its committees, and may punish by fine not exceeding one thousand dollars or imprisonment not exceeding ninety days, or both, any person not a member who has ... refused to obey its lawful summons or to answer lawful questions. Such powers, except the power to punish, may be conferred by law upon committees when the legislature is not in session. Punishment of contempt of an interim legislative committee shall be by judicial proceedings as prescribed by law.

This language first appeared in the 1885 constitution and was carried over to the 1968 constitution.

A committee that has been properly constituted has all the investigatory powers specified in § 5. *See Hagaman v. Andrews*, 232 So. 2d 1 (Fla. 1970). A committee that has been improperly formed has no investigatory powers. *See Johnston v. Gallen*, 217 So. 2d 319 (Fla. 1969). Although § 5 does not mention them, the Florida Supreme Court has held that subcommittees have the same investigatory powers as committees. *See Johnson v. McDonald*, 269 So. 2d 682 (Fla. 1972).

The legislature's investigatory power sets it apart from the courts, which have no ability to make independent inquiries. This is one reason why courts defer to the legislature. *See Publix Cleaners, Inc. v. Florida Dry Cleaning and Laundry Board*, 32 F. Supp. 31 (S.D. Fla. 1940). Another, of course, is the separation of powers doctrine (Art. II, § 3). *See* Ch. 2 of this book.

Like any power, the investigatory power is subject to abuse. In 1956, for example, the Florida Legislature created the notorious Johns Committee (named for its chairman, Sen. Charley Johns (D-Starke)) to investigate communists and homosexuals. Relishing its role, the committee "persecuted civil rights leaders, university professors, college students, public school teachers and state employees. . . . Niceties like due process or the right to counsel or civil liberties were ignored [and both] entrapment and blackmail [were employed]." Fred Grimm, "Committee's Innocent Victims Deserve an Apology," *South Florida Sun-Sentinel*, Feb. 24, 2019, at 25A.

(d) Requirements

Art. III, § 6 directs:

> Every law shall embrace but one subject and matter properly connected therewith, and the subject shall be briefly expressed in the title. No law shall be revised or amended by reference to its title only. Laws to revise or amend shall set out in full the revised or amended act, section, subsection or paragraph of a subsection. The enacting clause of every law shall read: "Be It Enacted by the Legislature of the State of Florida:".

The first three requirements—single subject, brief title, and prohibition on revision or amendment by title only—are products of the 1868 constitution. The enacting clause requirement originated with the 1838 constitution.

i. Single Subject

The single subject requirement is designed to prevent "logrolling" (*i.e.*, bills that have multiple subjects). This ensures that every idea stands or falls on its own merit. *See Department of Education v. Lewis*, 416 So. 2d 455 (Fla. 1982); *Hernandez-Molina v. State*, 860 So. 2d 483 (Fla. 4th Dist. Ct. App. 2003), *review denied*, 895 So. 2d 405 (Fla. 2005). The U.S. Constitution does not have a similar provision. As a result, logrolling is common in Congress.

Some wiggle room does exist. This is because Art. III, § 6 includes the words "and matter properly connected therewith." As a result, while bills are not allowed to contain multiple subjects, they can regulate a single subject in multiple ways.

The Florida Supreme Court has made it clear that the single subject requirement is satisfied so long as there is a logical connection between a law's different parts. *See Grant v. State*, 770 So. 2d 655 (Fla. 2000) (upholding statute dealing with arrests, gain time, and probation); *Smith v. Department of Insurance*, 507 So. 2d 1080 (Fla. 1987) (upholding statute capping tort damages, changing the financial responsibility requirements of doctors, freezing insurance rates, and requiring rebates); *State ex rel. Flink v. Canova*, 94 So. 2d 181 (Fla. 1957) (en banc) (upholding statute regulating drug stores and pharmacists). *See also Burch v. State*, 558 So. 2d 1, 2 (Fla. 1990) (upholding statute dealing with crime prevention studies, drug abuse education, entrapment, money laundering, safe neighborhoods, and vehicle forfeitures because "[e]ach of these areas bear a logical relationship to the single subject of controlling crime, whether by providing for imprisonment or through taking away the profits of crime and promoting education and safe neighborhoods.").

If a logical connection does not exist among a law's subjects, the law will be struck down. Thus, for example, in *Martinez v. Scanlan*, 582 So. 2d 1167 (Fla. 1991), a law dealing with both international trade and workers' compensation was held to violate § 6. Similarly, in *State v. Thompson*, 750 So. 2d 643 (Fla. 1999), a law dealing with career criminals and domestic violence was deemed unconstitutional.

However, because of the presumption that statutes are constitutional (discussed later in this chapter), any doubts will be resolved in the law's favor. *See, e.g., Whitsett v. State*, 913 So. 2d 1208, 1210 (Fla. 4th Dist. Ct. App. 2005) ("When reviewing legislation to determine whether the single subject rule was violated, the standard of review is highly deferential.").

A single subject challenge is viable only while a law remains a chapter law. This is known as a law's "window period." *See Henry v. State*, 765 So. 2d 736 (Fla. 1st Dist. Ct. App. 2000); *Diaz v. State*, 752 So. 2d 105 (Fla. 3d Dist. Ct. App.), *review denied*, 776 So. 2d 276 (Fla. 2000).

Chapter laws are incorporated annually into the Florida Statutes. The legislature then re-adopts the Florida Statutes at its next session "as the official statute law of the state." *See* Fla. Stat. § 11.2421. Doing so "cures" any underlying single subject violations and closes the window. *See State v. Johnson*, 616 So. 2d 1 (Fla. 1993); *Ellis v. Hunter*, 3 So. 3d 373 (Fla. 5th Dist. Ct. App.), *review denied*, 10 So. 3d 632 (Fla. 2009). In *Santos v. State*, 380 So. 2d 1284 (Fla. 1980), the court explained:

> The purpose of the requirement that each law embrace only one subject and matter properly connected with it is to prevent subterfuge, surprise, "hodge-podge" and log rolling in legislation. . . . When laws passed by the legislature are being codified for publication in the Florida Statutes, these restrictions do not apply. The legislature is free to use whatever

classification system it chooses. Article III, section 6 does not require sections of the Florida Statutes to conform to the single-subject requirement. The requirement applies to "laws" in the sense of acts of the legislature.

Id. at 1285.

The constitution contains a separate, and stricter, single subject requirement for citizen-initiated constitutional amendments. *See* Art. XI, § 3 (limiting such proposals to "one subject and matter directly [rather than just properly] connected therewith"), discussed in Ch. 23 of this book.

ii. Brief Title

All laws must include a brief title that gives a person of average intelligence reasonable notice of the law's subject matter. *See In the Matter of: Lowery Bros., Inc.*, 589 F.2d 851, 855 (5th Cir. 1979) ("The purpose of this constitutional mandate is to make certain that both the state legislature and the public are given adequate notice as to what a law entails."). Thus, for example, in *Rouleau v. Avrach*, 233 So. 2d 1 (Fla. 1970), a law titled "Occupational License Taxes Upon Those Engaged in the Practice of Law in Counties" was struck down because its title gave no hint that it included municipal occupational license taxes. Similarly, in *Tormey v. Moore*, 824 So. 2d 137 (Fla. 2002), a statute called the "Law Enforcement Protection Act" was deemed improper because while it did impose enhanced penalties for crimes against police officers, it also denied provisional sentencing credits to all murderers (not just those of police officers).

In *Williams v. State*, 370 So. 2d 1143 (Fla. 1979), the court devised the following test to determine whether a title is proper:

> The title of a statute need not index all of the statute's contents. The proper test is whether the title is so worded as not to mislead a person of average intelligence as to the scope of the enactment and is sufficient to put that person on notice and cause him to inquire into the body of the statute itself.

Id. at 1144.

As with single subject challenges, title challenges are permitted only during a chapter law's "window period."

iii. Amendments and Revisions

To prevent confusion, a law cannot amend or revise another law simply by referring to the latter's title. Instead, the affected language must be set out in full. *See Lipe v. City of Miami*, 141 So. 2d 738 (Fla. 1962). In *Deltona Corp. v. Florida Public Service Commission*, 220 So. 2d 905 (Fla. 1969), the court explained the reason for this rule:

> This constitutional provision was designed to prevent the enactment of amendatory statutes in terms so blind that the legislators themselves are sometimes deceived concerning their effect and the public fails to become advised of the

changes made in the law because of difficulty in making the necessary examination and comparison.

Id. at 908.

A law will not be declared invalid, even though it does not set out the affected language, if the change it is making is clear on its face. *See Webster v. North Orange Memorial Hospital Tax District*, 187 So. 2d 37 (Fla. 1966). The same is true for a law that is not intended to amend or revise an existing law and therefore does so, if at all, only by implication. *See State v. J.R.M.*, 388 So. 2d 1227 (Fla. 1980).

iv.   Enacting Clause

Every law must have an enacting clause. *See City of Winter Haven v. A. M. Klemm & Son*, 181 So. 153 (Fla.) (en banc), *reh'g denied*, 182 So. 841 (Fla. 1938). In the house, an amendment to delete a bill's enacting clause sometimes is used to force an immediate vote on a controversial measure.

In addition to assuring continuity and uniformity in bill format, the presence of an enacting clause alerts both legislators and the public that the measure under consideration is a proposed law, rather than a mere expression of the legislature's opinion or sentiment. Every state constitution has a similar requirement.

Enacting clauses are included in chapter laws but do not appear in the Florida Statutes. *See McCutcheon v. State*, 44 So. 3d 156 (Fla. 4th Dist. Ct. App.), *prohibition denied*, 46 So. 3d 566 (Fla. 2010), *review denied*, 75 So. 3d 1245 (Fla. 2011) (rejecting a pro se prisoner's argument that the lack of enacting clauses in the Florida Statutes invalidated the law used to convict him).

(e) Procedure

Art. III, § 7 provides:

> Any bill may originate in either house and after passage in one may be amended in the other. It shall be read in each house on three separate days, unless this rule is waived by two-thirds vote; provided the publication of its title in the journal of a house shall satisfy the requirement for the first reading in that house. On each reading, it shall be read by title only, unless one-third of the members present desire it read in full. On final passage, the vote of each member voting shall be entered on the journal. Passage of a bill shall require a majority vote in each house. Each bill and joint resolution passed in both houses shall be signed by the presiding officers of the respective houses and by the secretary of the senate and the clerk of the house of representatives during the session or as soon as practicable after its adjournment sine die.

In broad form, these requirements date to the 1838 constitution. In 1980, the constitution was amended to permit publication of a bill's title to count as its first reading.

Individual bills (back to 1998) can be located and tracked on the web sites of the house and senate. For a guide to conducting pre-1998 searches, see https://guides.law.fsu.edu/c.php?g=84905&p=547273.

i. Origination

Any bill, regardless of subject matter, may originate in either the house or senate. This marks a sharp break with federal practice. Under Art. I, § 7, cl. 1 of the U.S. Constitution, all bills raising money must start in the U.S. House of Representatives. This requirement follows British parliamentary practice, under which revenue bills must have their first reading in the House of Commons. Twenty state constitutions have an origination clause.

ii. Readings

The requirement that a bill be read on three separate days is designed to slow matters down, thereby giving legislators a chance to deliberate before they vote. See *State v. Carley*, 104 So. 577 (Fla. 1925) (en banc).

The reading rule is quite flimsy: the first reading is satisfied by publication of the bill's title in the journal; the second and third readings are by title only (unless 1/3 of the legislators request otherwise); and by a 2/3 vote, the need to wait three days can be waived. See *Florida Association of Professional Lobbyists, Inc. v. Division of Legislative Information Services of the Florida Office of Legislative Services*, 431 F. Supp. 2d 1228 (N.D. Fla. 2006). See also *State v. Kaufman*, 430 So. 2d 904 (Fla. 1983) (reading of bill's legislatively-assigned number is sufficient to constitute a reading).

The 1868 constitution was tougher: it required a bill's third reading to be "by sections" (*i.e.*, in full). The 1885 constitution went even further, requiring all three readings to be by sections, although it allowed the legislature to dispense with this rule for the first two readings by a 2/3 vote. In 1896, the constitution was changed to permit the first reading to be by title only, unless otherwise requested by 1/3 of the legislators. *See West v. State*, 39 So. 412 (Fla. 1905) (Div. B).

iii.   Passage

A majority of both the house and the senate must vote in favor of a bill for it to become law. Each legislator's vote must be recorded in the applicable journal.

iv.   Signing by Officers

The requirement that every passed bill must be signed by the legislature's four officers (clerk, president, secretary, speaker) ensures that the version presented to the governor accurately reflects what was approved. Although there is no fixed time for such signings, the last sentence of Art. III, § 7 requires the officers to act "as soon as practicable." *See also State ex rel. Thompson v. Davis*, 169 So. 199, 207 (Fla. 1936) (en banc) ("[Bills must be] signed by the legislative officers . . . within the reasonable limitations of time[.]").

In *Advisory Opinion to the Governor*, 154 So. 2d 838 (Fla. 1963), the secretary died before signing several passed bills. Given the circumstances, the court held that the signature of the remaining officers was sufficient.

(f) Gubernatorial Review

Art. III, § 8 gives the governor the power to veto legislation (in Latin, the word "veto" means "I forbid"). It also gives the legislature the power to override gubernatorial vetoes. Every one of Florida's constitutions has contained these two provisions, although the details have changed over time. *See Advisory Opinion to the Governor*, 12 So. 2d 583 (Fla. 1943); *Thompson v. State*, 47 So. 816 (Fla. 1908); *State ex rel. Boyd v. Deal*, 4 So. 899 (Fla. 1888); *In re Executive Communication Concerning Powers of Legislature*, 6 So. 925 (Fla. 1887).

i. Deadlines

As explained earlier in this chapter, a bill that has been approved by the legislature and signed by the officers is called an "enrolled" bill. Such a bill is not yet a law because it still must be submitted to the governor for his or her review. *See Amos v. Gunn*, 94 So. 615 (Fla. 1922).

Until a bill is presented to the governor, the legislature can recall it. *See Jinkins v. Entzminger*, 135 So. 785 (Fla. 1931) (Div. B). Once a bill is presented to the governor, this option disappears. *See State ex rel. Schwartz v. Bledsoe*, 31 So. 2d 457 (Fla. 1947) (en banc).

Under Art. III, § 8(a), the governor has seven consecutive days to review a bill. This time is increased to 15 consecutive days if, during the seven days, the legislature adjourns sine die or takes a recess of more than 30 days. *See Florida Society of Ophthalmology v. Florida Optometric Association*, 489 So. 2d 1118 (Fla. 1986). Because most bills are presented after adjournment sine die, the governor normally has 15 days to act.

The governor's time cannot be enlarged for any reason. *See State ex rel. Simmons v. Lee*, 160 So. 886 (Fla. 1935) (Div. A). In calculating the governor's time, the day of presentation is not included; the last day of the period is included; and the clock does not stop for weekends or holidays. *See In re Advisory Opinion to the Governor*, 131 So. 2d 196 (Fla. 1961); *Smithie v. State*, 101 So. 276 (Fla. 1924) (Div. A); *Croissant v. De Soto Improvement Co.,* 101 So. 37 (Fla. 1924) (en banc).

Florida's 7/15 formula is in line with other states, although a few are much more generous (Illinois, for example, gives its governor 60 calendar days). Art. I, § 7, cl. 2 of the U.S. Constitution allows the president 10 days (excluding Sundays).

Florida's 7/15 formula dates from the 1968 constitution. Earlier constitutions used different formulas—under a 1954 amendment, for example, the governor had to act in 5/20.

Because of their wording, the 1838, 1861, and 1865 constitutions allowed the governor to "pocket veto" bills. A pocket veto occurs when the legislature adjourns before the governor's time to act expires. In such situations, if the governor does nothing, the bill dies. This is because there is no one to whom the governor can send his or her veto.

To end pocket vetoes, the 1868 constitution was rewritten as follows:

> If any bill shall not be returned within five days after it shall have been presented to the Governor (Sundays excepted,) the same shall be a law, in like manner as if he had signed it. If the Legislature, by its final adjournment, prevent such action, such bill shall be a law unless the Governor, within ten days next after the adjournment, shall file such bill with his objections thereto in the office of the Secretary of State, who shall lay the same before the Legislature at its next session.

Because of this change, the governor finally had someone to send his or her veto (*i.e.*, the secretary of state). This provision was carried over to the 1885 and 1968 constitutions. The constitution now provides:

> When a bill or any specific appropriation of a general appropriation bill has been vetoed, the governor shall transmit signed objections thereto to the house in which the bill originated if in session. If that house is not in session, the governor shall file them with the custodian of state records, who shall lay them before that house at its next regular or special session, whichever occurs first, and they shall be entered on its journal.

Art. III, § 8(b). As explained in Ch. 14 of this book, the secretary of state is the "custodian of state records."

While Florida no longer allows pocket vetoes, several states still do (*e.g.*, Michigan, New Hampshire, Oklahoma). The president also has a pocket veto, but Congress normally gets around it by appointing one or more persons to accept the president's veto in its absence. The validity of this practice is unclear. *See Wright v. United States*, 302 U.S. 583 (1938), *partially overruling Bands of State of Washington v. United States*, 279 U.S. 655 (1929) ("The Pocket Veto Case").

ii. Options

When presented with a bill, the governor has three choices: sign it, do nothing, or veto it. *See* Art. III, § 8(a). Signing a bill, or doing nothing, results in it becoming a law. *Id.* Vetoing a bill returns it to the originating chamber for possible further action (*i.e.*, an override). *See* Art. III, § 8(b)–(c).

Since the passage of the 1968 constitution, governors have signed nearly all the bills presented to them (95%), only rarely failed to act (1%), and have used their veto power sparingly (4%). During his stormy tenure (1967–71), Gov. Claude Kirk averaged 27 vetoes a year. In contrast, Gov. Rick Scott (2011–19) averaged just seven vetoes a year. In 2019, Gov. Ron DeSantis vetoed just five bills while signing 189.

It is common for particularly important or popular bills to be signed twice: once officially, and then a second time in a staged ceremony attended by the media and the bill's sponsors and supporters. In 2018, Gov. Rick Scott held ceremonial bill signings at, among other places, a Hebrew school in Orlando, a restaurant in Miami, and a technology company in Fort Walton Beach.

By signing a bill, the governor places his or her stamp of approval on it. By doing nothing, the governor signals that he or she does not approve the bill but, for political reasons, has decided not to oppose it. Governors normally opt to do nothing for one of two reasons: 1) the bill is not worth fighting about; or, 2) the bill is worth fighting about but passed by such a large margin that opposing it would be futile.

Vetoing a bill means the governor is both opposed to it and ready for a fight. Normally, a governor will fight only when a bill's passage has been by a thin margin (meaning that a veto override is unlikely). Sometimes, however, a governor will veto a bill that commanded a large majority. This usually is done to score points with the public.

Signing a bill, or doing nothing, has the same effect: the bill becomes a law on its effective date (discussed below). *See State ex rel. Schwartz v. Bledsoe*, 31 So. 2d 457 (Fla. 1947) (en banc). And once made part of the Florida Statutes, it is impossible to know (unless one does detailed research) which of these options the governor chose. Vetoes, on the other hand, result in additional steps, as outlined below.

iii.   *Return and Reenactment of Vetoed Bills*

When the governor vetoes a bill, Art. III, § 8(b) requires him or her to "transmit signed objections thereto to the house in which the bill originated if in session. If that house is not in session, the governor shall file them with the custodian of state records. . . ."

The governor's reason(s) for vetoing a bill are memorialized in a "veto statement." There are no set rules for such statements, although they now normally take the form of a standard business letter. An example of a veto message can be found at https://www.flgov.com/wp-content/uploads/2013/05/SB718.pdf.

Once the veto statement is received, the legislature can attempt to override the governor's veto. The process for doing so is set out in Art. III, § 8(b)–(c):

> If the originating house votes to re-enact a vetoed measure, whether in a regular or special session, and the other house does not consider or fails to re-enact the vetoed measure, no further consideration by either house at any subsequent session may be taken. If a vetoed measure is presented at a special session and the originating house does not consider it, the measure will be available for consideration at any intervening special session and until the end of the next regular session. . . .

> If each house shall, by a two-thirds vote, re-enact the bill . . . the vote of each member voting shall be entered on the respective journals, and

the bill shall become law ..., the veto notwithstanding.

The 1838 constitution allowed the legislature to override the governor's veto by a simple majority. Since the 1861 constitution, a 2/3 vote has been required. This is in line with other states: 74% require a 2/3 vote; 14% a 3/5 vote; and 12% a majority vote. Art. I, § 7, cl. 2 of the U.S. Constitution allows Congress to override presidential vetoes by a 2/3 vote.

In 1997, a question arose regarding when a vetoed bill must be taken up by the legislature. In *Chiles v. Phelps*, 714 So. 2d 453 (Fla. 1998), the court, finding no deadline in the constitution, refused to impose one.

To address this situation, in 1998 the following sentence was added to Art. III, § 8(b): "If a vetoed measure is presented at a special session and the originating house does not consider it, the measure will be available for consideration at any intervening special session and until the end of the next regular session." Accordingly, the legislature now has until the end of the next regular session to override the governor's veto.

Veto overrides are extremely rare in Florida. Since 1986, only 13 vetoes have been overridden. Ten occurred during Gov. Charlie Crist's last two years in office (2010–11), and were political payback for his decision to leave the Republican party.

iv.   Line Item Vetoes

Florida allows the governor to "line item" veto appropriations (44 other states do likewise). This means that when presented with an appropriations bill (*i.e.*, a spending bill—see Art. III, § 12, discussed later in this chapter), the governor is permitted to go through it line-by-line and delete individual appropriations. *See Florida House of Representatives v. Martinez*, 555 So. 2d 839 (Fla. 1990); *Thompson v. Graham*, 481 So. 2d 1212 (Fla. 1985); *In re Advisory Opinion to the Governor*, 239 So. 2d 1 (Fla. 1970).

The Florida Constitution has granted governors line item veto power since 1875, making it one of the first to do so. It is important to keep in mind that the governor's line item veto power applies only to appropriations bills. For all other bills, the governor must accept or reject the entire bill.

There has been considerable litigation over the governor's line item veto power, most of which has involved "provisos." A proviso is a condition attached to a specific appropriation. *See, e.g., Chiles v. Milligan*, 659 So. 2d 1055 (Fla. 1995).

Governors are not permitted to add, change, or strike out a proviso. Thus, they must accept or delete each line item exactly as written. In *Florida Senate v. Harris*, 750 So. 2d 626 (Fla. 1999), the court explained:

   Article III, section 8(a) of the Florida Constitution provides in pertinent part that "[t]he governor may veto any specific appropriation in a general appropriation bill, but may not veto any qualification or restriction without also vetoing the appropriation to which it relates." As explained by this Court in *Brown v. Firestone*, 382 So.2d 654, 664 (Fla.1980), the governor's constitutional "veto power is intended to be a negative power, the power to nullify, or at least suspend, legislative intent. It is not designed to alter or amend legislative intent." *See also Chiles v. Children A, B, C, D, E, and F*, 589 So.2d 260, 265 (Fla.1991) ("[I]t is well settled that the executive branch does not have the power to use the veto to restructure an appropriation."). Thus, where the Legislature attaches "a rationally and directly related qualification or restriction to [an] appropriation . . . the governor [must] make the hard choice whether to give up the appropriation entirely or to follow the legislative direction for its use." *Brown*, 382 So.2d at 667.

Id. at 629. Provisos are discussed further later in this chapter.

The rationale behind the line item veto is that individual legislators try to obtain as much money for their constituents as possible (this is known as "bringing home the bacon"). Thus, it is up to the governor, the one official who represents all the people, to ensure that each appropriation represents a wise use of taxpayer money.

Much is made each year when the governor is presented with the state budget and strikes out different appropriations. Those whose programs are axed are quick to yell "foul" and claim the governor is playing politics. While this may be true, it also is true that even the most free-wheeling governors end up cutting very little. During their respective tenures, Gov. Jeb Bush (1999–2007) and Gov. Charlie Crist (2007–11) annually vetoed $250 million in appropriations. Gov. Rick Scott (2011–19) upped this figure to $295 million a year. While this sounds like a lot, it represents just 0.3% of the budget. In 2019, Gov. Ron DeSantis vetoed just $131 million in appropriations. This represented just 0.1% of the budget.

The U.S. Constitution does not allow line item vetoes. In 1996, President Bill Clinton convinced Congress to pass a line item veto law (every prior president had tried to obtain such legislation), but the statute was ruled unconstitutional in *Clinton v. City of New York*, 524 U.S. 417 (1998).

(g) Effective Date

Art. III, § 9 provides:

Each law shall take effect on the sixtieth day after adjournment sine die of the session of the legislature in which enacted or as otherwise provided therein. If the law is passed over the veto of the governor it shall take effect on the sixtieth day after adjournment sine die of the session in which the veto is overridden, on a later date fixed in the law, or on a date fixed by resolution passed by both houses of the legislature.

The 1885 constitution was the first to contain such language, which, as slightly modified, was carried over to the 1968 constitution. By keeping laws from going into effect immediately, the public is given time to learn about them. *See Pound v. Lee*, 154 So. 689 (Fla. 1934) (en banc).

Bills now typically specify when they become effective and usually select one of three dates: Jan. 1 (the start of the new calendar year), July 1 (the start of the state's new fiscal year), or Oct. 1 (the traditional date for new laws in the United States due to the schedules of printing houses). As a result, Art. III, § 9 has become largely a "fall back" provision in the rare event that a law does not contain an effective date or has an invalid one. *See, e.g., Berwald v. General Motors Acceptance Corp.*, 570 So. 2d 1109, 1110 n.1 (Fla. 5th Dist. Ct. App. 1990) ("GMAC correctly points out that while the bill . . . states an effective date of July 1, 1986 the governor did not sign the bill until July 2, 1986. Therefore, the effective date of the bill is August 6, 1986, or sixty days after the legislature adjourned *sine die*.").

The legislature is not limited in picking an effective date. *See, e.g., Kirk v. Brantley*, 228 So. 2d 278 (Fla. 1969) (Apr. 1); *Gaulden v. Kirk*, 47 So. 2d 567 (Fla. 1950) (en banc) (Nov. 1); *White v. Ballinger*, 33 So. 2d 157 (Fla. 1948) (Div. A) (Dec. 31). It also is permitted to tie the effective date to a future contingent event, such as when the law is approved by the governor or the voters. *See, e.g., Brown v. City of Tampa*, 6 So. 2d 287 (Fla. 1942) (en banc).

Following the Parkland mass shooting on Feb. 14, 2018, the legislature rushed through the "Marjory Stoneman Douglas High School Public Safety Act" (S.B. 7026). It became effective on Mar. 9, 2018, four days after it was approved by the senate, two days after it was approved by the house, and the same day it was signed by Gov. Rick Scott.

4.   TYPES OF LAWS

The Florida Legislature is authorized to pass five different types of laws: general, local, special, general laws of local application ("population acts"), and appropriations laws. As will be seen, each type of law has its own distinct constitutional requirements (although there also is a good deal of overlap).

(a) General Laws

Most of the laws now passed by the Florida Legislature are general laws (for the reasons why this is so, see the next section). Indeed, in the 2018 session, 96% of the bills filed, and 85% of the bills passed, were general law bills. As a result, a party claiming that a law is not a general law bears a heavy burden. *See License Acquisitions, LLC v. Debary Real Estate Holdings, LLC*, 155 So. 3d 1137 (Fla. 2014). To be procedurally valid, a general law only needs to meet the requirements contained in Art. III, §§ 6–9 (discussed above).

A general law is a law that applies uniformly throughout the state. In *McConihe v. State ex rel. McMurray*, 17 Fla. 238 (1879), the court explained:

Every law is *general* which includes in its provisions all persons or things of the same *genus*, and it is of uniform operation throughout the State, if it operates upon these persons or things equally in every locality. It is not necessary that all persons and things included in a general law should be placed precisely upon the same footing, without regard to differences in their character or capacities, provided all of the same class or kind are treated alike.

Id. at 251 (emphasis in original). *See also State ex rel. Landis v. Harris*, 163 So. 237, 240 (Fla. 1934) (en banc) ("A general law operates universally throughout the state, or uniformly upon subjects as they may exist throughout the state, or uniformly within permissible classifications by population of counties or otherwise, or is a law relating to a state function or instrumentality.").

A law that singles out a specific geographic area will be deemed a general law if it serves a statewide purpose. In *Schrader v. Florida Keys Aqueduct Authority*, 840 So. 2d 1050 (Fla. 2003), for example, the legislature passed a law permitting local governments in Monroe County to impose stricter waste water rules than those allowed in the rest of the state. In holding that this law was a general law, the court wrote:

In sum, if a law utilizes a classification that is geographical in its terms but the purpose of the statute is one of statewide importance and impact, and the classification is reasonably related to the law's purpose, it is a valid general law. . . . In this instance, the section of the statute being challenged is part of a general statutory scheme to environmentally protect areas which have been legislatively designated as being of "critical state concern."

Id. at 1056.

(b) Special and Local Laws

Like a general law, a special or local law must comply with the requirements of Art. III, §§ 6–9. It also, however, must comply with Art. III, §§ 10–11.

Initially, the Florida Legislature devoted most of its time to special and local laws. As counties and municipalities became more robust, the volume of such laws decreased. The 1968 constitution, which grants increased "home rule" powers to local governments, has accelerated this trend.

At times, the Florida Legislature still passes special or local laws. An example of a recent local law is Fla. Laws ch. 2015–198 (http://laws.flrules.org/2015/198), which changed the boundaries of West Palm Beach's water catchment area so that the Houston Astros and Washington Nationals could build a joint spring training baseball complex.

Because they are not included in the Florida Statutes, special and local laws are located using the annually-updated "Index to Special and Local Laws." It can be viewed at http://edocs.dlis.state.fl.us/fldocs/leg/divstatrev/indexlaws/IndexTSALL1845-1970.pdf (1845–1970) and http://edocs.dlis.state.fl.us/fldocs/leg/divstatrev/indexlaws/1971-2019.pdf (1971–2019).

i. *Defined*

Art. X, § 12(g) makes it clear that whenever the constitution uses the term "special law," local laws are included: " 'Special law' means a special or local law."

In *State ex rel. Gray v. Stoutamire*, 179 So. 730 (Fla. 1938) (en banc), the court distinguished special and local laws from general laws by writing:

[I]t has been stated that "a statute relating to * * * subjects or to persons or things as a class, based upon proper distinctions and differences that inhere in or are peculiar or appropriate to the class, is a 'general law'; while a statute relating to particular subdivisions or portions of the state, or to particular places of classified localities, is a 'local law'; and a statute relating to particular persons or things or other particular subjects of a class, is a 'special law.' " *State ex rel. v. Daniel*, 87 Fla. 270, 287, 99 So. 804, 809.

Id. at 732–33. *See also St. Johns River Water Management District v. Deseret Ranches of Florida, Inc.*, 421 So. 2d 1067, 1069 (Fla. 1982) (" '[S]pecial or local laws' as used in the constitution . . . refer ordinarily to laws relating to entities, interests, rights, and functions *other than those of the State*.") (emphasis in original).

A law that at the time of its enactment applies to only one party, but that can and likely will affect others as time goes by, will be treated as a general law rather than as a special or local law. *See License*

Acquisitions, LLC v. Debary Real Estate Holdings, LLC, 155 So. 3d 1137 (Fla. 2014); *Department of Legal Affairs v. Sanford-Orlando Kennel Club, Inc.*, 434 So. 2d 879 (Fla. 1983); *Biscayne Kennel Club, Inc. v. Florida State Racing Commission*, 165 So. 2d 762 (Fla. 1964).

On the other hand, a law that either cannot include other parties in the future (because of its express wording), or is unlikely to do so, will be deemed a special or local law. *See Florida Department of Business and Professional Regulation v. Gulfstream Park Racing Association, Inc.*, 967 So. 2d 802 (Fla. 2007); *City of Miami v. McGrath*, 824 So. 2d 143 (Fla. 2002); *Department of Business Regulation v. Classic Mile, Inc.*, 541 So. 2d 1155 (Fla. 1989).

ii.   Procedure

To validly pass a special or local law, Art. III, § 10 requires the legislature to do one of two things:

No special law shall be passed unless notice of intention to seek enactment thereof has been published in the manner provided by general law. Such notice shall not be necessary when the law, except the provision for referendum, is conditioned to become effective only upon approval by vote of the electors of the area affected.

The 1885 constitution was the first to require the legislature to notify the public about proposed special and local laws, and made the deadline for doing so "at least sixty days prior to the introduction into the

Legislature of such bill." In 1938, this provision was amended to dispense with the notice requirement when the law was made subject to a post-enactment referendum.

The notice requirement exists to give affected persons time to learn about the bill. *See North Ridge General Hospital, Inc. v. City of Oakland Park*, 374 So. 2d 461 (Fla. 1979), *appeal dismissed*, 444 U.S. 1062 (1980). The procedure for giving notice is set out in Fla. Stat. § 11.02:

> The notice required to obtain special or local legislation . . . shall be by publishing the identical notice in each county involved in some newspaper as defined in chapter 50 published in or circulated throughout the county or counties where the matter or thing to be affected by such legislation shall be situated one time at least 30 days before introduction of the proposed law into the Legislature or, there being no newspaper circulated throughout or published in the county, by posting for at least 30 days at not less than three public places in the county or each of the counties, one of which places shall be at the courthouse in the county or counties where the matter or thing to be affected by such legislation shall be situated. Notice of special or local legislation shall state the substance of the contemplated law, as required by § 10, Art. III of the State Constitution.

See also Fla. Stat. §§ 11.021 and 11.03.

If the legislature passes a special or local law without providing notice, a referendum must be held. Only if the vote is positive does the law go into effect. *See State v. County of Sarasota*, 62 So. 2d 708 (Fla. 1953) (en banc).

Art. VI, § 5(a) states: "[R]eferenda shall be held as provided by law." When a local law is on the ballot, Art. III, § 10 stipulates that only "the electors of the area affected" are eligible to vote. In *Barndollar v. Sunset Realty Corp.*, 379 So. 2d 1278 (Fla. 1979), the court invalidated a referendum that allowed both residents and non-residents to vote on a local law creating a historic preservation district.

iii. Prohibited Subjects

Art. III, § 11(a) contains a long list of subjects that cannot be regulated through either a special law or a local law. Art. III, § 11(a)(21) allows the legislature to add subjects "by a three-fifths vote of the membership of each house." (Once added, such subjects can only be removed by a similar 3/5 vote.) Pursuant to this power, the legislature has added a host of subjects, including county salaries, see Fla. Stat. § 145.16; public employee pensions, see Fla. Stat. § 112.67; and school taxes, see Fla. Stat. § 1011.77.

In *Lawnwood Medical Center, Inc. v. Seeger*, 990 So. 2d 503, 513 (Fla. 2008), the court explained that § 11(a) exists for three reasons: "to prevent state action benefiting local or private interests[; to] direct the Legislature to focus on issues of statewide importance[; and to] encourage[ ] uniformity in Florida law."

One of the earliest statements objecting to special or local laws is contained in the 1780 Massachusetts Constitution: "Government is instituted for the common good; for the protection, safety, prosperity and happiness of the people; and not for the profit, honor, or private interest of any one man, family, or class of men. . . ." Today, all but four state constitutions limit the use of special or local legislation. There is no such provision in the U.S. Constitution.

Florida's 1838 constitution prohibited the legislature from resorting to special or local laws when forming charities or dissolving private corporations. The 1861 constitution added contracts made by married women or minors; dams; ferries; illegitimate children; name changes; toll bridges; and towns. The 1865 constitution dropped the prohibitions on contracts made by married women and illegitimate children. The 1868 constitution placed all the prohibited subjects in one section and greatly revised them:

> The Legislature shall not pass special or local laws in any of the following enumerated cases; that is to say, regulating the jurisdiction and duties of any class of officers, or for the punishment of crime or misdemeanor; regulating the practice of courts of justice; providing for changing venue of civil and criminal cases; granting divorces; changing the names of persons; vacating roads, town plats,

streets, alleys, and public squares; summoning and empaneling grand and petit juries, and providing for their compensation; regulating county, township, and municipal business; regulating the election of county, township, and municipal officers; for the assessment and collection of taxes for State, county, and municipal purposes; providing for opening and conducting elections for State, county, and municipal officers, and designating the places of voting; providing for the sale of real estate belonging to minors or other persons laboring under legal disabilities; regulating the fees of officers.

The 1885 constitution tinkered with this list, adding adoptions and wills and restoring ferries and illegitimate children. The 1968 constitution added corporate privileges; disposal of public property; fishing and hunting; interest and liens on private contracts; refunds of fines, forfeitures, and penalties; and state-regulated occupations. It also dropped ferries; separated the topics into numbered paragraphs; gave the legislature the power to expand the list; and streamlined the language.

Numerous cases have litigated individual items on the list, with varying results. *See, e.g., Lee Memorial Health System v. Progressive Select Insurance Co.*, 260 So. 3d 1038 (Fla. 2018) (paragraph 9—contract liens—violated by local law creating Lee County health system and authorizing it to lien patient accounts); *Venice HMA, LLC v. Sarasota County*, 228 So. 3d 76 (Fla.), *reh'g denied*, 2017 WL 4545964 (Fla.

2017) (paragraph 12—corporate privileges—not violated by local law requiring Sarasota County to reimburse private hospitals for indigent care); *Kane v. Robbins*, 556 So. 2d 1381 (Fla. 1989) (paragraph 1—election of state officers—violated by local law requiring Martin County to hold non-partisan school board elections); *Sarasota County, Florida v. Barg*, 302 So. 2d 737 (Fla. 1974) (paragraph 7—conditions precedent for bringing civil actions—not violated by local law establishing Manasota Key Conservation District and requiring property owners to exhaust administrative remedies prior to filing suit); *State v. Leavins*, 599 So. 2d 1326 (Fla. 1st Dist. Ct. App. 1992) (paragraph 20—occupations regulated by state agencies—violated by local law curtailing oyster harvesting in Apalachicola Bay).

(c)   General Laws of Local Application

A general law of local application, more commonly known as a "population act," is a law that uses population as a trigger. Thus, for example, it may specify that it applies only to counties with more than 500,000 residents ("floor"); only to municipalities with less than 100,000 residents ("ceiling"); or only to districts with between 10,000 and 25,000 residents ("range").

Because population acts often were used to avoid the restrictions on special and local laws, the 1968 constitution added Art. III, § 11(b): "In the enactment of general laws on other subjects, political subdivisions or other governmental entities may be classified only on a basis reasonably related to the subject of the law." As a result, a population act: 1) may not be used to regulate any of the subjects listed in Art. III, § 11(a) (as discussed above); and, 2) may only be used to regulate other subjects when doing so is reasonable.

Even before the 1968 constitution, the Florida Supreme Court routinely scrutinized population acts to ensure that their line-drawing was appropriate and necessary. In *Vance v. Ruppel*, 215 So. 2d 309 (Fla. 1968), for example, the court encountered a population act that regulated constable fees. The law applied only to counties with between 350,000 and 385,000 residents. Based on the 1960 census, the law was operative only in Pinellas County, which had 374,665 residents. Given these facts, the court struck down the law:

> We conclude Ch. 67-719 is in effect a local act which attempts to regulate the fees of county officers and as such is violative of the requirements of . . . the State Constitution. . . . While on occasion we have sustained, as general laws, population acts, in all such instances we have been careful to adhere to the principle that the population classification bear a reasonable relation to the subject matter of the act and the public purpose to be effected thereby. *See Budget Commission of Pinellas County v. Blocker* (Fla.1952), 60 So.2d 193; *Walker v. Pendarvis* (Fla.1961), 132 So.2d 186. In the present case we fail to perceive existence of the necessary relationship between the classification factors involved and the purpose sought to be

accomplished by Ch. 67-719. We denote no reason justifying the distinctive regulation accorded constables' salaries falling within the population scheme here employed.

Id. at 310–11.

An otherwise proper population act will be invalidated if it uses a fixed date. In *City of Miami v. McGrath*, 824 So. 2d 143 (Fla. 2002), for example, the legislature passed a parking tax law that only applied to cities whose populations on Apr. 1, 1999 exceeded 300,000. In invalidating the statute, the court wrote:

Section 218.503(5)(a) is incapable of generic application to all municipalities that have a population of 300,000 or more because municipalities that reach this population threshold after April 1, 1999, are not eligible for inclusion in the class. Therefore, the April 1, 1999, deadline contained in the statute creates an arbitrary population classification.

Id. at 151.

Since the adoption of the 1968 constitution, population acts have become increasingly rare. In 1969, the number of such laws fell by 56% compared to 1967; by 1972, the drop was 76%. Today, population acts almost never are used. Nevertheless, they remain a favorite of the bar examiners.

(d) Appropriation Laws

Art. III, § 12 directs: "Laws making appropriations for salaries of public officers and other current expenses of the state shall contain provisions on no other subject." This restriction originated with the 1868 constitution and has appeared in every subsequent constitution. It often is described as a corollary to Art. III, § 6, which, as discussed above, prohibits laws from containing more than one subject.

An appropriation law is one that authorizes the spending of money. The importance of such laws is made clear by Art. VII, § 1(c): "No money shall be drawn from the treasury except in pursuance of appropriation made by law."

While the legislature regularly passes appropriation bills, the phrase "appropriation bill" most commonly is used to describe the annual general appropriation bill that funds the government (*i.e.*, the state budget). *See Florida Department of Education v. Glasser*, 622 So. 2d 944 (Fla. 1993). The state budget is discussed in Ch. 20 of this book.

Because the general appropriation bill lists thousands of items, legislators must trade votes to ensure their pet projects are included. This has led many observers to describe the general appropriation bill as a "Christmas tree bill," because it provides something for everyone.

Art. III, § 12 has not generated a great deal of litigation. What litigation has occurred has involved attempts to include substantive lawmaking in appropriation bills. Appropriations often include conditions or restrictions called "provisos." If the proviso constitutes mere "budgetary housekeeping," it will be upheld. But if the proviso makes new law, or changes existing law, it will be struck down.

In *Division of Administrative Hearings v. School Board of Collier County*, 634 So. 2d 1127 (Fla. 1st Dist. Ct. App. 1994), for example, an appropriation law altered the budgeting process of the Division of Administrative Hearings. In finding that this change did not violate § 12, the court wrote:

> Simply put, the appropriations provisos reflect only a new method of budgeting operating expenses for DOAH on an hourly basis rather than an agency lump-sum basis. The budgetary scheme differs from past methods of funding, but changes no substantive law. The method of budgeting costs is reasonably related to the appropriations, and requires an hourly reimbursement system that is more detailed than the previous system. The provisos concern *only* the appropriations process and related budgeting mechanisms.

Id. at 1129 (emphasis in original). *See also Department of Education v. School Board of Collier County*, 394 So. 2d 1010 (Fla. 1981) (proviso guaranteeing one-time 7.25% increase to budgets of certain school districts was permissible funding supplement that did not change existing law); *Browning v. Florida Prosecuting Attorneys Association, Inc.*, 56 So. 3d 873 (Fla. 1st Dist. Ct. App. 2011) (proviso prohibiting use of state monies to pay bar dues of prosecutors and public defenders upheld because it did no more than reiterate existing state law).

In contrast, the Florida Supreme Court struck down the proviso at issue in *Department of Education v. Lewis*, 416 So. 2d 455 (Fla. 1982). It prohibited the Florida Department of Education from giving money to any college or university that aided groups advocating unmarried sex. In finding it invalid, the court wrote: "[The] proviso is not directly and rationally related to the appropriation of state funds to postsecondary institutions and students." *Id.* at 460. *See also Chiles v. Milligan*, 682 So. 2d 74 (Fla. 1996); *City of North Miami v. Florida Defenders of the Environment*, 481 So. 2d 1196 (Fla. 1985); *Brown v. Firestone*, 382 So. 2d 654 (Fla. 1980).

When a proviso is invalidated, the remainder of the law remains unaffected unless severance is impossible. *See Moreau v. Lewis*, 648 So. 2d 124 (Fla. 1995); *In the Matter of the Executive Communication of February 19, 1872, Relative to the Constitutionality of the 3d Section of Appropriation Bill*, 14 Fla. 283 (1872); *Florida Public Employees Council 79, AFSCME v. Bush*, 860 So. 2d 992 (Fla. 1st Dist. Ct. App. 2003).

Two final points need to be mentioned. First, as explained earlier in this chapter, an appropriation bill is subject to the governor's line item veto power. Second, since the adoption of Art. III, § 19 in 1992, a general appropriation bill must follow a specific format and cannot be voted on until legislators have had at least 72 hours to review it. *See* Ch. 20 of this book.

5.   PRESUMPTION OF STATUTORY VALIDITY

A party that challenges the constitutionality of a state law bears a heavy burden. This is because all statutes come to court with a presumption of validity. *See, e.g., Wright v. City of Miami Gardens*, 200 So. 3d 765 (Fla. 2016); *License Acquisitions, LLC v. Debary Real Estate Holdings, LLC*, 155 So. 3d 1137 (Fla. 2014); *Lewis v. Leon County*, 73 So. 3d 151 (Fla. 2011).

In *State ex rel. Flink v. Canova*, 94 So. 2d 181 (Fla. 1957) (en banc), the court explained:

> Should any doubt exist that an act is in violation of . . . any constitutional provision, the presumption is in favor of constitutionality. To overcome the presumption, the invalidity must appear beyond reasonable doubt, for it must be assumed the legislature intended to enact a valid law. Therefore, the act must be construed, if fairly possible, as to avoid unconstitutionality and to remove grave doubts on that score.

Id. at 184–85. The assumption that the legislature intends to enact valid laws is grounded in Art. II, § 3 (separation of powers). *See* Ch. 2 of this book.

G.   NON-LAWMAKING DUTIES

Along with its lawmaking duties, the Florida Legislature has a host of non-lawmaking duties.

1.   IMPEACHMENTS

Art. III, § 17 gives the legislature the power to impeach and remove the governor, lieutenant governor, cabinet members, and justices and judges. Every one of Florida's previous constitutions has contained such a provision.

Impeachment is a two-step process. In many ways, it resembles a criminal proceeding. It begins in the house, which, by a 2/3 vote, can impeach any of the above-named officers "for misdemeanor in office." *See* Art. III, § 17(a). Once impeached, an officer is "disqualified from performing any official duties," see Art. III, § 17(b), and the governor is authorized to appoint a substitute. *Id*. If the governor is impeached, the lieutenant governor serves as the acting governor.

All impeachments are tried in the senate, where a 2/3 vote is needed to convict. *See* Art. III, § 17(c). The trial must be held within six months of the house's decision to impeach. *Id*. To accommodate this schedule, the senate can try impeachments even if the house is not in session. *Id*.

The chief justice of the Florida Supreme Court, or his or her designee, presides over the trial. *Id*. If the chief justice is on trial (something that has never happened), the governor presides. *Id*. During the trial, senators are on "their oath or affirmation," *id*., meaning they can be punished if they fail to live up to their oath (see Art. II, § 5(b), discussed in Ch. 2 of this book).

At the end of the trial, the senate can either convict or acquit. *See* Art. III, § 17(c). An acquittal restores the defendant to office. *See* Art. III, § 17(b). A conviction removes the defendant from office. *See* Art. III, § 17(c). If it votes to convict, the senate can further punish the defendant by making him or her ineligible "to hold any office of honor, trust or profit." *Id.*

The final sentence of § 17(c) states: "Conviction or acquittal shall not affect the civil or criminal responsibility of the officer." Thus, even if acquitted, the defendant remains subject to civil suits, criminal prosecution, and administrative sanctions (*e.g.*, having his or her occupational license suspended or revoked).

For defendants who have exhausted their other options, executive clemency normally offers one last bit of hope. *See* Ch. 7 of this book. Impeachment is the one time it does not. As Art. IV, § 8(a) makes clear, no pardon, commutation, or other relief is available "in cases where impeachment results in conviction."

When it was adopted in 1968, Art. III, § 17 did not include county judges. In 1978, a proposal to add them was part of a package of reforms that was rejected. In 1988, when this suggestion appeared on the ballot as a stand-alone amendment, it passed easily.

The bulk of Florida's impeachments have involved judges. In 1966, however, a provision was added to the constitution providing for an alternative method of removing justices and judges. *See* Ch. 15 of this book (discussing the Judicial Qualifications Commission). As a result, judicial impeachments now are rare. In 2017, the house was preparing to impeach Circuit Judge Mark Hulsey III of Jacksonville for allegedly making racist and sexist comments, but he resigned before the process got underway.

There is not a great deal of case law interpreting § 17. One issue that has been litigated is the meaning of the phrase "misdemeanor in office." The U.S. Constitution (see Art. II, § 4) uses the equally vague phrase "high crimes and misdemeanors." The Florida Supreme Court has held that the phrase means whatever the legislature decides it means. *See Forbes v. Earle*, 298 So. 2d 1 (Fla. 1974). It also has made it clear that the word "misdemeanor" is not to be interpreted in its ordinary criminal law sense, but rather includes any act of malfeasance, misfeasance, or nonfeasance. *See In re Investigation of Circuit Judge of the Eleventh Judicial Circuit of Florida*, 93 So. 2d 601 (Fla. 1957) (en banc).

An issue that has not been litigated is whether an impeached officer can continue to collect his or her salary. The practice has been to not pay the officer while impeached but to provide back pay if acquitted.

2.   REAPPORTIONMENT

(a) Basics

Every 10 years, the Florida Legislature is required to reapportion the state to account for population changes. The goal is to have each legislative district be of equal size, so that every voter's vote counts equally. *See Baker v. Carr*, 369 U.S. 186 (1962). *See also Wesberry v. Sanders*, 376 U.S. 1 (1964); *Reynolds v. Sims*, 377 U.S. 533 (1964).

The Florida Constitution requires the house to have 80–120 districts and the senate to have 30–40 districts. *See* Art. III, § 16(a). Since 1969, both the house (120) and the senate (40) have had the maximum number of districts allowed by the constitution. Thus, based on a projected 2020 population of 21.3 million, beginning in 2022 each house district will have 177,500 residents and each senate district will have 532,500 residents.

In addition to redistricting the state's legislative districts, the Florida Legislature is required to redistrict the state's congressional districts. Because each state receives two U.S. Senate seats regardless of its size, such redistricting affects only the U.S. House of Representatives.

Federal law sets the number of congressional districts at 435. *See* 2 U.S.C. §§ 2a–2c. Florida currently has 27 congressional districts, but the 2020 census is expected to boost this number to 29. Thus, beginning in 2022 each of Florida's congressional districts will have 734,500 residents.

(b) Process

The redistricting process is spelled out in Art. III, § 16(a)–(b):

1)   In each year ending in a "2," the legislature, during its regular session and using the most recent federal census, must produce a reapportionment plan.

2)   If a reapportionment plan is not agreed to by the end of the regular session, the governor must, within 30 days, call the legislature into a special apportionment session, which can last no longer than 30 days and which cannot take up any other business.

3)   If the special apportionment session adjourns without a plan, the attorney general must, within five days, petition the Florida Supreme Court.

4)   Within 60 days of the petition, the court must formulate a plan.

If, however, the legislature agrees on a plan, either at its regular session or during the special apportionment session, the attorney general must, within 15 days, ask the court whether the plan is valid. *See* Art. III, § 16(c). The court must render its decision within 30 days. *Id.* If the court upholds the plan, it becomes "binding upon all the citizens of the state." *See* Art. III, § 16(d).

If the court rules the plan is invalid, the governor must, within five days, call an extraordinary apportionment session, which cannot last longer than 15 days. *Id.* The purpose of this session is to fix the plan.

The attorney general must, within 15 days of the end of the extraordinary apportionment session, file the legislature's revised plan with the court. *See* Art. III, § 16(e). If a revised plan has not been agreed to, the attorney general must report this fact to the court. *Id.*

If the court determines that the revised plan is valid, the process ends. If, however, the court decides the revised plan is invalid, or there is no revised plan, then within 60 days it must produce its own plan. *See* Art. III, § 16(f).

In 2012, the court rejected parts of the legislature's plan. As a result, the legislature was forced to redraw it. *See In re Senate Joint Resolution of Legislative Apportionment 1176*, 83 So. 3d 597 (Fla.), *subsequent proceedings at In re Senate Joint Resolution of Legislative Apportionment 2-B*, 89 So. 3d 872 (Fla. 2012). To date, the court has never had to draw up its own plan.

(c) "Gerrymandering"

While Art. III, § 16 sets out a detailed process for reapportioning the state, it provides only limited guidance regarding the results to be achieved. *See* Art. III, § 16(a) ("The legislature . . . shall apportion the state in accordance with the constitution of the state and of the United States into . . . districts of either contiguous, overlapping or identical territory."). This has allowed extensive "gerrymandering" to take place. (Gerrymandering involves legislators drawing "safe" districts for themselves and their parties. Thus, instead of voters picking their legislators, legislators pick their voters. The term is named for Massachusetts Gov. Elbridge Gerry, a Democratic-Republican who in 1812 signed a law designed to keep the rival Federalists from gaining power in the state senate. The resulting districts were said to resemble a salamander.)

At the time of statehood (1845), Florida was controlled by the Democrats (Florida's other major party—the Whigs—held power from 1849 to 1853 but disbanded in 1856). Following the Civil War (1865), the Republicans became the dominant party. When Reconstruction ended (1877), the Democrats returned to power. In 1964, their grip on power began to slowly loosen due to the Civil Rights movement, the country's culture wars, and the state's changing demographics. *See* Peter Dunbar & Mike Haridopolos, *The Modern Republican Party in Florida* (University Press of Florida, 2019).

By 2010, the Florida house was 63% Republican and 37% Democrat and the Florida senate was 65% Republican and 35% Democrat. Florida's voters, however, were 41% Democrat, 36% Republican, and 23% Independent. Thus, the legislature should have been slightly Democratic. That it was not was due to the aggressive gerrymandering of the Republicans, who repeatedly outmaneuvered the Democrats when it came time to draw new legislative districts.

To put a stop to gerrymandering by either party, in 2010 a group called Fair Districts Florida ("FDF") proposed two constitutional amendments, one dealing with legislative districts and the other dealing with congressional districts. (FDF opted for two amendments instead of one to eliminate the possibility of a "single subject" violation. *See* Art. XI, § 3, discussed in Ch. 23 of this book.)

After making the ballot, see *Advisory Opinion to the Attorney General re Standards for Establishing Legislative District Boundaries*, 2 So. 3d 175 (Fla. 2009), these proposals passed easily. As a result, they now appear in the constitution as, respectively, Art. III, §§ 20 (congressional districts) and 21 (legislative districts).

Substantively, both sections are identical and provide as follows:

(a) No apportionment plan or district shall be drawn with the intent to favor or disfavor a political party or an incumbent; and districts shall not be drawn with the intent or result of denying or abridging the equal opportunity of racial or language minorities to participate in the political process or to diminish their ability to elect representatives of their choice; and districts shall consist of contiguous territory.

(b) Unless compliance with the standards in this subsection conflicts with the standards in subsection 1(a) or with federal law, districts shall be as nearly equal in population as is practicable; districts shall be compact; and districts shall, where feasible, utilize existing political and geographical boundaries.

(c) The order in which the standards within subsections 1(a) and (b) of this section are set forth shall not be read to establish any priority of one standard over the other within that subsection.

As can be seen, this language requires courts to review the legislature's handiwork from multiple perspectives. Thus, it is no longer enough for a district to have the proper number of residents. Now, it also must be drawn in a politically-neutral fashion.

Since its passage, § 20 has been the subject of two major lawsuits. First, in *Brown v. Secretary of State of the State of Florida*, 668 F.3d 1271 (11th Cir. 2012), the Eleventh Circuit rejected a preemption challenge based on the Elections Clause (Art. I, § 4, cl. 1) of the U.S. Constitution.

Second, in a lawsuit brought by the League of Women Voters, the Florida Supreme Court agreed that eight of Florida's 27 congressional districts evinced "partisan intent." *See League of Women Voters of Florida v. Detzner*, 172 So. 3d 363 (Fla. 2015). As a result, it ordered them redrawn. *See League of Women Voters of Florida v. Detzner*, 179 So. 3d 258 (Fla. 2015).

In *Rucho v. Common Cause*, 139 S. Ct. 2484 (2019), the U.S. Supreme Court held that gerrymandering challenges present non-justiciable political questions. As *Rucho* recognizes, see *id.* at 2507–08, its holding should have no effect in Florida because of §§ 20 and 21. Some observers, however, worry that it will.

3. COURT RULES

Art. V, § 2(a) states in part: "The supreme court shall adopt rules for the practice and procedure in all courts. . . . Rules of court may be repealed by general law enacted by two-thirds vote of the membership of each house of the legislature."

In 1956, as part of the amendment creating the district courts of appeal, see Ch. 15 of this book, the supreme court was made responsible for the state's practice and procedure rules. In 1972, the process was made subject to legislative oversight.

From 1973 to 2011, the legislature repealed 19 of the court's rules. In response, the court readopted five rules in full; readopted one rule in part; amended three rules, but in a manner different from the repealing legislation; accepted four of the repeals in full; and ignored six of the repeals.

The foregoing statistics caused some commentators to claim, to considerable fanfare, that the court was thwarting the legislature's (and, by extension, the public's) will 79% of the time. This led the legislature in 2012 to propose that § 2(a) be rewritten to read:

Rules of court may be repealed by general law that expresses the policy behind the repeal. The court may readopt the repealed rule only in conformity with the public policy expressed by the legislature. If the legislature determines that a rule has been readopted and repeals the readopted rule, the rule may not be readopted thereafter without prior approval of the legislature.

Although this proposal was rejected by the voters, the legislature and the court have continued to battle over specific rules. *See, e.g., DeLisle v. Crane Co.*, 258 So. 3d 1219 (Fla.), *reh'g denied*, 2018 WL 6433137 (Fla. 2018) (rejecting the legislature's attempt to change the test used to qualify expert witnesses from the *Frye* standard to the *Daubert* standard), *receded from by In re: Amendments to Florida Evidence Code*, 278 So. 3d 551 (Fla.), *reh'g denied*, 2019 WL 4127349 (Fla. 2019) (adopting the *Daubert* standard).

The legislature also can repeal the rules of the Judicial Qualification Commission. *See* Art. V, § 12(a)(4), discussed in Ch. 15 of this book.

4.   CLAIMS BILLS

A claims bill, also known as a private relief act, is a bill that compensates an individual, group, or business for injuries or losses caused by the negligence or error of a public officer or agency. It is most often used when a tort plaintiff has obtained a judgment against the government that exceeds the statutory caps contained in Fla. Stat. § 768.28. *See* Ch. 2 of this book.

After being introduced by a legislator, a claims bill is referred to the legislature's special masters. Following an investigation, during which evidence and witnesses can be subpoenaed, the special masters make written findings of fact and conclusions of law. In doing so, they are not bound by the case's prior proceedings.

Once the special masters have issued their reports, a claims bill proceeds in the same manner as any other bill. A local claims bill (*i.e.*, one seeking compensation from a county, municipality, or district, as opposed to the state) must comply with the publication/referendum provisions in Art. III, § 10.

Claims bills are not heard until a case's judicial proceedings have concluded. Once they are finished, a claimant has four years to start the claims bill process. *See* Fla. Stat. § 11.065(1). If a claims bill is not passed during a given legislative session, the process must be re-started in a future legislative session.

The senate has published a helpful guide explaining the claims bill process. *See* https://www.fl senate.gov/PublishedContent/ADMINISTRATIVE PUBLICATIONS/leg-claim-manual.pdf.

Since 1990, 850 claims bills have been introduced, although only 275 have passed. Nearly $375 million has been awarded, an average payout of $1.25 million.

A claims bill also can be used to obtain equitable relief. In 1994, for example, the legislature agreed to pay $2.1 million to compensate the victims of the 1923 Rosewood Massacre. During seven days of remarkable lawlessness, whites burned to the ground the African-American community of Rosewood in Levy County while government officials refused to intervene. The 1997 film *Rosewood*, starring Ving Rhames, presents a highly fictionalized account of the attack.

5.   AMENDMENTS TO THE FLORIDA CONSTITUTION

Art. XI, § 1 states: "Amendment of a section or revision of one or more articles, or the whole, of this constitution may be proposed by joint resolution agreed to by three-fifths of the membership of each house of the legislature. The full text of the joint resolution and the vote of each member voting shall be entered on the journal of each house."

Since the adoption of the 1968 constitution, the legislature has been the principal generator of constitutional amendments. Of the 185 that have made it to the ballot, 116 (62.7%) have come from the legislature. For a further discussion of the legislature's power to propose amendments, see Ch. 23 of this book.

6.   AMENDMENTS TO THE U.S. CONSTITUTION

Art. X, § 1 directs: "The legislature shall not take action on any proposed amendment to the constitution of the United States unless a majority of the members thereof have been elected after the proposed amendment has been submitted for ratification." This provision was declared unconstitutional in *Trombetta v. State of Florida*, 353 F. Supp. 575 (M.D. Fla. 1973). As a result, the Florida

Legislature can vote on a proposed amendment to the U.S. Constitution upon receipt.

Amendments to the U.S. Constitution proposed by Congress must be ratified by 75% of the states (38) to become effective. Each state's legislature casts the state's vote. Since Florida became a state in 1845, Congress has sent 17 proposed amendments to the states. Florida has voted for 10 (the 13th–15th, 18th–22nd, 24th, and 25th Amendments); rejected one (an unratified proposal limiting child labor); and failed to cast a vote on six (the 16th, 17th, 23rd, and 26th Amendments, the unratified District of Columbia Voting Rights Amendment, and the unratified Equal Rights Amendment ("ERA")).

In 1861, after Florida seceded from the Union, Congress sent to the states an amendment (known as the Corwin Amendment) that sought to institutionalize slavery. This proposal became moot with the ratification of the 13th Amendment.

In 1990, Florida voted for the 27th Amendment (delaying the effective date of congressional pay raises). After Congress sent it to the states in 1789, it became "lost." Rediscovered in 1982 by Gregory Watson, a student at the University of Texas, it was ratified in 1992. At present, it is the most recent amendment to the U.S. constitution.

The *Trombetta* case arose during Florida's consideration of the ERA. The house approved the ERA four times (1972, 1975, 1979, and 1982), but the senate consistently refused to bring it up for a vote. Although Congress's deadline for ratification expired in 1982, states continue to debate the ERA and two recently voted for it (Nevada in 2017 and Illinois in 2018). This brings the number of ratifications to 37. In Nov. 2019, Virginia's newly-elected Democratic legislators announced plans to ratify the amendment, which would bring the number of ratifications to the necessary number of 38. In the meantime, however, five states have rescinded their ratifications. Whether states can change their votes is an open question. *See National Organization for Women, Inc. v. Idaho*, 459 U.S. 809 (1982).

CHAPTER 14
EXECUTIVE

A. OVERVIEW

Art. IV describes Florida's executive. The job of the executive is to carry out the state's laws. Pursuant to Art. II, § 3, the executive is one of the three branches of Florida's state government.

B. HISTORY

Florida's executive branch includes the governor, the lieutenant governor, and the cabinet, which consists of the attorney general, the chief financial officer ("CFO"), and the commissioner of agriculture ("COA").

The positions of governor and attorney general have appeared in every one of Florida's constitutions.

The position of lieutenant governor originated with the 1865 constitution and was retained in the 1868 constitution. The 1885 constitution eliminated the office, but the 1968 constitution restored it. During periods when the constitution did not provide for a lieutenant governor, gubernatorial vacancies were filled by the president of the senate.

The position of CFO dates to 2002, when it was created by combining two offices (comptroller and treasurer) that had been in every one of Florida's constitutions.

The position of COA entered the constitution in 1885. However, its roots go back to the 1868 constitution, which created a commissioner of immigration (responsible for convincing foreigners to move to Florida to repopulate the state's war-devastated farms and plantations). In 1871, the title was changed to commissioner of lands and immigration when the office of surveyor-general (which had existed since 1824) was abolished. *See State ex rel. Mitchell v. Bloxham*, 7 So. 873 (Fla. 1890).

Florida's constitutions always have required the governor and the lieutenant governor to be elected. (In the territorial period, however, Florida's governors were presidential appointees.) In contrast, the attorney general, the comptroller, and the treasurer initially were appointed by the legislature. These offices became elective in the 1865 constitution, were changed to gubernatorial appointees in the 1868 constitution, and were changed back to elected positions in 1870. The commissioner of immigration, initially a gubernatorial appointee, also became elective in 1870.

C. "EXECUTIVE POWER"

Florida's constitution is unusual in that it does not place the power of the executive branch solely in the hands of the governor. This is true even though Art. IV, § 1(a) says: "The supreme executive power shall be vested in a governor." Instead, the constitution requires the governor to share executive power with the cabinet.

The phrase "executive power" is not defined in the constitution. When called on to interpret it, the Florida Supreme Court has given it a narrow construction. *See Whiley v. Scott,* 79 So. 3d 702 (Fla. 2011); *Florida House of Representatives v. Crist,* 999 So. 2d 601 (Fla. 2008), *cert. denied sub nom. Seminole Tribe of Florida v. Florida House of Representatives,* 555 U.S. 1212 (2009).

Florida's requirement that the governor share executive power with three other elected officials— each with his or her own agenda, aspirations, and political base (there is no requirement that cabinet members be from the same political party as the governor), and none of whom can be removed except by the legislature—is designed to hobble the governor. In 1970, Gov. Claude Kirk expressed his disdain for the cabinet (which at the time had six members) by describing the executive branch as "Snow White and the six dwarves."

The cabinet's existence means that Florida has a "weak governor" model of governance. Most states, in contrast, employ a "strong governor" model. (This is a recent development—until the 1950s, the weak governor model was dominant.) Although experts disagree over which state constitutions give their governors the most and least power, Hawaii and Maryland usually are included in the first group while North Carolina and Rhode Island typically appear in the second group.

In weak governor states, power rests with the legislature. Florida, however, has a hybrid legislature, see Ch. 13 of this book, making it a "weak legislature" state. No other state has both a weak governor and a weak legislature. The result is that lobbyists and staffers play an outsized role in Florida's state government. *See* Ch. 13 of this book.

D. GOVERNOR

1. DUTIES

(a) Military Affairs

Art. IV, § 1(a) makes the governor the "commander-in-chief of all military forces of the state not in active service of the United States," while Art. IV, § 1(d) authorizes him or her "to call out the militia to preserve the public peace, execute the laws of the state, suppress insurrection, or repel invasion." These powers are discussed in Ch. 2 of this book.

(b) Officers

i. Supervision

Art. IV, § 1 requires the governor to supervise the activities of all state and local officials:

(a) The governor shall ... commission all officers of the state and counties, and transact all necessary business with the officers of government. The governor may require information in writing from all executive or administrative state, county or

> municipal officers upon any subject relating to the duties of their respective offices. . . .

> (b)　The　governor　may　initiate　judicial proceedings in the name of the state against any executive or administrative state, county or municipal officer to enforce compliance with any duty or restrain any unauthorized act.

Two matters require elaboration. First, the word "commission" in paragraph (a) refers to written confirmation that the holder is authorized to exercise the state's sovereign power. *See* Fla. Stat. § 113.051. Thus, for example, non-commissioned personnel ("employees") cannot make binding state contracts. *See Dade County v. State*, 116 So. 72 (Fla. 1928) (en banc).

Second, although paragraph (b) authorizes the governor to sue only executive or administrative officers, the Florida Supreme Court has gotten around this limitation by invoking its "writ" jurisdiction. *See* Ch. 15 of this book. *See also Chiles v. Phelps*, 714 So. 2d 453 (Fla. 1998) (governor permitted to sue the legislature).

ii.　Vacancies

Art. IV, § 1(f) provides:

> When not otherwise provided for in this constitution, the governor shall fill by appointment any vacancy in state or county office for the remainder of the term of an appointive office, and for the remainder of the

term of an elective office if less than twenty-eight months, otherwise until the first Tuesday after the first Monday following the next general election.

This provision is implemented by Fla. Stat. § 100.111(1)(a). The governor's power to fill vacancies dates to the 1838 constitution:

Vacancies that happen in offices, the appointment to which is vested in the General Assembly, or given to the Governor, with the advice and consent of the Senate, shall be filled by the Governor during the recess of the General Assembly, by granting commissions, which shall expire at the end of the next session.

The 1861 and 1865 constitutions retained this language. The 1868 constitution changed it to: "When any office, from any cause, shall become vacant, and no mode is provided by this Constitution or by the laws of the State for filling such vacancy, the Governor shall have the power to fill such vacancy by granting a commission, which shall expire at the next election." The 1885 constitution carried over this wording.

Where it exists, the governor's power to fill vacancies is exclusive. *See In re Advisory Opinion to Governor, Request of February 25, 1975 (Sarasota County Tax Collector)*, 313 So. 2d 717 (Fla. 1975) (rejecting county commission's argument that Art. VIII, § 1(d) permitted it to make the appointment).

The governor has no power to fill municipal vacancies because Art. IV, § 1(f) is, by its express terms, limited to state and county offices. The governor similarly has no power to fill legislative vacancies because Art. III, § 15(d) states: "Vacancies in legislative office shall be filled only by election as provided by law." *See* Ch. 13 of this book. *See also State ex rel. Landis v. Bird*, 163 So. 248 (Fla. 1935) (en banc).

The governor does have the power to fill judicial vacancies, but must do so according to the procedures set forth in Art. V, § 11(a) (appellate courts) and (b) (trial courts). These provisions are discussed in Ch. 15 of this book.

iii. Suspensions

Art. IV, § 7 gives the governor the power to suspend state, militia, county, and municipal officers. This authority, which originated with the 1885 constitution, see *In re Advisory Opinion of Governor, Appointment of County Commissioners, Dade County*, 313 So. 2d 697 (Fla. 1975), may be used by the governor at any time. *See Bruner v. State Commission on Ethics*, 384 So. 2d 1339 (Fla. 1st Dist. Ct. App. 1980).

It has been held that school board members are county officers for § 7 purposes. *See In re Advisory Opinion to Governor—School Board Member—Suspension Authority*, 626 So. 2d 684 (Fla. 1993). The governor's suspension power also applies to members of constitutional commissions, see *In re Advisory Opinion to the Governor*, 52 So. 2d 646 (Fla. 1951), and special districts. *See, e.g.,* Fla. Att'y Gen. Op. 2011–12 (hospital district board member).

Sec. 7(a) expressly excludes state officers who are subject to impeachment (see Ch. 13 of this book) as well as active duty military officers. Although legislators are not mentioned, they also are excluded due to Art. III, § 4(d) (see Ch. 13 of this book).

To suspend a state, militia, or county officer, the governor must file with the custodian of state records (*i.e.*, the secretary of state) an executive order specifying at least one of the seven grounds listed in § 7(a): "malfeasance, misfeasance, neglect of duty, drunkenness, incompetence, permanent inability to perform official duties, or commission of a felony." In *Fair v. Kirk*, 317 F. Supp. 12 (N.D. Fla. 1970), *aff'd*, 401 U.S. 928, *reh'g denied*, 403 U.S. 941 (1971), a federal constitutional challenge to these grounds was rejected. For an example of a recent suspension order, see https://www.flgov.com/wp-content/uploads/orders/2019/EO_19-19.pdf (2019 order suspending Palm Beach County Supervisor of Elections Susan Bucher for incompetence, misfeasance, and neglect of duty).

The governor's suspension power is much more limited when it comes to municipal officers. Under paragraph (c), they can be suspended only if they are indicted for a crime. This nevertheless represents an expansion of the governor's power—under prior constitutions, governors had no power to suspend municipal officers. *See In re Opinion of the Justices*, 163 So. 410 (Fla. 1935). For a recent example of such a suspension order, see https://www.flgov.com/wp-content/uploads/orders/2019/EO_19-48.pdf (2019 order suspending Port Richey Mayor Dale Massad following his arrest on various charges, including attempted murder).

Where an officer is acting as both a county and a city officer, he or she is treated as a county officer for suspension purposes. *See In re Advisory Opinion to the Governor Request of July 12, 1976*, 336 So. 2d 97 (Fla. 1976).

When the governor suspends a state, militia, or county officer, he or she is authorized to name a replacement, who serves "for the period of suspension." Art. IV, § 7(a). When the governor suspends a municipal officer, however, he or she can name a replacement only if the power to do so is not "vested elsewhere by law or the municipal charter." Art. IV, § 7(c).

As new facts come to light (or previous facts are reassessed), the governor is permitted to add further grounds to the suspension order. *See Bass v. Askew*, 342 So. 2d 145 (Fla. 1st Dist. Ct. App. 1977). By the same token, the governor can lift the suspension and reinstate the officer. *See State ex rel. Hatton v. Joughin*, 138 So. 392 (Fla. 1931) (en banc), *reh'g denied*, 145 So. 174 (Fla. 1933) (en banc).

Suspended officers are tried by the senate. *See* Art. IV, § 7(b). *See also* Fla. Stat. §§ 112.40–112.52. Such trials result in either the removal or the reinstatement of the officer. If the officer is reinstated, he or she is entitled to back pay. *See Slaton v. Pizzi*, 163 So. 3d 655 (Fla. 3d Dist. Ct. App. 2015).

The courts have made it clear that suspensions and removals must be carried out in a manner that protects the officer's due process rights. *See Snipes v. Scott*, 2019 WL 163352 (N.D. Fla. 2019); *Israel v. DeSantis*, 269 So. 3d 491 (Fla. 2019). Referring a suspension case to a select committee, rather than the full senate, has been held not to violate due process. *See Sheffey v. Futch*, 250 So. 2d 907 (Fla. 4th Dist. Ct. App. 1971).

During his tenure as governor (2011–19), Rick Scott suspended 51 officers (an average of 6.4 suspensions per year). In his first year as governor (2019), Ron DeSantis suspended nine officers (four county, four municipal, and one district). *See* https://www.flgov.com/2019-executive-orders/.

(c) State Budget

In 1992, the Taxation and Budget Reform Commission recommended that Florida's budgeting process be overhauled. As a result, the last sentence of Art. IV, § 1(a) now makes the governor "the chief administrative officer of the state responsible for the planning and budgeting for the state." Accordingly, Art. III, § 19(a)(1) requires the governor to prepare a proposed budget each year. Likewise, Art. IV, § 13 requires the governor, working with other state officials, to address any deficits that occur during the year. Florida's budgeting process is described more fully in Ch. 20 of this book.

(d) "State of the State" Address

Art. IV, § 1(e) requires the governor "by message at least once in each regular session" to "inform the legislature concerning the condition of the state, propose such reorganization of the executive department as will promote efficiency and economy, and recommend measures in the public interest." This requirement originated with the 1838 constitution. The text of Gov. Ron DeSantis's 2019 "State of the State" address is available at https://www.flgov.com/2019/03/05/governor-desantis-state-of-the-state-address/.

Every state constitution requires the governor to give an annual address. For summaries of recent addresses, see https://www.nasbo.org/resources/state ofthestates. The federal constitution has a similar requirement. *See* Art. II, § 3, cl. 1 ("State of the Union"). Both governors and presidents use these occasions, which are extensively covered by the media, to lay out their legislative goals, explain their budget priorities, and push for specific action.

(e) Other Responsibilities

As discussed later in this chapter, Art. IV assigns additional duties to the governor (either independently or in conjunction with the cabinet). Other relevant sections (a few of which already have been discussed above) include:

1. Art. II, § 2, which gives the governor the power to temporarily move the seat of government. *See* Ch. 2 of this book.

2. Art. III, § 3(c)(1), which gives the governor the power to call the legislature into a special session. *See* Ch. 13 of this book.

3. Art. III, § 3(f), which gives the governor the power to adjourn the legislature if it becomes deadlocked. *See* Ch. 13 of this book.

4. Art. III, § 8, which gives the governor the power to veto legislation. *See* Ch. 13 of this book.

5. Art. III, § 16(a), which requires the governor to call the legislature into a special apportionment session if it fails to timely adopt a reapportionment plan. *See* Ch. 13 of this book.

6. Art. III, § 16(d), which requires the governor to call the legislature into an extraordinary apportionment session if its reapportionment plan is rejected by the Florida Supreme Court. *See* Ch. 13 of this book.

7. Art. III, § 17(c), which requires the governor to preside over impeachment trials of the chief justice of the Florida Supreme Court. *See* Ch. 13 of this book.

8. Art. III, § 19(a)(1), which requires the governor to annually prepare a proposed state budget. *See* Ch. 20 of this book.

9.   Art. V, § 11, which gives the governor the power to appoint justices and judges. *See* Ch. 15 of this book.

10. Art. V, § 12(a)(1)c. (judicial qualifications), Art. XI, § 2(a)(2) and (b) (constitution revision), and Art. XI, § 6(a)(1) (taxation and budget reform), which give the governor the power to appoint certain constitutional commissioners. *See* Chs. 15 and 23 of this book.

11. Art. IX, §§ 2 (state board of education), 7(c)–(d) (state university system), and 8(c) (state college system), which give the governor the power to appoint certain state education officials. *See* Ch. 18 of this book.

It should be noted that certain gubernatorial duties are specified only by statute. The signing of death warrants is a prime example. *See* Fla. Stat. § 922.052. For an example of a death warrant, see https://efactssc-public.flcourts.org/casedocuments/1960/71164/1960-71164_miscdoc_356641_e77.pdf (2019 death warrant of James Dailey).

2.   ADVISORY OPINIONS

Art. IV, § 1(c) allows the governor to request from the Florida Supreme Court an advisory opinion "as to the interpretation of any portion of this constitution upon any question affecting the governor's executive powers and duties." This power originated with the 1868 constitution and gives the governor a means for determining the scope of his or her authority. *See In the Matter of the Executive Communication of the 9th of November, A. D. 1868*, 12 Fla. 653 (1868).

It once was quite common for governors to request advisory opinions. Between 2000 and 2018, however, only six such requests were made. Each concerned the governor's power to fill vacancies. *See, e.g., Advisory Opinion to Governor re Judicial Vacancy Due to Resignation*, 42 So. 3d 795 (Fla. 2010). In 2019, Gov. Ron DeSantis requested an advisory opinion regarding the 2018 former felons' voting rights amendment (Art. VI, § 4(a)). *See* Ch. 3 of this book.

E. LIEUTENANT GOVERNOR

Art. IV, § 2 directs: "There shall be a lieutenant governor, who shall perform such duties pertaining to the office of governor as shall be assigned by the governor, except when otherwise provided by law, and such other duties as may be prescribed by law." As explained at the outset of this chapter, this provision was added by the 1968 constitution. Florida also had a lieutenant governor under the 1865 and 1868 constitutions. *See State ex rel. McQuaid v. County Commissioners of Duval County*, 3 So. 193 (Fla. 1887).

Florida is one of 45 states that has a lieutenant governor. In many states, the lieutenant governor has clearly-defined duties, the most common of which is presiding over the senate (28 states).

Neither the Florida Constitution nor the Florida Statutes assign any specific duties to the lieutenant governor. (The lieutenant governor was the president of the senate under both the 1865 and 1868 constitutions.) As a result, Florida governors typically place lieutenant governors in charge of specific policy issues; use them as legislative liaisons; and have them represent the state at official functions.

Fla. Stat. § 20.05(3) allows the governor to "assign the Lieutenant Governor, without Senate confirmation, the duty of serving as the head of any one department, the head of which is a secretary appointed by the Governor, notwithstanding any qualifications for appointment as secretary of the department." Until it was abolished in 1996, lieutenant governors frequently served as the head of the Florida Department of Commerce.

F. CABINET

1. COMPOSITION

Art. IV, § 4(a) provides: "There shall be a cabinet composed of an attorney general, a chief financial officer, and a commissioner of agriculture. In addition to the powers and duties specified herein, they shall exercise such powers and perform such duties as may be prescribed by law."

Florida's cabinet dates from the 1868 constitution, which provided for "a cabinet of administrative officers" appointed by the governor. Its eight members were the adjutant general, attorney general, commissioner of immigration, comptroller, secretary of state, superintendent of public instruction, surveyor-general, and treasurer. In 1870, these became elected offices. In 1871, as discussed above, the offices of the commissioner of immigration and the surveyor-general were merged and became the commissioner of lands and immigration.

The 1885 constitution authorized a six-member elected cabinet, consisting of the attorney general, comptroller, commissioner of agriculture, secretary of state, superintendent of public instruction, and treasurer. *See State ex rel. Russell v. Barnes*, 5 So. 698 (Fla. 1889). The 1968 constitution carried over this arrangement, but changed the superintendent of public instruction's title to "commissioner of education."

In 1978, the Constitution Revision Commission ("CRC") recommended that the cabinet be abolished to give the governor more power (and make it easier for the public to judge his or her performance). This proposal was defeated by a large margin.

In 1998, the CRC put forth a much more modest proposal. In addition to recommending that the commissioner of education and the secretary of state become gubernatorial appointees, it called for combining the comptroller and the treasurer into a single new office known as the chief financial officer. (The CRC had wanted to also make the commissioner of agriculture a gubernatorial appointee, but the state's farm interests objected.)

Following voter approval, the CRC's proposal took effect in 2003. As a result, the constitution now refers to the secretary of state as the "custodian of state records." To avoid deadlocks, the last sentence of § 4(a) provides: "In the event of a tie vote of the governor and cabinet, the side on which the governor voted shall be deemed to prevail."

Since 2015, Sen. Aaron Bean (R-Fernandina Beach) has been introducing legislation to again make the secretary of state an elected member of the cabinet, both to eliminate the possibility of ties and to reduce the governor's power when there is a tie.

No other state has an elected cabinet. Three states (Massachusetts, New Hampshire, and North Carolina), however, have elected executive councils that, in certain respects, resemble Florida's cabinet.

(a) Attorney General

Art. IV, § 4(b) makes the attorney general the state's chief legal officer. It also authorizes him or her to appoint the statewide prosecutor, who handles crimes that involve two or more judicial circuits. *See Scott v. State*, 102 So. 3d 676 (Fla. 5th Dist. Ct. App. 2012), *review denied*, 116 So. 3d 1263 (Fla. 2013). The position of statewide prosecutor was added to the constitution in 1986.

Also since 1986, Art. IV, § 10 has made the attorney general responsible for placing before the Florida Supreme Court citizen-initiated constitutional amendments. This duty is discussed further in Ch. 23 of this book.

The attorney general's other duties are codified in Fla. Stat. §§ 16.01–16.62. One of the attorney general's most important duties is spelled out in § 16.01(3):

> Notwithstanding any other provision of law, [the Attorney General] shall, on the written requisition of the Governor, a member of the Cabinet, the head of a department in the executive branch of state government, the Speaker of the House of Representatives, the President of the Senate, the Minority Leader of the House of Representatives, or the Minority Leader of the Senate, and may, upon the written requisition of a member of the Legislature, other state officer, or officer of a county, municipality, other unit of local government, or political subdivision, give an official opinion and legal advice in writing on any question of law relating to the official duties of the requesting officer.

Although attorney general opinions are not binding, they are highly persuasive and frequently are cited on issues that have not been judicially construed. They can be accessed at http://myflorida legal.com/opinions. Citations to them appear throughout this book ("Fla. Att'y Gen. Op.").

(b) Chief Financial Officer

Art. IV, § 4(c) makes the CFO the state's "chief fiscal officer" and orders him or her to "settle and approve accounts against the state . . . and . . . keep all state funds and securities." Additional duties are spelled out in Fla. Stat. §§ 17.001–17.68.

(c)   Commissioner of Agriculture

Art. IV, § 4(d) authorizes the COA to "supervis[e] matters pertaining to agriculture except as otherwise provided by law." Further duties are listed in Fla. Stat. §§ 19.12–19.54.

The COA more properly is known as the commissioner of agriculture and consumer services. This is because the COA is the head of the Florida Department of Agriculture and Consumer Services ("FDACS"). *See* Fla. Stat. § 20.14(1). In 1967, the legislature created the Office of Consumer Services and placed it under the COA. In 1969, the Florida Department of Agriculture was renamed the FDACS. Today, the FDACS's primary focus is consumer protection.

As part of their jobs, FDACS inspectors annually check Florida's 464,000 gas station fuel pumps to ensure they are accurate. An "approved" sticker is placed on all pumps that pass. In 2019, Nikki Fried, the newly-elected COA and the only Democrat in the cabinet, had new stickers printed up that featured her picture. Previous stickers had depicted just the department's logo. Republican lawmakers were so incensed by Fried's stickers (which they viewed as improper electioneering) that they passed a bill (S.B. 2502) that limits future stickers to "a combination of lettering, numbering, words, or the department logo." *See* Fla. Stat. § 525.07(1). Fried defended her stickers by saying, "[O]ur stickers have been placed up there so the consumers understand when they see fraud happening at the pump, they know exactly who to call."

2.   MEETINGS

The constitution does not specify how often the governor and the cabinet must meet. At one time, it was common for them to do so every two weeks. In recent years, they have met much less frequently: 15 times in 2014; 11 times in both 2016 and 2017; eight times in 2018; and 16 times in 2019.

3.   DUTIES

In addition to assigning them individual duties (as outlined above), the constitution gives the governor and the cabinet certain collective duties. These can be divided into two types: agency oversight and clemency.

(a)   Agency Oversight

Art. IV, § 4(e) makes the governor, the attorney general, and the CFO the State Board of Administration ("SBA"). The governor serves as the SBA's chair. *Id.* The SBA (https://www.sbafla.com/fsb/) was created in 1943 to provide investment services to Florida's state and local governments.

Art. IV, § 4(f) makes the governor and the cabinet the trustees of the internal improvement trust fund ("IITF") and the land acquisition trust fund ("LATF"). The governor serves as the chair of both funds. *Id.* The IITF (created 1855) and the LATF (created 1963) are discussed in Ch. 4 of this book. *See also* https://floridadep.gov/lands.

Art. IV, § 4(g) makes the governor and the cabinet the head of the Florida Department of Law

Enforcement (http://www.fdle.state.fl.us/) (created 1969). In 2018, § 4(g) was amended to require the department to include an Office of Domestic Security and Counterterrorism.

Lastly, Article IV, § 11 makes the governor and the cabinet the head of the Florida Department of Veterans' Affairs.

By statute, the governor and the cabinet also serve as the head of several other entities, including the Florida Department of Highway Safety and Motor Vehicles (see Fla. Stat. § 20.24(1)) and the Florida Department of Revenue (see Fla. Stat. § 20.21(1)).

(b) Clemency

Under Art. IV, § 8, the governor and the cabinet, sitting as the state's Executive Clemency Board, have the power to "grant full or conditional pardons, restore civil rights, commute punishment, and remit fines and forfeitures for offenses." When acting on his or her own, the governor can only "suspend collection of fines and forfeitures [and] grant reprieves not exceeding sixty days[.]" These matters are discussed further in Ch. 7 of this book.

G.　MECHANICS

1.　GOVERNOR

(a)　Qualifications

Art. IV, § 5(b) states: "When elected, the governor . . . must be an elector not less than thirty years of age who has resided in the state for the preceding seven years." All of Florida's previous constitutions have had similar requirements. Florida's provisions are typical of other states.

The requirements listed in § 5(b) are exclusive. As such, the legislature has no power to change them. *See Maloney v. Kirk*, 212 So. 2d 609 (Fla. 1968).

Art. II, § 1, cl. 5 of the U.S. Constitution requires the president to be 35, a 14-year resident of the country, and a natural born citizen.

(b) Disqualifications

Art. IV, § 5(b) prohibits a person "who has, or but for resignation would have, served as governor or acting governor for more than six years in two consecutive terms" from being "elected governor for the succeeding term." This provision is discussed in more detail later in this chapter.

The 22nd Amendment (ratified 1951) is stricter. It prohibits anyone from being elected president more than twice (or once, if the person has served as president or acting president for more than two years of a presidential term to which someone else was elected).

As noted in Ch. 13 of this book, both the Florida Constitution and the U.S. Constitution also contain general disqualification provisions that are applicable to all public offices.

(c) Elections

For many years, Florida held gubernatorial elections at the same time as presidential elections. In 1963, the dates of the former were changed so as not to conflict with the latter (thereby allowing voters to focus more closely on both races). *See* Art. IV, § 5(a) ("At a state-wide general election in each calendar year the number of which is even but not a multiple of four, the electors shall choose a governor. . . ."). Thus, while the next presidential election will be held in 2020, Florida's next gubernatorial election will occur in 2022.

In 1998, the constitution was changed to allow gubernatorial candidates to run in the primaries without a running mate. *See* Art. IV, § 5(a). In 2018, both Democrat Andrew Gillum and Republican Ron DeSantis named their running mates (respectively, Chris King and Jeanette Núñez) on Sept. 6, 2018, nine days after the gubernatorial primaries.

Nationally, 18 states (including Florida) allow gubernatorial candidates to pick their running mates after they have won the primary, while eight states hold separate primaries for the lieutenant governor. These 26 states then require gubernatorial and lieutenant gubernatorial candidates to run in the general election as a ticket. In 17 other states, lieutenant governors run by themselves in the general election. In the remaining two states that have lieutenant governors (Tennessee and West Virginia), there is no election because the position of lieutenant governor goes automatically to the senate president.

Florida gubernatorial candidates, much like presidential candidates, normally choose running mates who help "balance" the ticket. Most experts believe that doing so has no effect on an election's outcome. Indeed, it is rare for a lieutenant governor candidate to have much visibility. One exception is Sandra Mortham, who was tapped in 1997 by Jeb Bush (a full year before the election). Beleaguered by ethics investigations, Mortham withdrew from the ticket after just two months and later lost her secretary of state position to Katherine Harris.

Florida is one of 12 states that provides public financing to gubernatorial campaigns. *See* Art. VI, § 7. This provision is discussed in Ch. 3 of this book.

(d) Terms

Art. IV, § 5(a) sets the governor's term at four years. Every other Florida constitution has done likewise except for the 1861 constitution, which specified two-year terms. Currently, all but two states (New Hampshire and Vermont) have four-year gubernatorial terms.

Sec. 5(a) further provides that the terms of the "governor and [the] lieutenant governor and members of the cabinet [shall] begin[ ] on the first Tuesday after the first Monday in January of the succeeding year." *See also* Fla. Stat. § 100.041(1).

As noted earlier, Art. IV, § 5(b) limits the governor to two successive terms. Accordingly, Florida's governors must sit out one election cycle before seeking a third term. This requirement, which originated with the 1838 constitution, was omitted from the next three constitutions but was reinstated by the 1885 constitution.

In 1953, Gov. Daniel McCarty died nine months into his term. As a result, the Florida Supreme Court ordered a special election in 1954 to fill out his term. *See State ex rel. Ayres v. Gray*, 69 So. 2d 187 (Fla. 1953) (en banc). The winner was Sen. LeRoy Collins (D-Tallahassee). When Collins sought a full term in 1956, his eligibility was challenged because of the constitution's requirement that governors sit out one election after each term. In finding that Collins was eligible to run, the Florida Supreme Court wrote:

> Florida is committed to the general rule in this country that the right to hold office is a valuable one and should not be abridged except for unusual reason or by plain provision of law. We have no such provision and to interpolate one into the Constitution is contrary to every rule of constitutional interpretation.

Ervin v. Collins, 85 So. 2d 852, 858 (Fla. 1956) (en banc). As indicated above, the constitution now addresses this situation by making a partial term count as a full term only if it lasts at least two years.

Nationally, 14 states have no gubernatorial term limits; eight place a lifetime two-term limit on their governors, without regard to whether the terms are served separately or consecutively; one state requires its governors to sit out one election cycle after one term; 23 (including Florida) require their governors to sit out one election cycle after two consecutive terms; two limit their governors to eight years of service every 12 years; and two limit their governors to eight years of service every 16 years.

As explained earlier, the 22nd Amendment prohibits anyone from being elected president more than twice.

(e) Salary

Florida governors are paid $130,273 a year (32nd highest in the nation). Country-wide, gubernatorial salaries average $143,270 and range from a low of $70,000 (Maine) to a high of $201,680 (California). Since 2001, U.S. presidents have been paid $400,000 a year.

At $130,273, the governor is Florida's 1,168th highest paid public employee. The state's highest paid public employee currently is University of Florida football coach Dan Mullen ($6.07 million).

During his time in office (2011–19), Rick Scott refused to accept his salary, the only Florida governor ever to do so. With a net worth of $232 million, Scott also holds the distinction of being the richest governor in Florida's history.

(f) Office Location

Art. II, § 2 states: "The seat of government shall be the City of Tallahassee, in Leon County, where the offices of the governor, lieutenant governor, [and] cabinet members . . . shall be maintained. . . ." In addition to his main office in Tallahassee, Gov. Ron

DeSantis maintains "regional offices" in Jacksonville, Miami, Orlando, and Tampa.

(g) Vacancies

Art. IV, § 3 provides:

(a) Upon vacancy in the office of governor, the lieutenant governor shall become governor. Further succession to the office of governor shall be prescribed by law. A successor shall serve for the remainder of the term.

(b) Upon impeachment of the governor and until completion of trial thereof, or during the governor's physical or mental incapacity, the lieutenant governor shall act as governor. Further succession as acting governor shall be prescribed by law.

Fla. Stat. § 14.055 directs that if the governor's office becomes vacant and there is no lieutenant governor, the line of succession is: 1) the attorney general; 2) the CFO; 3) the COA; and, 4) a person chosen by the legislature. During earlier periods when the constitution did not provide for a lieutenant governor, the president of the senate was first in line, followed by the speaker of the house.

A vacancy in the office of the governor occurs when any of the conditions specified in Art. X, § 3 are met. *See* Ch. 2 of this book.

In some states (*e.g.*, California, Louisiana, Missouri), the governor's absence from the state automatically makes the lieutenant governor the acting governor. The Florida Constitution does not contain such a provision and the Florida Supreme Court has refused to read one into it. *See In re Advisory Opinion to the Governor*, 112 So. 2d 843 (Fla. 1959).

(h) Removals

The governor is one of the officers who can be removed by impeachment. *See* Art. III, § 17(a), discussed in Ch. 13 of this book.

Art. IV, § 3(b) allows the governor to be temporarily removed for mental or physical incapacity using an entirely different process:

> Incapacity to serve as governor may be determined by the supreme court upon due notice after docketing of a written suggestion thereof by three cabinet members, and in such case restoration of capacity shall be similarly determined after docketing of written suggestion thereof by the governor, the legislature or three cabinet members. Incapacity to serve as governor may also be established by certificate filed with the custodian of state records by the governor declaring incapacity for physical reasons to serve as governor, and in such case restoration of capacity shall be similarly established.

This provision, which applies only to the governor, was added by the 1968 constitution. It is modelled after the 25th Amendment (ratified 1967), which deals with presidential disability.

In 1998, as part of the restructuring of Florida's cabinet, the number of cabinet members needed to sign a notice of gubernatorial incapacity was reduced from four to three. This change makes the provision's use less likely. Previously, two-thirds of the cabinet's members had to sign off. Now, all do.

Florida's lone brush with gubernatorial mental incapacity is Gov. John Milton's decision to kill himself in the closing days of the Civil War. Contemporary reports describe Milton as having fallen into a deep depression prior to his death.

In 20 states, voters are permitted to "recall" governors prior to the expiration of their terms. In 2003, for example, California Gov. Gray Davis was recalled after he proved ineffective in handling the state's budget and electricity crises. He was replaced by movie star Arnold Schwarzenegger. There is no provision in Florida law for recalling governors.

2.   LIEUTENANT GOVERNOR

With only a few exceptions, the mechanics applicable to the governor, discussed above, also apply to the lieutenant governor, who is paid $124,851 a year. As explained in Ch. 2 of this book, a 2019 law allows the lieutenant governor to have his or her personal office in a city other than Tallahassee.

When the lieutenant governor's office was revived in 1968, no term limits were imposed. In 1992, a citizens' initiative petition proposed that multiple offices, including the lieutenant governor, be term limited. *See Advisory Opinion to the Attorney*

General—Limited Political Terms in Certain Elective Offices, 592 So. 2d 225 (Fla. 1991). As a result, Art. VI, § 4(c)(3) now limits the lieutenant governor to two terms, after which he or she must sit out one election cycle.

Another notable difference concerns vacancies. If the office of lieutenant governor becomes vacant, the governor appoints a replacement pursuant to Art. IV, § 1(f). Fla. Stat. § 14.055 adds an interesting gloss:

> [I]f after the appointment [of a lieutenant governor by the governor] a vacancy occurs in the office of Governor with more than 28 months remaining in the term, at the next statewide general election the electors shall choose a Governor and Lieutenant Governor to fill the remainder of the term in the manner provided in § 5, Art. IV of the State Constitution.

There is no fixed time in which the governor must fill a vacancy in the lieutenant governor's office. When Jennifer Carroll resigned as lieutenant governor in 2013 due to a gambling scandal, Gov. Rick Scott took nearly a year to replace her.

3. CABINET

The mechanics applicable to the governor, discussed above, generally also apply to the cabinet. However, Art. IV, § 5(b) adds: "The attorney general must have been a member of the bar of Florida for the preceding five years." The 1992 change that limits lieutenant governors to two consecutive terms, after which they must sit out a term, also applies to cabinet members. *See* Art. VI, § 4(c)(4). Cabinet members are paid $128,972 a year.

The constitution does not directly address cabinet vacancies. As a result, they are filled by the governor pursuant to Art. IV, § 1(f) (discussed above). In 2017, for example, Gov. Rick Scott appointed Jimmy Patronis to be the state's new CFO after Jeff Atwater resigned to become the new CFO of Florida Atlantic University.

Fla. Stat. § 16.02 (enacted 1845) adds: "In case of the disability of the Attorney General to perform any official duty devolving on him or her, by reason of interest or otherwise, the Governor or Attorney General of this state may appoint another person to perform such duty in the Attorney General's stead."

H. EXECUTIVE DEPARTMENTS

Art. IV, § 6 provides:

All functions of the executive branch of state government shall be allotted among not more than twenty-five departments, exclusive of those specifically provided for or authorized in this constitution. The administration of each department, unless otherwise provided in this constitution, shall be placed by law under the direct supervision of the governor, the lieutenant governor, the governor and cabinet, a cabinet member, or an officer or board appointed by and serving at the pleasure of the governor, except:

(a)   When provided by law, confirmation by the senate or the approval of three members of the cabinet shall be required for appointment to or removal from any designated statutory office.

(b)   Boards authorized to grant and revoke licenses to engage in regulated occupations shall be assigned to appropriate departments and their members appointed for fixed terms, subject to removal only for cause.

In 1943, the Florida Legislature created a Special Joint Economy and Efficiency Committee. Its 343-page report, released in 1945, was highly critical of Florida's government structure and called for consolidating the state's 123 agencies into 23 (instead, nearly 40 new ones were created over the next 25 years). Other critics included two University of Florida researchers, who recommended that Florida limit the number of its executive departments to 25. *See* Manning J. Dauer & William C. Havard, "The Florida Constitution of 1885—A Critique," 8 *U. Fla. L. Rev.* 1 (1955). Their suggestion became the basis for the cap in Art. IV, § 6.

To implement the 1968 constitution's cap, the legislature in 1969 passed a comprehensive reorganization act. *See* Fla. Stat. §§ 20.02–20.04. As a result, some 200 entities were either eliminated or consolidated into just 22 departments.

In 1988, the constitution was amended to authorize the creation of a Department of Elderly Affairs ("DEA") and a Department of Veterans' Affairs ("DVA") without having either count against the cap. *See* Fla. Const. Art. IV, §§ 11 (DVA) and 12 (DEA). In 1989, the legislature created the DVA. In 1991, it created the DEA. In 1995, it directed the DEA to use the word "Elder" instead of the word "Elderly" in its name. In 2018, Art. IV, § 11 was amended to make the DVA's existence permanent.

Florida currently has 23 executive departments. For the state's organizational chart, see http://www.oppaga.state.fl.us/government/storgchart.aspx. *See also* Fla. Stat. §§ 20.02–20.605.

CHAPTER 15
JUDICIARY

A. OVERVIEW

Art. V describes Florida's judiciary. The job of the judiciary is to interpret the state's laws. Pursuant to Art. II, § 3, the judiciary is one of the three branches of Florida's state government.

B. HISTORY

1. PRE-STATEHOOD

During Spain's first occupation of Florida (1513–1763), legal matters were handled by the governor, a military officer who lacked legal training. Although appeals were supposed to be heard in either Havana or Santo Domingo, most went directly to the Council of the Indies, the royal body in Madrid responsible for Spain's New World holdings.

Upon taking control of Florida (1763), the British, following their usual overseas practice, set up chancery courts for equity cases; common pleas courts for civil cases; general sessions courts for criminal cases; and vice-admiralty courts for maritime cases. Appeals were heard by the Privy Council in London.

The British courts were not retained when Spain regained control of Florida (1783). Instead, the Spanish again relied on their military governors, who sometimes received assistance from a law-trained advisor known as an "asesor." As before, appeals were supposed to go to Havana or Santo Domingo but normally were heard in Madrid.

In the U.S. territorial period (1821–45), Florida's principal courts were the superior courts. Located in Apalachicola, Key West, Pensacola, St. Augustine, and Tallahassee, each was allotted one judge appointed by the president. In 1824, appeals began to be heard by the territory's court of appeals, which was staffed by the superior courts' judges. While decisions involving federal law could be appealed to the U.S. Supreme Court, decisions involving territorial law were final.

Minor cases were heard by the county courts, whose judges were jointly appointed by the governor and the territorial council. Attached to each county court were justices of the peace. Some cities had their own courts, although their jurisdiction was largely limited to municipal ordinance offenses.

2. STATEHOOD TO 1972

When Florida became a state in 1845, the 1838 constitution went into effect. Its Art. V authorized a supreme court and three types of trial courts: chancery, circuit, and corporation.

For unknown reasons, neither the chancery courts nor the corporation courts were set up. As a result, cases pending in either the county courts or the superior courts were transferred to the new circuit courts, while cases pending in the court of appeals were transferred to the new supreme court. *See Stewart v. Preston*, 1 Fla. 1 (1846).

Cases involving federal law were transferred to the new U.S. District Court for the District of Florida. *See* 5 Stat. 788. Since 1962, Florida has had three federal district courts—designated Northern, Middle, and Southern—which sit, respectively, in Tallahassee, Orlando, and Miami. *See* 28 U.S.C. § 89. Until 1981, appeals from these courts were heard by the U.S. Court of Appeals for the Fifth Circuit in New Orleans. They now go to the U.S. Court of Appeals for the Eleventh Circuit in Atlanta. *See* 28 U.S.C. § 41.

Florida's 1861 and 1865 constitutions made no changes in Art. V, although the 1861 constitution did create specialized slave courts. In contrast, both the 1868 and 1885 constitutions made numerous changes to Art. V. Eventually, Florida found itself with more types of courts than any other state except New York.

By 1966, it was clear that Art. V needed to be entirely rewritten. Parochial concerns, however, repeatedly got in the way. Thus, when the 1968 constitution was placed before the public, Art. V was not ready and therefore was omitted.

In 1970, the legislature finally agreed on a new Art. V. The voters, however, rejected it because it did not go far enough. On Mar. 14, 1972, a much more comprehensive proposal passed by a vote of 933,221 to 390,223.

New Art. V went into effect on Jan. 1, 1973. *See* Art. V, § 20(j). When it did, 14 different types of courts were reduced to four. The county courts of record and the juvenile courts, for example, were merged into the circuit courts, see Art. V, § 20(d)(2);

the claims courts, justice of the peace courts, magistrates' courts, small claims courts, and small claims magistrates' courts were merged into the county courts, see Art. V, § 20(c)(4); and the county judges' courts were divided between the circuit courts and the county courts. *Id.*

A temporary exception was made for the municipal courts, which were permitted to keep operating until Jan. 3, 1977. At that time, they were merged into the county courts. *See* Art. V, § 20(d)(4).

3. CHANGES SINCE 1972

Since 1972, 16 amendments have appeared on the ballot proposing further changes to Art. V. Of these, 12 have passed. Most have been minor and non-controversial. Three, however, have been bitterly partisan.

In 2012, the legislature, upset that the supreme court's liberal members were blocking its agenda, placed on the ballot an amendment: 1) requiring justices to be confirmed by the senate; 2) making it easier for the legislature to repeal the supreme court's rules; 3) prohibiting the supreme court from readopting repealed rules except as directed by the legislature; and, 4) requiring judicial conduct investigators to divulge confidential information to the legislature. This proposal was rejected by a wide margin.

In 2014, the legislature, seeking to tilt the courts to the right, proposed an amendment allowing judicial vacancies to be filled "prospectively." This rather naked power grab was designed to ensure that Gov. Rick Scott (R), and not his successor (potentially a Democrat), would fill three supreme court seats scheduled to become vacant in 2019 (when, because of term limits, Scott also would be leaving office). This proposal was narrowly defeated.

(When Scott subsequently issued an executive order giving himself the right to make the appointments, the supreme court stopped him. *See League of Women Voters of Florida v. Scott*, 257 So. 3d 900 (Fla. 2018). As a result, Ron DeSantis, Scott's Republican successor, made the picks. In Jan. 2019, he chose three South Florida conservatives: Barbara Lagoa, Robert Luck, and Carlos Muñiz. With these appointments, the Florida Supreme Court was left with no liberal members.)

The third amendment, having to do with administrative agencies, passed.

As in most states, Florida's courts traditionally had deferred to administrative agencies regarding silent or ambiguous statutory provisions, so long as the agency's interpretation was reasonable and the statute was within the agency's jurisdiction. *See, e.g., Headley v. City of Miami, Florida*, 215 So. 3d 1 (Fla. 2017). Such deference often is called "*Chevron* deference," due to *Chevron U.S.A., Inc. v. Natural Resources Defense Council, Inc.*, 467 U.S. 837, *reh'g denied*, 468 U.S. 1227 (1984).

Convinced that *Chevron* deference gives too much power to administrative agencies, the 2018 Constitution Revision Commission persuaded voters to add the following language to the constitution: "In interpreting a state statute or rule, a state court or an officer hearing an administrative action pursuant to general law may not defer to an administrative agency's interpretation of such statute or rule, and must instead interpret such statute or rule de novo." *See* Art. V, § 21.

The amendment significantly changes Florida law. In *Kanter Real Estate, LLC v. Department of Environmental Protection*, 267 So. 3d 483 (Fla. 1st Dist. Ct. App.), *review dismissed*, 2019 WL 2428577 (Fla. 2019), the court, after acknowledging this fact, conducted its own inquiry and, disagreeing with the department, granted the plaintiff a permit to drill for oil in the Everglades.

C.   STRUCTURE

Art. V, § 1 arranges Florida's courts into a four-level pyramid. *See* https://www.flcourts.org/Florida-Courts. At the top is the supreme court. Below it, in descending order, are the district courts of appeal, circuit courts, and county courts. The supreme court and the district courts serve as the state's appellate courts, while the circuit courts and the county courts are its trial courts.

Sec. 1 prohibits the creation of other courts (to prevent the system from re-fragmenting). *See* *Simmons v. Faust*, 358 So. 2d 1358 (Fla. 1978). There are, however, three exceptions (all are discussed later in this chapter):

1) "Commissions established by law, or administrative officers or bodies[,] may be granted quasi-judicial power in matters connected with the functions of their offices." This provision was included in the 1972 overhaul.

2) "The legislature may establish by general law a civil traffic hearing officer system for the purpose of hearing civil traffic infractions." This provision was added in 1988.

3) "The legislature may, by general law, authorize a military court-martial to be conducted by military judges of the Florida National Guard, with direct appeal of a decision to the District Court of Appeal, First District." This provision was added in 1998.

D. FUNDING

When it was passed in 1972, Art. V, § 14 provided: "All justices and judges shall be compensated only by state salaries fixed by general law. The judiciary shall have no power to fix appropriations." Prior to 1972, some counties had supplemented judicial salaries, a practice prohibited by the first sentence. The second sentence was added to make it clear that judges cannot force the legislature to increase court funding.

In 1998, the section's first sentence became the first sentence of new paragraph (a), while the second sentence became the sole sentence of new paragraph (d). In-between these two sentences were inserted new paragraphs (b) and (c) (paragraph (a) also received additional language). These changes require:

1) The state to pay for the "courts system, state attorneys' offices, public defenders' officers, and court-appointed counsel."

2) The circuit clerks' offices to be funded through fees and fines, with the state making up any shortfall.

3) The counties to provide "facilities for the trial courts, public defenders' offices, state attorneys' offices, and the offices of the clerks of the circuit and county courts" and cover the "reasonable and necessary salaries, costs, and expenses of the state courts system to meet local requirements as determined by general law."

Prior to these changes, there had been a long-running dispute between the state and the counties as to who should pay for the trial courts (the state already was paying for the appellate courts). With the proposal's passage (following a vigorous get-out-the-vote campaign by the Florida Association of Counties), nearly $250 million in costs that had been shouldered by the counties was transferred to the state.

Sec. 14 is implemented by Fla. Stat. §§ 29.001–29.23. In 2018, Florida spent $2.78 billion on its court system. Of this amount, $1.45 billion (53%) came from the state, $901 million (32%) came from the counties, and $425 million (15%) came from litigants.

Despite the changes to § 14, Florida's court system remains woefully underfunded. In recent years, the problem has been exacerbated by the state using the surpluses generated by the circuit clerks (roughly $300 million a year) for non-court purposes. *See Crist v. Ervin*, 56 So. 3d 745 (Fla. 2010); *Florida Department of Revenue v. Forman*, 273 So. 3d 223 (Fla. 1st Dist. Ct. App.), *review denied*, 2019 WL 6319451 (Fla. 2019). Much of this surplus comes from the $1 billion in fees, fines, and penalties the courts annually impose on defendants. Because these amounts fall disproportionately on the poor (see Chs. 3 and 7 of this book), critics have accused Florida of engaging in "cash register justice."

E.   SUPREME COURT

1.   BASICS

Art. V, § 1 requires there to be "a supreme court," while Art. II, § 2 headquarters it at the seat of government (Tallahassee). A 2019 law, however, allows justices to keep a remote office in their home districts. *See* Fla. Stat. § 25.025 (making permanent a similar 2018 law). Most of the justices have availed themselves of this option and now travel to Tallahassee only to hear oral arguments and participate in court deliberations.

Art. V, § 3(a) provides that "[f]ive justices shall constitute a quorum" and "[t]he concurrence of four justices shall be necessary to a decision." It further provides that in the event of a recusal "for cause," lower court judges may be assigned to "temporary duty." The court fills recusals by calling up the chief judges of the district courts "on a rotating basis from the lowest numbered court to the highest ... repeating continuously." *See* Fla. Sup. Ct. Internal Op. R. § X.D. Temporary justices are known as "associate justices." *Id.*

Like many state supreme courts, the Florida Supreme Court has its own seal, which depicts Themis, the Greek goddess of justice. Above her is the court's motto in Latin: Sat Cito Si Recte ("Soon enough if done rightly"). For a further look at the court, see its web site: https://www.floridasupreme court.org/.

2. PERSONNEL

(a) Justices

Art. V, § 3(a) sets the supreme court's size at seven justices. This is the number used by most state supreme courts (five, however, have nine justices, while 16 have five justices).

From 1845 to 1851, Florida's four circuit court judges (elected by the legislature) acted as the supreme court. Beginning in 1852, the court was allotted three justices of its own. Subsequently, this number was changed to six (1902), then five (1911), then six again (1923), and finally seven (1940). Except for the chief justice, each justice is called "justice."

In 1927, when the court had six justices, the legislature authorized it to sit either together (*i.e.*, en banc) or in three-member divisions (designated "A" and "B"). In 1940, when the court's size was increased to seven, the chief justice was made a member of both divisions. The court has been prohibited from sitting in divisions since the creation of the district courts (1957).

Art. V, § 3(a) provides: "Of the seven justices, each appellate district shall have at least one justice elected or appointed from the district to the supreme court who is a resident of the district at the time of the original appointment or election." This requirement, adopted in 1976, ensures geographical balance.

Every two years, the court chooses a new chief justice. This highly unusual procedure is partially dictated by Art. V, § 2(b): "The chief justice of the supreme court shall be chosen by a majority of the members of the court."

Prior to the 1885 constitution, the chief justice was popularly elected. The 1885 constitution directed the justices to instead draw lots. This was accomplished by passing around a bible, or a brand-new law book, and having each justice open it to a random page. The justice whose page had the highest last digit, or whose first word began with the letter closest to "Z," was declared the winner.

According to a frequently repeated tale, in 1915 Justice William Ellis was in the lead with a "7" with only Justice Fenwick Taylor, the court's most senior member, still needing to cut. Taylor took the book, opened it, announced he had a "9," and then shut it before anyone could verify his claim. When he was asked why he had not challenged Taylor, Ellis replied: "I couldn't question the honesty of my father-in-law and the Dean of the Court."

A 1926 amendment substituted elections by the justices. This change marked the start of the court's biennial rotations. Traditionally, the most senior justice who has not yet served a term as chief justice is elected. Recently, however, this custom has not been followed. In Feb. 2016, Chief Justice Jorge Labarga was elected to a second consecutive term. In Mar. 2018, Justice Charles Canady was elected to a second non-consecutive term. In Oct. 2019, he was elected to a second consecutive term.

Pursuant to Art. V, § 2(b), the chief justice serves as the "chief administrative officer" of the courts. Since 1972, the chief justice has been assisted in this role by the Office of the State Courts Administrator (https://www.flcourts.org/Administration-Funding/Court-Administration-About-Us).

Under § 2(b), the chief justice has "the power to assign justices or judges, including consenting retired justices or judges, to temporary duty in any court for which the judge is qualified and to delegate to a chief judge of a judicial circuit the power to assign judges for duty in that circuit." For examples of such assignments, see *Physicians Healthcare Plans, Inc. v. Pfeifler*, 846 So. 2d 1129 (Fla. 2003) (retired judges used to help clear circuit court's docket); *Gore v. State*, 706 So. 2d 1328 (Fla. 1997) (county court judge allowed to hear circuit court cases).

Supreme court justices are paid $220,600 a year (fifth highest in the nation). As explained later in this chapter, they serve six-year terms, which are renewable, and must retire at 75.

(b) Clerk and Marshal

Art. V, § 3(c) requires the supreme court to appoint both a clerk and a marshal. The former handles the court's paperwork, while the latter is responsible for its security and serves process. For a further description of these offices, see the court's web site. *See also* Fla. Stat. §§ 25.241 (clerk) and 25.251 (marshal).

3.   JURISDICTION

Florida's 1838 constitution defined the supreme court's jurisdiction as follows:

> The Supreme Court, except in cases otherwise directed in this Constitution, shall have appellate jurisdiction only . . . provided that the said Court shall always have power to issue writs of injunction, mandamus, quo warranto, habeas corpus, and such other remedial and original writs as may be necessary to give it a general superintendence and control of all other Courts.

The 1861, 1865, 1868, and 1885 constitutions carried this language forward with only modest changes.

The court's jurisdiction began to change in 1957 with the creation of the district courts of appeal. Further changes were made in 1972 and 1980. All have been designed to limit the number of cases the court can hear. *See Wells v. State*, 132 So. 3d 1110 (Fla. 2014). As a result, the court now always includes a jurisdictional citation in its opening paragraph. A typical example can be found in *Allen v. State*, 261 So. 3d 1255 (Fla. 2019):

> Margaret Allen, a prisoner under sentence of death, appeals an order denying her motion for postconviction relief filed under Florida Rule of Criminal Procedure 3.851. We have jurisdiction. *See* art. V, § 3(b)(1), Fla. Const. For the reasons that follow, we affirm the circuit court's order denying Allen's motion for postconviction relief.

Id. at 1264.

A good sense of the court's jurisdiction can be gleaned from its 2018 docket. During that year, it added 2,161 new matters: 89 mandatory appeals (4.1%); 811 discretionary appeals (37.5%); 66 certified cases (3.1%); and 783 writ requests (36.2%). Of the remaining 412 matters (19.1%), nearly all (384) involved the court's supervisory responsibilities (*e.g.*, attorney suspension and disbarment petitions; bar applications; judicial conduct reviews; and rule changes).

(a) Mandatory Appeals

Pursuant to Art. V, § 3(b)(1), the supreme court must hear appeals from "final judgments of trial courts imposing the death penalty" or "decisions of district courts of appeal declaring invalid a state statute or a provision of the state constitution."

Similarly, Art. V, § 3(b)(2) requires the court to hear appeals from "[trial court] proceedings for the validation of bonds or certificates of indebtedness" or "action[s] of statewide agencies relating to rates or service of utilities providing electric, gas, or telephone service." At present, the only agency in Florida that has statewide authority over utilities is the Public Service Commission ("PSC") (http://www.psc.state.fl.us/).

The difference between paragraphs (b)(1) and (b)(2) is a small one. While the former is self-executing, the latter is not due to its opening qualifier: "When provided by general law. . . ." The legislature, however, has passed laws implementing paragraph (b)(2). *See* Fla. Stat. §§ 75.08 (bonds) and 350.128(1) (PSC).

As indicated above, the court docketed 89 mandatory appeals in 2018. These were distributed as follows: bond validation: one (1.1%); constitutional invalidity: 16 (18.0%); death penalty: 66 (74.2%); PSC: six (6.7%)

In only one instance (constitutional invalidity) does a mandatory appeal reach the supreme court by way of a district court. In the others, the appeal skips over the district court and arrives either from a circuit court (bond validation and death penalty) or an administrative agency (PSC).

(b) Discretionary Appeals

Under Art. V, § 3(b)(3), the supreme court can hear an appeal from a district court if the latter's decision

[1] expressly declares valid a state statute, or . . . [2] expressly construes a provision of the state or federal constitution, or . . . [3] expressly affects a class of constitutional or state officers, or . . . [4] expressly and directly conflicts with a decision of another district court of appeal or of the supreme court on the same question of law.

It is uncommon for the court to hear an appeal on the first, second, or third grounds. In 2018, for example, the court granted 811 discretionary appeals. Of these, six (0.7%) were for "statutory validity," 13 (1.6%) were for "constitutional construction," and six (0.7%) were for "class of officers." In contrast, 786 (96.9%) were for "direct conflict."

While the "statutory validity" and "constitutional construction" categories are self-explanatory and have caused little difficulty in practice, the "class of officers" category requires a word. Merely being a constitutional or state officer is not enough. Instead, the issue must affect the entire class. In *Spradley v. State*, 293 So. 2d 697 (Fla. 1974), the court explained:

A decision which "affects a class of constitutional or state officers" [is] one which . . . generally affects the entire class in some way unrelated to the specific facts of that case.

In the instant case, . . . any decision as to [the] possible non-compliance with [the] discovery rules by [Assistant State Attorney Jerry Stillson] did not affect any class of constitutional or state officers in any general way unrelated to the specific facts of this case. The decision affected only the rights of the parties directly involved. . . .

Id. at 701–02.

For cases in which an entire class of officers *was* affected, see, e.g., *Public Defender, Eleventh Judicial Circuit of Florida v. State*, 115 So. 3d 261 (Fla. 2013) (working conditions); *School Board of Palm Beach County v. Survivors Charter Schools, Inc.*, 3 So. 3d 1220 (Fla. 2009) (termination procedures).

That nearly all discretionary appeals granted review involve conflicts between district courts is attributable to the fact that no other mechanism exists for resolving such conflicts. In exercising its power, however, the supreme court has hewed closely to the requirements set out in the constitution: 1) the conflict must be express and direct (*i.e.*, it must be apparent when reading the majority opinion); 2) the conflict must be between two different district courts (*i.e.*, a conflict between two different panels of the same district court is not enough); and, 3) the conflict must be on the same question of law (*i.e.*, a conflict involving a question of fact is insufficient). *See Lee v. State*, 258 So. 3d 1297 (Fla.), *reh'g denied*, 2018 WL 6787405 (Fla. 2018); *Miles v. Weingrad*, 164 So. 3d 1208 (Fla. 2015); *Wallace v. Dean*, 3 So. 3d 1035 (Fla. 2009).

As noted above, a direct conflict also can exist between a district court's opinion and supreme court precedent. *See, e.g., Limones v. School District of Lee County*, 161 So. 3d 384 (Fla. 2015); *DK Arena, Inc. v. EB Acquisitions I, LLC*, 112 So. 3d 85 (Fla. 2013). For obvious reasons, such conflicts are relatively rare.

(c) Certified Cases

In certain instances, the constitution gives the supreme court the ability (but not the duty) to review "certified" cases:

(4)   May review any decision of a district court of appeal that passes upon a question certified by it to be of great public importance, or that is certified by it to be in direct conflict with a decision of another district court of appeal.

(5)   May review any order or judgment of a trial court certified by the district court of appeal in which an appeal is pending to be of great public importance, or to have a great effect on the proper administration of justice throughout the state, and certified to require immediate resolution by the supreme court.

(6)   May review a question of law certified by the Supreme Court of the United States or a United States Court of Appeals which is determinative of the cause and for which there is no controlling precedent of the supreme court of Florida.

Art. V, § 3(b)(4)–(6).

As can be seen, paragraph (b)(4) allows a district court to either ask the supreme court a specific question (if it is one "of great public importance") or to certify that its decision conflicts with the decision of another district court. In both instances, the district court already has ruled and is merely inviting the supreme court to review its decision. While the supreme court normally accepts such invitations, it does not have to and will decline if it finds that review is unnecessary. *See, e.g., Novack v. Novack*, 195 So. 2d 199, 200 (Fla. 1967) ("We have carefully considered the matters presented and have determined that a decision of this Court in these cases is neither justified nor required.").

Paragraph (b)(5) is quite different. It is invoked by the district court *before* it has heard the case, and asks the supreme court to accept immediate jurisdiction. This is done when the district court believes that the issues are critical and time is of the essence.

In the aftermath of the disputed 2000 presidential election, the district courts routinely utilized this "pass through" procedure. *See, e.g., Palm Beach County Canvassing Board v. Harris*, 772 So. 2d 1220 (Fla.), *cert. granted in part sub nom. Bush v. Palm Beach County Canvassing Board*, 531 U.S. 1004, *vacated, Bush v. Gore*, 531 U.S. 70 (2000). For more recent examples, see *Israel v. DeSantis*, 269 So. 3d 491 (Fla. 2019) (suspension of county sheriff by the governor); *Department of State v. Hollander*, 256 So. 3d 1300 (Fla. 2018) (removal of constitutional amendment from the ballot). Once again, the supreme court is under no obligation to accept the invitation. *See, e.g., Shaw v. Shaw*, 2014 WL 4403366, at *1 (Fla. 2014) ("Having reviewed the Second District's certification, as well as the dissenting opinion of Judge Altenbernd, we decline at this time to accept jurisdiction of the appeal under article V, section 3(b)(5). . . .").

Lastly, paragraph (b)(6), added in 1980, allows the supreme court to answer questions received from federal appellate courts. To invoke this procedure, four requirements must be met: 1) the question must be a question of law; 2) the inquiring court must be either the U.S. Supreme Court or a federal court of appeal; 3) the issue must be "determinative of the cause," meaning that the answer will resolve the case; and, 4) there cannot be a controlling Florida Supreme Court precedent.

This provision owes its existence to *Erie Railroad Co. v. Tompkins*, 304 U.S. 64 (1938). *Erie* held that federal courts sitting in diversity had to apply state law rather than federal common law. Anticipating that this change would cause federal courts to seek help on unsettled issues of state law, the Florida Legislature in 1945 passed a statute authorizing the Florida Supreme Court to provide answers. *See* 1945 Fla. Laws ch. 23098, § 1 (codified as Fla. Stat. § 25.031). Florida was the first state to have such a law; every state except North Carolina now has such a provision.

The procedure was used for the first time in *Sun Insurance Office, Ltd. v. Clay*, 133 So. 2d 735 (Fla. 1961). Since then, the Florida Supreme Court has received more than 125 requests (nearly all from the 11th Circuit). On very rare occasions, it has found a request to be improper. *See, e.g., Greene v. Massey,* 384 So. 2d 24, 27–28 (Fla. 1980) ("We have already stated that the decision of the District Court of Appeal, Second District, constitutes the law of the case. Since under the circumstances a response to the question posed would not be 'determinative of the cause,' we decline to undertake an academic discussion of the significance of a reversal 'in the interests of justice.'").

It is, of course, regrettable that paragraph (b)(6) is limited to federal appellate courts. Many states permit questions from federal district courts as well as other state supreme courts. A few (*e.g.,* Delaware, New Mexico, Oklahoma) go further and authorize them from tribal courts as well as from foreign country courts.

(d) Writs

Art. V, § 3(b)(7)–(9) grants the supreme court the power to issue four extraordinary writs (habeas corpus, mandamus, prohibition, and quo warranto), as well as "all writs necessary to the complete exercise of its jurisdiction."

A writ is a command from a court. In 2018, the Florida Supreme Court received 783 writ requests: 389 (49.7%) for habeas corpus; 245 (31.3%) for mandamus; 63 (8.0%) for prohibition; 33 (4.2%) for quo warranto; and 51 (6.5%) involving its "all writs" jurisdiction. It also received two coram nobis petitions, a common law writ used to correct factual errors. *See Wood v. State*, 750 So. 2d 592 (Fla. 1999).

The writ of habeas corpus is discussed in Ch. 7 of this book.

The writ of mandamus ("we order"), which can be directed to any state agency or officer, orders the respondent to perform a specific act. It may be used only when the respondent has failed or refused to do an act required by law (*i.e.*, a "ministerial act"). A mandamus action cannot involve a discretionary act or be used to establish a party's rights. *See Huffman v. State*, 813 So. 2d 10, 11 (Fla. 2000) ("[T]o be entitled to a writ of mandamus the petitioner must have a clear legal right to the requested relief, the respondent must have an indisputable legal duty to perform the requested action, and the petitioner must have no other adequate remedy available.").

The writ of prohibition bars a lower court from engaging in specific conduct. Such writs are issued by a superior court upon a showing that the lower court is "acting outside its jurisdiction." *Mandico v. Taos Construction, Inc.*, 605 So. 2d 850, 853 (Fla. 1992). As *Mandico* makes clear, the "writ is very narrow in scope and operation and [may] be . . . utilized only in emergency cases to prevent an impending injury where there is no other appropriate and adequate legal remedy." *Id.* at 854.

The writ of quo warranto ("by what right?") can be directed to any state agency or officer. It requires the respondent to explain its behavior. *See, e.g., Israel v. DeSantis*, 269 So. 3d 491 (Fla. 2019) (action challenging governor's decision to suspend county sheriff); *League of Women Voters of Florida v. Scott*, 232 So. 3d 264 (Fla. 2017) (action challenging governor's decision to fill judicial vacancies); *Florida House of Representatives v. Crist*, 999 So. 2d 601 (Fla. 2008), *cert. denied sub nom. Seminole Tribe of Florida v. Florida House of Representatives*, 555 U.S. 1212 (2009) (action challenging governor's decision to enter into a tribal gambling compact).

The "all writs" provision authorizes the supreme court to issue ancillary writs to preserve its jurisdiction. In *Shevin ex rel. State v. Public Service Commission*, 333 So. 2d 9 (Fla. 1976), the court offered two examples: "[A] stay of related proceedings in another court or [an order] transfer[ring such proceedings] here for consolidation." *Id.* at 12.

A party seeking an extraordinary writ can start its lawsuit at the supreme court. In *Harvard v. Singletary*, 733 So. 2d 1020 (Fla. 1999), however, the court made it clear that except in highly unusual circumstances, it will not hear such actions:

> Although we have original jurisdiction to issue writs of habeas corpus, prohibition, mandamus, and quo warranto, our jurisdiction is discretionary. *See* art. V, § 3(b)(7), (8), (9), Fla. Const. Our jurisdiction is also concurrent with the jurisdiction of the district courts of appeal and the circuit courts. *See* art. V, §§ 4(b)(3), 5(b). . . . For the reasons that follow, we decline to exercise our jurisdiction in this case and elect to transfer the petition [for habeas corpus] to a more appropriate court. By doing so, we are

exercising the discretion granted to us by the Florida Constitution.

We take the opportunity to explain that, in the future, we will likewise decline jurisdiction and transfer or dismiss writ petitions which, like the present one, raise substantial issues of fact or present individualized issues that do not require immediate resolution by this Court, or are not the type of case in which an opinion from this Court would provide important guiding principles for the other courts of this State. . . .

[W]e emphasize that this Court has not curtailed its own writ jurisdiction by this decision. On the contrary, we will continue to be vigilant to ensure that no fundamental injustices occur. If we determine that such an injustice may be occurring which cannot be appropriately addressed by transferring the petition, we may decide that action by this Court is necessary. . . .

Id. at 1021–24.

Because the supreme court can only hear appeals that meet the requirements specified in Art. V, § 3(b)(1)–(2) (mandatory appeals) or Art. V, § 3(b)(3) (discretionary appeals), some litigants have tried to use the extraordinary writs (particularly mandamus) as a "workaround." In *Mathews v. Crews*, 132 So. 3d 776 (Fla. 2014), the justices made it clear that they will not be fooled by such efforts:

We take this opportunity to caution all litigants that the writ of mandamus cannot be used to review an allegedly erroneous judicial decision. Moreover, mandamus or other writs cannot be used to circumvent the constitutional restrictions on this Court's jurisdiction to review certain types of district court of appeal decisions by extraordinary writ.

Id. at 779.

In contrast to extraordinary writs, the "all writs" clause does not provide an independent basis of supreme court jurisdiction. *See Williams v. State*, 913 So. 2d 541, 543 (Fla. 2005) ("[The] all writs provision, however, does not constitute a separate source of original or appellate jurisdiction. Rather, it operates as an aid to the Court in exercising its 'ultimate jurisdiction,' conferred elsewhere in the constitution. . . .").

At one time, the supreme court also could issue the extraordinary writ of certiorari. In 1980, however, a constitutional amendment stripped it of this power.

A writ of certiorari ("we wish to be informed") is an order to a lower court to send a case's file to a higher court. An appellate court that possesses this power (such as the U.S. Supreme Court) enjoys substantial control over its docket, because it can review any case. *See, e.g., Marshall v. Marshall*, 545 U.S. 1165 (2005) (granting certiorari in the famous Anna Nicole Smith will contest case, even though federal courts, by longstanding tradition, do not hear probate disputes.)

Ironically, the Florida Supreme Court championed the stripping of its certiorari power. Its reasons were twofold: to reduce its caseload and to make it clear that except in unusual cases, the district courts have the final word. *See Jenkins v. State*, 385 So. 2d 1356 (Fla. 1980).

The Florida Supreme Court is one of the few state supreme courts that cannot review cases by certiorari. The New Hampshire and West Virginia supreme courts also lack this power, but that is because their states do not have intermediate appellate courts.

(e) Advisory Opinions

In two instances, the constitution authorizes the Florida Supreme Court to issue advisory opinions.

First, Art. IV, § 1(c) permits the governor to request an advisory opinion "as to the interpretation of any portion of this constitution upon any question affecting the governor's executive powers and duties." *See* Ch. 14 of this book.

Second, Art. V, § 3(b)(10) requires the court to issue advisory opinions to the attorney general regarding citizen-initiated constitutional amendments. *See* Ch. 23 of this book.

4.   OTHER DUTIES

In addition to the foregoing, the Florida Constitution assigns the supreme court a variety of other duties.

(a) Gubernatorial Incapacity

Art. IV, § 3(b) provides:

> Incapacity to serve as governor may be determined by the supreme court upon due notice after docketing of a written suggestion thereof by three cabinet members, and in such case restoration of capacity shall be similarly determined after docketing of written suggestion thereof by the governor, the legislature or three cabinet members.

The subject of gubernatorial incapacity is examined in Ch. 14 of this book.

(b) Impeachments

Art. III, § 17(c) states: "All impeachments by the house of representatives shall be tried by the senate. The chief justice of the supreme court, or another justice designated by the chief justice, shall preside at the trial, except in a trial of the chief justice, in which case the governor shall preside." For a further discussion, see Ch. 13 of this book.

(c) Legislative Reapportionment

Art. III, § 16(c) and (e) requires the supreme court to review the legislature's reapportionment plans. Additionally, Art. III, § 16(f) empowers the court to promulgate such plans if the legislature's plans are declared invalid. Legislative reapportionment is discussed further in Ch. 13 of this book.

(d) Number of Judges

Art. V, § 9 requires the supreme court to annually advise the legislature in writing whether there is a need to "increas[e] or decreas[e] the number of judges or increas[e], decreas[e] or redefin[e] [the] appellate districts and judicial circuits." The court must do so "prior to the next regular session of the legislation." *Id.* This procedure (known as "certification") was adopted in 1972.

Traditionally, the court releases its report at the end of the year as an unsigned opinion. *See, e.g., In re: Certification of Need for Additional Judges*, 2019 WL 6336944, at *1 (Fla. 2019) ("In this opinion, we certify the need for two additional circuit court judgeships in the Ninth Judicial Circuit, one additional circuit court judgeship in the First Judicial Circuit, one additional circuit court judgeship in the Fourteenth Judicial Circuit, four additional county court judgeships in Hillsborough County, one additional county court judgeship in Orange County, one additional county court judgeship in Lee County, and no additional judgeships in the district courts of appeal. We decertify the need for two county court judgeships in Brevard County, one county court judgeship in Monroe County, and one county court judgeship in Collier County.").

In making its recommendations, the court uses "a verified objective weighted caseload methodology . . . supplemented by judgeship requests submitted by the lower courts, including . . . various secondary factors. These secondary factors [are] identified by each chief judge [and] reflect local differences. . . ." *Id.*

Once the court's report is received, Art. V, § 9 directs the legislature to consider it and gives it the option of "reject[ing] the recommendations or . . . implementing [them] in whole or in part; provided the legislature may create more judicial offices than are recommended by the supreme court or may decrease the number of judicial offices by a greater number than recommended by the court only upon a finding of two-thirds of the membership of both houses of the legislature . . . that such a need exists."

The legislature normally does its best to honor the court's recommendations. As a result, the number of judges has grown steadily. In 1972, Florida had 416 state judges: 20 on the district courts, 261 on the circuit courts, and 135 on the county courts. In 2019, Florida had 989 state judges: 64 on the district courts, 601 on the circuit courts, and 324 on the county courts.

As a safety measure (which so far has not been needed), § 9 allows the legislature to act on its own if the supreme court fails to make the necessary certification:

> If the supreme court fails to make findings as provided above when need exists, the legislature may by concurrent resolution request the court to certify its findings and recommendations and upon the failure of the court to certify its findings for nine consecutive months, the legislature may, upon a finding of two-thirds of

the membership of both houses of the legislature that a need exists, increase or decrease the number of judges or increase, decrease or redefine appellate districts and judicial circuits.

(e) Practice and Procedure Rules

Art. V, § 2(a) requires the supreme court to

adopt rules for the practice and procedure in all courts including the time for seeking appellate review, the administrative supervision of all courts, the transfer to the court having jurisdiction of any proceeding when the jurisdiction of another court has been improvidently invoked, and a requirement that no cause shall be dismissed because an improper remedy has been sought. The supreme court shall adopt rules to allow the court and the district courts of appeal to submit questions relating to military law to the federal Court of Appeals for the Armed Forces for an advisory opinion. Rules of court may be repealed by general law enacted by two-thirds vote of the membership of each house of the legislature.

The reference to the U.S. Court of Appeals for the Armed Forces was added in 1998.

Each year, the supreme court spends considerable time reviewing, modifying, and approving proposed rule changes. In 2018, for example, 1.9% of its docket was taken up with such matters.

As one would expect, most of the court's rule changes are routine. Two, however, have served as national models. In *In re Interest on Trust Accounts, A Petition of The Florida Bar*, 356 So. 2d 799 (Fla. 1978), the court pioneered the rule requiring that the interest on lawyers' trust accounts be used to fund legal aid programs. Similarly, in *In re Petition of Post-Newsweek Stations, Florida, Inc.*, 370 So. 2d 764 (Fla. 1979), the court adopted a rule making Florida the first state to allow cameras inside courtrooms.

Deciding whether a rule is substantive or procedural can be tricky. In *Benyard v. Wainwright*, 322 So. 2d 473 (Fla. 1975), the court explained:

Substantive law prescribes the duties and rights under our system of government. The responsibility to make substantive law is in the legislature within the limits of the state and federal constitutions. Procedural law concerns the means and method to apply and enforce those duties and rights. Procedural rules concerning the judicial branch are the responsibility of this Court, subject to repeal by the legislature in accordance with our constitutional provisions.

Id. at 475.

In close cases, the court usually defers to the legislature. *See, e.g., Abdool v. Bondi*, 141 So. 3d 529 (Fla. 2014) (upholding statute expediting executions); *Williams v. Law*, 368 So. 2d 1285 (Fla. 1979) (upholding statute requiring taxes to be challenged within 60 days of assessment). Where, however, a law clearly is procedural, it will be struck down. *See, e.g., Massey v. David*, 979 So. 2d 931 (Fla.

2008) (statute restricting taxable court costs); *State v. Raymond*, 906 So. 2d 1045 (Fla. 2005) (statute denying pre-trial release). In such instances, the court sometimes adopts the stricken provision as a new procedural rule. *See, e.g., In re Amendments to Florida Evidence Code*, 278 So. 3d 551 (Fla.), *reh'g denied*, 2019 WL 4127349 (Fla. 2019) (expert witnesses); *Avila South Condominium Association, Inc. v. Kappa Corporation*, 347 So. 2d 599 (Fla. 1977) (class actions).

In recent times, there has been considerable tension between the court and the legislature over § 2(a). As a result, in 2004 the legislature considered a constitutional amendment stripping the court of its rulemaking power. As explained earlier in this chapter, in 2012 a watered-down version of this proposal made it to the ballot but was rejected.

(f)   Revenue Shortfalls

Art. IV, § 13 directs: "In the event of revenue shortfalls . . . the chief justice of the supreme court shall implement all necessary reductions for the judicial budget." Revenue shortfalls (*i.e.,* budget deficits) are discussed in Ch. 20 of this book.

(g)   Supervision of the Bar

Art. V, § 15 gives the supreme court "exclusive jurisdiction to regulate the admission of persons to the practice of law and the discipline of persons admitted."

The 1838, 1861, 1865, and 1885 constitutions were silent on these matters. The 1868 constitution provided: "Attorneys at law, who have been admitted to practice in any court of record in any State of the Union, or to any United States Court, shall be admitted to practice in any court of this State, on producing evidence of having been so admitted."

For most of Florida's history, the legislature took the lead in attorney licensing and discipline. *See, e.g., Petition of Florida State Bar Association*, 186 So. 280 (Fla. 1938). *See also State ex rel. Clyatt v. Hocker*, 22 So. 721 (Fla. 1897).

Matters began to change in 1949, when the court approved a petition requiring all Florida attorneys to belong to The Florida Bar ("TFB") (https://www.floridabar.org/). *See Petition of Florida State Bar Association*, 40 So. 2d 902 (Fla. 1949) (en banc). Previously, the Florida State Bar Association, founded in Jacksonville in 1907, had been a voluntary organization.

Further change came in 1954, when the court, in an attorney disciplinary case, asserted itself even more forcefully:

It is well settled that the legislature may impose minimum character and scholastic requirements as a prerequisite for admission to the bar, but the decisions [of other jurisdictions] generally hold that when it comes to establishing and upholding the highest standards of professiona. conduct and protecting the public from the unscrupulous practitioner, that duty rests upon the courts.

State ex rel. Florida Bar v. Murrell, 74 So. 2d 221, 223 (Fla. 1954) (en banc).

Finally, in 1956, as part of the amendment creating the district courts, the supreme court was given control of both attorney admissions and discipline:

> The supreme court shall have exclusive jurisdiction over the admission to the practice of law and the discipline of persons admitted. It may provide for an agency to handle admissions subject to its supervision. It may also provide for the handling of disciplinary matters in the circuit courts and the district courts of appeal, or by commissions consisting of members of the bar to be designated by it, the supreme court, subject to its supervision and review.

As can be seen, this language, in shortened form, was retained when Art. V was amended in 1972.

Today, the Florida Supreme Court fulfills its § 15 responsibilities with the help of the TFB and the Florida Board of Bar Examiners ("FBBE") (https://www.floridabarexam.org/). In 2018, the court's docket included 294 matters filed by TFB and 41 filed by the FBBE.

Despite the power given to it by § 15, in 2014 the court ruled that it could not admit unlawful aliens unless the legislature passed a law allowing it to do so. *See Florida Board of Bar Examiners re Question as to Whether Undocumented Immigrants are Eligible for Admission to The Florida Bar*, 134 So. 3d 432 (Fla. 2014). This rather odd holding was forced by a quirk in the federal immigration laws. In response to the court's ruling, the legislature quickly made the necessary change. *See* Fla. Laws ch. 2014–35 (adding paragraph (3) to Fla. Stat. § 454.021).

(h) Supervision of the Bench

Art. V, § 12 gives the supreme court the power to discipline judges. It also gives the court oversight power with respect to the rules used to investigate judges. These subjects are discussed later in this chapter.

(i) Constitution Revision Commission

Lastly, Art. XI, § 2(a)(4) authorizes the chief justice, with the "advice" of the court's other justices, to appoint three persons to the Constitution Revision Commission ("CRC"). The CRC meets once every 20 years and has 37 members. *See* Ch. 23 of this book.

F. DISTRICT COURTS OF APPEAL

Sitting just below the supreme court are the district courts of appeal. Until 1957, the supreme court was Florida's only appellate court. By 1955, it was handling 1,225 cases a year, more than three times the workload of other state supreme courts. To remedy this situation, in 1956 the constitution was amended to create intermediate appellate courts. Florida used California's district courts as its model.

The amendment had a second goal: making it "more convenient [for] parties and their lawyers" to take appeals. *See Maryland Casualty Co. v. Marshall*, 106 So. 2d 212, 215 (Fla. 1st Dist. Ct. App. 1958). At present, every major Florida city is within 200 miles of its district court.

When Florida's district courts were created, only 13 states had intermediate appellate courts. Today, 40 do.

1. BASICS

Art. V, § 1 leaves it to the legislature to decide how many district courts the state should have and where they should be located. In making the latter choice, the legislature must "follow[ ] county lines." *Id.*

There presently are five district courts of appeals. *See* Fla. Stat. §§ 35.01–35.05. Each is designated by a number, as follows:

First District (https://www.1dca.org/): Tallahassee (created 1957) (originally 37 counties, now 32 counties). At one time, the First District's courthouse was two blocks from the supreme court. In 2010, however, it moved to a new courthouse located on the outskirts of town.

Second District (https://www.2dca.org/): Lakeland (1957) (originally 28 counties, now 14 counties). Since 1980, the Second District has operated a branch in Tampa, the only district court to have a second location. (All oral arguments take place in Tampa.) Because of southwest Florida's growing population, the

Second District is likely to be divided in the future, resulting in a sixth district court.

Third District (https://www.3dca.flcourts. org/): Miami (1957) (Miami-Dade and Monroe Counties). The Third District's territory has not changed since its creation.

Fourth District (https://www.4dca.org/): West Palm Beach (1965) (created from six Second District counties). The Fourth District originally sat in Vero Beach but its headquarters was changed to Palm Beach County in 1967.

Fifth District (https://www.5dca.org/): Daytona Beach (1979) (created from five First District counties and eight Second District counties). A bitter fight broke out during the court's creation, and for a time its headquarters was expected to be in Orlando (with the Second District's moving to Tampa). *See* https://www. 5dca.org/About-the-Court/Court-History. *See also In re Advisory Opinion to Governor— Request of June 29, 1979*, 374 So. 2d 959 (Fla. 1979).

Florida currently is the only state to call its intermediate courts "district courts of appeal." A common mistake, made by both lawyers and non-lawyers, is adding an "s" to the word "appeal." *See, e.g., Koontz v. St. Johns River Water Management District*, 570 U.S. 595, 610 (2013).

2.   PERSONNEL

(a)   Judges

Art. V, § 4(a) stipulates: "[Each] district court of appeal shall consist of at least three judges. Three judges shall consider each case and the concurrence of two shall be necessary to a decision."

Art. V, § 2(c) provides: "A chief judge for each district court of appeal shall be chosen by a majority of the judges thereof or, if there is no majority, by the chief justice [of the Florida Supreme Court]." It also states: "The chief judge [of a district court] shall be responsible for the administrative supervision of the court."

As explained earlier in this chapter, there currently are a total of 64 district court judges. *See* Fla. Stat. § 35.06 (authorizing 15 judges for the First District, 16 for the Second, 10 for the Third, 12 for the Fourth, and 11 for the Fifth).

District court judges are paid $169,554 a year. As explained later in this chapter, they serve six-year terms, which are renewable, and must retire at 75.

Pursuant to Rule 2.220(c) of the Florida Rules of Judicial Administration, the Florida Conference of District Court of Appeal Judges (no web site) "conduct[s] conferences and institutes for continuing judicial education and . . . provide[s] forums in which the district court of appeal judges of Florida may meet and discuss mutual problems and solutions."

(b) Clerks and Marshals

Art. V, § 4(c) requires each "district court of appeal [to] appoint a clerk and a marshal who shall hold office during the pleasure of the court and perform such duties as the court directs. . . . The marshal shall have the power to execute the process of the court. . . ." These positions perform the same functions as their supreme court counterparts (discussed earlier in this chapter). *See also* Fla. Stat. §§ 35.22–35.24 (district court clerks) and § 35.26 (district court marshals).

3. JURISDICTION

As noted earlier, the district courts are designed to be the final arbiter of most cases. This is because most cases concern the application of settled law. Thus, rather than making law (the supreme court's principal function), the district courts' main purpose is to correct errors made by the trial courts. *See Ansin v. Thurston*, 101 So. 2d 808 (Fla. 1958).

In 2018, 21,178 new appeals were filed in the district courts, of which 9,356 (44.2%) were civil and 11,822 (55.8%) were criminal. The First District had the most filings (5,516), while the Third District had the fewest (2,621).

(a) Appeals from Circuit Courts: Final Judgments and Orders

In Florida, every litigant is entitled to one appeal "as a matter of right." Thus, all final judgments and orders issued by the circuit courts are appealable to the district courts. *See* Art. V, § 4(b)(1). As such, there is no need, nor any procedure, for circuit courts to pose certified questions to the district courts. *See Florida Department of Health and Rehabilitative Services v. State*, 616 So. 2d 66 (Fla. 1st Dist. Ct. App. 1993).

(b) Appeals from Circuit Courts: Interlocutory Orders

Art. V, § 4(b)(1) also authorizes the district courts to "review interlocutory orders . . . to the extent provided by rules adopted by the supreme court." The supreme court has read this section to be exclusive. *See State v. Gaines*, 770 So. 2d 1221 (Fla. 2000) (invalidating statute allowing government to take interlocutory appeals of orders suppressing evidence in criminal cases); *State v. Smith*, 260 So. 2d 489 (Fla. 1972) (invalidating statute allowing government to take interlocutory appeals in criminal cases).

Interlocutory appeals are governed by Rule 9.130 of the Florida Rules of Appellate Procedure. It permits such appeals in civil cases from orders that:

(A) concern venue;

(B) grant, continue, modify, deny, or dissolve injunctions, or refuse to modify or dissolve injunctions;

(C) determine: (i) the jurisdiction of the person; (ii) the right to immediate possession of property, including but not limited to orders that grant, modify, dissolve, or refuse to grant, modify, or dissolve writs of replevin, garnishment, or attachment; (iii) in family law matters: a. the right to immediate monetary relief; b. the rights or obligations of a party regarding child custody or time-sharing under a parenting plan; or c. that a marital agreement is invalid in its entirety; (iv) the entitlement of a party to arbitration, or to an appraisal under an insurance policy; (v) that, as a matter of law, a party is not entitled to workers' compensation immunity; (vi) whether to certify a class; (vii) that, as a matter of law, a party is not entitled to absolute or qualified immunity in a civil rights claim arising under federal law; (viii) that a governmental entity has taken action that has inordinately burdened real property within the meaning of section 70.001(6)(a), Florida Statutes; (ix) the issue of forum non conveniens; (x) that, as a matter of law, a party is not entitled to immunity under section 768.28(9), Florida Statutes; (xi) that, as a matter of law, a party is not entitled to sovereign immunity; or (xii) that, as a matter of law, a settlement agreement is unenforceable, is set aside, or never existed;

(D) grant or deny the appointment of a receiver, or terminate or refuse to terminate a receivership; or

(E) grant or deny a motion to disqualify counsel.

Similar provisions are contained in Rule 9.140, which concerns appeals from non-final criminal orders.

(c) Appeals from County Courts

As authorized by Art. V, § 4(b)(1), the legislature has given the district courts the power to hear appeals from county courts in two instances:

1) If a county court invalidates a provision of the Florida Constitution or a state statute. *See* Fla. Stat. § 26.012(1)(b). *See also Fieselman v. State*, 566 So. 2d 768 (Fla. 1990).

2) If a county court certifies that its judgment or order raises a question of great public importance or affects the uniform administration of justice. *See* Fla. Stat. §§ 34.017(1) and 35.065. If the district court declines to take up the question, the appeal is transferred to the appropriate circuit court. *See* Fla. Stat. § 34.017(4)(b). For an example of a county court certifying a question and the district court granting review, see *Moore v. State Farm Mutual Automobile Insurance Co.*, 916 So. 2d 871 (Fla. 2d Dist. Ct. App. 2005).

(d) Appeals from Administrative Agencies

Art. V, § 4(b)(2) provides: "District courts of appeal shall have the power of direct review of administrative action, as prescribed by general law."

In most instances, appeals from agency decisions go to the district court in whose territory the agency is headquartered. *See* Fla. Stat. § 120.68(2)(a). There are, however, some exceptions to this rule.

First, as explained earlier, appeals from the PSC go directly to the Supreme Court. *See* Art. V, § 3(b)(2).

Second, Art. V, § 1 requires all court-martial appeals to go to the First District. Similarly, Fla. Stat. § 440.271 requires all workers' compensation appeals to go to the First District. In both instances, the reason is the same: to build-up the court's expertise and assure consistent decisions. *See Rollins v. Southern Bell Telephone and Telegraph Co.*, 384 So. 2d 650 (Fla. 1980).

Third, appeals from agencies that are not subject to Florida's Administrative Procedure Act ("APA"), see Fla. Stat. §§ 120.50–120.81, go to circuit court. As a practical matter, the only agencies not subject to the APA are those created by municipalities. *See* Fla. Stat. § 120.52(1).

As will be recalled from the discussion earlier in this chapter, Art. V, § 21 requires an agency's statutory interpretations to be reviewed de novo.

(e) Writs

Art. V, § 4(b)(3) authorizes a district court to issue "writs of habeas corpus[,] mandamus, certiorari, prohibition, quo warranto, and other writs necessary to the complete exercise of its jurisdiction." These writs are the same ones that the supreme court can issue (except certiorari).

District courts grant certiorari in two instances: 1) when a trial court has "departed from the essential requirements of the law" and the error cannot be corrected by any other means ("common law certiorari"); and, 2) to review appellate decisions issued by circuit courts ("second appeal certiorari"). *See, e.g., Allstate Insurance Co. v. Langston*, 655 So. 2d 91 (Fla. 1995); *Florida Wellness & Rehabilitation Center, Inc. v. Mark J. Feldman, P.A.*, 276 So. 3d 884 (Fla. 3d Dist. Ct. App. 2019). The ability of circuit courts to issue appellate decisions is discussed later in this chapter.

4.   EN BANC PROCEEDINGS

Pursuant to Art. V, § 4(a) district courts sit in panels of three, with two votes necessary for a decision. The composition of each panel is determined primarily, but not entirely, by random assignment. *See, e.g., Russo v. Blanks*, 2018 WL 5391775 (Fla. 2018), at https://efactssc-public.flcourts.org/Case Documents/2018/886/2018-886_Petition_70035_ PETITION2DMANDAMUS.pdf (petitioner's brief explaining how assignments are made in the Third District).

There are times, however, when all members of a district court will hear a case. Such proceedings are rare (typically occurring just two or three times a year), and generally are granted when different panels have come to opposite conclusions on the same question of law. In this way, a district court can harmonize its case law.

Intra-district conflicts should not be confused with *inter*-district conflicts. In the former, there is a conflict within a single district court. In the latter, there is a conflict between two different district courts. While the en banc procedure can cure the first type of conflict, it cannot cure the second. As explained earlier in this chapter, inter-district conflicts are cured by the supreme court and make up the bulk of its work.

A party seeking en banc review normally files a "petition for rehearing and rehearing en banc." The former asks the panel to reconsider its decision, while the latter asks the full court to review the panel's opinion. *See* Fla. R. App. Proc. Rules 9.330–9.331.

5.   PER CURIAM AFFIRMED OPINIONS

The most controversial aspect of the district courts is their extensive use of per curiam affirmed ("PCA") opinions. The statistics of the First District are typical. From May 2018 to May 2019, it disposed of 5,068 cases. To do so, it wrote 992 opinions and issued 1,852 PCA opinions and 304 per curiam denied ("PCD") opinions (a PCD is the same as a PCA but is used when a writ is requested). Most of its remaining dispositions—1,920—consisted of "housekeeping" orders. Thus, of the 3,148 cases that the First District disposed of by opinion, 2,156 (68.5%) were by PCA or PCD.

A PCA opinion begins with the words per curiam ("by the court"). The word "affirmed" then follows. That is the entire opinion, and it has two important consequences. First, it requires the losing attorney to explain to his or her client why its appeal merited just one word. Second, it forecloses the ability to pursue a further appeal. This is because the supreme court has held that PCA opinions do not provide the "clear grounds" needed to establish the court's jurisdiction. *See Wells v. State*, 132 So. 3d 1110 (Fla. 2014); *Gandy v. State*, 846 So. 2d 1141 (Fla. 2003); *Jenkins v. State*, 385 So. 2d 1356 (Fla. 1980).

Lawyers repeatedly have called on the supreme court to ban PCA opinions. The district courts have fought to keep them, insisting they are only way they can keep up with their workloads. They also have criticized lawyers for routinely taking appeals when the correctness of the trial court's decision was obvious.

Rule 9.330(a)(2)(D) of the Florida Rules of Appellate Procedure permits lawyers to ask for a written opinion after receiving a PCA opinion, but makes it clear that such requests will be granted only when a written opinion would provide:

(i)   a legitimate basis for supreme court review;

(ii)   an explanation for an apparent deviation from prior precedent; or

(iii) guidance to the parties or lower tribunal when: a. the issue decided is also present in other cases pending before the court or another district court of appeal; b. the issue

> decided is expected to recur in future cases;
> c. there are conflicting decisions on the
> issue from lower tribunals; d. the issue
> decided is one of first impression; or e. the
> issue arises in a case in which the court has
> exclusive subject matter jurisdiction.

PCA opinions usually include a "string" of citations. The supreme court has held that the inclusion of a string cite does not provide a basis for review

> unless one of the cases cited as controlling
> authority is pending before this Court, or has
> been reversed on appeal or review, or receded
> from by this Court, or unless the citation
> explicitly notes a contrary holding of another
> district court or of this Court. *See Jollie v. State*,
> 405 So.2d 418, 420 (Fla.1981).

The Florida Star v. B.J.F., 530 So. 2d 286, 288 n.3 (Fla. 1988).

Lastly, it should be noted that while the Florida Supreme Court cannot review a PCA opinion, the U.S. Supreme Court can. *See Davis v. State*, 953 So. 2d 612, 614 (Fla. 2d Dist. Ct. App. 2007) (Altenbernd, J., concurring) ("Mr. Davis attempted to have the United States Supreme Court review our affirmance. That court does have the power, by writ of certiorari, to review a decision from a Florida district court of appeal even when no written opinion is issued. That power is very rarely exercised.").

6.   PRECEDENTIAL VALUE OF DECISIONS

A district court opinion binds the circuit and county courts within the district. It also binds the circuit and county courts in every other district that has not ruled on the question. *See Brannon v. State*, 850 So. 2d 452 (Fla. 2003); *Pardo v. State*, 596 So. 2d 665 (Fla. 1992). In the event of a conflict between two district courts, circuit and county courts must follow their own district court. *Id.*

District court decisions have no binding effect on either the supreme court or other district courts. *Id.* Of course, they can and often are cited as persuasive authority. *See, e.g., Amos v. Amos*, 99 So. 3d 979, 980 (Fla. 1st Dist. Ct. App. 2012) ("We hold that an intentional dissipation of assets more than two years prior to the filing of a petition . . . may fall within the catchall of [Fla. Stat. § 61.075(1)(j)]. In doing so, we follow the Fifth District in *Beers v. Beers*, 724 So.2d 109 (Fla. 5th DCA 1998). . . .").

G.   CIRCUIT COURTS

1.   BASICS

Art. V, § 5(a) provides: "There shall be a circuit court serving each judicial circuit." As noted at the outset of this chapter, circuit courts have been a part of Florida's judiciary since the state's formation, although their number, jurisdiction, and operations have changed significantly over time.

The 1838 constitution directed the legislature to divide the state "into at least four convenient

Circuits, and until other Circuits shall be provided for by the General Assembly, the arrangement of the Circuits shall be the Western, Middle, Eastern and Southern Circuits, and for each Circuit there shall be appointed a Judge[.]" The 1861 and 1865 constitutions simply directed the state to have "convenient circuits."

The 1868 constitution authorized seven circuits and, for the first time, numbered them. In 1870, the legislature reduced the state to five circuits, but the 1885 constitution bumped this figure back up to seven.

As Florida's population grew and new counties were created, the number of circuits, as well as their boundaries, changed repeatedly. By 1911, the legislature had increased the number of circuits to 11. By 1919, there were 15, and by 1928 there were 28. A 1934 constitutional amendment reduced the number to 15. A 1950 amendment increased it to 16.

The 1956 amendment establishing the district courts capped the circuit courts at 16. The 1968 constitution increased this number to 20. The 1972 amendment to Art. V did away with the cap. *See* Art. V, § 1 ("The legislature shall, by general law, divide the state into . . . judicial circuits following county lines.").

At present, there are 20 circuits, see Fla. Stat. § 26.021, as follows:

First Circuit (https://www.firstjudicialcircuit. org/): 24 judges—Escambia, Okaloosa, Santa Rosa, and Walton Counties.

Second Circuit (http://2ndcircuit.leoncountyfl. gov/): 16 judges—Franklin, Gadsden, Jefferson, Leon, Liberty, and Wakulla Counties.

Third Circuit (http://www.jud3.flcourts.org/): seven judges—Columbia, Dixie, Hamilton, Lafayette, Madison, Suwannee, and Taylor Counties.

Fourth Circuit (http://www.jud4.org/): 35 judges—Clay, Duval, and Nassau Counties.

Fifth Circuit (https://www.circuit5.org/): 31 judges—Citrus, Hernando, Lake, Marion, and Sumter Counties.

Sixth Circuit (http://www.jud6.org/): 45 judges—Pasco and Pinellas Counties.

Seventh Circuit (http://www.circuit7.org/): 27 judges—Flagler, Putnam, St. Johns, and Volusia Counties.

Eighth Circuit (https://circuit8.org/): 13 judges—Alachua, Baker, Bradford, Gilchrist, Levy, and Union Counties.

Ninth Circuit (https://www.ninthcircuit.org/): 44 judges—Orange and Osceola Counties.

10th Circuit (http://www.jud10.flcourts.org/): 28 judges—Hardee, Highlands, and Polk Counties.

11th Circuit (https://www.jud11.flcourts.org/): 80 judges—Miami-Dade County.

12th Circuit (http://www.jud12.flcourts.org/): 22 judges—DeSoto, Manatee, and Sarasota Counties.

13th Circuit (http://www.fljud13.org/): 45 judges—Hillsborough County.

14th Circuit (https://www.jud14.flcourts.org/): 11 judges—Bay, Calhoun, Gulf, Holmes, Jackson, and Washington Counties.

15th Circuit (https://www.15thcircuit.com/): 35 judges—Palm Beach County.

16th Circuit (http://www.keyscourts.net/): four judges—Monroe County.

17th Circuit (http://www.17th.flcourts.org/): 58 judges—Broward County.

18th Circuit (https://flcourts18.org/): 26 judges—Brevard and Seminole Counties.

19th Circuit (http://www.circuit19.org/): 19 judges—Indian River, Martin, Okeechobee, and St. Lucie Counties.

20th Circuit (https://www.ca.cjis20.org/home/main/homepage.asp): 31 judges—Charlotte, Collier, Glades, Hendry, and Lee Counties.

In 2018, 762,685 new cases were filed in the circuit courts:

Criminal: 177,419 (23.3%)

Civil: 180,881 (23.7%)

Family: 278,317 (36.5%)

Probate: 126,068 (16.5%)

The 11th Circuit had the greatest number of new cases (92,701), while the 16th Circuit had the smallest (3,918).

For efficiency's sake, circuit courts typically arrange themselves into divisions. *See* Art. V, § 7; Fla. Stat. § 43.30 (allowing all courts except the supreme court to sit in divisions; although authorized, no district court sits in divisions). The typical circuit court is divided into four divisions: civil, criminal, family, and probate. Larger circuits often have additional divisions. *See, e.g.*, http://www. jud6.org/GeneralPublic/CourtDivisions.html (divisions page of the Sixth Circuit); https://www. jud11.flcourts.org/About-the-Court/Court-Divisions (divisions page of the 11th Circuit).

As has been noted elsewhere, "[T]he assignment of a circuit judge to a particular division does not limit that judge's jurisdiction; he or she continues to possess the authority to exercise the full power conferred on the circuit courts by the state." *Willie v. State*, 600 So. 2d 479, 481 (Fla. 1st Dist. Ct. App. 1992). *See also Baudanza v. Baudanza*, 78 So. 3d 656 (Fla. 4th Dist. Ct. App. 2012).

In addition to divisions, many circuits have specialized "problem-solving" programs that function as "courts within courts." Defendants who qualify for them are diverted from the criminal justice system and provided with individualized treatment plans. Such efforts go by a variety of names, including drug court, DUI court, mental health court, and veterans' court. Florida was the first state to have such courts (beginning, in 1989, with a drug court in Miami-Dade County). Today, similar programs can be found throughout the country (in 2018, for example, Las Vegas established a gambling court to handle criminal cases involving compulsive gamblers).

2.   PERSONNEL

(a) Judges

The number of circuit court judges is set by statute, see Fla. Stat. § 26.031, and varies considerably (as indicated by the list above). As explained earlier in this chapter, there currently are a total of 601 circuit court judges.

Originally, the constitution specified the number of judges per circuit. In 1956, all circuits were allotted one judge for every 50,000 inhabitants. In 1972, the annual "certification" system described earlier in this chapter was adopted. *See* Art. V, § 9.

Art. V, § 2(d) directs: "A chief judge in each circuit shall be chosen from among the circuit judges as provided by supreme court rule. The chief judge shall be responsible for the administrative supervision of the circuit courts and county courts in his [or her] circuit." The administrative duties of circuit court chief judges are spelled out in Fla. Stat. § 43.26.

Circuit court judges are paid $160,688 a year. As explained later in this chapter, they serve six-year terms, which are renewable, and must retire at 75. For a further look at circuit court judges, see the web site of the Florida Conference of Circuit Judges (https://flcircuitconference.com/).

(b) Clerks

As discussed earlier in this chapter, the supreme court and the district courts choose their clerks. In contrast, Art. V, § 16 provides that the clerks of the circuit courts

> shall be selected pursuant to the provisions of Article VIII section 1. Notwithstanding any other provision of the constitution, the duties of the clerk of the circuit court may be divided by special or general law between two officers, one serving as clerk of court and one serving as ex officio clerk of the board of county commissioners, auditor, recorder, and custodian of all county funds. There may be a clerk of the county court if authorized by general or special law.

In relevant part, Art. VIII, § 1(d) states:

> There shall be elected by the electors of each county, for terms of four years . . . a clerk of the circuit court. Unless otherwise provided by special law approved by vote of the electors or pursuant to Article V, section 16, the clerk of the circuit court shall be ex officio clerk of the board of county commissioners, auditor, recorder and custodian of all county funds. Notwithstanding subsection 6(e) of this article, a county charter may not abolish the office of . . . clerk of the circuit court; transfer the duties of [the clerk] to

another officer or office; change the length of the four-year term of office; or establish any manner of selection other than by election by the electors of the county.

Art. VIII, § 1(d) was amended in 2018 at the suggestion of the Constitution Revision Commission (see Ch. 16 of this book). Previously, it had read:

[W]hen provided by county charter or special law approved by vote of the electors of the county, any county officer may be chosen in another manner therein specified, or any county office may be abolished when all the duties of the office prescribed by general law are transferred to another office. When not otherwise provided by county charter or special law approved by vote of the electors, the clerk of the circuit court shall be ex officio clerk of the board of county commissioners, auditor, recorder and custodian of all county funds.

For a further discussion, see the web sites of the Florida Clerks of Court Operations Corporation (https://flccoc.org/) and the Florida Court Clerks & Comptrollers (https://www.flclerks.com/). A list of the individual clerks and their web sites can be found at https://www.flclerks.com/page/FindaClerk.

3.   JURISDICTION

Fla. Stat. § 26.012(5) provides: "A circuit court is a trial court." Pursuant to Art. V, § 5(b), the jurisdiction of the circuit courts must "be uniform throughout the state."

Despite being trial courts, circuit courts have three kinds of jurisdiction: original, appellate, and writ.

(a) Original

Art. V, § 5(b) states: "The circuit courts shall have original jurisdiction not vested in the county courts. . . ." This provision is implemented by Fla. Stat. § 26.012(2), which makes the circuit courts competent:

(a)   In all actions at law not cognizable by the county courts;

(b)   Of proceedings relating to the settlement of the estates of decedents and minors, the granting of letters testamentary, guardianship, involuntary hospitalization, the determination of incompetency, and other jurisdiction usually pertaining to courts of probate;

(c)   In all cases in equity including all cases relating to juveniles except traffic offenses as provided in chapters 316 and 985;

(d)   Of all felonies and of all misdemeanors arising out of the same circumstances as a felony which is also charged;

(e)   In all cases involving legality of any tax assessment or toll or denial of refund, except as provided in § 72.011;

(f)   In actions of ejectment; and

(g) In all actions involving the title and boundaries of real property.

In most civil cases, the dividing line between the circuit courts and the county courts is the amount of damages sought by the plaintiff (as explained below, by 2023 the county courts' jurisdiction will be $50,000). Similarly, in most criminal cases, the dividing line is whether the defendant is charged with a felony or a misdemeanor.

As has been recognized repeatedly, the circuit courts are courts of general jurisdiction. *See, e.g., Allstate Insurance Co. v. Kaklamanos*, 843 So. 2d 885 (Fla. 2003); *Curtis v. Albritton*, 132 So. 677 (Fla. 1931) (en banc); *Chapman v. Reddick*, 25 So. 673 (Fla. 1899). As such, they "have authority over any matter not expressly denied them by the constitution or applicable statutes." *Department of Revenue v. Kuhnlein*, 646 So. 2d 717, 720 (Fla. 1994), *cert. denied sub nom. Adams v. Dickinson*, 515 U.S. 1158 (1995).

(b) Appellate

Art. V, § 5(b) gives the circuit courts "jurisdiction of appeals when provided by general law."

In larger circuits, appeals are heard by three-judge panels. *See, e.g.*, https://www.jud4.org/Appeals (appellate page of the Fourth Circuit); http://www.17th.flcourts.org/circuit-appellate-panel/ (appellate page of the 17th Circuit). In smaller circuits, appeals are heard by one judge. Although this practice has been criticized, smaller circuits would be hard pressed if they had to convene appellate panels.

Unlike district courts, which can sit en banc to resolve intra-district conflicts, a similar mechanism does not exist for appellate circuit courts to resolve conflicts. *See* J. Sebastien Rogers, *The Chasm in Florida Appellate Law: Intra-Circuit Conflicting Appellate Decisions*, 92 Fla. B.J. 52 (Apr. 2018).

i.   *Appeals from County Courts*

Fla. Stat. § 26.012(1) provides:

Circuit courts shall have jurisdiction of appeals from county courts except:

(a) Appeals of county court orders or judgments where the amount in controversy is greater than $15,000. This paragraph is repealed on January 1, 2023.

(b) Appeals of county court orders or judgments declaring invalid a state statute or a provision of the State Constitution.

(c)   Orders or judgments of a county court which are certified by the county court to the district court of appeal to be of great public importance and which are accepted by the district court of appeal for review.

The 1868 constitution gave circuit courts appellate jurisdiction over the county courts "in all civil cases arising in the county court in which the amount in controversy is one hundred dollars and upwards, and in all cases of misdemeanor." The 1885 constitution expanded this language:

The Circuit Courts ... shall have final appellate jurisdiction in all civil and criminal cases arising in the County Court, or before the County Judge, of all misdemeanors tried in Criminal Courts, of judgments or sentences of any Mayor's Court, and of all cases arising before Justices of the Peace in counties in which there is no County Court; and supervision and appellate jurisdiction of matters arising before County Judges pertaining to their probate jurisdiction, or to the estates and interests of minors, and of such other matters as the Legislature may provide.

The 1968 constitution streamlined this language:

The circuit courts ... shall have final appellate jurisdiction in all civil and criminal cases arising in the county court, or before county judges' courts, of all misdemeanors tried in criminal courts of record, and of all cases arising in municipal courts, small claims courts, and courts of justices of the peace.

The 1972 amendments to Art. V shortened the language to its present form.

ii.   *Appeals from Administrative Agencies*

Art. V, § 5(b) states: "The circuit courts ... shall have the power of direct review of administrative action prescribed by general law." As a practical matter, this means the circuit courts have jurisdiction to review appeals from all agencies *not* subject to the APA. (As explained earlier in this chapter, appeals from agencies that *are* subject to the APA go to the district courts.)

The following agencies are not subject to the APA:

[A] municipality or legal entity created solely by a municipality; a legal entity or agency created in whole or in part pursuant to part II of chapter 361; a metropolitan planning organization created pursuant to § 339.175; a separate legal or administrative entity created pursuant to § 339.175 of which a metropolitan planning organization is a member; an expressway authority pursuant to chapter 348 or any transportation authority or commission under chapter 343 or chapter 349; or a legal or administrative entity created by an interlocal agreement pursuant to § 163.01(7), unless any party to such agreement is otherwise an agency as defined in this subsection.

Fla. Stat. § 120.52(1)(c).

Fla. Stat. § 26.012(1) additionally grants "circuit courts . . . jurisdiction of appeals from final administrative orders of local government code enforcement boards."

As will be recalled, Art. V, § 21 requires an agency's statutory interpretations to be reviewed de novo.

iii. Appeals from Civil Traffic Infraction Hearing Officers

As explained later in this chapter, in 1988 the constitution was amended to permit civil traffic infraction hearing officers. *See* Art. V, § 1. Pursuant to Fla. Stat. § 318.33, appeals from these cases go to the circuit courts.

(c) Writs

Art. V, § 5(b) gives the circuit courts "the power to issue writs of mandamus, quo warranto, certiorari, prohibition and habeas corpus, and all writs necessary or proper to the complete exercise of their jurisdiction." For a discussion of these writs, see the earlier sections of this chapter.

H.   COUNTY COURTS

1.   BASICS

Art. V, § 6(a) stipulates: "There shall be a county court in each county." Fla. Stat. § 34.01(5) adds: "A county court is a trial court."

In larger counties, the county court typically is divided into civil and criminal divisions. It also may operate out of multiple courthouses. *See*, *e.g.*, http://www.17th.flcourts.org/10-county-court-civil-and-criminal/ (county court page of Broward County). *See also* Fla. Stat. § 34.181 (permitting county courts to have branch locations).

The county courts are the workhorses of Florida's court system. In 2018, 2,663,654 new lawsuits were filed in them: 2,085,835 civil cases (78.3%) and 577,819 criminal cases (21.7%). This accounts for 77.7% of all new trial court filings in Florida. This large volume of cases is the result of the county courts having jurisdiction over numerous minor matters.

2. PERSONNEL

(a) Judges

Art. V, § 6(b) states: "There shall be one or more judges for each county court as prescribed by general law." Pursuant to this provision, Fla. Stat. § 34.022 specifies the number of county court judges. At present, 31 of Florida's 67 county courts have one judge; 26 have two to nine judges; three have 10 to 14 judges; and seven have 15 or more judges. Miami-Dade (43) and Broward (32) Counties have the most county court judges. As explained earlier in this chapter, there are a total of 324 county judges.

County court judges are paid $151,822 a year. As explained later in this chapter, they serve six-year terms, which are renewable, and must retire at 75. For a further look at county court judges, see the web site of the Conference of County Court Judges of Florida (https://floridacountyjudges.com/).

(b) Clerks

As previously noted, the clerk of the circuit court serves as the clerk of the county courts in his or her jurisdiction except when otherwise provided by law. *See* Art. V, § 16; Fla. Stat. § 34.031. No county court currently has its own clerk.

3. JURISDICTION

Art. V, § 6(b) provides: "The county courts shall exercise the jurisdiction prescribed by general law. Such jurisdiction shall be uniform throughout the state."

Fla. Stat. § 34.01(1) gives the county courts jurisdiction:

(a) In all misdemeanor cases not cognizable by the circuit courts.

(b) Of all violations of municipal and county ordinances.

(c) Of all actions at law, except those within the exclusive jurisdiction of the circuit courts, in which the matter in controversy does not exceed, exclusive of interest, costs, and attorney fees: 1. If filed on or before December 31, 2019, the sum of $15,000. 2. If filed on or after January 1, 2020, the sum of $30,000. 3. If filed on or after January 1, 2023, the sum of $50,000.

(d) Of disputes occurring in the homeowners' associations as described in § 720.311(2)(a), which shall be concurrent with [the] jurisdiction of the circuit courts.

Additionally, Fla. Stat. § 34.01(2) allows county courts to hear uncontested divorces, while Fla. Stat. § 34.011 gives them jurisdiction over landlord-tenant disputes (so long as the amount in controversy does not exceed their jurisdiction). Fla. Stat. § 34.01(4) gives county courts equity jurisdiction in all cases they are competent to hear.

The county courts also are where one finds "small claims court." This phrase refers to the simplified procedure used by county courts to hear civil disputes involving amounts up to $5,000 (up to $8,000 beginning on Jan. 1, 2020).

In 1988, to take some of the burden off the county courts, the constitution was amended to permit the appointment of civil traffic infraction hearing officers. *See* Art. V, § 1. This provision is implemented by Fla. Stat. §§ 318.30–318.38.

Fla. Stat. § 318.32 describes the jurisdiction of hearing officers:

(1) Hearing officers shall be empowered to accept pleas from and decide the guilt or innocence of any person, adult or juvenile, charged with any civil traffic infraction and shall be empowered to adjudicate or withhold adjudication of guilt in the same manner as a county court judge under the statutes, rules, and procedures presently existing or as subsequently amended, except that hearing officers shall not:

(a) Have the power to hold a defendant in contempt of court, but shall be permitted to file a motion for order of contempt with the appropriate state trial court judge;

(b)   Hear a case involving a crash resulting in injury or death;

(c)   Hear a criminal traffic offense case or a case involving a civil traffic infraction issued in conjunction with a criminal traffic offense; or

(d)   Have the power to suspend or revoke a defendant's driver license pursuant to § 316.655(2).

(2)   This section does not prohibit a county court judge from exercising concurrent jurisdiction with a civil traffic hearing officer.

(3)   Upon the request of the defendant contained in a Notice of Appearance or a written plea, the case shall be assigned to a county court judge regularly assigned to hear traffic matters.

Hearing officers are appointed by the chief judges of the circuit courts, see Fla. Stat. § 318.35, and must be lawyers. *See* Fla. Stat. § 318.34. These part-time positions, which typically pay $50–$75 an hour, often are used by lawyers as stepping stones to judicial office. At present, every circuit has such officers, although the number varies from fewer than five (in 14 circuits) to as many as 29 (in the 11th Circuit). For a further discussion, see Rule 6.630 of the Florida Rules of Traffic Court.

I. OTHER COURTS

In addition to its federal and states courts, Florida has three other types of courts: military, religious, and tribal. *See Florida's Other Courts: Unconventional Justice in the Sunshine State* (Robert M. Jarvis ed., University Press of Florida, 2018).

1. MILITARY

Florida's military courts have the power to punish members of the Florida National Guard (except when they are in the active service of the United States). *See* Fla. Stat. §§ 250.35–250.37. *See also Waterman v. State*, 654 So. 2d 150 (Fla. 1st Dist. Ct. App. 1995) (affirming order reducing National Guardsman's rank and forfeiting his pay for misconduct during Hurricane Andrew).

A military court convened to hear charges against a service member is known as a court-martial. There are three types of courts-martial: general (felonies), special (misdemeanors), and summary (minor violations). Since 1998, Art. V, § 1 has required court-martial appeals to be heard by the First District in Tallahassee. Another 1998 change authorizes the Florida Supreme Court and the district courts to seek advisory opinions from the U.S. Court of Appeals for the Armed Forces. *See* Art. V, § 2. To date, this provision has not been used.

2. RELIGIOUS

Many religious groups in Florida have their own courts. Pursuant to both the First Amendment and

Art. I, § 3, such courts have exclusive jurisdiction in purely ecclesiastical matters. *See, e.g., Crowder v. Southern Baptist Convention*, 828 F.2d 718 (11th Cir. 1987), *cert. denied*, 484 U.S. 1066 (1988); *Diocese of Palm Beach, Inc. v. Gallagher*, 249 So. 3d 657 (Fla. 4th Dist. Ct. App.), *review denied*, 2018 WL 4050485 (Fla. 2018), *cert. denied*, 139 S. Ct. 1601 (2019). For a further discussion, see Ch. 11 of this book.

3.   TRIBAL

Both of Florida's federally-recognized Indian tribes (the Miccosukees and the Seminoles) have their own courts (the former since 1981, the latter since 2015). Although these courts are not mentioned in the Florida Constitution, in certain instances federal law ousts the jurisdiction of Florida's state courts. *See, e.g., Miccosukee Tribe of Indians of Florida v. United States*, 2000 WL 35623105 (S.D. Fla. 2000) (criminal law); *Billie v. Stier*, 141 So. 3d 584 (Fla. 3d Dist. Ct. App.), *review denied*, 157 So. 3d 1041 (Fla. 2014) (family law).

J.   ADMINISTRATIVE TRIBUNALS

As noted earlier, Art. V, § 1 authorizes the legislature to grant "[c]ommissions . . . or administrative officers or bodies . . . quasi-judicial power in matters connected with the functions of their offices." Pursuant to this provision, in 1974 Florida established the Division of Administrative Hearings ("DOAH"). The DOAH is part of the state's Department of Management Services and is modelled after California's Office of Administrative Hearings.

The DOAH was created to ensure "administrative due process." *See* Fla. Stat. § 120.515. Prior to the DOAH, government agencies frequently operated without published policies and hearings challenging their decisions often were conducted by the agency's own employees. In addition, hearing procedures varied greatly among agencies. The result was a system of administrative adjudication that lacked accountability, impartiality, and transparency.

The DOAH is staffed by 32 administrative law judges ("ALJ") and 32 compensation claims judges ("JCC"). ALJs hear challenges to state agency rules and the processes used to promulgate them. *See* Fla. Stat. § 120.56. They also handle certain types of individual claims, including: 1) awards under the state's birth-related neurological injury compensation plan; 2) child support enforcement orders; 3) educational placements (for students with special needs); 4) involuntary mental health commitments; 5) license revocations; 6) school personnel firings; and, 7) state contract bidding protests. *See* Fla. Stat. §§ 120.569, 120.57, 120.60, and 120.651. JCCs, on the other hand, exclusively hear workers' compensation cases. *See* Fla. Stat. § 440.45(2)(a).

The head of the DOAH is its chief administrative law judge. *See* Fla. Stat. § 120.65(1). He or she is appointed by the Administration Commission (consisting of the governor and the cabinet—see Fla. Stat. § 14.202) and must be confirmed by the senate. *Id.* In addition to overseeing the DOAH, the chief judge hires the ALJs. *See* Fla. Stat. § 120.65(4). Both the chief judge and the ALJs must be lawyers. *Id.* JCCs also must be lawyers, but they are appointed by the governor for four-year renewable terms. *See* Fla. Stat. § 440.45. ALJs and JCCs earn $124,564 a year.

In a typical year, 6,300 new ALJ cases, and 70,000 new JCC petitions, are filed. Although the DOAH's offices are in Tallahassee, hearings take place throughout the state (extensive use is made of videoconferencing).

Appeals from ALJ decisions go to the district court "where the agency maintains its headquarters or where a party resides or as otherwise provided by law." Fla. Stat. § 120.68(2)(a). In contrast, appeals from JCC decisions go to the First District in Tallahassee. *See* Fla. Stat. § 440.271. As will be recalled, Art. V, § 21 requires an agency's statutory interpretations to be reviewed de novo.

For a further look at ALJs and JCCs, see the web sites of the DOAH (https://www.doah.state.fl.us/ALJ/) and the Office of the Judges of Compensation Claims (https://www.jcc.state.fl.us/jcc/).

A point not made by the constitution, but important from a practice standpoint, bears mentioning. When a Florida agency (either through the DOAH or by some other means) provides a process for challenging its decisions, a party must use it. This is due to the "exhaustion of administrative remedies" doctrine:

[T]he doctrine of exhaustion of administrative remedies precludes judicial intervention where available administrative remedies can afford the relief a litigant seeks. Thus, one seeking judicial review of administrative action must first exhaust the administrative remedies that are available and adequate to afford the relief sought, and a reviewing court may not entertain a suit where the complaining party has not exhausted the available administrative remedies. Hence, it is appropriate to dismiss a suit when a party fails to exhaust his or her administrative remedies.

The exhaustion of administrative remedies rule serves a number of policies: full development of a factual record, conservation of judicial resources, avoiding premature interruption of the administrative process, and enabling the agency to apply its discretion and expertise in the first instance to technical subject matter. Additionally, the exhaustion doctrine promotes judicial efficiency by giving the agency an opportunity to correct its own mistakes, thereby mooting controversies and eliminating the need for court intervention; and in some contexts, judicial restraint through the doctrine of exhaustion of remedies may be necessary to support the integrity of the administrative process and to allow the executive branch to carry out its responsibilities as a coequal branch of government.

John Bourdeau et al., "Administrative Law" § 406, *in* 2 *Florida Jurisprudence 2d* 464–65 (2014) (footnotes omitted).

In carrying out their duties, all quasi-judicial officials must abide by Art. I, § 18, which directs: "No administrative agency, except the Department of Military Affairs in an appropriately convened court-martial action as provided by law, shall impose a sentence of imprisonment, nor shall it impose any other penalty except as provided by law." This provision was added during the 1968 revision of the constitution. In 1998, it was amended to make it clear that courts-martial are excluded.

Despite the clarity of § 18, there are a surprising number of cases in which administrative officers have attempted to impose unauthorized penalties. *See, e.g., Moore v. Pearson*, 789 So. 2d 316 (Fla. 2001); *Crary v. Tri-Par Estates Park and Recreation District*, 267 So. 3d 530 (Fla. 2d Dist. Ct. App. 2019); *Florida Elections Commission v. Davis*, 44 So. 3d 1211 (Fla. 1st Dist. Ct. App.), *review dismissed*, 49 So. 3d 746 (Fla. 2010). *See also Fernandez v. School Board of Miami-Dade County, Florida*, 201 F. Supp. 3d 1353 (S.D. Fla. 2016).

The proper procedure, if criminal wrongdoing is suspected, is for an administrative officer to refer a case to the appropriate state attorney for prosecution. *See, e.g., State v. Avatar Development Corp.*, 697 So. 2d 561 (Fla. 4th Dist. Ct. App.), *review granted*, 703 So. 2d 475 (Fla. 1997), *approved*, 723 So. 2d 199 (Fla. 1998).

K. JUSTICES AND JUDGES

1. ELIGIBILITY

Art. V, § 8 sets out the eligibility requirements for justices and judges:

> No person shall be eligible for office of justice or judge of any court unless the person is an elector of the state and resides in the territorial jurisdiction of the court. No justice or judge shall serve after attaining the age of seventy-five years except upon temporary assignment. No person is eligible for the office of justice of the supreme court or judge of a district court of appeal unless the person is, and has been for the preceding ten years, a member of the bar of Florida. No person is eligible for the office of circuit judge unless the person is, and has been for the preceding five years, a member of the bar of Florida. Unless otherwise provided by general law, no person is eligible for the office of county court judge unless the person is, and has been for the preceding five years, a member of the bar of Florida. Unless otherwise provided by general law, a person shall be eligible for election or appointment to the office of county court judge in a county having a population of 40,000 or less if the person is a member in good standing of the bar of Florida.

The requirements for being an elector are set out in Art. VI, §§ 2 and 4. *See* Ch. 3 of this book. A justice or judge must meet the applicable eligibility requirements at the time he or she is sworn in. *See*

Advisory Opinion to the Governor re Commission of Elected Judge, 17 So. 3d 265 (Fla. 2009) (bar membership); *Miller v. Menendez*, 804 So. 2d 1243 (Fla. 2001) (residency); *In re Advisory Opinion to the Governor*, 192 So. 2d 757 (Fla. 1966) (bar admission). Unless filling a vacancy, new jurists are sworn in on the first Tuesday after the first Monday in January. *See* Fla. Stat. § 100.041(1).

There were no judicial eligibility requirements in Florida's first three constitutions. Florida's 1868 constitution required both supreme court justices and circuit court judges to be attorneys and at least 25 years old. The 1885 constitution retained these requirements.

In 1956, the constitution was amended to require supreme court justices and district court judges to have been attorneys for at least 10 years. In 1966, two different amendments were passed. The first required circuit court judges to have been attorneys for at least five years, while the second authorized the legislature to require county court judges to be attorneys.

The 1972 overhaul of Art. V required county judges to be attorneys. Since 1984, county court judges have had to be attorneys for at least five years except in counties with a population of 40,000 or less, where they only need to be lawyers. At present, there are 20 such counties, all located in the northern part of the state.

In 2018, the retirement age for all justices and judges was raised from 70 to 75. Florida is one of 31 states that has a mandatory judicial retirement age (nationwide, such laws range from 70 to 90). There is no mandatory retirement age for federal judges.

2. VACANCIES; TERMS; RETENTION; ELECTIONS

Art. V, § 11(a)–(b) directs the governor to fill all judicial vacancies from lists of candidates supplied by the appropriate Judicial Nominating Commission ("JNC"). These lists must contain at least three, but not more than six, names. *Id*. Art. V, § 11(d) specifies: "There shall be a separate judicial nominating commission as provided by general law for the supreme court, each district court of appeal, and each judicial circuit for all trial courts within the circuit." Thus, there currently are 26 JNCs. For a list of them, see https://www.floridabar.org/directories/jnc/. Pursuant to Fla. Stat. § 43.291, each JNC must have nine members appointed by the governor, at least six of whom must be lawyers.

Art. V, § 11(c) requires JNCs to make nominations within 30 days of a vacancy, after which the governor must make his or her choice within 60 days. When necessary, the governor can extend the JNC's time by 30 days. *Id*. For a further discussion of these requirements, see *League of Women Voters of Florida v. Scott*, 257 So. 3d 900 (Fla. 2018); *Pleus v. Crist*, 14 So. 3d 941 (Fla. 2009); *In re Advisory Opinion to the Governor (Judicial Vacancies)*, 600 So. 2d 460 (Fla. 1992).

Since their creation in 1972, the JNCs have remained, from a constitutional perspective, largely unchanged. Minor technical modifications were made in 1984, 1996, and 1998. Among other things, these amendments increased the number of candidates to be forwarded to the governor (from three to six); required the adoption of uniform operating rules; and made the JNC process more transparent.

Statutorily, however, the JNCs underwent a significant change in 2001. Prior to that time, three JNC members were selected by the governor, three were selected by The Florida Bar, and the remaining three were selected by the other six. By changing the law to allow the governor to pick all nine members, the JNCs have become little more than gubernatorial rubber stamps.

A regular term for both justices and judges is six years. *See* Art. V, § 10(a) (supreme court justices and district court judges) and § 10(b)(3)c (circuit court and county court judges). However, justices or judges who are appointed to fill vacancies hold office only until the next general election "occurring at least one year after the date of appointment." *See* Art. V, § 11(a)–(b). This seemingly straightforward provision has proven contentious in practice (and subject to considerable political manipulation), as the following cases demonstrate: *Advisory Opinion to the Governor re Judicial Vacancy Due to Resignation*, 42 So. 3d 795 (Fla. 2010); *Advisory Opinion to the Governor re Appointment or Election of Judges*, 983 So. 2d 526 (Fla. 2008); *Advisory Opinion to the Governor re Sheriff and Judicial Vacancies Due to Resignations*, 928 So. 2d 1218 (Fla. 2006). *See also Scott v. Trotti*, 283 So. 3d 340 (Fla. 1st Dist. Ct. App.), *review granted*, 2018 WL 3831299 (Fla.), *and review dismissed as improvidently granted*, 271 So. 3d 904 (Fla. 2018).

Once the initial term of a supreme court justice or district court judge expires, he or she can seek a new six-year term. *See* Art. V, § 10(a). In such instances, the voters are asked whether they wish to "retain" the candidate. Because only two choices appear on the ballot—"yes" or "no"—the justice or judge quite literally runs on his or her record.

The "merit retention" of supreme court justices and district court judges became part of Florida's constitution in 1976. A 14th Amendment challenge was rejected in *Holley v. Askew*, 583 F.2d 728 (5th Cir. 1978). Since the introduction of the retention system, no justice or judge has been turned out of office, although a few justices have been the subject of concerted removal campaigns because of their views on specific issues (*e.g.*, Rosemary Barkett (anti-death penalty) and Leander Shaw (pro-abortion)).

When the initial term of a circuit court or county court judge expires, he or she can seek election to a new six-year term. *See* Art. V, § 10(b)(1)–(2). Such elections are "non-partisan," meaning that no party affiliation appears next to any candidate's name. Since 2000, voters in every circuit have had the option of choosing their "circuit court judges and county court judges by merit selection and retention rather than by election." Art. V, § 10(b)(3). To date, no circuit's voters have approved such a change.

Florida's present judicial selection system is the result of a long series of changes:

1)   The 1838 constitution originally called for the legislature to appoint circuit court judges (who, as explained earlier, doubled as supreme court justices) for an initial term of five years, after which they would hold office for life. Before this system could be fully implemented, it was discarded in favor of having the people elect circuit judges to eight-year terms (1848), a figure later reduced to six years (1852). The 1852 amendment also authorized separate supreme court justices elected to six-year terms.

2)   The 1861 constitution authorized the governor to appoint, with the consent of 2/3 of the senate, both supreme court justices and circuit court judges to six-year terms.

3)   The 1865 constitution authorized the governor to appoint, with senate consent, supreme court justices to six-year terms and the people to elect circuit court judges to six-year terms.

4)   The 1868 constitution authorized the governor to appoint, subject to senate confirmation, both supreme court justices and circuit court judges, the former for life and the latter to eight-year terms.

5)   The 1885 constitution authorized the people to elect supreme court justices to six-

year terms; the governor to appoint, subject to senate confirmation, circuit court judges to six-year terms; and the people to elect county court judges to four-year terms.

By the time of the 1968 constitution, all Florida jurists were popularly elected, with each serving six-year terms except for county court judges, whose terms remained four years. A 1978 proposal to lengthen the terms of county court judges was narrowly defeated. In 1998, the same suggestion passed easily.

At present, Florida is one of 24 states that uses merit selection/retention for its supreme court justices and one of 10 states that uses a combination of merit selection/retention and non-partisan elections for its lower courts.

In the federal system, Art. III judges are appointed by the president with the advice and consent of the U.S. Senate and have life tenure. Non-Art. III judges may or may not be appointed by the president, may or may not be subject to senate confirmation, and do not have life tenure.

3.   DISCIPLINE

Florida's jurists can be disciplined in two different ways. First, as explained in Ch. 13 of this book, they can be impeached. *See* Art. III, § 17.

Florida's 1838 constitution authorized impeachment for serious offenses, vaguely defined as "misdemeanor[s] in office." For less serious offenses, such as willful neglect of duty, a justice or judge could be removed by the governor

> on the address of two-thirds of each House of the General Assembly; provided, however, that the cause or causes shall be stated at length in such address, and entered on the journals of each House; and provided further, that the cause or causes shall be notified to the Judge so intended to be removed, and he shall be admitted to a hearing in his own defense, before any vote for such address shall pass. . . .

The 1861 and 1865 constitutions carried over this language. The 1868 constitution made impeachment the sole means for removing justices and judges. The 1885 constitution retained this rule.

As an overtly-political process employing an ill-defined standard, impeachments are a poor way to determine whether a justice or judge should remain on the bench. Additionally, impeachments have only two possible outcomes: acquittal or conviction. In many instances, action that stops short of removal is more appropriate. This is particularly true for jurists with mental health or substance abuse problems.

Given the foregoing, in 1966 the constitution was amended to provide a second method of judicial discipline. At the heart of this process is the Judicial Qualifications Commission ("JQC") (https://florida jqc.com/). *See* Art. V, § 12; Fla. Stat. § 43.20. Since the 1972 overhaul of Art. V, the JQC's procedures have undergone multiple technical changes (1974, 1976, 1996, and 1998).

The existence of the JQC has made judicial impeachments extremely rare. Indeed, the last Florida state judge to be impeached was Lake City circuit court judge Samuel Smith in 1978 for drug trafficking.

The JQC has

> jurisdiction over justices and judges regarding allegations that misconduct occurred before or during service as a justice or judge if a complaint is made no later than one year following service as a justice or judge. [It also has] jurisdiction regarding allegations of incapacity during service as a justice or judge.

Art. V, § 12(a)(1).

The JQC consists of six judges (two each from the district courts, circuit courts, and county courts); four lawyers; and five public members. The judges are selected by their fellow judges. *See* Art. V, § 12(a)(1)a. The attorneys are selected by the board of governors of The Florida Bar. *See* Art. V, § 12(a)(1)b. The public members are selected by the governor. *See* Art. V, § 12(a)(1)c. JQC members serve staggered terms and must step down after six years. *See* Art. V, § 12(a)(2). The process for removing JQC members is spelled out in Art. V, § 12(a)(3).

The JQC chooses its chair, see Art. V, § 12(a)(2), and sets its rules. *See* Art. V, § 12(a)(4). The rules can "be repealed by general law enacted by a majority vote of the membership of each house of the legislature, or by the supreme court, five justices concurring." *Id.*

To ensure that the JQC can perform its duties, the constitution requires "all executive, legislative and judicial agencies, including grand juries," to turn over any information requested by the JQC. *See* Art. V, § 12(a)(5). This same section provides: "At any time, on request of the speaker of the house of representatives or the governor, the commission shall make available all information in the possession of the commission for use in consideration of impeachment or suspension, respectively."

Administratively, the JQC is divided into an investigation panel and a hearing panel. The former is authorized "to receive or initiate complaints, conduct investigations, dismiss complaints, and upon a vote of a simple majority of the panel submit formal charges to the hearing panel." *See* Art. V, § 12(b). The latter is authorized

> to receive and hear formal charges from the investigative panel and upon a two-thirds vote of the panel recommend to the supreme court the removal of a justice or judge or the involuntary retirement of a justice or judge for any permanent disability that seriously interferes with the performance of judicial duties. Upon a simple majority vote of the membership of the hearing panel, the panel may recommend to the supreme court that the justice or judge be subject to appropriate discipline.

Id.

Upon receiving a recommendation from the JQC's hearing panel, the supreme court may accept, reject, or modify in whole or in part the findings, conclusions, and recommendations of the commission and it may order that the justice or judge be subjected to appropriate discipline, or be removed from office. . . . After the filing of a formal proceeding and upon request of the investigative panel, the supreme court may suspend the justice or judge from office, with or without compensation, pending final determination of the inquiry.

Art. V, § 12(c)(1). Until charges are filed at the supreme court, the JQC process is confidential. *See* Art. V, § 12(a)(4).

Art. V, § 12(c)(1) allows the supreme court to reprimand, fine, suspend, or remove the defendant from the bench. *See, e.g.*, *Inquiry Concerning a Judge No. 18–63—Re: Maria Ortiz*, 2019 WL 364277 (Fla. 2019) (county court judge suspended for 90 days without pay, fined $5,000, and publicly reprimanded for failing to properly fill out her financial disclosure forms); *Inquiry Concerning a Judge No. 16–534—Re: Dana Marie Santino*, 257 So. 3d 25 (Fla. 2018) (county court judge removed from office for campaign violations). The court also can award costs to the prevailing party. *See* Art. V, § 12(c)(2).

If the JQC recommends that action be taken against a supreme court justice, the entire court is disqualified and the matter is heard by the seven most senior circuit court judges. *See* Art. V, § 12(e).

A justice or judge who is cleared by the JQC remains subject to impeachment. This is made clear by Art. V, § 12(d): "The power of removal conferred by this section shall be both alternative and cumulative to the power of impeachment."

Since its creation, the JQC has filed charges against more than 200 judges (including several supreme court justices). For a list of such actions going back to 2000, see https://www.floridasupreme court.org/News-Media/Judicial-Discipline-JQC-Cases/JQC-Case-Archive.

Federal judges are subject to discipline pursuant to the Judicial Conduct and Disability Act of 1980, 28 U.S.C. §§ 351–364. However, because they are appointed for life, they can be removed only by Congress. *See* U.S. Const. Art. II, § 4. Two Florida federal judges have been removed: Halsted Ritter (Southern District—impeached 1936 for favoritism and practicing law while on the bench, convicted 1936) and Alcee Hastings (Southern District— impeached 1988 for perjury and conspiring to solicit a bribe, convicted 1989). A third Florida federal judge (Charles Swayne of the Northern District) was impeached for abusing his office (1904) but was acquitted (1905).

4.   PROHIBITED ACTIVITIES

Art. V, § 13 currently reads: "All justices and judges shall devote full time to their judicial duties. They shall not engage in the practice of law or hold office in any political party." Effective December 31, 2022, this language will be changed to read:

(a) All justices and judges shall devote full time to their judicial duties. A justice or judge shall not engage in the practice of law or hold office in any political party.

(b) A former justice or former judge shall not lobby for compensation on issues of policy, appropriations, or procurement before the legislative or executive branches of state government for a period of six years after he or she vacates his or her judicial position. The legislature may enact legislation to implement this subsection, including, but not limited to, defining terms and providing penalties for violations. Any such law shall not contain provisions on any other subject.

Paragraph (a) first appeared in the constitution in 1956. It was carried over, with slight changes, in the 1972 overhaul of Art. V. Paragraph (b) was added in 2018. As explained in Ch. 2 of this book, in 2022 the same six-year "cooling off" period will apply to former state, county, and local officials. *See* Art. II, re-designated § 8(f).

5.   CONSERVATORS OF THE PEACE

Art. V, § 19 declares: "All judicial officers in this state shall be conservators of the peace." This language originated with the 1861 constitution and has appeared in every subsequent constitution.

The term "conservator of the peace" (Latin: *Custodes pacis*) has no precise modern meaning, although it often is equated with the term "law enforcement officer." It generally is understood as giving judges the authority to carry weapons, make arrests, hold persons in custody, and take whatever other steps are necessary to maintain public order. *See* Fla. Stat. §§ 790.061 and 901.01. *See also Ex parte Sirmans*, 116 So. 282 (Fla. 1927) (Div. B); *Edge-Gougen v. State*, 182 So. 3d 730 (Fla. 1st Dist. Ct. App. 2015); Fla. Att'y Gen. Op. 84–22.

L. STATE ATTORNEYS

Art. V, § 17 provides:

> In each judicial circuit a state attorney shall be elected for a term of four years. Except as otherwise provided in this constitution, the state attorney shall be the prosecuting officer of all trial courts in that circuit and shall perform other duties prescribed by general law; provided, however, when authorized by general law, the violations of all municipal ordinances may be prosecuted by municipal prosecutors. A state attorney shall be an elector of the state and reside in the territorial jurisdiction of the circuit; shall be and have been a member of the bar of Florida for the preceding five years; shall devote full time to the duties of the office; and shall not engage in the private practice of law. State attorneys shall appoint such assistant state attorneys as may be authorized by law.

This provision was adopted as part of the 1972 overhaul of Art. V. It assumed its present wording following amendments in 1986 (adding the statewide prosecutor) and 1998 (removing gendered pronouns).

Originally, state attorneys were called solicitors, and the 1838 constitution provided:

There shall be one Solicitor for each Circuit, who shall reside therein, to be elected by the joint vote of the General Assembly, who shall hold his office for the term of four years; and shall receive for his services a compensation to be fixed by law.

The 1861 constitution placed the election of solicitors in the hands of each circuit's voters. The 1865 constitution made no changes. The 1868 constitution renamed the position "state attorney" and authorized the governor to appoint state attorneys subject to senate confirmation. The 1885 constitution made no changes. In 1944, state attorneys again were made elective officials.

The title "state attorney" is an uncommon one (only six other states use it). In most jurisdictions, the position is called "county attorney," "district attorney," or "prosecuting attorney." South Carolina, however, still refers to its prosecutors as "solicitors."

Although they are elected by circuit, state attorneys are state officers. See *Johns v. State*, 197 So. 791 (Fla. 1940) (Div. B). They also are constitutional officers. See *Austin v. State ex rel. Christian*, 310 So. 2d 289 (Fla. 1975).

In *Valdes v. State*, 728 So. 2d 736 (Fla. 1999), the petitioner challenged his conviction for premediated murder on separation of powers grounds. In turning aside this argument, the court wrote:

The crux of Valdes' claim appears to be that the state attorney violates constitutional principles by performing the executive function of charging crimes. In support of his claim, Valdes argues that the location of the section creating the office of state attorney in the Judiciary Article, article V, establishes that state attorneys were intended to a part of the judicial branch of government, and thus cannot perform the executive function of charging crimes. . . .

As this Court explained in *The Office of the State Attorney v. Parrotino*, 628 So.2d 1097, 1099 (Fla.1993), state attorneys fulfill a unique role, which is both quasi-judicial and quasi-executive. This unique role is due to the tradition of their exclusive discretion in prosecution, combined with their status as officers of the court. The office of state attorney thus "shares some attributes of the executive" by virtue of its power as the prosecuting authority to determine whom and how to prosecute, as well as some attributes of the judicial branch, such as judicial immunity. *Id.* at 1099 n.2. Nothing about the placement of the constitutional provision in article V providing for the creation of the state attorneys undermines these long-held principles.

Id. at 738–39.

Fla. Stat. § 27.02(1) defines the duties of state attorneys:

The state attorney shall appear in the circuit and county courts within his or her judicial circuit and prosecute or defend on behalf of the state all suits, applications, or motions, civil or criminal, in which the state is a party. . . .

[T]he state attorney shall appear in the circuit and county courts within his or her judicial circuit for the purpose of prosecuting violations of special laws and county or municipal ordinances punishable by incarceration if the prosecution is ancillary to a state prosecution or if the state attorney has contracted with the county or municipality for reimbursement for services rendered in accordance with § 27.34(1).

In 2018, Florida's 20 state attorneys had a collective budget of $473 million and prosecuted 370,000 felony cases, 645,000 misdemeanor cases, and 99,000 juvenile cases. By law, appeals are conducted by the attorney general's office. *See* Fla. Stat. §§ 16.01(4) and 27.05. State attorneys also handle certain types of civil cases. *See*, *e.g.*, Fla. Stat. §§ 75.05(1) (bond validations) and 394.467(6) (involuntary mental health commitments). Except when authorized by statute, state attorneys have no power to initiate civil or administrative proceedings. *See State v. General Development Corp.*, 469 So. 2d 1381 (Fla. 1985).

Each state attorney is aided by between 15 and 250 assistant state attorneys ("ASAs"). Statewide, there are 2,200 ASAs. ASAs are hired by, and serve at the pleasure of, their state attorneys. *See* Fla. Stat. § 27.181(1).

State attorneys are paid $169,554 a year. *See* Fla. Stat. § 27.35. The salaries of ASAs are set by their state attorneys. *See* Fla. Stat. § 27.181(3). By law, ASAs cannot be paid more than their state attorneys. *Id.* In 2019, the legislature raised the minimum salary of all ASAs to $50,000.

For a list of Florida's state attorneys, see https://www.yourfpaa.org/public-information/state-attorneys. For a further look at them, see the web site of the Florida Prosecuting Attorneys Association (https://www.yourfpaa.org/). *See also* http://www.oppaga.state.fl.us/profiles/1023/. Another helpful web site is the National District Attorneys Association (https://ndaa.org/).

Federal criminal defendants are prosecuted by U.S. Attorneys. *See* https://www.justice.gov/usao. The web sites of Florida's three U.S. Attorney's offices are: https://www.justice.gov/usao-sdfl (Southern District); https://www.justice.gov/usao-mdfl (Middle District); and https://www.justice.gov/usao-ndfl (Northern District).

M.   PUBLIC DEFENDERS

Art. V, § 18 states:

In each judicial circuit a public defender shall be elected for a term of four years, who shall perform duties prescribed by general law. A public defender shall be an elector of the state and reside in the territorial jurisdiction of the circuit and shall be and have been a member of the Bar of Florida for the preceding five years.

Public defenders shall appoint such assistant public defenders as may be authorized by law.

This provision was added as part of the 1972 overhaul of Art. V.

An indigent defendant had no right to appointed counsel under Florida's first four constitutions. The 1885 constitution changed this by providing: "In all criminal cases prosecuted in the name of the State, where the defendant is insolvent or discharged, the State shall pay the legal costs and expenses, including the fees of officers, under such regulations as shall be prescribed by law." In 1894, the duty to pay was placed on the county where the crime was committed. *See In re Advisory Opinion to the Governor*, 16 So. 410 (Fla. 1895).

Notwithstanding the foregoing, Florida routinely failed to provide lawyers to criminal defendants. This changed after the U.S. Supreme Court began holding that such appointments were mandated by the Sixth Amendment. *See, e.g., Powell v. Alabama*, 287 U.S. 45 (1932) (capital cases); *Gideon v. Wainwright*, 372 U.S. 335 (1963) (felony cases); *Application of Gault*, 387 U.S. 1 (1967) (juvenile delinquency cases); *Argersinger v. Hamlin*, 407 U.S. 25 (1972) (misdemeanor cases in which the defendant faces the possibility of incarceration).

In 1963, in response to the *Gideon* decision, the Florida Legislature appropriated $186,250 to create public defender offices in each of the state's 16 judicial circuits (thereby making Florida the first state to have a statewide public defender system).

When Art. V was overhauled in 1972, these offices were constitutionalized. *See* Fla. Att'y Gen. Op. 85–103. Florida now annually spends $232 million on its public defender system.

Florida is the only state that elects its public defenders. Three states (California, Nebraska, Tennessee) have a mix of appointed and elected public defenders. In all other states, public defenders are gubernatorial appointees. Florida elects its public defenders because at the time of the 1963 statewide public defender bill, four large counties (Broward, Dade, Hillsborough, and Pinellas) had their own locally-appointed public defenders and objected to making them gubernatorial appointees.

Fla. Stat. § 27.51 specifies the duties of public defenders and limits them to: 1) felony cases; 2) misdemeanor cases (unless, prior to trial, the judge enters an "order of no imprisonment"); 3) juvenile delinquency cases; and, 4) involuntary mental health cases. Unless authorized by statute, public defenders cannot represent parties in civil cases. *See* Fla. Stat. § 27.51(1)(d). Fla. Stat. § 27.52(2)(a) establishes the requirements for being declared indigent.

If the public defender is unable to represent a defendant due to a conflict of interest, the case is assigned to the Office of Criminal Conflict and Civil Regional Counsel ("OCCCRC"). *See* Fla. Stat. § 27.511. Each of Florida's five appellate districts has its own OCCCRC. *Id. See* http://www.oppaga.state.fl. us/profiles/1022/02/.

In 2018, Florida's 20 public defenders represented 536,000 defendants in 670,000 cases. To improve efficiency and save money, appeals are conducted only by certain public defender offices. *See* Fla. Stat. § 27.51(4) (appeals in the First District handled by Second Circuit public defenders; Second District/10th Circuit; Third District/11th Circuit; Fourth District/15th Circuit; Fifth District/Seventh Circuit).

Since 1985, habeas corpus appeals by indigent death row inmates who have exhausted their direct appeals have been handled by the Office of Capital Collateral Regional Counsel ("OCCRC"). *See* Fla. Stat. § 27.702. There is an OCCRC office in each of Florida's three federal districts. *See* Fla. Stat. § 27.701. *See also* http://www.oppaga.state.fl.us/profiles/1025/.

Public defenders are aided by between 15 and 200 assistant public defenders ("APDs"). Statewide, there are 1,725 APDs (including 125 appellate APDs). APDs are hired by, and serve at the pleasure of, their public defenders. *See* Fla. Stat. § 27.53(1).

Public defenders are paid $169,554 a year. *See* Fla. Stat. § 27.5301(1). The salaries of APDs are set by their public defenders. *See* Fla. Stat. § 27.5301(2). By law, APDs cannot be paid more than their public defenders. *Id*. In 2019, the legislature raised the minimum salary of all APDs to $50,000.

For a list of Florida's public defenders, see https://flpda.org/home. For a further look at them, see the web site of the Florida Public Defender Association (https://www.flpda.org/home). *See also* http://www.

oppaga.state.fl.us/profiles/1024/. Another helpful web site is the National Association for Public Defense (https://www.publicdefenders.us/).

Indigent defendants in federal cases are represented by federal public defenders. For a look at them, see https://www.uscourts.gov/services-forms/defender-services. The web sites of Florida's three federal public defender offices are: https://fpdsouthflorida.org/ (Southern District); https://flm.fd.org/ (Middle District); and https://fln.fd.org/ (Northern District).

PART IV
LOCAL GOVERNMENTS

CHAPTER 16
COUNTIES

A. OVERVIEW

Art. VIII takes up the subject of local government. It begins with § 1(a), which requires "[t]he state [to] be divided . . . into political subdivisions called counties." This pattern is followed in every other state, although Alaska has "boroughs" and Louisiana has "parishes."

B. BASICS

In France, a *conté* was an area controlled by a count. In England, however, land was divided into *shires* overseen by earls. As a result, the first eight counties established in the United States (in Virginia in 1634) were called shires. Within a decade, all had been renamed counties.

At the beginning of the British occupation (1763), Florida was split into two halves known, respectively, as East Florida and West Florida. When Florida became a U.S. territory in 1821, Andrew Jackson, Florida's military governor, scrapped these designations and issued the following order:

> All the country lying between the Perdido and Suwaney rivers, with all the islands therein, shall form one county to be called Escambia. All the country lying east of the river Suwaney and every part of the ceded territories, not designated as belonging to the former county, shall form a county to be called St. Johns.

Over time, as Florida's population grew, new counties were added. As a result, Florida now has 67 counties. Texas (254) has the most counties, while Delaware (three) has the fewest. The average number of counties per state is 62. There are 3,142 counties in the United States.

Geographically speaking, Florida's largest county is Palm Beach—it encompasses 2,034 square miles. At 240 square miles, Union is Florida's smallest county. Nationally, the North Slope in Alaska is the largest county (94,763 square miles) and Kalawao in Hawaii is the smallest (12 square miles). The average county in the United States covers 1,124 square miles; in Florida, the figure is 805 square miles.

By population, Florida's largest county is Miami-Dade. It has 2.7 million residents. At 8,900 residents, Liberty is Florida's smallest county. Nationally, Los Angeles is the largest (10.1 million residents) and Kalawao is the smallest (90 residents). On average, counties in the United States have 100,000 residents. Florida's average is 313,000 residents.

Based on annual median household income, St. Johns is Florida's richest county ($74,000) and Madison is its poorest ($32,000). Nationally, Loudoun in Virginia is the richest ($130,000) and Sumter in Alabama is the poorest ($21,000). (Annual median income in the United States is $61,000. Florida's annual median household income is $53,000, which ranks 39th nationally.)

Florida's counties are represented by the Florida Association of Counties ("FAC") (founded in 1929 as the State Association of County Commissioners) (http://www.fl-counties.com/). Biennially, the FAC publishes the *Florida County Government Guide.* The FAC is a member of the National Association of Counties (founded 1935) (https://www.naco.org/).

Information about Florida's counties can be found on their individual web sites. *See* https://www.stateof florida.com/florida-counties.aspx. Demographic data is available at https://www.enterpriseflorida.com/data-center/florida-communities/floridas-counties/.

Although counties have been mentioned in every one of Florida's constitutions, the 1885 constitution was the first to devote an entire article to them. Nevertheless, it continued to treat counties as mere administrative units of the state, with county officials little more than locally-based state agents. *See Stephens v. Futch*, 74 So. 805 (Fla. 1917).

The 1968 constitution abandoned the 1885 constitution's views, an acknowledgment of the vast expansion of county responsibilities. The current constitutional provisions affecting counties are put into effect by Fla. Stat. chs. 124–164.

Counties are one of the two types of "general purpose" local governments that exist in Florida. The other are municipalities, discussed in Ch. 17 of this book.

As the "upper level" local government, counties typically are responsible for such things as airport and seaport operations, emergency management services, health care, public housing, and solid waste disposal. In contrast, municipalities, as the "lower level" local government, usually focus on more day-to-day concerns, such as code enforcement, fire and police protection, sanitation, and zoning.

C. EXISTENCE

Art. VIII, § 1(a) provides: "Counties may be created, abolished or changed by law, with provision for payment or apportionment of the public debt." Thus, only the legislature may create, change, or abolish a county. If a county is abolished, its debt either must be paid off or transferred to another government unit.

1. CREATION

As noted above, Florida's first two counties were established in 1821. By 1900, the state had 45 counties. Between 1905 and 1925, an additional 22 counties were created, bringing the state to its current total of 67. The last county to be formed was Gilchrist (Dec. 4, 1925).

Over the years, various attempts have been made to create other counties. For example:

1)   In 1828, the territorial council voted to create a new county near Tallahassee named after Richard Call, Gen. Andrew Jackson's aide. The bill was vetoed, however, by Gov. William DuVal, who detested Jackson. In 1822, Florida's third and fourth counties were named for DuVal and Jackson, although the former now

misspells DuVal's name by failing to capitalize the "V."

2) In 1915, the Florida Legislature agreed to create Bloxham County from land located in Levy and Marion Counties, but local voters rejected the idea. This county was intended to honor former Florida Gov. William Bloxham.

3) In 1965, Reps. Lynwood Arnold (D-Jacksonville) and George Stallings (D-Jacksonville) proposed dividing Dade County into three new counties: Dade, Kennedy (for Pres. John F. Kennedy), and Miami Beach. Their bill died in committee.

4) In 1993, the residents of Atlantic Beach, Jacksonville Beach, and Neptune Beach, in three straw polls, voted overwhelming to create a new county (Ocean) from land located in Duval and St. Johns Counties. This led Rep. Joseph Arnall (D-Jacksonville Beach) to ask the Florida Institute of Government (https://iog.fsu.edu/) to study the idea. Although it reported back favorably, the plan failed to advance.

5) In 1999, Sen. Roberto Casas (R-Hialeah) introduced a bill to make the City of Hialeah (in Miami-Dade) a county (Casas argued that Hialeah was being ignored by county officials). Casas's bill died in committee.

Most Florida counties (43) are named for notable people, including explorers, military heroes, Native Americans, religious figures, and statesmen. Twenty pay tribute to Florida's natural resources. Three use political slogans: Dixie, Liberty, and Union. The meaning of one county's name (Sarasota) is uncertain—the most likely explanation is that it refers to the Spanish explorer Hernando de Soto, who visited the area in 1539. De Soto, also spelled DeSoto, is the acknowledged namesake of DeSoto and Hernando Counties.

Four counties no longer have their original names: Dade (now Miami-Dade); Mosquito (Orange); New River (Bradford); and St. Lucie (Brevard) (in 1905, a new, smaller St. Lucie County was created in the same general vicinity). In addition, Hernando County, founded in 1843, had its name changed to Benton in 1844 and back to Hernando in 1850.

2. ABOLITION

To date, only one Florida county has been abolished. In 1832, Fayette County (named for the Marquis de Lafayette) was created from the eastern half of Jackson County. In 1834, it was merged back into Jackson County. In 1853, Lafayette's name was revived when a new county was created from land in Madison County.

3. CHANGE

Although the Florida Legislature has not created a new county since 1925, it has continued to make small adjustments in the borders of individual counties. In 1991, for example, it transferred Naverre Beach from Escambia County to Santa Rosa County. In 1994, it changed the line separating Citrus and Levy Counties from the Withlacoochee River's north bank to its "thread" (*i.e.*, middle). In 2007, it transferred 1,949 acres of land (known as "The Wedge") from Palm Beach County to Broward County. And in 2012, it transferred 129 acres from St. Lucie County to Martin County. For the current boundaries of every county, see Fla. Stat. §§ 7.01–7.67.

D.   SEAT

Art. VIII, § 1(k) provides:

In every county there shall be a county seat at which shall be located the principal offices and permanent records of all county officers. The county seat may not be moved except as provided by general law. Branch offices for the conduct of county business may be established elsewhere in the county by resolution of the governing body of the county in the manner prescribed by law. No instrument shall be deemed recorded until filed at the county seat, or a branch office designated by the governing body of the county for the recording of instruments, according to law.

The county seat normally is the county's largest city. (In this respect Wakulla is unique—it is the only Florida county whose seat, Crawfordville, is not a city.) A list of Florida's county seats can be found at

https://en.wikipedia.org/wiki/List_of_counties_in_
Florida.

Because being the county seat once brought both economic benefits and prestige, fights to be named the county seat were common in Florida's early history, and nearly half (31) the counties changed their seats at least once between 1824 and 1965. (Brevard and Orange Counties did so five times.) Since 1965, however, no county has changed its seat (the last one to do so was Gulf County, which in 1965 moved its seat from Wewahitchka to Port St. Joe). For the procedures for changing a county's seat, see Fla. Stat. §§ 138.01–138.12.

The requirement that a county's principal offices be located at its seat became an issue when Volusia County decided to build its new jail 11 miles from its seat. In *Volusia County v. State*, 417 So. 2d 968 (Fla. 1982), the Florida Supreme Court held that it could do so either by expanding its seat's limits or by designating the new jail a "branch jail." *See also* Fla. Att'y Gen. Op. 91–71.

In 1998, the constitution was amended to allow counties to create "branch offices" to help residents save time. Of course, the advent of the internet has greatly reduced the average citizen's need to personally visit government offices.

E. HOME RULE POWERS

The Florida Constitution divides counties into two types: "charter" and "non-charter." At one time, the differences between them were significant, because charter counties had "home rule" powers (*i.e.*, local autonomy) and non-charter counties did not. The 1968 constitution granted home rule powers to both, but with a subtle difference. While charter counties have home rule powers to the extent *not prohibited* by state law, non-charter counties have home rule powers to the extent *provided by* state law. *See* Art. VIII, § 1(f)–(g). *See also Shands Teaching Hospital and Clinics, Inc. v. Mercury Insurance Co. of Florida*, 97 So. 3d 204 (Fla. 2012) (describing the home rule powers of charter counties); *Tallahassee Memorial Regional Medical Center, Inc. v. Tallahassee Medical Center, Inc.*, 681 So. 2d 826 (Fla. 1st Dist. Ct. App. 1996) (describing the home rule powers of non-charter counties).

Today, there are six key differences between charter and non-charter counties:

1)   Organization. Charter counties have much greater flexibility in how they organize themselves and deliver services to their residents. *See* Art. VIII, § 1(e).

2)   Salaries. In charter counties, local officials set their salaries. In non-charter counties, the legislature performs this task. *See* Fla. Stat. §§ 145.011–145.19. (In 2018, the salaries of Florida's county commissioners ranged from $6,000 to $99,000.)

3)   Ordinances. In charter counties, the county charter resolves conflicts between county and municipal ordinances. *See* Art. VIII, § 1(g). *See also City of Coconut Creek v. Broward*

County Board of County Commissioners, 430 So. 2d 959 (Fla. 4th Dist. Ct. App. 1983). In non-charter counties, the municipal ordinance prevails if there is a conflict. *See* Art. VIII, § 1(f). *See also Misty's Cafe, Inc. v. Leon County*, 640 So. 2d 170 (Fla. 1st Dist. Ct. App.), *review denied*, 650 So. 2d 990 (Fla. 1994).

4)   Taxes. Charter counties are permitted to impose "municipal utility taxes" in unincorporated areas. Non-charter counties lack this authority. *See* Ch. 21 of this book.

5)   Public Participation. Charter county residents often can make changes to their county's charter through initiative petitions. In addition, Fla. Stat. § 100.361 allows charter county residents to "recall" officials before the end of their terms. In 2011, for example, Miami-Dade County's voters ousted Mayor Carlos Alvarez and Commissioner Natacha Seijas.

6)   Special Laws. Charter counties cannot be regulated by special laws unless their residents agree. *See* Art. VIII, § 1(g). Non-charter counties lack this protection.

Although only 20 of Florida's 67 counties are chartered, they account for 80% of the state's population. A list of Florida's charter counties can be found at https://www.fl-counties.com/charter-county-information. The most recent county to become a charter county is Wakulla (2008). The process for becoming a charter county is set forth in Art. VIII, § 1(c) and Fla. Stat. §§ 125.60–125.64. *See also*

Maxwell v. Lee County, 714 So. 2d 1043 (Fla. 2d Dist. Ct. App. 1998).

The 1885 constitution made no allowance for charter counties. As a result, in 1956 the Florida Legislature recommended that a provision be added authorizing Dade County (now Miami-Dade County) to become a charter county. After surviving a taxpayer challenge, see *Gray v. Golden*, 89 So. 2d 785 (Fla. 1956) (en banc), this proposal was approved by the voters. The 1968 constitution recognizes Miami-Dade's chartered status. *See* Art. VIII, § 6(e)–(f). *See also Metropolitan Dade County v. City of Miami*, 396 So. 2d 144 (Fla. 1980).

F. CONSOLIDATION

The 1968 constitution permits cities and counties to "consolidate," thereby allowing taxpayers to save money through the elimination of duplicate offices. *See* Art. VIII, § 3. To date, however, no such mergers have occurred. Although proposals to consolidate the City of Tallahassee and Leon County have been made repeatedly (1971, 1973, 1976, 1980, 1986, 1992), each has failed. In 2017, an FBI investigation into public corruption in Tallahassee briefly revived interest in the idea.

Florida's only consolidation, involving the City of Jacksonville and Duval County, occurred in 1967 under the 1885 constitution. The 1968 constitution preserves this arrangement. *See* Art. VIII, § 6(e); *Jackson v. Consolidated Government of City of Jacksonville*, 225 So. 2d 497 (Fla. 1969). As has been explained elsewhere: "Jacksonville is a case where the governments, both of the City and of the County, had deteriorated to such a point that action was an imperative. It was a reform born of crisis." Frank P. Sherwood, *County Governments in Florida* 109 (iUniverse, 2008).

No Florida county is considered a likely candidate for future consolidation. *See id.* at 96. Outside Florida, consolidations have proven more popular. Prominent examples include Anchorage, Denver, Honolulu, Indianapolis, Kansas City, Louisville, Nashville, New Orleans, Philadelphia, and San Francisco.

G. COMMISSIONERS

The 1885 constitution required each county to be run by a board of county commissioners appointed by the governor and confirmed by the senate. In 1900, commissioners became elective. In 1944, the terms of commissioners were increased from two years to four years.

The 1968 constitution kept these provisions largely intact. As a result, Art. VIII, § 1(e) reads:

Except when otherwise provided by county charter, the governing body of each county shall be a board of county commissioners composed of five or seven members serving staggered terms of four years. After each decennial census the board of county commissioners shall divide the county into districts of contiguous territory as nearly equal in population as practicable. One commissioner residing in each district shall be elected as provided by law.

Most of Florida's counties (57) have five-member commissions. Seven have seven-member commissions (Hillsborough, Leon, Manatee, Orange, Palm Beach, Pinellas, and Volusia) (of these, all are charter counties except Manatee). Per their charters, three counties have commissions with more than seven members: Broward (nine), Duval (20), and Miami-Dade (14). For a list of each county's commissioners, see http://www.fl-counties.com/ directory.

Currently, 38 counties use "at large" elections (meaning that all citizens vote for all commissioners); 23 counties use "single member" districts (each citizen votes for only his or her district's commissioner); and six use a hybrid system. *See, e.g., Brinkmann v. Francois*, 184 So. 3d 504 (Fla. 2016) (describing Broward County's "single member" district system).

As originally worded, Art. VIII, § 1(e) required (except in charter counties) that counties hold "at large" elections for five commissioners. In 1984, these requirements were changed to allow both "at large" and "single member" districts and either five or seven commissioners. *See* Fla. Stat. §§ 124.01–124.03.

Under Art. VIII, § 1(e), commissioners are the county's "legislative branch." Accordingly, they are responsible for the county's finances, see Art. VIII, § 1(b), and pass county ordinances. *See* Art. VIII,

§ 1(h)–(j). County ordinances do not become effective until they are filed with the state. *See* Art. VIII, § 1(i).

Traditionally, commissioners also served as the county's "executive branch." *See* Fla. Stat. § 125.01. However, since 1974 it has been possible to shift this responsibility to either an appointed county administrator or manager, see Fla. Stat. §§ 125.70–125.74, or an elected executive. *See* Fla. Stat. §§ 125.83–125.86. At present, 10 counties still use the traditional model; 54 use the appointed administrator/manager model; and three (Duval, Miami-Dade, and Orange) use the elected executive model.

The constitution does not term-limit county commissioners. However, a charter county can impose such limits. *See Telli v. Broward County*, 94 So. 3d 504 (Fla. 2012). All county commissioners are subject to the governor's suspension powers (Art. IV, § 7). *See* Ch. 14 of this book.

H. OFFICERS

In addition to commissioners, the 1885 constitution required every county to have the following elected officers:

> A Clerk of the Circuit Court, a Sheriff, Constables, a County Assessor of Taxes, a Tax Collector, a County Treasurer, a Superintendent of Public Instruction, and a County Surveyor. The term of office of all county officers mentioned in this section shall be four years, except that of County Assessor of Taxes, County

Tax Collector and County Treasurer, who shall be elected for two years. Their powers, duties and compensation shall be prescribed by law.

Because of changes made in 2018 (discussed below), this provision (Art. VIII, § 1(d)) now reads:

There shall be elected by the electors of each county, for terms of four years, a sheriff, a tax collector, a property appraiser, a supervisor of elections, and a clerk of the circuit court. Unless otherwise provided by special law approved by vote of the electors or pursuant to Article V, section 16, the clerk of the circuit court shall be ex officio clerk of the board of county commissioners, auditor, recorder and custodian of all county funds. Notwithstanding subsection 6(e) of this article, a county charter may not abolish the office of a sheriff, a tax collector, a property appraiser, a supervisor of elections, or a clerk of the circuit court; transfer the duties of those officers to another officer or office; change the length of the four-year term of office; or establish any manner of selection other than by election by the electors of the county.

The 2018 changes, recommended by the Constitution Revision Commission ("CRC"), rewrote paragraph (d) to: 1) require that all five officers be elected; 2) prohibit the elimination of any of them; and, 3) include, with respect to circuit court clerks, a reference to Art. V, § 16 (discussed in Ch. 15 of this book). As a result, by 2024 all Florida counties will be required to elect their officers. *See* Art. VIII, § 1, note

1. For a list of each county's officers, see http://www. fl-counties.com/directory.

The CRC's proposal was challenged by Broward, Miami-Dade, and Volusia Counties—Broward because it did not have an elected tax collector; Miami-Dade because it did not have an elected sheriff, supervisor of elections, or tax collector; and Volusia because it did not have an elected tax collector. In *County of Volusia v. Detzner*, 253 So. 3d 507 (Fla. 2018), the Florida Supreme Court refused to strike the amendment from the ballot.

Elected county officers are not term-limited and a county cannot impose such limits. *See Telli v. Broward County*, 94 So. 3d 504 (Fla. 2012). They are, however, subject to the governor's suspension powers (Art. IV, § 7). *See* Ch. 14 of this book.

I.   INTER-LOCAL AGREEMENTS

Art. VIII, § 4 provides:

By law or by resolution of the governing bodies of each of the governments affected, any function or power of a county, municipality or special district may be transferred to or contracted to be performed by another county, municipality or special district, after approval by vote of the electors of the transferor and approval by vote of the electors of the transferee, or as otherwise provided by law.

This provision originated with the 1968 constitution and applies to both charter and non-charter counties. *See Sarasota County v. Town of*

Longboat Key, 355 So. 2d 1197 (Fla. 1978). As is obvious, it also authorizes municipalities and special districts to enter into transfer agreements.

Most of the litigation generated by this provision has concerned when a dual referendum must be held. In answering this question, the courts have made it clear that such votes are necessary only when there is an *actual* transfer of power. *See, e.g., City of Palm Beach Gardens v. Barnes*, 390 So. 2d 1188 (Fla. 1980) (law enforcement services); *Palm Beach County v. City of Boca Raton*, 995 So. 2d 1017 (Fla. 4th Dist. Ct. App. 2008), *review denied*, 10 So. 3d 631 (Fla. 2009) (emergency dispatch system).

J.   LOCAL OPTION

Art. VIII, § 5 allows each county to decide for itself whether to

1)   permit or ban alcohol sales (defined as "intoxicating liquors, wines or beers") (paragraph (a)); and,

2)   impose waiting periods on firearm sales that take place within the county (paragraph (b)).

Paragraph (a) originated with the 1885 constitution and was retained by the 1968 constitution. At present, only three small counties in north Florida are still "dry": Lafayette, Liberty, and Washington. Each, however, allows packaged beer sales.

Paragraph (b), which was added to the constitution in 1998 to close the "gun show loophole," is discussed in Ch. 8 of this book.

CHAPTER 17
MUNICIPALITIES

A. OVERVIEW

Art. VIII, § 2 provides:

(a) ESTABLISHMENT. Municipalities may be established or abolished and their charters amended pursuant to general or special law. When any municipality is abolished, provision shall be made for the protection of its creditors.

(b) POWERS. Municipalities shall have governmental, corporate and proprietary powers to enable them to conduct municipal government, perform municipal functions and render municipal services, and may exercise any power for municipal purposes except as otherwise provided by law. Each municipal legislative body shall be elective.

(c) ANNEXATION. Municipal annexation of unincorporated territory, merger of municipalities, and exercise of extra-territorial powers by municipalities shall be as provided by general or special law.

The 1868 constitution was the first to mention municipalities. The current language originated in the 1885 constitution.

As § 2(a) indicates, each municipality must have a charter. At a minimum, a charter must "prescribe[ ] the [municipality's] form of government[,] clearly define[ ] the responsibility for legislative and

executive functions[, and] not prohibit the ...
municipality from exercising its powers to levy any
tax authorized by the Constitution or general law."
Fla. Stat. § 165.061(1)(e).

B. BASICS

In everyday conversation, one rarely hears the
word "municipality." Instead, most people use the
word "city." In some states (*e.g.*, Michigan, New York,
Pennsylvania), the words "city," "town," and "village"
have specific legal meanings. In such jurisdictions,
how an area is classified determines its duties,
powers, and rights.

Florida does not draw such distinctions. *See*, *e.g.*,
Fla. Stat. § 180.01 ("The term 'municipality,' as used
in this chapter, shall mean any city, town, or village
duly incorporated under the laws of the state.").
Thus, for example, in Palm Beach County one finds
the City of Boca Raton, the Town of Jupiter, and the
Village of Tequesta. Despite their different names, all
are municipalities.

The United States has 35,637 municipalities.
Florida has 412 municipalities, consisting of 283
cities, 107 towns, and 22 villages. Its five largest
municipalities are Jacksonville (population 926,000),
Miami (466,000), Tampa (399,000), Orlando
(298,000), and St. Petersburg (273,000).
(Tallahassee, Florida's capital, is seventh at
196,000.) Florida's smallest municipality, with a
population of 11, is Marineland.

Florida's municipalities are represented by the Florida League of Cities ("FLC") (established 1922) (https://www.floridaleagueofcities.com/). The FLC is affiliated with the National League of Cities (founded 1924) (https://www.nlc.org/).

For a further look at Florida's municipalities, see Fla. Stat. chs. 165–185. For the web sites of specific municipalities, see https://www.floridaleagueofcities. com/research-resources/municipal-directory.   For municipal legislative materials, see the Municipal Code Corporation's library (https://library.municode. com/).

C.   CREATION AND DISSOLUTION

As explained in Ch. 16 of this book, Florida is divided into 67 counties. Parts of a county not within a municipality are "unincorporated." When the residents of such an area decide to form a municipal government, the area becomes "incorporated." Thus, a city, town, or village is an incorporated part of a county. In such areas, residents are subject to two local, general-purpose governments: the county and the municipality.

Residents typically incorporate because they want a "grass roots" government to which they can bring basic concerns. Thus, municipalities tend to deal with "day-to-day" issues, such as fire and police protection. In areas without a municipality, these issues are handled by the county.

In 2018, 10.6 million Floridians lived in incorporated areas and 10.3 million lived in unincorporated areas. Palm Beach (39), Miami-Dade (34), and Broward (31) Counties have the most municipalities. In contrast, nine counties have just one municipality and 12 have just two municipalities. Four Florida municipalities straddle two counties: Fanning Springs, Flagler Beach, Longboat Key, and Marineland.

As Art. VIII, § 2(a) explains, municipalities can only be created or dissolved by the Florida Legislature. Under Fla. Stat. § 165.041, creation requires: 1) passage of a special act; and, 2) the holding of a local election. *See also* Fla. Stat. § 165.061 (setting minimum population requirements for proposed municipalities).

Florida's oldest municipalities are Pensacola and St. Augustine. Both were incorporated in 1822. Other 19th century incorporations include Tallahassee (1825), Key West (1828), Jacksonville (1832), Tampa (1855), Orlando (1875), and Miami (1896).

Since 1973, there have been 32 incorporations. Florida's newest municipality (2017) is Indiantown in Martin County (population 6,000) (see http://laws. flrules.org/2017/195). It was created after residents decided they wanted more control over the area's land use rules.

Disincorporation of a municipality is governed by Fla. Stat. § 165.051. It authorizes dissolution "by either [a] special act of the Legislature . . . or [an] ordinance of the governing body of the municipality, approved by a vote of the qualified voters." The most recent Florida municipality to disincorporate is the

Town of Hastings in St. Johns County. In 2017, its residents voted to disincorporate because of the town's increasingly shaky finances.

Since 1847, more than 150 Florida municipalities have disincorporated, although only 11 have done so since 1973. Various municipalities (*e.g.*, Marathon, Marco Island, Opa-locka) have considered the idea, however, and in 1997 Miami held a referendum asking voters whether they wanted to abolish the city and merge with the county (the idea lost overwhelmingly).

As explained above, the constitution prohibits a municipality from dissolving unless its debt either is assumed or paid off. Typically, the outstanding balance is transferred to the acquiring government. When the Town of Hastings dissolved in 2017, for example, its debt ($911,000) was assumed by St. Johns County.

Conversely, the residents of the acquired government may or may not be made liable for the acquiring government's pre-existing debt. *See, e.g.,* *Hayes v. Walker*, 44 So. 747, 750 (Fla. 1907) (Div. A) (upholding a law authorizing the City of Tampa to annex Fort Brooke on the condition that the latter's residents "shall not be liable for nor taxed to pay any existing bonded indebtedness of the city of Tampa").

The Florida Supreme Court has recognized that the establishment and disestablishment of municipalities is a legislative prerogative. *See State v. North Bay Village*, 34 So. 2d 876 (Fla. 1948) (Div. A). *See also Sullivan v. Volusia County Canvassing*

Board, 679 So. 2d 1206 (Fla. 5th Dist. Ct. App. 1996) (legislature had power to ratify election process that created the City of Deltona, notwithstanding alleged notice and ballot irregularities). As such, it generally has rejected incorporation and disincorporation challenges.

D. POWERS

In *City of Clinton v. Cedar Rapids and Missouri River Railroad Co.*, 24 Iowa 455 (1868), Chief Justice Dillon held that municipalities have no inherent powers ("Dillon's Rule"). In *Jacksonville Electric Light Co. v. City of Jacksonville*, 18 So. 677 (Fla. 1895), the Florida Supreme Court adopted Dillon's Rule. The U.S. Supreme Court did likewise in *Hunter v. City of Pittsburgh*, 207 U.S. 161 (1907).

Florida's 1968 constitution rejects Dillon's Rule. As a result, Florida's municipalities now possess all powers "except as otherwise provided by law." *See* Art. VIII, § 2(b). Thus, unless the legislature has passed a contrary law, or has preempted the field, a municipality is free to act. *See, e.g.*, *D'Agastino v. City of Miami*, 220 So. 3d 410 (Fla. 2017) (state's "Police Officers' Bill of Rights" law did not negate city's power to investigate police misconduct). *See also City of Hollywood v. Mulligan*, 934 So. 2d 1238, 1243 (Fla. 2006) ("In Florida, a municipality is given broad authority to enact ordinances. . . . [Thus], a municipality may legislate concurrently with the Legislature on any subject which has not been expressly preempted to the State."). *But see Masone v. City of Aventura*, 147 So. 3d 492 (Fla. 2014) (city's "red light" traffic ordinance conflicted with state law); *City of Palm Bay v. Wells Fargo Bank, N.A.*, 114 So. 3d 924 (Fla. 2013) (city ordinance giving "super priority" status to municipal code enforcement liens was preempted by state's property laws). *See also City of South Miami v. DeSantis*, 408 F. Supp. 3d 1266 (S.D. Fla. 2019) (upholding state's "sanctuary city" ban).

In exercising its powers, a municipality must be acting for a "municipal purpose." *See City of Ocala v. Nye*, 608 So. 2d 15 (Fla. 1992). The phrase "municipal purpose" has been interpreted liberally. *See, e.g., City of Winter Park v. Montesi*, 448 So. 2d 1242 (Fla. 5th Dist. Ct. App.), *review denied*, 456 So. 2d 1182 (Fla. 1984) (city allowed to compete with private photographer in selling pictures of local sinkhole that had become global phenomenon).

On rare occasions, a municipal act has been found to have no municipal purpose. In *State v. City of Orlando*, 576 So. 2d 1315 (Fla. 1991), for example, the Florida Supreme Court held that no municipal purpose was served by the city issuing revenue bonds solely to make money:

[B]orrowing money for the primary purpose of reinvestment is not a valid municipal purpose as contemplated by article VIII, section 2(b). A municipality exists in order to provide services to its inhabitants. As noted in then-Chief Justice McDonald's dissenting opinion in *State v. City of Panama City Beach*, 529 So.2d 250 (Fla.1988), we "see no valid public purpose in investing for investing's sake. Making a profit on an investment is an aspect of commerce more properly left to commercial banking and business entities." 529 So.2d at 257 (McDonald, C.J., dissenting). . . .

Id. at 1317.

E. OFFICERS

The last sentence of Art. VIII, § 2(b) requires "[e]ach municipal legislative body [to] be elective." In all other respects, municipalities are free to structure themselves as they wish.

Four basic models of municipal government exist: council-weak mayor; council-strong mayor; commission; and council-manager. In the 19th century, the predominant form of municipal government was the council-weak mayor model. Today, the council-manager model is the dominant form. Many smaller municipalities, however, still use the council-weak mayor model. Others have hybrid systems that borrow different elements from the various models.

In the council-weak mayor model, the council runs the municipality. The mayor is simply one of the council's members, and the position, largely ceremonial, rotates according to a set schedule.

In the council-strong mayor model, the mayor is the municipality's chief executive officer. He or she exercises considerable day-to-day authority (including the power to hire and fire municipal employees) and often has veto power when it comes to council decisions.

In the commission model, the commission's members collectively set the municipality's policies. Each commissioner, however, also in in charge of one or more departments. Proponents of this system believe it increases accountability.

Lastly, in the council-manager model, the council sets the municipality's policies, which are then implemented by a professional manager appointed by the council.

Regardless of which model is chosen, officers are responsible for overseeing their municipalities. This includes adopting a budget, levying taxes, and passing ordinances. For a further discussion of these duties, see *The Florida Municipal Officials' Manual* (published by the FLC), which can be found at https://www.floridaleagueofcities.com/docs/default-source/Pubs/floridamunicipalofficialsmanual.pdf?sfvrsn=70d6ded5_0.

F. BORDERS

As noted at the beginning of this chapter, Art. VIII, § 2(c) leaves it to the Florida Legislature to regulate the annexation of unincorporated territory by municipalities; the merger of municipalities; and the exercise of extra-territorial powers by municipalities. If it so chooses, it can delegate these responsibilities. *See, e.g., Pinellas County v. City of Largo*, 964 So. 2d 847 (Fla. 2d Dist. Ct. App. 2007) (upholding law giving counties the power to adjust municipal borders).

1. ANNEXATIONS

Municipalities can try to expand their borders by annexing any surrounding territory that is unincorporated. *See* Fla. Stat. § 171.043(1) ("The total area to be annexed must be contiguous to the municipality's boundaries at the time the annexation proceeding is begun and reasonably compact, and no part of the area shall be included within the boundary of another incorporated municipality."). *See also Town of Baldwin v. Consolidated City of Jacksonville*, 610 So. 2d 95 (Fla. 1st Dist. Ct. App. 1992).

Normally, the residents of the area to be annexed must vote to become part of the municipality. *See* Fla. Stat. § 171.0413(2)(e). *See also Capella v. City of Gainesville*, 377 So. 2d 658 (Fla. 1979). A vote is not necessary in two instances: 1) when the annexation is ordered by the legislature, see, e.g., *North Ridge General Hospital, Inc. v. City of Oakland Park*, 374 So. 2d 461 (Fla. 1979), *appeal dismissed*, 444 U.S. 1062 (1980); or, 2) when all the landowners in a specific unincorporated area request that a neighboring municipality annex them and the municipality agrees. *See* Fla. Stat. § 171.044.

Although it is not specifically mentioned in the constitution, a municipality also can have its borders reduced. "Contractions," also called "deannexations," are regulated by Fla. Stat. §§ 171.051–171.091.

In 2014, Florida state officials came very close to disincorporating the City of Hampton (population 475) in Bradford County. In 1993, it had annexed a

1,260-foot stretch of U.S. Highway 301 so that its police department could ticket passing motorists. (The highway was one mile outside the city's limits.) In 2012, the city collected $211,000 from such tickets (60% of its budget), making it one of the state's most notorious "speed traps." To avoid disincorporation, the city agreed to retract its annexation of the highway and disband its police force.

2.   MERGERS

Municipalities also can try to expand their borders by merging with other municipalities. The voters in both municipalities must approve such plans. *See* Fla. Stat. § 165.041(2).

3.   EXTRA-TERRITORIAL POWERS

At times, municipalities seek to exercise control over a surrounding unincorporated area, either to protect their own residents or those of the unincorporated area. Because such control is disfavored, it must be expressly authorized. For an example of such an authorization, see Fla. Stat. § 163.3171(1).

CHAPTER 18
SCHOOLS

A. OVERVIEW

Art. IX deals with education. While most of its provisions focus on pre-kindergarten to 12th grade ("PK–12"), higher education also is addressed.

Florida's public education system is the third largest in the country. Its 4,200 PK–12 schools, 28 colleges, and 12 universities collectively serve 2.9 million PK–12 students and 800,000 higher education students. Annually, Florida spends $25.7 billion on PK–12 education and $12.8 billion on higher education. For a further look at Florida's public education system, see the web site of the Florida Department of Education (http://www.fldoe.org/).

B. HISTORY

When Florida became a U.S. territory in 1821, it had no public schools. As a result, in 1827 Congress ordered 40 acres in each Florida township to be set aside for public education. *See* 4 Stat. 201. It expected these lands, known as "sixteenth-section lands," to be leased, with the proceeds used to create permanent local school funds.

Florida's 1838 constitution acknowledged Congress's plan and directed the state "to take such measures as may be necessary to preserve from waste or damage all land so granted and appropriated. . . ." Otherwise, it said nothing at all about education. The 1861 and 1865 constitutions carried over this language without making any changes.

In contrast, the 1868 constitution:

1) Declared education to be a "paramount duty of the State."

2) Required the government "to make ample provision for the education of all . . . children . . . without distinction or preference."

3) Ordered the legislature to create "a uniform system" of free public schools, including a state university, and provide for their "liberal maintenance."

4) Placed responsibility for Florida's schools in the hands of an elected superintendent of public instruction, who also was made the president of the state's new education board.

5) Created a state school fund and a state school tax.

The 1868 constitution also required distributions from the state fund to be tied to a county's school-age population; prohibited counties from receiving state school money unless they levied a local school tax and kept their schools open at least three months a year; and required the governor to appoint a "superintendent of common schools" in each county.

Today, the framework established by the 1868 constitution remains largely intact. The only significant change, a product of the 1885 constitution, is the dividing of the state into school districts based on county boundaries, with each district having an elected school board.

All state constitutions contain provisions on education. In contrast, the U.S. constitution says nothing about the subject. This is because education traditionally has been viewed as a state responsibility. Since 1965, however, Washington has played a significant role in education. *See* https://www.ed.gov/ (web site of the U.S. Department of Education). Indeed, 61% of the money spent on higher education in Florida in 2018 came from federal sources.

C.   PUBLIC EDUCATION

1.   FUNDING

(a) Appropriations

As noted above, the 1868 constitution required the state to make "ample provision" for education and ensure the "liberal maintenance" of schools. The 1885 constitution dropped the former phrase but kept the latter one.

The 1968 constitution deleted the words "liberal maintenance." In their place, an entirely new standard appeared: "Adequate provision shall be made by law for a uniform system of free public schools and for the establishment, maintenance and operation of institutions of higher learning and other public education programs that the needs of the people may require." *See* Art. IX, § 1.

In *Coalition for Adequacy and Fairness in School Funding, Inc. v. Chiles*, 680 So. 2d 400 (Fla. 1996), the plaintiffs

asked the trial court to declare that an adequate education is a fundamental right under the Florida Constitution, and that the State has failed to provide its students that fundamental right by failing to allocate adequate resources for a uniform system of free public schools as provided for in the Florida Constitution.

Id. at 402.

The trial court rejected these requests. On appeal, the Florida Supreme Court affirmed:

As the trial court correctly noted, "[t]here is no textually demonstrable guidance in Article IX, section 1, by which the courts may decide, a priori, whether a given overall level of state funds is 'adequate,' in the abstract." . . . .

We agree with the rationale expressed in the trial court's order, which stated:

While the courts are competent to decide whether or not the Legislature's distribution of state funds to complement local education expenditures results in the required "uniform system," the courts cannot decide whether the Legislature's appropriation of funds is adequate in the abstract, divorced from the required uniformity. To decide such an abstract question of "adequate" funding, the courts would necessarily be required to subjectively evaluate the Legislature's value judgments as to the spending priorities to be assigned to the state's many needs, education being one among them. In short, the Court would have to usurp and oversee the appropriations power, either directly or indirectly, in order to grant the relief sought by Plaintiffs.

Id. at 406–07.

In response, the 1998 Constitution Revision Commission ("CRC") proposed, and the voters approved, numerous changes to Art. IX, § 1. As a result, paragraph (a) now declares education to be "a fundamental value of the people of the State of Florida"; requires the state to provide schools that are "efficient, safe, secure, and high quality"; and promises students "a high quality education." The amendment also revived the 1868 constitution's "paramount duty" language but wedded it to the 1968 constitution's "adequate provision" language, resulting in a particularly odd standard: "It is, therefore, a paramount duty of the state to make adequate provision for the education of all children residing within its borders." *Id.*

Although the CRC's amendment attracted broad support, it did not lead to an increase in school funding. This caused the *Coalition* plaintiffs to file a new lawsuit. After a 10-year battle, the courts again held that § 1 leaves it to the legislature to decide how much money should be spent on education. *See Citizens for Strong Schools, Inc. v. Florida State Board of Education*, 262 So. 3d 127 (Fla. 2019).

Compared to other states, Florida's per pupil spending is very low. In 2018, for example Florida spent $8,881 per pupil, placing it 42nd among states (Utah was last at $6,575). In contrast, New York, which ranked first, spent $21,206 per pupil. To account for differences in the cost of living, the newspaper *Education Week* re-calculated these figures. Although Florida's spending increased to $9,737 per pupil, this was still less than half the amount spent by Vermont, which came in first at $20,795 (Utah remained last at $7,207). It also was significantly below the national average of $12,526.

Other studies, using such factors as graduation rates, teacher salaries, and test scores, also place Florida among the "also-rans." In 2018, for example, *Education Week* ranked Florida 26th, *USA Today* ranked Florida 29th, *U.S. News & World Report* ranked Florida 40th, and the web site *WalletHub* ranked Florida 47th.

In 2008, the Taxation and Budget Reform Commission proposed that Florida's schools spend at least 65% of their money on classroom instruction. Concluding that the amendment exceeded the commission's authority, the Florida Supreme Court struck it from the ballot. *See Ford v. Browning*, 992 So. 2d 132 (Fla. 2008).

Rather than provide more funds to Florida's public schools, the Florida Legislature has encouraged students to go to private schools. As discussed below, it has done so by: 1) creating a variety of voucher programs (officially called "scholarships"); and, 2) authorizing charter schools. According to critics, these initiatives have resulted in the diversion of billions of tax dollars to institutions that operate with little accountability or oversight. Proponents, however, argue that these options—part of the national "school choice" movement (see https://www.edchoice.org/)—place each child in the learning environment that best meets his or her needs.

(b) Vouchers

Florida leads the nation when it comes to school vouchers (it outspends Ohio, which is second, by a three-to-one margin). However, its first voucher—the Opportunity Scholarship Program ("OSP"), begun in 1999, see Fla. Stat. § 1002.38—was struck down in *Bush v. Holmes*, 919 So. 2d 392 (Fla. 2006). Under it, students attending "failing" public schools were given the choice of transferring to a different public school or attending private school at public expense. According to the court, this second option "violate[d] [the constitution] by devoting the state's resources to the education of children . . . through means other than a system of free public schools." *Id.* at 407. Several pages later, however, the court pointedly limited its ruling to the OSP: "We reject the suggestion by the State and amici that other publicly funded educational and welfare programs would necessarily be affected by our decision." *Id.* at 412.

Relying on this language, the Florida Legislature decided to keep its other voucher program, which provides funding for disabled students (McKay scholarships, started 2002—see Fla. Stat. § 1002.39). In 2014, it created a voucher program for special needs students (Gardiner scholarships—see Fla. Stat. § 1002.385), and in 2018 authorized another for students who have been bullied (Hope scholarships— see Fla. Stat. § 1002.40). In 2018, 41,393 students (31,044 McKay/10,258 Gardiner/91 Hope) received vouchers worth a total of $293 million. Nearly all were used at religious schools (80%—this figure has remained constant over time).

In 2019, the Florida Legislature established yet another new voucher program (Family Empowerment scholarships—see Fla. Stat. § 1002.394). It is expected to send 18,000 economically-disadvantaged students to private schools at a cost of $200 million a year.

Under a slightly different plan—the Florida Tax Credit ("FTC") Scholarship (started 2001—see Fla. Stat. § 1002.395)—businesses that provide private school scholarships to low-income students are given tax breaks. In 2018, 108,098 students received FTC scholarships. In exchange, 250 companies claimed $641 million in tax breaks.

In *Citizens for Strong Schools, Inc. v. Florida State Board of Education*, 262 So. 3d 127 (Fla. 2019), the court upheld both the FTC and McKay scholarships (the plaintiffs did not challenge the Gardiner or Hope scholarships). In June 2019, the Florida Education Association ("FEA") announced that it was considering filing a lawsuit to stop the Family Empowerment scholarships. In the meantime, Florida's original voucher program—the OSP—still exists. However, students now can use it only to attend a different public school. In 2018, the program cost $15 million and served 2,595 students.

Because so many Florida students use vouchers to attend religious schools, many observers believe they violate Art. I, § 3 of the Florida Constitution, which prohibits public money from being spent on religious institutions. To date, the Florida Supreme Court has sidestepped this issue, although it may have to confront it if: 1) the FEA goes ahead with its Family Empowerment lawsuit; and, 2) the U.S. Supreme Court preserves § 3-type bans in its upcoming *Espinoza* decision. *See* Ch. 11 of this book.

(c) Charter Schools

In *School Board of Palm Beach County v. Survivors Charter Schools, Inc.*, 3 So. 3d 1220 (Fla. 2009), the Florida Supreme Court held that charter schools are constitutional. In addition to decrying their cost (which is footed by taxpayers), critics insist that charter schools are no more innovative than public schools (charter schools typically claim they are highly innovative); are not properly staffed or run (at least 373 Florida charter schools have closed since 1998, often with little or no notice); and primarily benefit their owners (many of whom also are the schools' landlords—this allows them to collect both rent and tuition). Nevertheless, charter schools have been warmly embraced by Florida's politicians, who have received $13 million in campaign donations from them.

Charter schools were authorized by the Florida Legislature in 1996. *See* Fla. Stat. § 1002.33. At present, Florida's 650 charter schools enroll 290,000 students, accounting for 10% of the state's PK–12 students. In 2018, more than $2 billion in taxpayer money was spent on Florida's charter schools. Nationally, only California and Texas have more charter schools.

Initially, only school districts could authorize charter schools. In 2006, the Florida Legislature transferred this power to the newly-created Florida Schools of Excellence Commission. This law was declared unconstitutional in *Duval County School Board v. State, Board of Education*, 998 So. 2d 641 (Fla. 1st Dist. Ct. App. 2008). As a result, a charter school's application now goes first to the school district. If it votes to deny the application, the applicants can appeal to the Charter School Appeal Commission (an advisory body that includes both charter school operators and school districts) and then to the State Board of Education. *See School Board of Palm Beach County v. Florida Charter Education Foundation, Inc.*, 213 So. 3d 356 (Fla. 4th Dist. Ct. App.), *review denied*, 2017 WL 4129202 (Fla. 2017). *See also School Board of Hillsborough County v. Tampa School Development Corp.*, 113 So. 3d 919 (Fla. 2d Dist. Ct. App. 2013).

In 2018, the CRC recommended that school districts be stripped of their power to approve and supervise charter schools. The Florida Supreme

Court struck this proposal from the ballot because its summary did not clearly explain its purpose. *See Detzner v. League of Women Voters of Florida*, 256 So. 3d 803 (Fla. 2018).

In *School Board of Collier County v. Florida Department of Education*, 279 So. 3d 281 (Fla. 1st Dist. Ct. App. 2019), *appeal filed*, SC19–1649 (Fla.), the court upheld a 2017 statute (see Fla. Laws ch. 2017-116) that requires school districts to share their tax dollars with charter schools:

> While charter schools are statutorily considered to be public schools, the reality is that they do compete with the traditional public schools in their districts. Indeed, section 1002.33(2)(c)2., Florida Statutes (2017), sets forth that one of the purposes of charter schools is to "[p]rovide rigorous competition within the public school district to stimulate continual improvement in all public schools." Given such, the State's constitutional duty to make adequate provision for Florida's public schools must be interpreted to mean that the State has a duty to ensure that charter schools are not neglected by the school boards. By requiring that charter schools receive a certain portion of capital millage funds, the State is . . . fulfilling the purpose of article IX, section 1.

Id. at *7.

2. UNIFORMITY

As explained earlier, the 1868 constitution was the first to require public schools to be "uniform." The 1885 constitution retained this provision, but added a racial spin: "White and colored children shall not be taught in the same school, but impartial provision shall be made for both." After the U.S. Supreme Court outlawed segregated education in *Brown v. Board of Education of Topeka, Shawnee County, Kansas*, 347 U.S. 483 (1954), this language was eliminated. The requirement that schools be uniform, however, was carried over to the 1968 constitution. *See* Art. IX, § 1(a).

In *San Antonio Independent School District v. Rodriguez*, 411 U.S. 1, *reh'g denied*, 411 U.S. 959 (1973), the U.S. Supreme Court held that Texas's reliance on property taxes to fund its schools did not violate the 14th Amendment, even though schools in rich neighborhoods received up to 40% more money than schools in poor neighborhoods. In a rare step, Justice Brennan, one of the decision's dissenters, wrote a law review article urging parents to seek relief in state courts. *See* William J. Brennan, "State Constitutions and the Protection of Individual Rights," 90 *Harv. L. Rev.* 489 (1977). In *Edgewood Independent School District v. Kirby*, 804 S.W.2d 491 (Tex. 1991), the Texas Supreme Court, relying on the Texas constitution, struck down the very system that had been upheld in *Rodriguez*.

To address the disparities in its school districts, Florida in 1945 adopted the State Foundation Program Fund. This was replaced in 1947 with the

Minimum Foundation Program, which in 1973 became the Florida Education Finance Program ("FEFP"). According to the Florida Legislature's policy statement, the FEFP exists "to guarantee to each student in the Florida public education system the availability of programs and services appropriate to his or her educational needs which are substantially equal to those available to any similar student notwithstanding geographic differences and varying local economic factors."

The FEFP allocates money to school districts based on student enrollment, adjusted for geographical differences, diseconomies of scale (to help small school districts), and the number of students needing special services. It also considers the "required local effort" (*i.e.*, the amount of money raised by each school district through property taxes). Such money is combined with the state's contribution to make up each year's FEFP.

Whether the FEFP delivers on its promise of equal education is a much-debated issue, and one that has been litigated frequently. Each time, the courts have deferred to the legislature. In *St. Johns County v. Northeast Florida Builders Association, Inc.*, 583 So. 2d 635 (Fla. 1991), for example, the Florida Supreme Court wrote:

> The Florida Constitution only requires that a system be provided that gives every student an equal chance to achieve basic educational goals prescribed by the legislature. The constitutional mandate is not that every school district in the state must receive equal funding nor that each

educational program must be equivalent. Inherent inequities, such as varying revenues because of higher or lower property values or difference in millage assessments, will always favor or disfavor some districts.

Id. at 641. *See also Florida Department of Education v. Glasser*, 622 So. 2d 944, 950 (Fla. 1993) (Kogan, J. concurring) ("The uniformity clause is not and never was intended to require that each school district be a mirror image of every other one."); *Undereducated Foster Children of Florida v. Florida Senate*, 700 So. 2d 66, 67 (Fla. 1st Dist. Ct. App. 1997) ("Appellants' second claim would require a constitutional guarantee of equal educational performance . . . rather than a right to uniform educational opportunity. A plain reading of Article IX, Section 1, contemplates protection of the latter, not the former.").

3.   CLASS SIZE

In yet another effort to improve Florida's schools, a 2002 citizens' initiative petition asked voters to limit the size of PK–12 classes. After making the ballot, see *Advisory Opinion to the Attorney General re Florida's Amendment to Reduce Class Size*, 816 So. 2d 580 (Fla. 2002), the proposal narrowly passed. As a result, Art. IX, § 1(a) caps "core" classes at 18 students (PK-grade 3), 22 students (grades 4–8), and 25 students (grades 9–12). Extracurricular classes are excluded from the caps. To give the state time to adjust its budget, the amendment called for the caps to be phased in over eight years (*i.e.*, by the start of the 2010–11 school year).

By early 2010, the amendment had cost the state $15.8 billion. To rein in future costs, the Florida Legislature in 2010 proposed a constitutional amendment increasing the caps to 21 (PK-grade 3, up from 18), 27 (grades 4–8, up from 25), and 30 (grades 9–12, up from 25). After surviving a court challenge, see *Florida Education Association v. Florida Department of State*, 48 So. 3d 694 (Fla. 2010), the proposal was defeated.

Since the 2010 vote, the Florida Legislature has made numerous changes in the amendment's implementing legislation, including, most notably, reducing the number of core classes from 849 to 288 (among the classes affected: anatomy, calculus, and Spanish). *See Kunz v. School Board of Palm Beach County*, 237 So. 3d 1026 (Fla. 4th Dist. Ct. App. 2018) (refusing to second-guess these changes). Even with these changes, the amendment so far has cost the state $42 billion ($39.5 billion for more teachers and $2.5 billion for more classrooms).

4.   VOLUNTARY PRE-KINDERGARTEN

Florida's compulsory education law (Fla. Stat. § 1003.21) requires children to begin attending school at age six and continue until at least age 16. Believing that children would benefit from an earlier starting date, a 2002 citizens' initiative called on the state to offer free voluntary pre-kindergarten ("VPK") beginning at age four. *See Advisory Opinion to the Attorney General re: Voluntary Universal Pre-*

Kindergarten Education, 824 So. 2d 161 (Fla. 2002). As a result, Art. IX, § 1(b) now reads in pertinent part: "Every four-year old child in Florida shall be provided by the State a high quality pre-kindergarten learning opportunity in the form of an early childhood development and education program which shall be voluntary, high quality, free, and delivered according to professionally accepted standards." Paragraph 1(c) allows the state to pay for such schooling using funds from "existing education, health, and development programs."

To date, Florida's legislature has done very little to support VPK. Indeed, out of 45 states that have VPK, Florida's spending per child ranks 41st; its policies meet just two of the 10 benchmarks set by the National Institute for Early Education (http://nieer. org/); and unlike 28 states, Florida does not require VPK teachers to have a bachelor's degree. As a result, 41% of the children who participated in Florida's VPK program in 2018 were not ready for kindergarten.

5.   OPERATIONS

As explained at the outset of this chapter, the general features of Florida's public education system largely have been in place since the 1868 constitution. This is immediately apparent when one looks at Art. IX, § 2, which continues to provide for a state board of education ("BOE") and a state commissioner of education ("COE") (the successor office to the state superintendent of public instruction—the name was changed by the 1968 constitution).

In 1998, as part of an overhaul of the state cabinet, see Ch. 14 of this book, the BOE's composition was changed from the governor and the cabinet to seven members serving staggered four-year terms who are appointed by the governor and confirmed by the senate. In addition, the COE was changed from an elected official to a BOE appointee.

Art. IX, § 4 continues to provide for a school board in each school district, with school districts organized along county lines. Paragraph (a) requires each school board to have at least five members, who must be chosen in non-partisan elections for staggered four-year terms. At present, 58 school boards have five members, six have seven members, one (Orange County) has eight members, and two (Broward and Miami-Dade Counties) have nine members. For a list of Florida's school boards, see the web site of the Florida School Boards Association (https://fsba.org/).

The requirement that school board elections be non-partisan (meaning that candidates run without party affiliations) was added in 1998. Recently, there has been a growing effort to amend paragraph (a) to also term limit school board members. *See, e.g.*, S.J.R. 274 (2019) (proposing that school board members be limited to eight years).

Paragraph (a) also permits two contiguous school districts to combine into a single district if their respective voters agree. To date, no school districts have taken this step, which is intended to improve economies of scale and eliminate needless duplication.

Paragraph (b) empowers school boards to oversee the schools in their district, set local school taxes, and participate in joint education programs with other school districts.

Art. IX, § 5 likewise is a holdover. It requires each school district to have a superintendent of schools. Except when changed by either a local law or a resolution of the school board approved by the district's voters, superintendents are elected for four-year terms.

The 1868 constitution made superintendents gubernatorial appointees. The 1885 constitution made them popularly elected. Beginning in 1956, the constitution was changed to allow school districts to appoint their superintendents. Today, 26 of Florida's school districts, comprising 82% of Florida's population, have appointed superintendents. For a list of Florida's superintendents, see http://www. fldoe.org/accountability/data-sys/school-dis-data/ superintendents.stml. Alabama and Florida are the only two states that still let voters decide if they want appointed or elected superintendents. Nationally, 99% of superintendents are appointed.

Appointed superintendents are not subject to the governor's suspension powers (discussed in Ch. 14 of this book) because they serve at the pleasure of the school board. *See In re Advisory Opinion to the Governor*, 298 So. 2d 366 (Fla. 1974). Nevertheless, shortly after taking office in 2019, Gov. Ron DeSantis announced that he was investigating whether he could remove Robert Runcie, Broward County's appointed superintendent, over his handling of the 2018 mass shooting at Parkland's Marjory Stoneman Douglas high school.

6.   REVENUE

As noted earlier, in 2018 Florida spent $25.7 billion on its public schools. Of this amount, 48% came from local sources (*i.e.*, property taxes), 40.5% came from state sources (*i.e.*, sales taxes and lottery proceeds), and 11.5% came from federal sources. *See* the Florida Department of Education's *2019–20 Funding for Florida School Districts* report, available at http://www.fldoe.org/core/fileparse.php/7507/urlt/ Fefpdist.pdf.

Art. IX, § 6 requires there to be a separate state school fund: "The income derived from the state school fund shall, and the principal of the fund may, be appropriated, but only to the support and maintenance of free public schools." As explained earlier, the school fund originated with the 1868 constitution.

Pursuant to Art. X, § 15 (discussed in Ch. 13 of this book), Florida's schools receive the Florida Lottery's annual net proceeds, which in 2018 came to $1.9 billion. *See* http://www.fldoe.org/core/fileparse.php/ 7507/urlt/Lotbook.pdf (2017–18 Florida Department of Education lottery handbook). Since its inception in 1988, the lottery has generated $35.3 billion for education.

In voting for the lottery, the public was told that it would be used for "educational enhancements" rather than as a substitute for previously-existing funding. *See Advisory Opinion to the Attorney General re Requirement for Adequate Public Education Funding*, 703 So. 2d 446 (Fla. 1997). At the time the lottery began, the state's contribution to education was 64%. Given that it now is just 40.5%, many people view the lottery as having been a "bait-and-switch." The Florida Legislature has used the money it has not spent on education for multiple purposes, including tax cuts for corporations.

In 2004, the constitution was amended to allow pari-mutuels in Broward and Miami-Dade Counties to have slot machines. *See* Ch. 13 of this book. The taxes generated by these machines (currently $199.2 million a year) also go to education. *See* Art. X, § 23(b).

D.   HIGHER EDUCATION

1.   STATE UNIVERSITIES

The 1868 constitution required the legislature to create and support a free university. The 1885 constitution dropped this language. The 1968 constitution reinstated it, but substituted the phrase "institutions of higher learning."

In 1905, the Buckman Act (named for Rep. Henry Buckman (D-Jacksonville)) consolidated the state's six higher education institutions into three: the University of the State of Florida (the future University of Florida) for white men; the Florida

Female College (the future Florida State University) for white women; and the State Normal School for Colored Students (the future Florida Agricultural & Mechanical University) for African-American men and women.

To administer these institutions, the Buckman Act created the Board of Control ("BOC"). In 1965, the BOC was replaced by the Board of Regents ("BOR"). In 2001, the Florida Legislature abolished the BOR after clashes over affirmative action (which the regents supported and the legislature opposed).

Objecting to the BOR's elimination, U.S. Sen. Bob Graham (D-Fla.) launched a successful campaign to bring it back as the Board of Governors ("BOG") and make it independent from the legislature. *See Advisory Opinion to the Attorney General re Local Trustees and Statewide Governing Board to Manage Florida's University System*, 819 So. 2d 725 (Fla. 2002).

With the passage of Graham's amendment, Art. IX, § 7 was added to the Florida Constitution. Paragraph (a) states that its goal is "to achieve excellence through teaching students, advancing research and providing public service for the benefit of Florida's citizens, their communities and economies."

Paragraph (b) creates "a single state university system comprised of all public universities," run by the BOG but with each university having its own Board of Trustees ("BOT") (as had been the case under the BOR).

Paragraph (c) requires each BOT to have 13 members, consisting of six citizens appointed by the governor; five citizens appointed by the BOG; the chair of the university's faculty senate; and the president of the university's student government. The 11 citizen members, who must be confirmed by the senate, serve five-year staggered terms.

Paragraph (d) requires the BOG to have 17 members: 14 citizens appointed by the governor; the COE; the chair of the advisory council of faculty senates; and the president of the Florida Student Association. The 14 citizen members, who must be confirmed by the senate, serve staggered seven-year terms. In addition to overseeing the BOTs, paragraph (d) requires the BOG to define a "distinctive mission" for each university, provide "well-planned coordination and operation" of the entire university system, and avoid "wasteful duplication of facilities or programs."

Although Art. IX, § 7 has been held to be self-executing, see *NAACP, Inc. v. Florida Board of Regents*, 876 So. 2d 636 (Fla. 1st Dist. Ct. App.), *review dismissed*, 882 So. 2d 386 (Fla. 2004), the sparseness of its language has required the courts to repeatedly determine its specific effect. *See, e.g., Graham v. Haridopolos*, 108 So. 3d 597 (Fla. 2013) (power to control tuition and fees remains with the legislature); *Florida Carry, Inc. v. University of North Florida*, 133 So. 3d 966 (Fla. 1st Dist. Ct. App. 2013) (power to ban or allow guns on campus remains with the legislature); *Couchman v. University of Central Florida*, 84 So. 3d 445 (Fla. 5th Dist. Ct. App. 2012) (power to adopt and enforce student conduct codes rests with the BOG). For a further discussion, see *University of South Florida Board of Trustees v. CoMentis, Inc.*, 861 F.3d 1234 (11th Cir. 2017).

In 2018, a new paragraph (e) was added to § 7. As a result, when a university wants to "raise, impose, or authorize any fee" that requires board approval, a simple majority no longer is sufficient. Instead, it now takes a double super-majority: nine trustees (69.2%) and 12 governors (70.6%).

As noted at the outset of this chapter, Florida currently has 12 state universities. For a list of them, see Fla. Stat. § 1000.21(6).

2. STATE COLLEGES

Florida's first public college was Palm Beach Junior College, established in 1933. In 1939, a new law permitted any county, or group of counties, with at least 50,000 residents to petition the BOE for a college. In the 1950s, the term "junior college" began to be replaced by "community college."

In 1955, the Community College Council ("CCC") was created and directed to prepare a long-range plan for the state. Two years later, it issued a report calling for 28 community colleges to be in operation by 1967. It also recommended that they be strategically placed around the state, to give residents easy driving access to them. In 1972, with the opening of Pasco-Hernando Community College, the CCC's goal was realized.

In 1979, the legislature replaced the CCC with the Community College Coordinating Board ("CCCB"). In 1983, the CCCB was replaced by the State Board of Community Colleges ("SBCC"), which was given the task of "overseeing and coordinating the individually governed public community colleges."

In 2001, at the same that it abolished the BOR, the legislature eliminated the SBCC and transferred its duties to the BOE. It also changed the name of St. Petersburg Junior College to "St. Petersburg College" and allowed it to begin offering a limited number of four-year programs. Today, all of Florida's community colleges are authorized to grant both associate and bachelor degrees. *See* Fla. Stat. § 1007.33. As a result, all but two have dropped the word "community" from their names. *See* Fla. Stat. § 1000.21(3). Nationally, 23 states (including Florida) have taken such steps, primarily to make four-year degrees more affordable. In keeping with the traditional mission of community colleges (*i.e.*, preparing students for careers), such programs focus on "workforce-critical" areas (*e.g.*, computer science, law enforcement, and nursing).

In 2018, Florida's public college system received its own constitutional section. *See* Art. IX, § 8. This change was long overdue, as the public college system was the only public education entity not mentioned in the constitution.

Paragraph (a) sets out its goals, which are

to achieve excellence and to provide access to undergraduate education to the students of this state; to originate articulated pathways to a baccalaureate degree; to ensure superior commitment to teaching and learning; and to respond quickly and efficiently to meet the demand of communities by aligning certificate and degree programs with local and regional workforce needs[.]

Paragraph (b) creates "a single state college system comprised of all public community and state colleges" run by the BOE but with each college having its own BOT.

Paragraph (c) authorizes the governor to appoint trustees to staggered four-year terms, subject to confirmation by the senate. It also requires trustees to be residents of their colleges' "service delivery area[s]."

Lastly, paragraph (d) places the BOE in charge of the state college system.

E.   APPOINTIVE EDUCATION BODIES

As explained in Ch. 13 of this book, the constitution limits most offices to four years. Art. IX, § 3 creates an exception for appointive education bodies: "Members of any appointive board dealing with education may serve terms in excess of four years as provided by law." This exception has been part of the constitution since 1964.

The constitution does not provide any guidelines for determining whether a given body is sufficiently education-related to qualify for this exception. In *Nohrr v. Brevard County Educational Facilities*

Authority, 247 So. 2d 304 (Fla. 1971), the Florida
Supreme Court, without elaboration, applied the
exception to the Brevard County Educational
Facilities Authority, a local entity in charge of
arranging school construction financing.

CHAPTER 19
SPECIAL DISTRICTS

A. OVERVIEW

Although the Florida Constitution makes only passing reference to them, special districts (also known as "special purpose districts," "special service districts," and "special taxing districts," but often officially designated "authorities") represent an important part of local governance in Florida. *See Canaveral Port Authority v. Department of Revenue*, 690 So. 2d 1226, 1232 (Fla. 1996) ("Special districts have been given very substantial governmental responsibilities[, particularly when it comes to] transportation, health care, and public safety matters.").

B. DEFINITIONS

The Florida Constitution does not define the phrase "special district." However, Fla. Stat. § 189.012(6) does:

> "Special district" means a unit of local government created for a special purpose, as opposed to a general purpose, which has jurisdiction to operate within a limited geographic boundary and is created by general law, special act, local ordinance, or by rule of the Governor and Cabinet. The term does not include a school district, a community college district, a special improvement district created pursuant to § 285.17, a municipal service taxing

or benefit unit as specified in § 125.01, or a board which provides electrical service and which is a political subdivision of a municipality or is part of a municipality.

Special districts are either "dependent" or "independent," as explained by Fla. Stat. § 189.012:

(2) "Dependent special district" means a special district that meets at least one of the following criteria:

(a) The membership of its governing body is identical to that of the governing body of a single county or a single municipality.

(b) All members of its governing body are appointed by the governing body of a single county or a single municipality.

(c) During their unexpired terms, members of the special district's governing body are subject to removal at will by the governing body of a single county or a single municipality.

(d) The district has a budget that requires approval through an affirmative vote or can be vetoed by the governing body of a single county or a single municipality. . . .

(3) "Independent special district" means a special district that is not a dependent special district as defined in subsection (2). A district that includes more than one county is an independent special district unless the district

lies wholly within the boundaries of a single municipality.

C. PURPOSE

A special district can be set up in Florida for nearly any purpose. For example, a group of citizens may decide to create a special district to preserve their local history. As is obvious, such a district has a single mission and only one priority. In contrast, a county or municipality has many missions and many priorities (which must be constantly juggled). Thus, a special district is useful when citizens want to ensure that a specific issue receives focused and on-going attention. In addition, persons who are chosen to lead special districts often have demonstrated expertise in the district's subject matter.

The principal reason why special districts are formed, however, is money. By creating a special district, taxpayers know in advance what their money will be used for (because of the restricted nature of a special district). This is not true when it comes to money paid to a county or municipality (or any general purpose governmental entity). By the same token, because only taxpayers within the special district's territory are required to support it, special districts help to keep down county and municipal taxes. *See State v. Sarasota County*, 372 So. 2d 1115 (Fla. 1979).

D. OPERATIONS

The United States has 51,296 special districts. Illinois leads the nation with 4,090 special districts.

Since 1950, special districts have been the fastest growing type of local government entity, registering a 300% increase.

The most common type of special district are fire control districts. Indeed, the country's first special district was the Union Fire Company of Philadelphia, which was set up by Benjamin Franklin in 1736. (Residents who failed to pay its fees received no fire protection.) In Florida, the first special districts were road districts. *See* 1822 Fla. Terr. Acts 95. Because these districts lacked taxing authority, they conscripted men and fined those who did not show up $1 for each missed day. *Id.* at 98.

Today, Florida has 1,729 active special districts, of which 1,092 are independent and 637 are dependent. The oldest Florida special district still in existence is the Hastings Drainage District in Putnam and St. Johns Counties. It was created on July 1, 1913. Two other districts notable for their longevity are the South Florida Conservancy District (1919) and the Florida Inland Navigation District (1927).

Florida's special districts vary greatly in terms of budget, personnel, and size. While some are professionally managed, operate with large budgets and staffs, and set and collect taxes, others are run by volunteers, have either no budgets or very limited ones, and lack taxing authority (thus, the term "special taxing district" is accurate only some of the time). The five most common types of special districts in Florida are: community developments districts (662), community redevelopment districts (224), housing authorities (91), drainage and water control districts (83), and fire control districts (63).

Depending on their enabling legislation, special districts may have appointed or elected leaders (some have a combination). While taxes often are used to finance special districts, they also may receive money from bonds, donations, grants, investments, leases, revenue sharing (*i.e.*, they may be funded by other government entities), and user fees.

The Florida Department of Economic Opportunity ("FDEO") maintains a comprehensive list of Florida's special districts with links to their individual web sites. *See* http://specialdistrictreports.floridajobs. org/. (By law, every special district must have a functioning web site and is required to post certain information on it. *See* Fla. Stat. § 189.069.) The FDEO also produces an on-line handbook that assists special districts in carrying out their duties. *See* http://www.floridajobs.org/community-planning-and-development/special-districts/special-district-accountability-program/florida-special-district-handbook-online.

Fla. Stat. ch. 189 applies to all special districts. Other chapters apply only to certain types of special districts. Examples include 161 (beach and shore preservation districts); 163 (community redevelopment districts and neighborhood improvement districts); 190 (community development districts); 191 (fire control districts); 298 (drainage and water control districts); 374 (navigation districts); 388 (mosquito control districts); 418 (recreation districts); and 582 (soil and water conservation districts).

E. CONSTITUTIONAL REFERENCES

The 1968 constitution is the first one to mention special districts. No article or section, however, is specifically devoted to them. Instead, references are scattered throughout the text. For example:

1)   Art. I, § 24 requires special districts to have open meetings and records. *See* Ch. 5 of this book.

2)   Art. II, § 8 requires elected officers in special districts having ad valorem taxing authority to comply with the constitution's financial disclosure and lobbying rules. *See* Ch. 2 of this book.

3)   Art. III, § 11(a)(1) allows special, local, and general laws of local application to be passed concerning the election and duties of special district officers. Pursuant to Art. III, § 11(a)(21), however, the legislature has placed certain limitations on these powers with respect to independent special districts. *See* Fla. Stat. §§ 189.031(2) and 190.049. *See also* Ch. 13 of this book.

4)   Art. III, § 14 authorizes the creation of special district civil service systems. *See* Ch. 2 of this book.

5) Art. VII, § 8 allows the state to appropriate money to special districts. *See* Ch. 21 of this book.

6) Art. VII, § 9 allows special districts to impose taxes (when authorized by law) and sets their maximum ad valorem millage rates. *See* Ch. 21 of this book.

7) Art. VII, § 10 prohibits special districts from becoming joint owners with, or investors in, private businesses, or using their credit or taxing powers to assist such entities (subject to certain very limited exceptions). *See* Ch. 21 of this book.

8) Art. VII, § 12 allows authorized special districts to issue bonds. *See* Ch. 22 of this book.

9) Art. VII, § 19 exempts special districts from the supermajority voting requirements needed to impose, authorize, or raise taxes or fees. *See* Ch. 21 of this book.

10) Art. VIII, § 4 permits special districts to enter into inter-local agreements. *See* Ch. 16 of this book.

11) Lastly, special districts are mentioned in two of the constitution's schedules (Art. VIII, § 6 and Art. XII, § 15). *See* Ch. 24 of this book.

A constitutional provision does not have to expressly mention a special district for it to apply to a special district. In *Eldred v. North Broward*

Hospital District, 498 So. 2d 911 (Fla. 1986), for example, the question arose whether the constitution's sovereign immunity provision (Art. X, § 13), and the legislature's subsequent partial waiver of it in tort cases pursuant to Fla. Stat. § 768.28 (discussed in Ch. 2 of this book), apply to special districts. In answering this question in the affirmative, the Florida Supreme Court wrote:

> The provisions of the 1968 Constitution leave no doubt that special taxing districts are included as one of four types of local governmental entities, along with counties, school districts, and municipalities. In our view, the legislature clearly intended the provisions of section 768.28(2) to include special taxing districts within the phrase "independent establishments of the state."

Id. at 914.

F. WATER MANAGEMENT DISTRICTS

Because the word "district" is included in their name, Florida's five water management districts ("WMDs") often are incorrectly viewed as just another type of special district. In fact, they occupy their own unique niche. *See* Fla. Att'y Gen. Op. 90–66 (observing that WMDs are regional entities that stand apart from both state and local government). In certain instances, however, the legislature has chosen to treat WMDs as special districts. *See, e.g.*, Fla. Stat. § 189.012(7) (making WMDs subject to the Uniform Special District Accountability Act.). Despite this fact, WMDs are not special districts because local voters have no say over their creation, operation, dissolution, or tax rates. WMDs are discussed further in Ch. 21 of this book.

PART V
GOVERNMENT FINANCES

CHAPTER 20
BUDGETING

A. OVERVIEW

The Florida Constitution requires the state to annually adopt a balanced budget. *See* Art. VII, § 1(d) ("Provision shall be made by law for raising sufficient revenue to defray the expenses of the state for each fiscal period."). Such a requirement has been included in every one of Florida's constitutions. Until 1971, however, Florida was on a two-year budget cycle. Today, most states (31), including Florida, approve a new budget every year.

In 1845, Florida's state budget was $25,000. This figure grew to $150,000 in 1860; $500,000 in 1865; and $1.5 million in 1885. By 1925, the state budget was $5.5 million, a figure that rose to $6 million in 1935. Since the end of World War II, Florida's state budget has escalated even more rapidly:

1945 $11 million

1955 $175 million

1965 $1.1 billion

1975 $2.3 billion

1985 $14.7 billion

1995 $38.8 billion

2005 $63.1 billion

2015 $71.0 billion

2019 $91.0 billion

Nationally, Florida's state budget is eclipsed only by California ($214.8 billion), New York ($175.5 billion), and Texas ($125.4 billion). On a per capita basis, however, Florida ranks 50th in state spending. The 2019 federal budget was $4.45 trillion.

B. BUDGET PROCESS

Until 1992, the Florida Constitution did not say anything about the state's budget process. In that year, the Taxation and Budget Reform Commission ("TBRC") recommended that it be constitutionalized. As a result: 1) Art. III, § 19 was adopted ("State Budgeting, Planning and Appropriations Processes"); and, 2) a new sentence was inserted in Art. IV, § 1(a) ("The governor shall be the chief administrative officer of the state responsible for the planning and budgeting for the state.").

In 2006, two further sections were added to Art. III, § 19: (i) ("Government Efficiency Task Force") and (j) ("Joint Legislative Budget Commission").

The foregoing provisions are implemented by Fla. Stat. chs. 215–216.

Since 1925, Florida's fiscal year has run from July 1 to June 30. *See* Fla. Stat. § 215.01. Previously, Florida's finances were on a calendar-year basis. Today, most states use a July 1 fiscal year. The federal government, however, uses an October 1 fiscal year. Since 1960, Florida's budget always has been finalized before July 1 (except in 1992, when it was finalized on July 1).

Although Florida's budget process is complex, for present purposes it can be summarized as follows (the timeline below is followed in odd-numbered years; in even-numbered years, it starts 60 days earlier because the annual legislative session begins in January rather than in March—see Art. III, § 3(b)):

1) <u>August</u>: The Legislative Budget Commission ("LBC"), see Art. III, § 19(j), Fla. Stat. § 11.90, prepares a Long-Range Financial Outlook Report ("LRFOR"). This document forecasts Florida's finances for the next three years. *See* Art. III, § 19(c)(1); Fla. Stat. § 216.012(1). In developing it, the LBC is expected to seek input from the public as well as other government stakeholders. *See* Art. III, § 19(c)(2).

2) <u>September</u>: Using the LRFOR, state agencies, as well as the judiciary, prepare their own Long-Range Program Plans ("LRPPs"). These documents, which cover five years, identify each entity's priorities, needs, and goals. *See* Fla. Stat. § 216.013(1)–(2).

3) <u>October</u>: State agencies, as well as the judiciary, use the LRFOR and their LRPPs to prepare their Legislative Budget Requests ("LBRs"). *See* Art. III, § 19(a)(3); Fla. Stat. § 216.023(1).

4) <u>November–January</u>: State agencies, as well as the judiciary, defend their LBRs during

legislative committee hearings and public hearings. *See* Fla. Stat. §§ 216.131 and 216.172.

5) <u>February</u>: The governor releases his or her proposed budget. By law, this must occur at least 30 days before the start of the legislative session. *See* Fla. Stat. § 216.162(1).

6) <u>March–April</u>: The legislature, using the governor's budget as a starting point, drafts its own budget. In doing so, it must follow the formatting rules contained in Art. III, § 19(b) (these rules are designed to increase the budget's transparency).

7) <u>April–May</u>: Near the end of the legislative session, joint budget conference committees resolve differences between the house and senate's budget bills. The result of these negotiations is a conference committee report. Seventy-two hours after it is released, it can be voted on. (This three-day "cooling off" period is mandated by Art. III, § 19(d). *See also* Fla. Stat. § 216.178(1).) If either the house or the senate fail to adopt the report, the conference process starts over.

8) <u>May–June</u>: The budget is delivered to the governor for approval. In reviewing it, the governor can "line-item veto" specific appropriations. A 2/3 majority vote is

needed to restore such items. *See* Ch. 14 of this book (discussing Art. III, § 8).

Within 120 days of the start of each fiscal year, the Office of Planning and Budgeting is required to issue a final budget report "that reflects the net appropriations for each budget item." *See* Art. III, § 19(e); Fla. Stat. § 216.178(2). Florida's final 2019 budget can be found at http://floridafiscalportal. state.fl.us/Document.aspx?ID=19778&DocType= PDF.

For a further look at Florida's budgeting processing, see, e.g., *Corcoran v. Geffin*, 250 So. 3d 779 (Fla. 1st Dist. Ct. App. 2018); *Crews v. Florida Public Employers Council 79, AFSCME*, 113 So. 3d 1063 (Fla. 1st Dist. Ct. App. 2013).

C.   REVENUE SHORTFALLS

As explained at the start of this chapter, Florida must end each fiscal year in the "black" (*i.e.*, deficits are not allowed). Except for Vermont, all states have such a requirement (the level of stringency, however, varies—Florida is considered a "high stringency" state). The U.S. Constitution does not have such a provision. As a result, 28 states, including Florida, have called for a federal balanced budget amendment.

In 1987, the Florida Legislature passed a law giving the governor the power to reduce the state budget whenever deficits threatened. *See* Fla. Att'y Gen. Op. 87–57. Four years later, with the state facing a $622 million deficit, Gov. Lawton Chiles announced that the state's guardian ad litem program (a $3.5 million expense) would be cut. In response, a Miami lawyer named Karen Gievers sued Chiles.

In *Chiles v. Children A, B, C, D, E and F*, 589 So. 2d 260 (Fla. 1991), the Florida Supreme Court agreed that the budget reduction law violated Art. II, § 3:

> The central issue in this case is whether the legislature, in passing section 216.221 [in 1987], violated the doctrine of separation of powers by assigning to the executive branch the broad discretionary authority to reapportion the state budget. . . . To permit the [executive] to reduce specific appropriations in general appropriations bills . . . allow[s] the legislature to abdicate its lawmaking function and . . . enable[s] [the executive] to amend the law without resort to the constitutionally prescribed lawmaking process. This delegation strikes at the very core of the separation of powers doctrine, and for this reason section 216.221 must fail as unconstitutional.

Id. at 263, 265–66.

Thus, as the final piece of its 1992 recommendations, the TBRC proposed new Art. IV, § 13 ("Revenue Shortfalls"):

> In the event of revenue shortfalls, as defined by general law, the governor and cabinet may establish all necessary reductions in the state budget in order to comply with the provisions of Article VII, Section 1(d). The governor and

cabinet shall implement all necessary reductions for the executive budget, the chief justice of the supreme court shall implement all necessary reductions for the judicial budget, and the speaker of the house of representatives and the president of the senate shall implement all necessary reductions for the legislative budget. Budget reductions pursuant to this section shall be consistent with the provisions of Article III, Section 19(h).

These procedures, which to date have not been used, are spelled out in greater detail in Fla. Stat. § 216.221.

D. OTHER MATTERS

1. "RAINY DAY" FUND

Art. III, § 19(g) requires the state to have a "rainy day" fund (formally known as a "budget stabilization" fund). The fund's balance must be between 5% and 10% "of the last completed fiscal year's net revenue collections for the general revenue fund." *Id.*

New York set up the country's first rainy day fund in 1946. Florida set up its fund in 1959, after a brutally cold winter destroyed the state's 1957–58 citrus crop. Today, all states have rainy day funds, although some are better capitalized than others. (Alaska and Wyoming have particularly strong funds, while Illinois and Pennsylvania have particularly weak ones.)

In 2018, state rainy day funds collectively totaled $59.9 billion. Florida's fund contained $1 billion. This represented a significant decrease from 2016, when it stood at $3.5 billion. Among the reasons for the drop: Hurricane Irma (2017) and the mass shooting at Parkland's Marjory Stoneman Douglas high school (2018), which led to increased school security costs throughout the state.

In 2019, Florida's rainy day fund stood at $1.4 billion, enough to run the state for 16 days. In 2002, the fund had enough money to run the state for 33 days. For a further look at Florida's rainy day fund, see Fla. Stat. §§ 215.18, 215.32, 216.221, 216.222, and 252.37. *See also* Art. VII, § 1(e) (requiring budget surpluses to "be transferred to the budget stabilization fund until the fund reaches the maximum balance specified in Section 19(g) of Article III, [after which any further surpluses must be] refunded to taxpayers as provided by general law.").

2. TRUST FUNDS

In its effort to make Florida's budget more transparent, the TBRC took specific aim at the state's numerous trust funds. *See* Art. III, § 19(f)(1) ("No trust fund of the State of Florida or other public body may be created or re-created by law without a three-fifths vote of the membership of each house of the legislature in a separate bill for that purpose only.") and (f)(2) ("[Except as provided in paragraph (3),] State trust funds shall terminate not more than four years after the effective date of the act authorizing the initial creation of the trust fund. By law the legislature may set a shorter time period for which any trust fund is authorized.").

In explaining its opposition to such funds, the TBRC wrote:

> [O]ver 50% of the Approved Budget for fiscal year 1990–91 was from trust funds. . . . In the last ten years, the percentage of trust fund appropriations has increased from 48% to 60% of the state budget and the percentage of the General Revenue Fund appropriations has decreased from 52% to 38%. However, the Commission found that the General Revenue Fund serves as the primary reporting vehicle for government operations. Thus, the hundreds of trust funds currently in existence serve only to make reporting the actual revenues and finances of the state virtually impossible. . . .

Secretary of State v. Milligan, 704 So. 2d 152, 154 (Fla. 1st Dist. Ct. App. 1997), *review denied*, 725 So. 2d 1109 (Fla. 1998) (quoting the TBRC's final resolution). *See also American Bankers Insurance Co. v. Chiles*, 675 So. 2d 922, 924 (Fla. 1996) ("[T]he intent of article III, section 19 is to make it more difficult for the legislature to create trust funds and to make those funds more accountable by subjecting them to the detailed planning and appropriation process created in subsections (a) through (h) of the constitutional provision.").

Despite the TRBC's efforts, trust funds continue to make up a substantial portion of Florida's revenues (25.4% in 2019).

3. LONG-RANGE PLAN

Art. III, § 19(h) requires the state to prepare, and then update biennially, a long-range plan. This provision is implemented by Fla. Stat. chs. 186–187. The plan is intended to "provide[ ] long-range guidance for the orderly social, economic, and physical growth of the state." *See* Fla. Stat. § 186.007(1). The plan's current goals are set out in Fla. Stat. § 187.201.

4. GOVERNMENT EFFICIENCY TASK FORCE

Since 2006, the constitution has required the quadrennial establishment of a Government Efficiency Task Force ("GETF"). *See* Art. III, § 19(i) and Fla. Stat. § 11.9005 (requiring the GETF to have 15 members: five appointed by the governor, five by the president of the senate, and five by the speaker of the house). As Fla. Stat. § 11.9005(5) explains, "The task force shall develop recommendations for improving governmental operations and reducing costs."

To date, the GETF has met three times (2007–08, 2011–12, and 2015–16). The GETF's 2016 final report, proposing 29 changes expected to save $2 billion annually, appears at https://www.splcenter. org/sites/default/files/2016-getf-final-report.pdf. Information about the 2019–20 GETF can be found at https://www.dms.myflorida.com/other_programs/ government_efficiency_task_force.

5.　REVENUE SHARING

Art. VII, § 8 permits the legislature to distribute state funds to "counties, school districts, municipalities or special districts upon such conditions as may be provided by general law." A 1980 amendment added the section's final sentence: "These conditions may include the use of relative ad valorem assessment levels determined by a state agency designated by general law." Thus, a local government that keeps it property taxes artificially low (as many school districts were doing prior to 1980) can be penalized.

This section is best understood by comparing it to Art. VII, § 7, which requires the state to distribute pari-mutuel taxes equally among Florida's 67 counties. *See* Ch. 13 of this book.

6.　PUBLIC EMPLOYEE PENSIONS

Art. X, § 14, added in 1976 due to the increasingly generous retirement benefits being given to firefighters and police officers, provides:

A governmental unit responsible for any retirement or pension system supported in whole or in part by public funds shall not after January 1, 1977, provide any increase in the benefits to the members or beneficiaries of such system unless such unit has made or concurrently makes provision for the funding of the increase in benefits on a sound actuarial basis.

As is obvious, this section affects both state and local budgeting.

In *Florida Association of Counties, Inc. v. Department of Administration, Division of Retirement*, 595 So. 2d 42 (Fla. 1992), the Florida Supreme Court explained that "sound actuarial basis" means "a retirement program [is] funded in such a way that the retirement fund is able to meet its continuing obligations as and when they mature." *Id.* at 43–44. Thus, a pension plan does not have to be currently fully-funded to be sound. In *Branca v. City of Miramar*, 634 So. 2d 604 (Fla. 1994), the court held that § 14 applies to both existing and new retirement programs.

Florida's public pension system—the fourth largest in the nation—covers 643,000 current workers and 415,000 retirees. A 2019 report by the state's auditor described the system as "stable." Nevertheless, with assets of $161 billion, it is only 84% funded. Moreover, since 2009 its unfunded liabilities have doubled to $29 billion.

CHAPTER 21
TAXES

A. OVERVIEW

Art. VII explains how the government gets the money it needs to operate. While the first half of Art. VII authorizes the government to impose taxes, the second half permits it to issue bonds. Taxes are used to pay for ordinary ("recurring") expenses, such as salaries and benefits. Bonds, on the other hand, are used to pay for extraordinary ("non-recurring") expenses, such as buildings and roads. This chapter focuses on taxes. Ch. 22 looks at bonds.

In recent times, Florida's politicians have shied away from raising taxes. To fill the resulting revenue gap, they have turned to fees. Accordingly, fees are discussed at the end of this chapter.

Taxes represent a government levy on some portion of a person's (or a company's) wealth. Depending on how one counts, Florida has thousands of taxes—on everything from beer (48 cents per gallon) to cell phones (14.8 cents per dollar) to cigarettes ($1.34 per pack). Although the constitution only discusses certain taxes, it requires all taxes to be authorized by law. *See* Art. VII, § 1(a) ("No tax shall be levied except in pursuance of law.").

B. HISTORY

Sixty-five years ago, a trio of authors wrote: "Florida's tax structure has developed without an overall plan or philosophy." Wilson K. Doyle et al.,

The Government and Administration of Florida 112 (1954). In fact, nothing could be further from the truth. Throughout its history, Florida has been guided by three principles when it comes to taxes: 1) keep them as low as possible; 2) craft them to be as attractive as possible to out-of-staters; and, 3) make it as difficult as possible to increase them.

In 1924, for example, when Floridians were deciding whether to pass a constitutional amendment banning income and inheritance taxes, one newspaper urged its readers to do so by writing:

> If you wish to extend a cordial invitation to investors to come to Florida and make this state their permanent home, vote "YES" on the proposition to prevent the Legislature from ever imposing taxes on inheritances and incomes.

> A vote in favor of the amendment will insure that your own income will not be taxed in this state and that a very large number of wealthy people will be induced to come to Florida where they will become heavy investors and large taxpayers, thus lightening your own tax burdens and, what is more, contribute to the more rapid development of the whole state.

"Editorial," *Miami Herald*, Nov. 3, 1924, at 1.

In more recent times, the constitution has become even more tax adverse. A 1996 amendment prohibits any change in the constitution that would result in the creation of a new state tax or fee unless it is approved by 2/3 of the voters. *See* Art. XI, § 7. Similarly, a 2018 amendment prohibits any state fee or tax from being imposed or raised unless it is approved by 2/3 of the legislature. *See* Art. VII, § 19.

In 2018, Florida was ranked the fourth most "tax friendly" state in the country, just behind: 1) Alaska, 2) Wyoming, and, 3) South Dakota. In 2019, Pres. Donald Trump and First Lady Melania Trump changed their domiciles to Florida to avoid New York's high taxes.

While playing for the New York Yankees (and living in an apartment in Trump Tower in Manhattan), shortstop Derek Jeter tried to claim he was a Florida resident to avoid paying New York taxes. The New York tax authorities disputed Jeter's claim and took him to court. In 2007, the two sides reached a confidential settlement.

Like most states, Florida's tax system places a disproportionate burden on part-time residents (who do not receive the same tax breaks as full-time residents); the poor (due to the system's regressive nature—Florida's tax system is the country's third most regressive); and tourists (who pay high taxes on hotel rooms and rental cars).

Taxes do more than simply fund the government. They also promote political agendas and reflect social values. In 1889, for example, Florida adopted a "poll tax." Its express purpose was to keep blacks from voting.

The poll tax required all adults (regardless of financial circumstances) to pay $1 a year. Those who failed to comply were prohibited from voting. While the poll tax was facially neutral, it rarely was applied

to poor whites. Other southern states quickly
followed Florida's lead. As a result, poll taxes became
one of the hallmarks of the Jim Crow era. In 1964,
the 24th Amendment outlawed their use in federal
elections. Two years later, the U.S. Supreme Court
banned them in state elections. *See Harper v.
Virginia Board of Elections*, 383 U.S. 663 (1966).

C. TYPES

The Florida Constitution specifically mentions
nine types of taxes: documentary stamp, estate,
income, inheritance, license, motor fuel, pari-mutuel,
personal property, and real property. It also
authorizes the legislature to create "other" types of
taxes. *See* Art. VII, § 1(a). The most important of
these other taxes are sales taxes. For a detailed look
at Florida's taxes, see the *2019 Florida Tax
Handbook*, available at http://edr.state.fl.us/Content/
revenues/reports/tax-handbook/taxhandbook2019.
pdf.

1. DOCUMENTARY STAMP TAXES

In Florida, certain types of transactions are subject
to a "documentary stamp tax." *See* Fla. Stat. § 201.01.
The tax applies to assignments, deeds, and
easements affecting land, as well as to contracts for
gas, mineral, oil, and timber rights. *See* Fla. Stat.
§ 201.02. In all counties except Miami-Dade, the rate
is 70 cents per $100 of value. *Id*. In Miami-Dade, the
rate is 60 cents per $100 of value for single family
homes and $1.05 per $100 of value for all other types
of property. *See* Fla. Stat. § 201.031.

The tax also applies to bonds, liens, mortgages, and notes. The rate for these items is 35 cents per $100 of value with a cap of $2,450 for notes. *See* Fla. Stat. §§ 201.07 and 201.08.

Florida instituted the documentary stamp tax in 1931 and initially set the rate at 10 cents per $100 of value. In 2018, the tax generated $911.2 million. Neither the federal government nor any other state has such a tax.

The Florida Constitution mentions the documentary stamp tax in Art. X, § 28(a) (see Ch. 4 of this book, discussing the Land Acquisition Trust Fund), although it uses the more generic phrase "excise tax." An excise tax is any tax that is levied on the seller rather than the buyer (although the seller typically passes the cost of the tax on to the buyer as part of the sales price). Alcohol, cigarette, and gasoline taxes are examples of excise taxes. For a further look at the documentary stamp tax, see http://floridarevenue.com/taxes/taxesfees/Pages/doc_stamp.aspx.

2. ESTATE TAXES

Art. VII, § 5(a) provides: "No tax upon estates . . . shall be levied by the state, or under its authority, in excess of the aggregate of amounts which may be allowed to be credited upon or deducted from any similar tax levied by the United States or any state."

An estate tax is a tax on a decedent's assets that is imposed prior to their distribution to the decedent's beneficiaries. Opponents of such taxes often call them "death taxes," suggesting (incorrectly) that the government is charging people to die. Proponents defend them by pointing out that only America's richest families pay estate taxes.

The federal estate tax exempts the first $11.4 million of a person's estate. Amounts above this figure are taxed at rates that begin at 18% and top out at 40%. In most instances, assets passed on to a spouse or charity are exempt from the federal estate tax.

The federal estate tax was adopted in 1916. By that time, 43 states had their own estate tax. Florida did not, and used this fact to appeal to wealthy northerners. To stop the flow of money southward (Alabama also did not have an estate tax), states with estate taxes convinced Congress in 1924 to give every estate a federal tax credit for any state estate taxes it paid. Florida, realizing the threat this change posed, responded by challenging the federal credit in court.

In *State of Florida v. Mellon*, 273 U.S. 12 (1927), the U.S. Supreme Court upheld the federal credit. As a result, in 1930 the Florida Constitution was amended to allow a state estate tax up to the amount of the federal credit. For obvious reasons, such a tax is known as a "pick up" or "sponge" tax.

In 2001, as part of an overhaul of the federal tax code, Congress phased out the federal credit. With its demise, Florida was forced to stop collecting its estate tax (as of Dec. 31, 2004) because § 5(a) ties Florida's estate tax to the federal credit. Nevertheless,

Florida's estate tax remains on the books. *See* Fla. Stat. §§ 198.01–198.44.

Nationally, estate taxes now largely are a relic—only 13 states still have them (at 20%, Washington's is the highest). Nevertheless, some observers have called for Florida to reinstate its estate tax, pointing out that doing so would generate $580 million a year.

3.   INCOME TAXES

(a) Personal Income Taxes

Art. VII, § 5(a) prohibits income taxes on "natural persons who are residents or citizens of the state . . . in excess of the aggregate of amounts which may be allowed to be credited upon or deducted from any similar tax levied by the United States or any state." At present, taxpayers in six states get a break on their state income taxes by being able to deduct a portion of their federal income taxes (Alabama, Iowa, Louisiana, Missouri, Montana, and Oregon).

Florida initially had a personal income tax ("PIT"), but abolished it in 1855 because of its high administrative costs. As explained above, in 1924 both income taxes and inheritance taxes were constitutionally banned.

In 1994, fearing that the Florida Legislature was warming up to the idea of a PIT (it was not), a citizens' group called the Tax Cap Committee proposed that any new state tax or fee "imposed . . . by any amendment to this constitution . . . be null, void and without effect . . . unless . . . approved by not fewer than two-thirds of the voters." After failing to make the 1994 ballot for technical reasons, see *Advisory Opinion to the Attorney General re Tax Limitation*, 644 So. 2d 486 (Fla. 1994), a reworked version appeared on the 1996 ballot. *See Advisory Opinion to the Attorney General re Tax Limitation*, 673 So. 2d 864 (Fla. 1996). On election day, it passed handily. It generally is agreed that this provision (now Art. XI, § 7) shuts the door on Florida having a PIT.

Florida is one of just eight states that does not have a PIT—the others are Alaska, Nevada, South Dakota, Tennessee (as of 2021), Texas, Washington, and Wyoming. (New Hampshire sometimes is added to this list because it does not tax salaries. It does, however, tax dividends and investment income.) The federal government has had a PIT since 1913.

It is estimated that a Florida PIT would generate $5.9 billion a year. The lack of a PIT is one reason why Florida perennially is short of money and, consequently, has limited public services. On the flip side, not having a PIT is very beneficial to high-wage workers. In 2014, for example, outfielder Giancarlo Stanton signed a 13-year, $325 million contract with the Miami Marlins. In 2017, he waived his "no-trade" clause and agreed to be dealt to the New York Yankees. If he remains in New York for the remainder of the contract (he can "opt out" after the 2020 season), Stanton will pay $29 million in New York state and local income taxes, money he would have saved had he stayed in Miami.

(b) Corporate Income Taxes

Although Florida does not tax personal income, in 1971 the constitution was amended to authorize a corporate income tax ("CIT"). *See* Art. VII, § 5(b).

Gov. Reubin Askew campaigned for this change by buying two identical $6 pink dress shirts, one from a Sears store in Atlanta and the other from a Sears store in Miami Beach. As he went around Florida, Askew held the two shirts up and asked audiences how they differed. When they could not come up with an answer, Askew explained that while Sears was paying Florida nothing in CITs, it was paying Georgia nearly $500,000 a year in CITs.

Florida's CIT is limited to a maximum of 5% of net income unless a higher amount is approved by 3/5 of the legislature. *See* Art. VII, § 5(b). In addition, at least $5,000 of such income must be made exempt. *Id.* In 1972, the legislature set the CIT's rate at 5% and the exempted amount at $5,000. In 1984, it raised the rate to 5.5%. The exempted amount remained $5,000 until 2011, when it was increased to $25,000. In 2012, it was doubled to $50,000. *See* http://floridarevenue.com/taxes/taxesfees/Pages/corporate.aspx.

Forty-four states (including Florida) have CITs, which range from 3% (in North Carolina) to 12% (in Iowa). The federal government has had a CIT since 1909. In 2017, it was reduced from 35% to 21%.

Florida's CIT annually generates $2.4 billion. While running for governor in 2010, Republican Rick Scott pledged to eliminate Florida's CIT within seven years (part of his "7-7-7" plan to create 700,000 new jobs in seven years). Although Scott failed to get rid of the CIT, he did convince the legislature to raise the exempted amount to $50,000. During his 2018 gubernatorial campaign, Andrew Gillum (D) called for increasing the CIT's rate to 7.75% to produce an extra $1 billion a year for education. His opponent Ron DeSantis (R) promised to keep the rate at 5.5%.

4.   INHERITANCE TAXES

In contrast to estate taxes (discussed above), which are paid by decedents, inheritance taxes are paid by beneficiaries. Art. VII, § 5(a) prohibits inheritance taxes. This provision was added to the constitution in 1924.

At present, only six states have inheritance taxes. Nebraska has the highest rate—it taxes beneficiaries who are not relatives 18% on amounts above $10,000. There is no federal inheritance tax.

5.   LICENSE TAXES

Certain types of property (*e.g.*, airplanes, boats, cars) pay license taxes in exchange for being allowed to operate in Florida. *See* Art. VII, § 1(b). Such taxes, which generate $1.4 billion a year, are discussed later in this chapter.

6.   MOTOR FUEL TAXES

Florida heavily taxes motor fuel (41.4 cents per gallon)—only eight states charge more. At 58.7 cents per gallon, Pennsylvania has the highest motor fuel taxes in the country. The federal government also taxes motor fuels: 18.4 cents per gallon on gasoline and 24.4 cents per gallon on diesel fuel.

The Florida motor fuel tax is authorized by Fla. Stat. § 206.41. Fla. Stat. § 206.01(9) defines "motor fuels" as "all gasoline products or any product blended with gasoline or any fuel placed in the storage supply tank of a gasoline-powered motor vehicle."

The constitution refers to the motor fuel tax in two places: Art. VII, § 17(b) and Art. XII, § 9(c). The former, adopted in 1988, allows such taxes to be used to finance transportation bonds. The latter, a carryover from the 1885 constitution, requires two cents of such taxes (known as the "constitutional fuel tax") to be used for roads and local transportation infrastructure projects. *See* Fla. Stat. § 206.47 (detailing how such taxes are allocated).

In 1919, Oregon became the first state to have a motor fuel tax (a penny a gallon). In 1921, Florida began taxing motor fuels at the same rate. Today, Florida annually collects $2.7 billion in motor fuel taxes. Due to the increasing use of alternative fuels, as well as the development of ride-sharing services such as Lyft and Uber, some observers believe that motor fuel taxes have outlived their usefulness. For a further look at Florida's motor fuel tax, see the Florida Department of Transportation's *Transportation Tax Sources Primer* (2019), available at https://fdotwww.blob.core.windows.net/sitefinity/docs/default-source/comptroller/2019-transportation-tax-source-primer.pdf?sfvrsn=43ccaffd_2.

7.   PARI-MUTUEL TAXES

Art. VII, § 7 states: "Taxes upon the operation of pari-mutuel pools may be preempted to the state or allocated in whole or in part to the counties. When allocated to the counties, the distribution shall be in equal amounts to the several counties."

The term "pari-mutuel" refers to the type of betting system used at dog tracks, horse tracks, and jai-alai frontons. The taxes generated by these venues go first to the state. If the state decides to share any portion of them, it must give an equal amount to each county. This requirement was added to the constitution in 1940 at the insistence of the state's small northern counties, which lacked such venues. In 1968, when it appeared that this provision might be dropped from the constitution, such counties began bonding pari-mutuel income to tie the legislature's hands. *See State v. Gadsden County*, 229 So. 2d 587 (Fla. 1969).

Florida started taxing pari-mutuels in 1931 (the year dog and horse tracks were legalized; jai-alai was legalized in 1935). At one time, pari-mutuel taxes were a significant contributor to the state's bottom line; in 1988, for example, they brought in $130 million. Since then, all three sports have declined in popularity. As a result, in 2018 pari-mutuel taxes totaled just $25.8 million.

To stay afloat, pari-mutuels increasingly have turned to poker. In addition, a 2004 constitutional amendment allows the pari-mutuels in Broward and Miami-Dade Counties to have slot machines.

Pursuant to Art. X, § 23(b), slot taxes must be used to "supplement public education funding statewide." *See* Ch. 18 of this book. Fla. Stat. § 551.106 sets the slot tax rate at 35%. Such taxes generate $199.2 million a year. For a further discussion of Florida's pari-mutuels, see Ch. 13 of this book. As it points out, betting on dog racing is being phased out and will be illegal in Florida after 2020.

8.   PERSONAL PROPERTY TAXES

There are two types of personal property: intangible and tangible. Examples of the former include an interest in a partnership (such as a law firm); copyrights, patents, and trademarks; life insurance policies; and stocks and bonds. Examples of the latter include clothing, electronics, furniture, jewelry, and vehicles.

Although real property (*i.e.*, land and buildings) is tangible, it always is treated as its own category. This is because personal property is movable and real property is not.

(a) Intangible Property Taxes

Intangible property taxes are mentioned in two different sections of the constitution: Art. VII, § 2 and Art. VII, § 9(a). The former caps the state tax rate on intangible property at "two mills" (*i.e.*, $2 per $1,000 of value). The latter prohibits local governments from taxing intangible property. These provisions were added to the constitution in 1944.

Florida began collecting intangible taxes in 1931 to fill a $1 million shortfall in the state's budget. Because they generated very little money, were difficult to enforce, and were an obstacle to luring wealthy retirees to the state, they were repealed effective January 1, 2007. *See* Fla. Stat. ch. 199. At the time, the rate was 50 cents per $1,000 of value. Thus, for example, a person who owned $1 million in stocks was taxed $500 a year. Florida was the last state to have an intangible property tax; in its final year, it generated $130 million.

The federal government does not have an intangible property tax. It does, however, have a capital gains tax, which operates somewhat like an intangible property tax.

(b) Tangible Property Taxes

Tangible property taxes are referenced seven times in the Florida Constitution:

1) Art. VII, § 1(a): Prohibits the state from imposing such taxes. As a result, only local governments can tax tangible property. This provision was added to the constitution in 1940.

2) Art. VII, § 3(b): Grants an exemption from such taxes "to every head of a family residing in this state, household goods and personal effects to the value fixed by general law, not less than one thousand dollars[.]" This provision first appeared in

the 1868 constitution and has been included in every succeeding constitution.

3) Art. VII, § 3(c): Allows counties and municipalities to exempt from such taxes both new businesses and existing businesses that agree to expand their operations. This provision was added to the constitution in 1980.

4) Art. VII, § 3(e)(1): Exempts the first $25,000 of tangible personal property from such taxes. This provision was added to the constitution in 2008.

5) Art. VII, § 3(e)(2): Permits "solar devices" and "renewable energy source devices" to be exempted from such taxes. This provision was added to the constitution in 2016. Unless extended, it will expire on Dec. 31, 2037. *See* Art. XII, § 34.

6) Art. VII, § 4(c): Permits "tangible personal property held for sale as stock in trade and livestock" to be "[1] valued for taxation at a specified percentage of its value, . . . [2] classified for tax purposes, or . . . [3] exempted from taxation." This provision was added to the constitution in 1966. Like most states, Florida currently does not tax a business's inventory. *See* Fla. Stat. § 192.001(11)(d).

7) Art. VII, § 9(b): Limits the rate local governments can tax tangible personal property to 10 mills (*i.e.*, $10 per $1,000 of

value). This provision was added during the constitution's 1968 revision.

From the beginning, enforcing the tangible property tax against individuals was difficult, expensive, and time-consuming. It also produced relatively little money ($40 million a year) while turning nearly every Floridian into a tax cheat (due to under-reporting). As a result, Florida stopped collecting the tax from individuals in 1967. *See* Fla. Stat. § 192.001(11)(d).

Such taxes still apply to businesses, although in 2008 the first $25,000 of assets (*e.g.*, furniture, machinery, office supplies, signs, and tools) was made exempt. *See* Fla. Stat. § 196.183(1). As a result, only about 5% of all Florida businesses are required to pay it. *See further* http://floridarevenue.com/property/Pages/Taxpayers_TangiblePersonal Property.aspx.

Including Florida, 43 states currently tax tangible property. While such taxes represent just 7% of Florida's property tax base, they make up 29% of Louisiana's property tax base (the national average is 10%). The federal government does not have such a tax.

9. REAL PROPERTY TAXES

The primary source of revenue for local governments in Florida is real property taxes. This is the result of Art. VII, § 1(a) and Art. VII, § 9(a). The former provides: "No state ad valorem taxes shall be levied upon real estate. . . ." The latter adds:

"Counties, school districts, and municipalities shall, and special districts may, be authorized by law to levy ad valorem taxes. . . ." Taken together, these two provisions mean that only local governments can tax real property. Most states handle real property taxes in the same way.

Taxing land is attractive because it can neither flee nor hide. Thus, from the government's standpoint, real property is the easiest, most cost-effective asset to tax. Despite this fact, the federal government does not tax real property.

Nationally, real property tax rates range from a low of 0.27% (in Hawaii) to a high of 2.44% (in New Jersey). Thus, a home valued at $226,800 (the U.S. median) annually pays $612 in Hawaii and $5,534 in New Jersey. The typical American homeowner pays $2,279 a year in real property taxes.

At 0.98%, Florida's real property tax rate ranks 26th in the country. Tax rates in Florida, however, vary widely: from 0.55% in Walton County to 1.38% in Hendry County. The typical Florida homeowner pays $1,702 a year in real property taxes.

Florida provides certain landowners (primarily homeowners who live in the state year-round) with tax breaks that help keep down the cost of real property taxes. These breaks are discussed later in this chapter.

In 2018, Florida's various local governments collectively levied $33.2 billion in real property taxes: counties, $12.8 billion; municipalities, $5.2 billion; school districts, $13.1 billion; and special districts,

$2.1 billion. For a further look at these and other local government taxes, see the *2018 Local Government Financial Information Handbook* at http://edr.state.fl.us/Content/local-government/reports/lgfih18.pdf.

10. SALES TAXES

As noted above, Florida levies numerous taxes that are not specifically mentioned in the constitution. The most important of these is the sales tax. *See* Fla. Stat. §§ 212.01–212.211. Sales taxes now are the leading source of tax revenue for Florida's state government.

Florida's first sales tax, enacted in 1949, was 3%. This figure was increased to 4% in 1968, 5% in 1982, and 6% in 1988. Florida allows counties to "tack on" sur-taxes (which currently range from 0.5% to 2.5%). As a result, sales taxes in Florida currently range from 6% (in Citrus County) to 8.5% (in Hillsborough County). The average rate is 7%.

Closely related to sales taxes are "use taxes." Such taxes are applied when an item is purchased outside Florida, does not pay the state's sales tax, and later is used within the state.

Sales taxes are a common means of raising revenue, and only five states do not have them (Alaska, Delaware, Montana, New Hampshire, and Oregon). In other states, sales taxes range from 2.9% to 7.25% (not including local sur-taxes). The federal government does not charge a sales tax. In recent years, many proposals have been floated for a national sales tax—such plans usually are coupled with a call to eliminate (or at least sharply reduce) the federal income tax.

In 2018, Florida's sales tax generated $25.2 billion. This amounted to 77% of the state's total tax revenues. Like the rest of Florida's tax laws, the sales tax is riddled with exemptions and loopholes, most of which are the product of special interest legislation (see, e.g., Fla. Stat. § 212.04(2)(a)(5), which prohibits sales taxes on Super Bowl tickets). It is estimated that if all the exemptions and loopholes were abolished, Florida would collect an additional $43.7 billion a year.

Sales taxes are not imposed on groceries or medicine. *See* http://floridarevenue.com/Forms_library/current/dr46nt.pdf. Despite this fact, sales taxes are highly regressive. This is because the poor spend a greater percentage of their income than the rich. As a result, the Florida Legislature now regularly authorizes sales tax "holidays" on back-to-school items (since 1998) and hurricane supplies (since 2005). Michigan and Ohio held the nation's first sales tax holidays in 1980 (on automobile sales); today, 17 states (including Florida) have tax holidays. While most exempt the same things as Florida, several give breaks to more unusual goods, such as energy-efficient appliances (Maryland, Missouri, and Texas) and guns (Louisiana and Mississippi).

To make the rich pay more, the Florida Legislature in 1987 extended the sales tax to a broad range of services (including legal services). Although the

Florida Supreme Court ruled that the tax was constitutional, see *In re Advisory Opinion to the Governor, Request of May 12, 1987*, 509 So. 2d 292 (Fla. 1987), the tax provoked fierce protests and was repealed after just six months. Had it remained in place, it now would be producing $31 billion a year. For a further look at Florida's sales tax, see http://floridarevenue.com/taxes/taxesfees/Pages/sales_tax.aspx.

D. MECHANICS

1. AD VALOREM AND NON-AD VALOREM TAXES

Taxes are calculated on either an ad valorem (Latin for "according to value") or non-ad valorem basis. When an item is taxed on its value, the tax increases as the item's value increases. In contrast, non-ad valorem taxes ignore an item's value and instead require payment of a fixed amount.

A good example of ad valorem taxes are real property taxes. If such taxes are 2%, a parcel of land worth $10,000 pays $200 in taxes; a parcel of land worth $100,000 pays $2,000 in taxes; and a parcel of land worth $1,000,000 pays $20,000 in taxes.

Art. VII, § 1(b) requires certain types of property to be taxed on a non-ad valorem basis: "Motor vehicles, boats, airplanes, trailers, trailer coaches and mobile homes, as defined by law, shall be subject to a license tax for their operation in the amounts and for the purposes prescribed by law, but shall not be subject to ad valorem taxes." Thus, a private jet worth $5 million pays the same amount of taxes as a private jet worth $50 million.

Sec. 1(b) traces its origins to 1930, when the following provision was inserted in the constitution:

> Motor Vehicles, as property, shall be subject to only one form of taxation which shall be a license tax for the operation of such motor vehicles, which license tax shall be in such amount and levied for such purpose as the Legislature may, by law, provide, and shall be in lieu of all ad valorem taxes assessable against motor vehicles as personal property

In 1965, mobile homes, trailer coaches, and trailers were added to the list after the Florida Supreme Court decided they were not motor vehicles. *See Palethorpe v. Thomson*, 171 So. 2d 526 (Fla. 1965). Airplanes and boats were included as part of the constitution's 1968 revision to entice wealthy northerners to move to Florida. *See Department of Revenue v. Florida Boaters Association, Inc.*, 409 So. 2d 17 (Fla. 1981).

2. TAX RATES

Art. VII, § 2 provides in part: "All ad valorem taxation shall be at a uniform rate within each taxing unit. . . ." Thus, when a tax is based on value, the government must apply the same rate (percentage) to all taxpayers.

Art. VII, § 9(b) limits how much taxing units can charge:

Ad valorem taxes . . . shall not be levied in excess of the following millages upon the assessed value of real estate and tangible personal property: for all county purposes, ten mills; for all municipal purposes, ten mills; for all school purposes, ten mills; for water management purposes for the northwest portion of the state lying west of the line between ranges two and three east, 0.05 mill; for water management purposes for the remaining portions of the state, 1.0 mill; and for all other special districts a millage authorized by law approved by vote of the electors who are owners of freeholds therein not wholly exempt from taxation. A county furnishing municipal services may, to the extent authorized by law, levy additional taxes within the limits fixed for municipal purposes.

A "mill" (from the Latin *millesimum*, meaning "one-thousandth") is an abstract unit of currency equal to one-tenth of a dime. Put another way, 1,000 mills equal a dollar. Thus, if a piece of land is worth $100,000 and has a mill rate of five, it would pay 500,000 mills (100,000 × 5). Converted into dollars, 500,000 mills equal $500 (500,000 ÷ 1,000). It is easier, however, to just remember that one mill equals $1 of tax for every $1,000 of value.

As can be seen, § 9(b) (added to the constitution in 1968) caps the millage rate of counties, municipalities, and school districts at 10 mills; caps the millage rate of water management districts at 0.05 or 1.0 depending on their location; and lets the voters decide the maximum millage rate of special districts. It also allows, in areas where the county is providing municipal services (because there is no municipality in the area) to increase its millage rate to compensate it for such services, up to a maximum of 10 mills. *See* Fla. Stat. § 200.071(3).

In 1922, a constitutional amendment authorized the creation of school districts and set their millage rates at 10. This likely is the reason why counties and municipalities also are capped at 10 mills.

Millage rates in Florida vary widely. In Miami-Dade County, for example, the total millage rate ranges from just under 17 (in rural areas) to nearly 26 (in the City of Opa-locka). The millage rate in the City of Miami is 21.8256. This works out to $2,182.56 in taxes for a house with an assessed value of $100,000.

While most millage rates are set by local officials, the millage rates of Florida's five water management districts ("WMD") are determined by the legislature. Fla. Stat. § 373.503(3)(a) currently sets the following rates: 1) Northwest Florida WMD (Pensacola region): 0.05 mills; 2) Suwannee River WMD (Lake City region): 0.75 mills; 3) St. Johns River WMD (Jacksonville region): 0.6 mills; 4) Southwest Florida WMD (Tampa region): 1.0 mills; and, 5) South Florida WMD (Miami region): 0.8 mills.

Millage rates, of course, are only relevant with respect to ad valorem taxes. When it comes to non-ad valorem taxes (often called "assessments" rather than taxes), all taxpayers are charged the same amount. *See* Fla. Stat. §§ 197.3631 and 197.3632. Many local governments assess property owners to defray the cost of their fire-rescue departments. *See*, *e.g.*, *City of Cooper City v. Joliff*, 227 So. 3d 633 (Fla. 4th Dist. Ct. App. 2017), *review denied*, 2018 WL 3201729 (Fla. 2018).

3.   VALUATIONS

The amount of ad valorem tax that is due is determined by two factors: the tax rate and the value of the property being taxed.

State tax rates are set by the legislature. Local tax rates are set by local governments. *See* Fla. Stat. §§ 200.001, 200.011, and 200.065.

Property values, on the other hand, are determined by the county property appraiser. *See* Fla. Stat. § 192.001(3). Art. VIII, § 1(d) requires each county to have an elected property appraiser. For a further discussion of these officials, see the web site of the Florida Association of Property Appraisers (https://www.fapa.net/). For a list of Florida's property appraisers, see http://floridarevenue.com/property/Pages/LocalOfficials.aspx.

Art. VII, § 4 requires the property appraiser to assign to all property subject to ad valorem taxes a "just valuation." As a practical matter, this means "fair market value," or the amount a willing buyer and a willing seller would agree on in an arms-length transaction. As explained earlier in this chapter, Florida currently imposes ad valorem taxes only on business assets and real estate.

A property owner who disagrees with the property appraiser's valuation may appeal to the local Value Adjustment Board ("VAB"). Each county has its own VAB, which consists of two county commissioners, one school board member, and two citizens. *See* http://floridarevenue.com/property/Pages/VAB.aspx. To initiate an appeal, a property owner files a petition with the clerk of the circuit court. *See* http://floridarevenue.com/property/Documents/pt101.pdf.

4.   EXEMPTIONS

Art. VII, § 3(a) exempts six types of property from ad valorem taxation:

[1] All property owned by a municipality and used exclusively by it for municipal or public purposes shall be exempt from taxation. A municipality, owning property outside the municipality, may be required by general law to make payment to the taxing unit in which the property is located. Such portions of property as are used predominantly for [2] educational, [3] literary, [4] scientific, [5] religious or [6] charitable purposes may be exempted by general law from taxation.

The first of these exemptions (for municipally-owned property) is automatic. The other five require, and have received, legislative authorization. *See* Fla. Stat. §§ 196.192, 196.196, and 196.198. *See also* http://floridarevenue.com/property/Documents/dr50 4.pdf. All six exemptions have been a part of the constitution since 1868.

The municipal exemption has generated numerous fact-specific lawsuits. A good example is *Florida Department of Revenue v. City of Gainesville*, 918 So. 2d 250 (Fla. 2005). In that case, the court held that the city could be taxed on property it was using to provide telecommunications services to its citizens because "telecommunications services have historically been provided by the private sector." *Id.* at 265.

The other exemptions have generated an even greater number of fact-specific lawsuits. In *Sarasota City v. Sarasota Church of Christ, Inc.*, 667 So. 2d 180 (Fla. 1995), for example, the court held that the city could impose a storm water management tax on all property owners, including houses of worship.

As the constitution indicates, only property being used for an exempt purpose receives an exemption. Thus, for example, a not-for-profit hospital that built a four-story building, rented the first floor to private doctors, and used the remaining three floors for its own purposes was ordered to pay taxes on 25% of the building. *See Underhill v. Edwards*, 400 So. 2d 129 (Fla. 5th Dist. Ct. App.), *review denied*, 411 So. 2d 381 (Fla. 1981).

The constitution permits counties and municipalities to grant ad valorem property tax exemptions to "new businesses and expansions of existing businesses," see Art. VII, § 3(c) (added 1980), as well as to the owners of "historic properties." *See* Art. VII, § 3(d) (added 1992; amended 1998).

In 2008, "real property dedicated in perpetuity for conservation purposes, including real property encumbered by perpetual conservation easements or by other perpetual conservation protections," also was made exempt from property taxes. *See* Art. VII, § 3(f).

It is important to keep in mind that whenever property is taken off the tax rolls through exemption (or, as discussed below, immunity or classification), the amount of taxes paid by those properties left on the tax rolls must increase if the government is to reap the same amount of tax revenues. (Alternatively, the government can cut expenses, or reduce services, to make up the difference.) It has been estimated, for example, that Fla. Stat. § 196.197, which exempts not-for-profit hospitals from property taxes, costs local governments $200 million a year.

5. IMMUNITY

Property that belongs to a superior sovereign cannot be taxed by an inferior sovereign because it is immune from such taxes. *See, e.g., Russell v. Southeast Housing, LLC*, 162 So. 3d 262 (Fla. Dist. Ct. App. 2015), *review denied*, 2016 WL 1065886 (Fla. 2016) (Monroe County prohibited from taxing the U.S. Navy's local housing complex). Sovereigns of equal dignity, however, can tax each other. *See Joiner v. Pinellas County*, 279 So. 3d. 860 (Fla. 2d Dist. Ct. App. 2019), *appeal filed*, SC19–1819 (Fla.) (Pinellas County required to pay Pasco County property taxes).

In *McCulloch v. Maryland*, 17 U.S. (4 Wheat.) 316 (1819), the U.S. Supreme Court used the principle of tax immunity to invalidate Maryland's tax on the Second Bank of the United States. Nevertheless, it is common today for a superior sovereign to make payments "in lieu of taxes" to an inferior sovereign to reimburse it for its costs. This is done, for example, where the inferior sovereign provides fire, police, or sanitation services to the superior sovereign's property.

6. CLASSIFICATION

Certain types of property receive a tax break by having their value ignored: "Agricultural land, land producing high water recharge to Florida's aquifers, or land used exclusively for noncommercial recreational purposes may be classified by general law and assessed solely on the basis of character or use." Art. VII, § 4(a). *See also* Fla. Stat. § 193.461(5) (defining the term "agricultural land").

Although the agricultural land tax break, adopted in 1959, was intended to help farmers, it has become a favorite of real estate developers. By placing a small herd of "rent-a-cows" on a piece of land until construction begins, a developer can claim the land is being used for agricultural purposes. It is estimated that rent-a-cows cost Florida $500 million a year in lost tax revenues.

The constitution similarly grants classification to three other types of properties: 1) land used for conservation purposes, see Art. VII, § 4(b); 2) historic properties when authorized by a county or municipality, see Art. VII, § 4(e); and, 3) certain working waterfront properties (*e.g.*, vessel repair facilities), see Art. VII, § 4(j).

7. HOMESTEADS

By far, the most confusing aspect of ad valorem taxes is the treatment accorded to "homestead properties." As pointed out in Ch. 12 of this book, to qualify as a homestead a property must be: 1) located in Florida; 2) owned by a natural person; and, 3) be the owner's actual principal residence. As further explained in Ch. 12, there currently are 4.3 million homestead properties in Florida.

A homestead property receives two kinds of benefits. First, as discussed in Ch. 12, it is protected from being sold out from under its owner by the owner's creditors (except "super creditors"). *See* Art. X, § 4(a).

The second type of benefit a homestead property receives, and the one that is relevant here, is a break on property taxes. This tax break saves the average Floridian $700 a year.

Art. VII, § 6(a) shields the first $25,000 of assessed value from ad valorem taxes. When the 1968 constitution was adopted, the shielded amount was $5,000 (the same as in 1934, when the exemption was first added to the constitution), but a 1980 amendment increased this figure to $25,000. Only one such exemption is permitted per individual or family unit. *See* Art. VII, § 6(b). The legislature can extend this exemption, either partially or fully, to renters who pay ad valorem taxes. *See* Art. VII, § 6(c). To date, however, it has not done so.

It is important to note that § 6 does *not* provide a $25,000 reduction in one's property taxes. If it did, almost no one would have to pay property taxes. Rather, it reduces the amount of *property value* that is subject to taxation. Thus, for example, a homestead property worth $125,000 will be taxed as if it was worth $100,000. If the tax rate is 2%, this results in a savings of $500 (*i.e.*, a $2,000 tax bill instead of a $2,500 tax bill).

Since 1980, § 6 has been amended repeatedly (1998, 2006, 2008, 2012, 2016). As a result, certain homestead owners can shield additional amounts of assessed value:

1)   Those who are 65 or older can shield an extra $50,000 if their income does not exceed $20,000 and their counties or municipalities allow such shielding (see paragraph (d)(1) and Fla. Stat. § 196.075).

2)   Those who are 65 or older, have lived in the same house for at least 25 years, and whose income does not exceed $20,000, may shield their home's entire value (up to $250,000) if their counties or municipalities allow such shielding (see paragraph (d)(2) and Fla. Stat. § 196.075).

3)   Veterans who are 65 or older and who are disabled due to combat are entitled to an extra discount equal to the percentage of

their disability (see paragraph (e) and Fla. Stat. § 196.082).

4)   The surviving spouse of a veteran who dies while on active duty is entitled to ad valorem tax relief up to the amount set by the legislature (see paragraph (f)(1) and Fla. Stat. § 196.081 (setting the exemption at 100%)).

5)   The surviving spouse of a first responder who dies in the line of duty is entitled to ad valorem tax relief up to the amount set by the legislature (see paragraph (f)(2) and Fla. Stat. § 196.081 (setting the exemption at 100%)).

6)   A totally and permanently disabled first responder whose injuries were sustained in the line of duty is entitled to ad valorem tax relief up to the amount set by the legislature (see paragraph (f)(3) and Fla. Stat. § 196.102 (setting the exemption at 100%)).

In addition to the exemptions and discounts contained in § 6, other constitutional provisions contain further tax breaks. For example:

1)   Pursuant to Art. VII, § 3(b), widows and widowers, as well as persons who are blind or permanently disabled, are entitled to a $500 exemption. This exemption first appeared in the 1885 constitution and originally was set at $200.

2) Pursuant to Art. VII, § 3(g), members of the armed forces (including reservists) who serve outside the United States are entitled to an exemption based on how many days they are deployed. This exemption is only available in years when the person is deployed in military operations recognized ("designated") by the legislature. This provision was added in 2016.

3) Pursuant to Art. VII, § 4(f), a county may grant a discount to homestead property that includes "living quarters for one or more natural or adoptive grandparents or parents of the owner of the property or of the owner's spouse if at least one of the grandparents or parents for whom the living quarters are provided is 62 years of age or older." The amount of this discount cannot exceed the lesser of "(1) The increase in assessed value resulting from construction or reconstruction of the property [or] (2) Twenty percent of the total assessed value of the property as improved." This provision was added in 2002 and often is referred to as the "granny flat" tax exemption.

4) Pursuant to Art. VII, § 4(i), the legislature can exempt from a homestead property's value: "(1) Any change or improvement to real property used for residential purposes made to improve the property's resistance to wind damage[; and,] (2) The installation

of a solar or renewable energy source device." These exemptions were added to the constitution in 2008. Unless renewed, the latter exemption, which also is available to non-homestead properties, will expire on Dec. 31, 2037. *See* Art. XII, § 34.

In 1992, a citizens' group known as Save Our Homes ("SOH") proposed that annual homestead valuation increases be limited to 3% or the percent change in the Consumer Price Index ("CPI"), whichever is less. (Since 1992, the yearly change in the CPI has averaged 2.26%, with the biggest jump—3.8%—coming in 2008.) After making the ballot, see *In re Advisory Opinion to the Attorney General—Homestead Valuation Limitation*, 581 So. 2d 586 (Fla. 1991), and then being allowed to stay on the ballot, see *Florida League of Cities v. Smith*, 607 So. 2d 397 (Fla. 1992), the amendment narrowly was approved. *See* Art. VII, § 4(d).

In many ways, SOH's proposal resembled California's controversial Proposition 13 (1978), which capped yearly property increases at 2%. For obvious reasons, SOH did not highlight the fact that the primary beneficiaries would be millionaire homeowners. Instead, its ads claimed that "little old ladies" were being forced out of their homes. It was not until the closing days of the campaign that the public began to catch on, and it has been suggested that if the election had come just a few weeks later, the amendment would have lost.

The following example shows how SOH works. Assume a homestead in "year one" is worth $100,000.

Also assume that over the next five years, its value increases 15% each year but the CPI increases only 2% each year. Lastly, assume the tax rate remains steady at 2%. By the end of the sixth year, the homeowner will have saved $4,891.23:

Year	Market Value (15% annual increase)	Assessed Value (2% annual Increase)	Taxes Without SOH	Taxes With SOH
2	$115,000	$102,000	$2,300	$2,040
3	$132,250	$104,040	$2,645	$2,080.80
4	$152,087.50	$106,120.80	$3,041.75	$2,122.42
5	$174,900.63	$108,243.22	$3,498.01	$2,164.86
6	$201,135.72	$110,408.08	$4,022.71	$2,208.16

Although the foregoing example uses a 15% yearly increase in the home's value, it does so simply to make the illustration clearer. In the real world, home values rarely increase by very much. Indeed, from 1970 to 1990, the average home's value increased 2% a year while inflation increased 6% a year. Very high-end homes (particularly those on the water) did beat inflation, and, as explained above, it was these owners who were behind the SOH amendment.

The SOH amendment had an unforeseen consequence, one that by the early 2000s had become a significant problem: it trapped owners in their homes. This is because if they sold their homes, they lost their accumulated SOH savings. This was particularly bad for "empty-nesters" who wanted to trade down to a smaller home; growing families who wanted to trade up to a bigger home; and real estate agents, who were losing commissions due to the freeze in the marketplace.

To fix this problem, in 2007 the Florida Legislature proposed an amendment to Art. VII, § 4(d) allowing homeowners to keep some of their savings (known as "portability") if they moved. It also increased the § 6(a) homestead exemption from $25,000 to $50,000. Rather than wait until election day, the legislature called a special election (Jan. 2008), at which the measure passed.

The 2008 amendment, dubbed the "Portability of Save Our Homes" amendment, contains the following restrictions:

1) Portability is available only up to $500,000 and is determined by subtracting the assessed value of the former home from its market value and applying that amount to the new home. *See* Art. VII, § 4(d)(8). Thus, if a homeowner sells a home with a market value of $200,000 and an assessed value of $100,000 and then buys a new home for $300,000, the new home will receive $100,000 in portability credits, meaning that it will be assessed (in the first year of ownership) at $200,000, after which the SOH cap will apply. To qualify for portability, an owner must replace a Florida homestead with another Florida homestead within two years.

2) The second $25,000 exemption applies to assessed values between $50,000 and $75,000. *See* Art. VII, § 6(a). Thus, a homestead property worth $40,000 receives only the first $25,000 exemption but a homestead property worth $100,000 receives both exemptions.

3) The second $25,000 exemption does not apply to school taxes. *Id*. Thus, while it is common to refer to the current homestead exemption as a $50,000 exemption, its true value is closer to $40,000.

4) A special "recapture" rule results in some homeowners seeing their taxes increase even when the market falls. This occurs when a property is not assessed at its full market value. Assume, for example, that a homestead property is worth $100,000. Over the next three years, its market value doubles to $200,000 and its assessed value increases by 2% a year to $106,120.80. In the fourth year, however, the market crashes, resulting in the home's market value falling to $150,000. Even though the owner has lost 25% of his or her equity, the assessed value will still go up.

To complete the hypothetical, assume further that the CPI in the crash year is 1%. This means the house's assessed value will increase by $1,061.21 ($106,120.80 to $107,182.01). If the tax rate remains steady at 2%, the owner's taxes will go up by $21.22 ($2,122.42 to $2,143.64). While this is a very modest increase, it will come as a shock to the typical owner, who will be expecting his or her property taxes to drop $530.61 (to equal the 25% drop in equity).

In 2012, an amendment that would have allowed the legislature to change the recapture rule was rejected. Had it passed, it also would have given first-time buyers an additional homestead exemption equal to 50% of their home's value (up to their county's median home value). This exemption would have been reduced 20% each year, causing it to disappear after five years.

There are several other things one should know about the SOH tax breaks:

1)   When a homestead property is remodeled, renovated, or otherwise substantially changed, the property appraiser is authorized to increase the assessed value of the home without regard to the SOH cap. *See* Art. VII, § 4(d)(5). Routine maintenance does *not* trigger reassessment. In the past, property appraisers primarily relied on building permits to learn about changes. Today, they increasingly are using unmanned aerial vehicles (*i.e.*, drones).

2)   When a homestead property is sold, the buyer does not "inherit" the seller's assessed value. Instead, the property appraiser will adjust the property to reflect its fair market value, which may or may not be the same as the sales price. *See* Art. VII, § 4(d)(3).

3) New homestead property is assessed at fair market value "as of January 1st of the year following the establishment of the homestead." *See* Art. VII, § 4(d)(4).

4) Renting out a homestead property for more than 30 days a year for two consecutive years automatically terminates the exemption. *See* Fla. Stat. § 196.061(1). Exceptions exist for members of the armed forces. *See* Fla. Stat. §§ 196.061(2) and 196.071.

5) Homestead property is protected automatically from forced sales under Art. X, § 4(a). In contrast, a homeowner must apply for homestead property tax breaks under Art. VII, §§ 3, 4, and 6. Such applications are made to the county property appraiser and must be renewed annually. *See* Fla. Stat. § 196.011. Whenever there is a question regarding a homeowner's entitlement to a specific tax break, the burden of proof is on the homeowner. *See* Fla. Stat. § 196.015. *See also Garcia v. Andonie*, 101 So. 3d 339 (Fla. 2012); *Zingale v. Powell*, 885 So. 2d 277 (Fla. 2004).

6) Fla. Stat. ch. 196 contains various additional tax breaks for homestead property that are not mentioned in the constitution. *See*, *e.g.*, Fla. Stat. § 196.101(1) ("Any real estate used and

owned as a homestead by any quadriplegic is exempt from taxation.").

7) Falsely claiming a homestead exemption is a misdemeanor and is punishable by up to one year in jail and a fine of up to $5,000. *See* Fla. Stat. § 196.131(2). Other potential penalties include having a tax lien placed on the property; being "back taxed" for up to 10 years; being required to pay penalties of up to 50% of the unpaid taxes for each year; and being charged interest at a rate of 15% per year. *See* Fla. Stat. §§ 193.155(9)(a) and 196.161(1)(a)–(b).

8) Increases in non-homestead and business property valuations are capped at 10% a year (except as to school taxes). *See* Art. VII, § 4(g)–(h). These provisions are designed to protect part-time residents and business owners. The rejected 2012 amendment discussed above would have changed the cap to 5%.

In 2018, the Florida Legislature proposed increasing the homestead exemption to $75,000. Surprisingly, this idea was defeated. It was the only amendment on the 2018 ballot that failed to win approval.

Although SOH favors long-time Florida residents over newcomers and out-of-staters, constitutional challenges based on this fact have been unsuccessful. *See, e.g., Lanning v. Pilcher*, 16 So. 3d 294 (Fla. 1st Dist. Ct. App.), *review denied*, 37 So. 3d 847 (Fla.), *cert. denied*, 562 U.S. 1062 (2010); *Reinish v. Clark*, 765 So. 2d 197 (Fla. 1st Dist. Ct. App.), *review dismissed*, 773 So. 2d 54 (Fla. 2000), *review denied*, 790 So. 2d 1107 (Fla.), *cert. denied*, 534 U.S. 993 (2001).

For a further look at Florida's homestead exemptions, see http://floridarevenue.com/property/Pages/Taxpayers_Exemptions.aspx. *See also* Fla. Stat. §§ 193.155, 196.031, and 196.041.

8.   COLLECTIONS

(a) Generally

State taxes are collected by the Florida Department of Revenue ("FDOR") (http://florida revenue.com/pages/default.aspx). In contrast, local taxes are collected by the county tax collector. *See* Fla. Stat. § 192.001(4). Pursuant to Art. VIII, § 1(d), each county is required to have its own elected tax collector. As Fla. Stat. § 197.332 explains, a county tax collector collects taxes on behalf of all the local governments within his or her jurisdiction. For a further discussion, see the web site of the Florida Tax Collectors Association (https://floridataxcollectors.com/). A list of tax collectors by county can be found at https://floridataxcollectors.com/your-tax-collector/.

In 1992, the constitution was amended to require the Florida Legislature to promulgate a Taxpayer's Bill of Rights ("TBR"). *See* Art. I, § 25. The TBR's text appears in Fla. Stat. § 213.015. Notwithstanding the TBR, a taxpayer who wishes to challenge a tax on the grounds of illegality or illegal assessment must first pay so much of the tax as is not disputed. *See* Art. VII, § 13; Fla. Stat. § 194.171. *See also Bystrom v. Diaz*, 514 So. 2d 1072 (Fla. 1987).

The actual process of collecting taxes varies depending on the tax. Sales taxes, for example, are collected by the seller at the time of the transaction. The seller is then required to remit the taxes to the FDOR. Large merchants (those who annually collect more than $1,000 in sales taxes) must remit payments monthly; smaller merchants are required to do so quarterly, semi-annually, or annually.

County tax collectors, on the other hand, send out real property tax bills once a year in November. *See* https://floridarevenue.com/property/Documents/tax calendar.pdf. In the case of mortgaged properties, the bill normally goes to the bank holding the mortgage, which pays it from an escrow fund established by the property owner. For a sample property tax bill, see https://www.broward.org/RecordsTaxesTreasury/ TaxesFees/Documents/SampleTaxNotice.pdf.

(b) Tax Sales

If a property owner fails to pay his or her property taxes by their due date (*i.e.*, Apr. 1 of the year following the year in which they are assessed), the county tax collector will place a lien on the property. *See* Fla. Stat. § 197.122. If the lien remains unpaid after 60 days (*i.e.*, by June 1), the tax collector will hold a public auction (known as a *tax lien sale*). *See* Fla. Stat. § 197.432. Such sales normally are conducted over the internet.

The winning bidder pays the taxes (plus interest and costs) and, in exchange, receives a tax lien certificate. If, after two years, the certificate holder remains unpaid, he or she can force the property to be sold at a public auction (known as a *tax deed sale*). *See* Fla. Stat. § 197.502. The auction is conducted by the circuit court clerk, either in person or electronically. *See* Fla. Stat. § 197.542. If there are no bidders, the certificate holder gets the property. *Id.* Otherwise, the winning bidder gets the property, the certificate holder gets the proceeds (up to what he or she is owed), and any excess is distributed to the property owner or other lienholders. *See* Fla. Stat. § 197.582.

Nationally, 19 states conduct tax lien sales and 29 states conduct tax deed sales. Two states (Florida and Ohio) conduct both types of sales. Because they offer investors the chance to earn above-market interest (up to 18% in Florida), tax sales are quite popular. But unless one knows what one is doing, it is easy to lose money. This can occur, for example, if the property owner decides to abandon the property, no bidder purchases it, and it turns out not to be worth what the certificate holder paid for it.

E.   FEES

As noted at the outset of this chapter, the public's aversion to taxes has caused politicians to turn increasingly to fees. A fee is "any charge or payment required by law, including any fee for service, fee or cost for licenses, and charge for service." Art. VII, § 19(d)(1). Thus, for example, a motorist who needs to obtain, renew, or replace his or her driver's license is required to pay a fee to do so. *See* Fla. Stat. § 322.21(b) ($48 for a new license), (c) ($48 for a renewed license), and (e) ($25 for a replacement license).

The Florida Constitution mentions fees in several different provisions:

1) Art. IV, § 9: Requires all hunting and fishing fees to be prescribed by general law and the revenues generated by them (currently $62 million a year) to be appropriated to the Florida Fish and Wildlife Conservation Commission "for the purposes of management, protection, and conservation of wild animal life and fresh water aquatic life . . . [and] marine life as provided by law."

2) Art. V, § 14(b): Requires "the offices of the clerks of the circuit and county courts performing court-related functions" to be funded through "adequate and appropriate filing fees for judicial proceedings and service charges and costs for performing court-related functions as required by general law."

3) Art. VII, § 1(e): Defines the phrase "state revenues" as the "taxes, fees, licenses, and charges for services imposed by the legislature on individuals, businesses, or agencies outside state government."

4) Art. VII, § 15(a): Allows student fees to be used to pay for "revenue bonds . . . issued to establish a fund to make loans to students determined eligible as prescribed by law. . . ."

5) Art. VII, § 19: Prohibits the imposition of any new state fees, or the raising of any existing ones, unless 2/3 of the legislature agrees. It also requires a state "fee imposed, authorized, or raised under this section [to] be contained in a separate bill that contains no other subject."

6) Art. IX, § 7(e): Requires a state university that wishes "to raise, impose, or authorize any fee, as authorized by law, [to obtain] at least nine affirmative votes of [its] board of trustees . . . if approval by the board of trustees is required by general law, and at least twelve affirmative votes of the [state] board of governors, if approval by the board of governors is required by general law. . . ."

7) Art. XI, § 7: Prohibits the imposition of any new state fee that requires a change to the constitution unless the fee is approved by 2/3 of the voters.

Fees can be divided into three types: impact, service, and user. Developers, for example, can be charged impact fees to help defray the cost of new infrastructure. *See* Fla. Stat. § 163.31801. Thus, if a developer plans to build 100 new houses, the affected county or municipality (or both) can charge it for the cost of the new roads, sewers, and other items that the houses will require. *See St. Johns County v. Northeast Florida Builders Association, Inc.*, 583 So. 2d 635 (Fla. 1991).

A service fee is a fee charged for a specific government service, such as the issuing of a driver's license.

A user fee is a fee charged for using government property. For example, one must pay a fee to enter Florida's state parks. *See* https://www.floridastate parks.org/fees.

To be valid, a fee must be reasonably priced; provide a special benefit to the payor; and cannot be used to fund unrelated activities. *See Collier County v. State*, 733 So. 2d 1012 (Fla. 1999); *City of Daytona Beach Shores v. State*, 483 So. 2d 405 (Fla. 1985); *City of Miami v. Haigley*, 143 So. 3d 1025 (Fla. 3d Dist. Ct. App. 2014). *See also* Fla. Att'y Gen. Op. 91–55 ("Escambia County may not impose a user fee on tickets sold to civic center events in order to fund the Historic Pensacola Preservation Board and The Arts Council of Northwest Florida when such fee has no relation to the use of the facility."). These requirements have been adopted as "best practices" by the Government Finance Officers Association. *See* https://www.gfoa.org/establishing-government-charges-and-fees.

CHAPTER 22
BONDS

A. OVERVIEW

When the government decides to undertake a construction project—*e.g.*, a hospital, prison, or road—it normally raises the money it needs by issuing bonds. A bond is simply a loan, which the government promises to repay at a specified rate of interest.

Bonds cannot be used by the government to pay for ordinary ("recurring") expenses (*e.g.*, salaries and benefits). *See Cheney v. Jones*, 14 Fla. 587 (1874). Instead, such expenses must be paid for through taxes. Thus, bonds are reserved for extraordinary ("non-recurring") expenses, often referred to as "brick and mortar" projects. *See State v. City of Orlando*, 576 So. 2d 1315 (Fla. 1991) (city's plan to issue bonds and use the proceeds to make more money by taking advantage of price differences in the markets— "arbitraging"—was improper because no capital improvement project was involved or even contemplated).

Art. VII, § 11 authorizes the state to issue bonds, while Art. VII, §§ 10(c) and 12 permits local governments to issue bonds. As will be seen below, several other provisions of the Florida Constitution also are relevant.

B. BASICS

Bonds (sometimes called "certificates of indebtedness" or "tax anticipation certificates") can be divided into two primary types: general obligation ("G.O.") and revenue. When the former is used, the government makes all its assets available for repayment. It also promises to raise taxes if necessary. As a result, the bond is said to be backed by the "full faith and credit" of the government. (Because of these guarantees, G.O. bonds also are known as "hell or high water" bonds.)

A revenue bond, on the other hand, carries no assurances. Instead, the investor is paid back only if the underlying project generates enough money to cover the debt. Thus, the investor must carefully evaluate the project's chances for success.

A third type of bond, known as a special obligation ("S.O.") bond, is a variation of a revenue bond. It pledges money from a revenue source other than the project but does not invoke the government's full faith and credit power. Gasoline and parking taxes often are used to fund S.O. bonds.

Because G.O. bonds carry less risk than revenue bonds, their interest rates are lower. Thus, a cautious investor ordinarily buys G.O. bonds, while an investor seeking profits normally purchases revenue bonds.

Except when the constitution provides otherwise, G.O. bonds must be approved by the voters. This is because the public is likely to end up paying for such bonds through higher future taxes. No such vote is needed for a revenue bond because the public is not at risk—if the project does not generate enough funds, the investor is stuck footing the bill.

To help investors, bonds are "rated" by credit rating agencies. The three largest rating agencies in the United States are Fitch (https://www.fitch ratings.com), Moody's (https://www.moodys.com/), and Standard & Poor's ("S & P") (https://www. standardandpoors.com). Collectively, they rate 95% of all U.S. bonds. A higher rating denotes lower risk, while a lower rating indicates higher risk. The amount of interest that a bond pays is determined in large part by its rating, although other factors—such as its length—also are important.

The top rating given by both Fitch and S & P is "AAA." Moody's equivalent is "Aaa." These ratings mean that the issuer's finances are extremely strong and the likelihood of repayment is excellent. Such bonds are "investment grade." At the other end of the spectrum, bonds rated "CCC" (by Fitch or S & P) or "Caa2" (by Moody's) are extremely speculative and often are referred to as "junk bonds." These bonds pay the highest interest rates but also carry the most risk and are not suitable for most investors.

All bonds have what is known as a "face value." This is the bond's par or principal value. Thus, for example, a $100 bond is a bond that, upon first being issued, costs $100 to buy and will pay $100 when it "matures" (*i.e.*, becomes due). The typical bond matures in 5–30 years, although in recent times both California and Ohio have issued 100-year bonds. Bonds that have no maturity date (*i.e.*, that give the issuer the right to decide when to pay them back) are said to be perpetual and are called "consols" (short for consolidated). In 1751, Great Britain issued consols that it did not pay off until 2015.

Paying back a bond is known as "redeeming" or "retiring" it. Bonds typically are redeemed when their maturity date is reached. Sometimes, however, bonds are paid back early. If the government's future finances prove stronger than expected, for example, it may choose to retire its bonds (assuming they permit early redemption).

More often, however, the government redeems a bond because interest rates have fallen, meaning that new bonds with a lower interest rate can be issued and the proceeds used to pay off the older bonds. This is known as "refunding" and can result in significant savings. The constitution permits the government to refund G.O. bonds without voter approval. *See* Art. VII, §§ 11(a) and 12(b).

Until a bond is paid off, interest is paid to the bondholder. The interest rate is set at the time the bond is first offered for sale and is paid on the bond's face value. Depending on the bond, interest may be remitted on a monthly, quarterly, semi-annual, or annual basis. The rate of interest is known as the "coupon" (at one time, bonds came with actual coupons that had to be sent in to the issuer). Bonds that do not pay regular interest are known as "zero coupon" bonds. Such bonds effectively roll their interest payments into their face value.

Most bonds are "negotiable," meaning they can be sold by the original purchaser and resold by subsequent purchasers. Just like any other security, the price a bond commands on the secondary market is subject to supply and demand. If interest rates fall, for example, a bond normally will trade at a "premium" (*i.e.*, above its face value). On the other hand, if the issuer experiences financial problems and seems likely to default, the bond will trade at a "discount."

Because bonds are sold at different times for different prices, investors often talk about a bond's "yield." A bond's yield is determined by considering such factors as its face value, selling price, maturity date, how much interest is left to be paid, and whether it is tax exempt. (Different yield formulas use different combinations.) Knowing a bond's yield gives an investor a better sense of its current value.

Government bonds often come to market through public auctions. In contrast, corporate bonds usually are purchased by a syndicate of banks or brokerage houses who then resell them to the public (a process known as "underwriting"). Insurance companies, mutual funds, and pension plans tend to be the biggest purchasers of bonds.

Bonds invariably raise a host of legal issues (usually having to do with securities and tax law). Accordingly, specialized bond lawyers are hired to prepare the underlying paperwork, which includes a formal opinion attesting to the bond's legality and tax status (*i.e.*, fully-exempt, partially exempt, or non-exempt). For more information, see the web site of the National Association of Bond Lawyers (https://www.nabl.org/).

Before a government bond can be sold, it must be "validated" by the courts. The validation process is described later in this chapter. Because market conditions can change rapidly, bond validation cases receive expedited treatment.

Government bonds, colloquially known as "municipal bonds" or "munis," are particularly attractive to investors because their interest often is exempt from federal, state, and local income taxes. *See Department of Revenue of Kentucky v. Davis*, 553 U.S. 328 (2008). They also tend to be a safe investment. However, in 2016 Puerto Rico defaulted on its bonds, worth $74 billion. *See Puerto Rico v. Franklin California Tax-Free Trust*, 136 S. Ct. 1938 (2016).

C. HISTORY

Government bonds in this country trace their start to 1817, when New York issued $7 million in bonds (paying 6% interest) to finance the building of the 360-mile Erie Canal. The tolls collected from the canal's users not only allowed the bonds to be paid off in a mere 15 years, they helped subsidize an additional 600 miles of canals.

Today, the government bond market consists of more than 50,000 issuers. Currently, these entities have $1.1 trillion in bonded debt. In Florida, the state government has $21 billion in outstanding bonds. Florida's local governments owe an additional $7 billion. At \$28 billion, Florida is the 13th most bond-indebted state in the country (California is first at \$209 billion). On a per capita basis, however, Florida, at \$1,415, ranks 46th (Alaska, at \$10,576, ranks first).

Florida's bond history begins in 1833, when it chartered the Union Bank of Florida and authorized \$3 million in bonds to capitalize it. Two years later, it endorsed bonds for the Bank of Pensacola (\$500,000) and the Southern Life Insurance and Trust Company (\$400,000). The Panic of 1837 caused all three institutions to fail. When the territorial government was pressed to honor these bonds, it responded by passing Resolution 9 (1842): "Resolved, That the Territorial Legislature does not possess nor was it ever invested [by Congress] with the authority to pledge the faith of the Territory so as to render the citizens of the Territory responsible for the debts or engagements of any corporation chartered by said Territorial Legislature." Upon becoming a state in 1845, a second reason for not paying was offered: the debt was a territorial one, for which the new state had no responsibility.

Repudiation again became an issue following the end of the Civil War. In 1865, Florida had \$2.1 million in public debt, including \$1.8 million in outstanding bonds. Although this amount was tiny compared to the rest of the Confederacy, it represented an enormous number in Florida, where the value of taxable property had fallen by 52.9%.

For a time, the question of whether to honor the state's debt was a heated one, with many Floridians believing it should be paid back because it represented "honest debt." Uncertain what to do, the delegates to the 1865 constitutional convention voted 25–21 to put the question to the people.

Subsequently, however, the delegates learned that Pres. Andrew Johnson had sent a telegram to Gov. William Holden of North Carolina making repudiation a prerequisite for readmission to the Union. As a result, the delegates took a new vote and decided, 33–9, to repudiate Florida's debt. The adoption of the 14th Amendment (1868) settled the matter (see § 4): "[N]either the United States nor any State shall assume or pay any debt or obligation incurred in aid of insurrection or rebellion against the United States [and] all such debts, obligations and claims shall be held illegal and void."

The first Florida constitution to specifically mention government-issued bonds was the 1868 constitution: "The Legislature shall have power to provide for issuing State bonds bearing interest, for securing the debt [of this State,] and for the erection of State buildings, support of State institutions, and perfecting public works." This provision was a tacit acknowledgment that the Civil War had left Florida battered and in need of massive rebuilding. It also, however, opened the door to breathtaking acts of graft, mismanagement, and theft, most of which involved the railroad industry. *See, e.g., Holland v. State*, 15 Fla. 455 (1876).

As a result, the delegates to the 1885 constitutional convention severely restricted the state's ability to issue bonds: "The legislature shall have power to provide for issuing State bonds only for the purpose of repelling invasion or suppressing insurrection, or for the purpose of redeeming or refunding bonds already issued, at a lower rate of interest."

Because the delegates' focus was on the state's profligacy, the 1885 constitution said nothing about local governments bonds. Thus, when Florida experienced a sudden land boom in 1920, local governments began issuing bonds at a furious pace. The bursting of this bubble in 1926, followed closely by the Great Depression in 1929, had severe consequences:

> Florida led the nation in number of school taxing districts in default, placed third in the reclamation and irrigation district default race, lapped the field in the county default event, and also pulled handsomely ahead in the defaulting cities and towns event. In short, Florida won the national grand championship with points to spare. . . . [A]s of Jan. 1, 1936 bond defaults had already occurred in 47 out of Florida's 67 counties, in 204 out of its 514 municipalities, in 79 . . . of its reclamation, levee, irrigation, and drainage districts, and in 28 of its special assessment districts, for a total default record of 621. The nearest other states on total figures were Arkansas with 290 defaults, Louisiana with 256, North Carolina with 250, Texas with 247, Michigan with 217, and California with 184.

Grover C. Herring & George John Miller, "Florida Public Bond Financing—Comments on the Constitutional Aspects," 21 *U. Miami L. Rev.* 1, 4–5 & n.10 (1966).

In response, the constitution was amended in 1930 to limit the bonding authority of local governments:

> The Legislature shall have power to provide for issuing State bonds only for the purpose of repelling invasion or suppressing insurrection, and the Counties, Districts or Municipalities of the State of Florida shall have power to issue bonds only after the same shall have been approved by a majority of the votes cast in an election in which a majority of the freeholders who are qualified electors residing in such Counties, Districts, or Municipalities shall participate, to be held in the manner to be prescribed by law; but the provisions of this Act shall not apply to the refunding of bonds issued exclusively for the purpose of refunding of the bonds or the interest thereon of such Counties, Districts, or Municipalities.

In *State v. City of Miami*, 152 So. 6 (Fla. 1933) (en banc), the Florida Supreme Court held that local government revenue bonds were unaffected by the 1930 amendment. Using similar reasoning, it held that the state also could issue revenue bonds. *See Hopkins v. Baldwin*, 167 So. 677 (Fla. 1936) (en banc).

To further get around the constitution's restrictions, amendments began to be added authorizing S.O. bonds for highways (1942—from gas taxes); schools (1952—from motor vehicle registration fees); and conservation projects (1963—from general revenues).

By 1966, when the Constitution Revision Commission began work on what would become the 1968 constitution, Florida had just $2.6 billion in public debt, of which 27% was held by the state and 73% by local governments. Moreover, 82% of this debt was revenue bonds. Thus, Floridians faced very little risk in the event of a bond default. On the other hand, the lack of bond debt was a sign that many projects were not getting built, particularly those that could not use revenue bonds. In addition, Florida was paying more than other jurisdictions for the projects that were getting built. In a 1960 study comparing Connecticut and Florida, for example, Connecticut was found to be paying 3.25% interest while Florida was paying 4.13% interest.

To address these matters, the 1968 constitution greatly liberalized the rules governing government bonds. To avoid upending any existing bonds, it also reaffirmed all bonds issued under the 1885 constitution. *See* Art. XII, § 9.

D. STATE BONDS

Art. VII, § 11 allows the state to issue bonds. This provision is implemented by the State Bond Act. *See* Fla. Stat. §§ 215.57–215.835. Responsibility for overseeing state bonds is vested in the Division of Bond Finance ("DBF") (https://www.sbafla.com/bond/), an agency of the State Board of

Administration. *See* Fla. Stat. §§ 215.62 and 215.69. The chair of the DBF is the governor. *See* Fla. Stat. § 215.62(1).

The *State of Florida 2018 Debt Report* can be found at https://www.sbafla.com/fsb/Portals/FSB/Content/Performance/DAR2018.pdf?ver=2018-12-14-115233-417. As it indicates, Florida has $21 billion of bonded debt ($17.5 billion in G.O. bonds and $3.5 billion in revenue bonds). Education (48%) and transportation (40%) projects account for most of the state's debt. In 2018, the state's bond rating was AAA/Aaa.

1.   GENERAL OBLIGATION BONDS

Under Art. VII, § 11(a), state G.O. bonds can be used "to finance or refinance the cost of state fixed capital outlay projects authorized by law, and purposes incidental thereto, upon approval by a vote of the electors." They also can be used to refund existing G.O. bonds. *Id*. As explained above, refunding does not require voter approval.

State G.O. bonds cannot be used for non-construction purposes. In *Division of Bond Finance v. Smathers*, 337 So. 2d 805 (Fla. 1976), the Florida Legislature voted to use state G.O. bonds for debt servicing. Calling the plan "violative of Article VII, Section 11(a) on its face," *id*. at 807, the Florida Supreme Court struck it down.

The requirement that all projects funded though state G.O. bonds be "authorized by law" was added in 1984. As is obvious, it places a further check on the state's bonding power.

To ensure that the state's G.O. bond debt remains manageable, paragraph (a) provides: "The total outstanding principal of state bonds issued pursuant to this subsection shall never exceed fifty percent of the total tax revenues of the state for the two preceding fiscal years, excluding any tax revenues held in trust under the provisions of this constitution." The state currently is well below this figure (21%).

Paragraphs (b) and (c) are technical in nature and concern the payment of interest and the sale of G.O. bonds:

(b)   Moneys sufficient to pay debt service on state bonds as the same becomes due shall be appropriated by law.

(c)   Any state bonds pledging the full faith and credit of the state issued under this section or any other section of this constitution may be combined for the purposes of sale.

In addition to Art. VII, § 11(a)–(c), two other sections of the constitution address state G.O. bonds: Art. VII, § 14 (added 1970) and Art. VII, § 17 (added 1988).

Sec. 14(a) allows state G.O. bonds to be issued, *without an election*,

to finance the construction of air and water pollution control and abatement and solid waste disposal facilities and other water facilities authorized by general law . . . to be operated by any municipality, county, district or authority, or any agency thereof . . . or by any agency of the State of Florida.

Paragraphs (b)–(e) add various qualifications, including limiting the amount of such bonds to "fifty per cent of the total tax revenues of the state for the two preceding fiscal years."

Although paragraph (a) makes it clear that the listed facilities are to be self-financing, the added security of the state's taxing power has sharply reduced the borrowing costs of local governments. In 1980, § 14 was amended to include "other water facilities."

Soon after it was added, § 14 was challenged because of its lack of an election requirement. In *State v. Division of Bond Finance of the Department of General Services*, 278 So. 2d 614 (Fla. 1973), the court brushed aside this challenge:

[I]n adopting Article VII, Section 14, by a statewide election, the sovereign people of this State intended to provide an alternative method of financing state bonds without a referendum in certain particular instances. The people of this State created a specific exception to the requirement of an election in this type of bond validation proceeding.

Id. at 618.

Turning to Art. VII, § 17, its paragraph (a) allows state bonds to be issued, *without an election*, "to finance or refinance the cost of acquiring real property or the rights to real property for state roads as defined by law, or to finance or refinance the cost of state bridge construction, and purposes incidental to such property acquisition or state bridge construction."

As paragraph (b) makes clear, these bonds are payable primarily from "motor fuel or special fuel taxes" but are "additionally . . . secured by the full faith and credit of the state," which explains the inclusion of the "without an election" language. Paragraph (c) limits the amount of bonds that can issued under this section to "ninety percent of the pledged revenues available for payment of such debt service requirements, as defined by law."

2. REVENUE BONDS

Art. VII, § 11(d) and (f) regulates state revenue bonds. The former paragraph allows the government to issue such bonds "without a vote of the electors to finance or refinance the cost of state fixed capital outlay projects authorized by law, and purposes incidental thereto, and shall be payable solely from funds derived directly from sources other than state tax revenues." The latter paragraph requires "[e]ach project, building, or facility to be financed or refinanced with revenue bonds issued under this section [to] first be approved by the Legislature by an act relating to appropriations or by general law."

The requirement that all projects funded though state revenue bonds be "authorized by law" was added as part of the previously-discussed 1984 G.O. bonds amendment.

As explained above, Art. VII, § 11(b) requires the legislature to appropriate funds to pay the debt service (*i.e.*, interest) on G.O. bonds. This provision also applies to revenue bonds.

In addition to Art. VII, § 11(d) and (f), two other sections of the constitution deal with state revenue bonds: Art. VII, § 15 (added 1972) and Art. VII, § 16 (added 1980).

Sec. 15(a) allows state revenue bonds to be used "to establish a fund to make loans to students . . . who have been admitted to . . . any public or private institutions of higher learning, junior colleges, health related training institutions, or vocational training centers . . . [as] prescribed by law." Paragraph (b) allows any excess interest money generated by the fund to be used "for such other related purposes as may be provided by law."

As is obvious, § 15 modifies Art. VII, § 11(d), which limits revenue bonds to "state fixed capital outlay projects."

Similarly, § 16(a) allows state revenue bonds to be issued, *without an election*, to "finance or refinance housing and related facilities in Florida." Paragraph (b) prohibits "the full faith and credit of the state" from being "pledged to secure such . . . bonds," although other sources of revenue can be used. Paragraph (c) limits the amount of bonds that can be issued under this section to "the pledged revenues available for payment of such debt service requirements, as defined by law."

Sec. 16 modifies Art. VII, § 11(d), which limits revenue bonds to "state fixed capital outlay projects." The "without an election" language appears to have been included to emphasize that these are revenue bonds and not G.O. bonds. The bonds under this section are administered by the Florida Housing Finance Corporation (https://www.floridahousing. org/).

3.   SPECIAL OBLIGATION BONDS

Art. VII, § 11(e) allows the state to issue S.O. bonds for specified projects:

> Bonds pledging all or part of a dedicated state tax revenue may be issued by the state in the manner provided by general law to finance or refinance the acquisition and improvement of land, water areas, and related property interests and resources for the purposes of conservation, outdoor recreation, water resource development, restoration of natural systems, and historic preservation.

Paragraph (e) was added to the constitution in 1998. Upon its addition, what had been paragraph (e) became paragraph (f).

E.   **LOCAL BONDS**

Two different sections of the constitution regulate local government bonds: Art. VII, § 10(c) (revenue bonds, including, by implication, S.O. bonds) and Art. VII, § 12 (G.O. bonds). These provisions are implemented by, among others, Fla. Stat. chs. 132

(refunding bonds), 159 (county bonds), 166 (municipal bonds), 189 (special district bonds), and 1010 (school bonds).

As explained above, the 1885 constitution did not address the bonding powers of local governments (which allowed them to run wild in the 1920s), while the 1930 amendment made it impossible for local governments to issue G.O. bonds. The drafters of the 1968 constitution sought to strike a balance. They also wanted to overturn recent court decisions that had made it harder for local governments to issue revenue bonds on behalf of private companies. (Such financing is known as "conduit" financing. Local governments often use conduit financing to attract or retain businesses, who benefit by obtaining capital at a reduced cost. Conduit bonds typically are referred to as "industrial development bonds," "industrial revenue bonds," or "private activity bonds.")

Since 1973, local governments have been required to report, on an annual basis, their debt levels to the Florida Department of Financial Services. *See* Fla. Stat. § 218.32. These reports (going back to 2009) can be found at https://apps.fldfs.com/LocalGov/Reports/default.aspx.

In examining these reports, one recent study has found that six cities have especially high levels of bonded debt: Cape Coral, Fort Myers, Hollywood, Jacksonville, Miami, and Pembroke Pines.

1. GENERAL OBLIGATION BONDS

Art. VII, § 12 permits local governments to issue "bonds, certificates of indebtedness or any form of tax anticipation certificates, payable from ad valorem taxation and maturing more than twelve months after issuance only":

(a) to finance or refinance capital projects authorized by law and only when approved by vote of the electors who are owners of freeholds therein not wholly exempt from taxation; or

(b) to refund outstanding bonds and interest and redemption premium thereon at a lower net average interest cost rate.

Both paragraphs have been the subject of litigation. Paragraph (a)'s first requirement—that local government G.O. bonds be used only for "capital projects"—was tested in *County of Palm Beach v. State*, 342 So. 2d 56 (Fla. 1976). In that case, bonds were issued to finance "the cost of the acquisition, maintenance and preservation" of beaches and parks. The Florida Supreme Court approved the bonds after concluding that the term "maintenance" could be read to mean "capital maintenance."

Paragraph (a)'s second requirement—that elections be limited to "freeholders" (*i.e.*, property owners)—was struck down in *State v. City of Miami Beach*, 245 So. 2d 863 (Fla. 1971). Relying on a recent U.S. Supreme Court decision, see *City of Phoenix, Arizona v. Kolodziejski*, 399 U.S. 204 (1970), the Florida Supreme Court held that this requirement violated the U.S. Constitution. As a result, all area residents must be allowed to vote in such referendums. *See State v. City of Miami*, 260 So. 2d 497 (Fla. 1972). *See also Fair v. Fair*, 317 F. Supp. 859 (M.D. Fla. 1970).

The Florida Supreme Court has made it clear that only a simple majority is needed to approve a proposed local government G.O. bond. As will be recalled, the constitution's 1930 amendment required a "majority of a majority." In holding that this standard no longer applies, the court in *State v. City of St. Augustine*, 235 So. 2d 1 (Fla. 1970), explained:

> It is abundantly clear that the requirement contained in the 1930 Amendment to the 1885 Constitution that bonds must be approved by a majority of the qualified freeholder electors in an election in which a majority of such electors participated was intentionally and deliberately omitted from the 1968 Constitution. . . .

> After 1930 many bond elections in the state failed by reason of voter apathy. The major problem in the issuance of public obligations was securing participation in an election by a majority of freeholders. Failure to participate became the accepted method in many areas of defeating local bond issues. To overcome this situation the Legislature provided for the re-registration of freeholders as a basis for determining the number qualified to participate in a given bond election. Such cumbersome and costly procedures were, in our judgment and we so hold, intentionally and deliberately

eliminated in the Constitution of 1968 by eliminating the requirements of participation found in the 1885 Constitution.

Id. at 4–5 (footnotes omitted).

With respect to paragraph (b) (refunding), the court has held that it applies only to G.O. bonds. *See Jacksonville Shipyards, Inc. v. Jacksonville Electric Authority*, 419 So. 2d 1092 (Fla. 1982); *State v. City of Sunrise*, 354 So. 2d 1206 (Fla. 1978).

The question of when a referendum must be conducted has been litigated repeatedly. Each time, the court has held that an election is necessary only when the bonds at issue directly impact the local government's ad valorem (*i.e.*, property) taxes. *See Strand v. Escambia County*, 992 So. 2d 150 (Fla. 2008); *Boschen v. City of Clearwater*, 777 So. 2d 958 (Fla. 2001); *Frankenmuth Mutual Insurance Co. v. Magaha*, 769 So. 2d 1012 (Fla. 2000).

2. REVENUE BONDS

When authorized by law, Art. VII, § 10(c) allows local governments to issue revenue bonds

(1) . . . to finance or refinance the cost of capital projects for airports or port facilities, or (2) . . . to finance or refinance the cost of capital projects for industrial or manufacturing plants to the extent that the interest thereon is exempt from income taxes under the then existing laws of the United States, when, in either case, the revenue bonds are payable solely from revenue derived

from the sale, operation or leasing of the projects.

Paragraph (1) is self-explanatory.

As explained above, paragraph (2) authorizes conduit financing. When such financing is used, the interest to be paid must be exempt from federal income tax. *See International Brotherhood of Electrical Workers, Local Union No. 177 v. Jacksonville Port Authority*, 424 So. 2d 753, 756 (Fla. 1982) ("[A]rticle VII, section 10(c) only requires tax-exempt status in cases arising under clause (2) pertaining to industrial or manufacturing plants. Article VII, section 10(c)(1) does not demand that bonds for airports and ports be eligible for the tax exemption.").

The reason for this requirement was explained by the Florida Supreme Court in *Linscott v. Orange County Industrial Development Authority*, 443 So. 2d 97 (Fla. 1983):

The Constitution of 1885, article IX, section 10, prohibited government bodies from obtaining money for, or pledging the public credit to, any private entity. Under case law, revenue bonds payable solely from capital project revenues (non-recourse bonds) were held to be pledges of the public credit and were prohibited unless it could be shown that the capital project served a predominantly or paramount public purpose. *Contrast State v. Town of North Miami*, 59 So.2d 779 (Fla.1952), where non-recourse revenue bonds were held to

be invalid because they served a predominantly
private purpose with only incidental public
benefit *and State v. Board of Control*, 66 So.2d
209 (Fla.1953), where the bonds were validated
because they served a predominantly public
purpose with only incidental private benefit. . . .

Town of North Miami, and its progeny, began
to have a significant effect on Florida's economic
development in the 1960s because of a ruling by
the Internal Revenue Service, later codified,
which made the interest on industrial revenue
bonds exempt from federal income tax. As a
result of this ruling, Florida was placed at a
competitive disadvantage with other states
which could offer tax exempt, non-recourse
revenue bonds to private entities for capital
projects. *See, for example, State v. Jacksonville
Port Authority*, 204 So.2d 881 (Fla.1967), where
non-recourse bonds for a major port expansion
were held to be invalid. Significantly,
Jacksonville Port Authority was decided in July,
1967, when the Florida Legislature was
considering revisions to the Constitution of
1885. The legislative interest in the economic
impact of *Jacksonville Port Authority* was
evidenced by the immediate passage of
legislation attempting to nullify the court ruling.
See 204 So.2d at 892. Concurrently, in August,
1967, each house adopted joint resolutions
proposing revisions to the constitutional
provisions prohibiting the pledge of public credit
to private entities. In pertinent part, the thrust
of the Senate version was to overturn

Jacksonville Port Authority; that of the House version to overturn *Town of North Miami*. These differing versions, subsections 10(c)(1) and (2) respectively, became House Joint Resolution No. 1-2X 559–60, Laws of Florida (1968), which was submitted to, and approved by, the voters of Florida in November, 1968.

Id. at 99–100 (footnotes omitted).

The terms "industrial plant" and "manufacturing plant" are not defined in the constitution. However, Fla. Stat. § 159.27(5) includes a lengthy (and expansive) list. Moreover, the Florida Supreme Court has made it clear that this list is not exclusive. *See, e.g., State v. Leon County*, 400 So. 2d 949 (Fla. 1981) (nursing home); *Nohrr v. Brevard County Educational Facilities Authority*, 247 So. 2d 304 (Fla. 1971) (college cafeteria). As a result, most projects will qualify if they fulfill a "public purpose." *See, e.g., Donovan v. Okaloosa County, Florida*, 82 So. 3d 801 (Fla. 2012) (approving use of local revenue bonds for a beach restoration project).

A rare example of a project failing to qualify is *Orange County Industrial Development Authority v. State*, 427 So. 2d 174 (Fla. 1983). In refusing to approve $9 million in industrial revenue bonds for a commercial television station, the Florida Supreme Court first held that the project was neither an industrial plant nor a manufacturing plant:

We do not believe that the legislature intended to define "industrial or manufacturing plant" to include a commercial television station. Several indicators bear this out.

First, television stations are not included among the projects specifically designated as permissible under . . . § 159.27(5), Fla.Stat. (1981).

Second, . . . on its face, an industrial or manufacturing plant does not subsume within it a television broadcast facility. To hold otherwise would be to give the words an unreasonable construction. . . .

Third, . . . [the] dictionary definition of "industry" includes requirement of the employment of a large personnel as well as capital. WEBSTER'S THIRD NEW INTERNATIONAL DICTIONARY 1155–56 (1976). The relatively small number of persons employed at the broadcast facility hardly qualifies as a large number of personnel. . . .

Id. at 177.

The court next found that the project did not do enough to satisfy the public purpose requirement:

The Outlet Company [the station's owner] would save around $300,000 per year for the life of the bonds. There will be no benefit to the public other than the improved local news coverage which might produce a more informed citizenry in the central Florida area, a minimal increase in employment, limited economic prosperity to the community, and an alleged advancement of the general welfare of the people. A broad, general public purpose, though, will not constitutionally sustain a project that in terms of direct, actual use, is purely a private enterprise.

Id. at 179.

Unless a separate deal is struck providing otherwise, a private entity that uses local government bonds to finance a project remains liable for all applicable property taxes. *See* Art. VII, § 10(c) ("If any project so financed, or any part thereof, is occupied or operated by any private corporation, association, partnership or person pursuant to contract or lease with the issuing body, the property interest created by such contract or lease shall be subject to taxation to the same extent as other privately owned property."). *See also Volusia County v. Daytona Beach Racing and Recreational Facilities District*, 341 So. 2d 498 (Fla. 1976), *appeal dismissed*, 434 U.S. 804 (1977); *Dade County v. Pan American World Airways, Inc.*, 275 So. 2d 505 (Fla. 1973).

A private project financed by local revenue bonds does not have to be located within the issuing entity's jurisdiction. *See State v. City of Riviera Beach*, 397 So. 2d 685 (Fla. 1981) (permitting city to issue revenue bonds for a private waste plant to be built outside its borders).

F.   OTHER LIMITATIONS

As explained earlier in this chapter, the territory's investments were wiped out by the Panic of 1837. To prevent future losses, the 1838 constitution provided: "The General Assembly shall not pledge the faith and credit of the State to raise funds in aid of any corporation whatsoever." This language was carried over to the 1861 and 1865 constitutions.

The 1868 constitution changed this provision to read: "No tax shall be levied upon persons for the benefit of any chartered company of the State, or for paying the interest on any bonds issued by said chartered companies, or by counties or by corporations, for the above-mentioned purposes."

Because of the problems that arose after the Civil War, the 1885 constitution went even further:

The credit of the State shall not be pledged or loaned to any individual, company, corporation or association; nor shall the State become a joint owner or stockholder in any company, association or corporation. The Legislature shall not authorize any county, city, borough, township or incorporated district to become a stockholder in any company, association or corporation, or to obtain or appropriate money for, or to loan its credit to, any corporation, association, institution or individual.

The 1968 constitution largely retained this wording but, as described above, added a provision that allows local governments to issue revenue bonds for private companies. As a result, Art. VII, § 10 now reads as follows:

Neither the state nor any county, school district, municipality, special district, or agency of any of them, shall become a joint owner with, or stockholder of, or give, lend or use its taxing power or credit to aid any corporation, association, partnership or person; but this shall not prohibit laws authorizing:

(a) the investment of public trust funds;

(b) the investment of other public funds in obligations of, or insured by, the United States or any of its instrumentalities;

(c) the issuance and sale by any county, municipality, special district or other local governmental body of . . . revenue bonds. . . .

(d) a municipality, county, special district, or agency of any of them, being a joint owner of, giving, or lending or using its taxing power or credit for the joint ownership, construction and operation of electrical energy generating or transmission facilities with any corporation, association, partnership or person.

Paragraph (d) was added in 1974, a response to the 1973 world oil embargo.

Thus, § 10 prohibits the government from going into business with a private party except when the purpose is to generate or transmit electricity. Other types of relationships, however, are permissible (*e.g.*, customer, landlord, tenant). *See, e.g., Jackson-Shaw Co. v. Jacksonville Aviation Authority*, 8 So. 3d 1076 (Fla. 2008); *City of West Palm Beach v. Williams*, 291 So. 2d 572 (Fla. 1974); *Bannon v. Port of Palm Beach District*, 246 So. 2d 737 (Fla. 1971). For a further look at the limitations imposed by § 10, see Fla. Stat. § 215.47.

Matters become trickier when the government uses its credit or taxing powers and a private company benefits. A good example is *Poe v. Hillsborough County*, 695 So. 2d 672 (Fla. 1997). The county, the city, and the city's sports authority agreed to issue tax-backed bonds to build a new stadium for the Tampa Bay Buccaneers. They also agreed that the first $2 million generated each year by "non-Bucs events" held at the stadium would go to the team.

The plaintiff claimed that the deal violated § 10. In rejecting this contention, the Florida Supreme Court focused on the fact that the public would benefit by keeping the team in Tampa:

> Poe's criticisms of the terms of the lease agreement, and the "$2 million in non-Buc revenue" clause in particular, may well be valid. However, once a trial court has found that a "paramount public purpose" exists, the court cannot micromanage the arms-length business negotiations of the parties. . . . In addition, we reject Poe's contention that even when a project serves a paramount public purpose that only bonds which are to be repaid from revenues derived from the project itself may be validated if a private entity also derives some benefit from the project. *See State v. City of Miami*, 379 So.2d 651 (Fla.1980); *State v. Sunrise Lakes Phase II Special Recreation Dist.*, 383 So.2d 631

(Fla.1980); *Panama City v. State*, 93 So.2d 608 (Fla.1957).

Id. at 679.

The trial court's finding that the stadium served a "paramount public purpose" requires a word of explanation. In assessing whether the government can participate in a project that involves a private party, courts use one of two standards: "public purpose" or "paramount public purpose." The difference was explained by the Florida Supreme Court in *State v. Osceola County*, 752 So. 2d 530 (Fla. 1999):

> If the County has not exercised its taxing power or pledged its credit, the obligation must merely serve a public purpose. On the other hand, if the County has used either its taxing power or pledge of credit to support the issuance of the bonds, the purpose of the obligation must serve a paramount public purpose and any benefits to a private party must be incidental.

Id. at 536. *See also State v. JEA*, 789 So. 2d 268 (Fla. 2001). Thus, because the bonds in *Poe* involved the use of tax monies, the stadium had to serve a paramount public purpose and the benefit to the Buccaneers had to be incidental. According to the court, both conditions were met.

The plaintiff in *Poe* did not challenge the bonds under Art. VII, § 12. This is because, as the court explains, the tax used to fund the bonds—a 30-year, half-penny infrastructure sales surtax—was approved by the county's voters. *See Poe*, 695 So. 2d at 674.

G.   VALIDATION PROCEEDINGS

As mentioned at the outset of this chapter, government bonds must be "validated" before being offered for sale. The procedures to be followed in such cases are set forth in Fla. Stat. §§ 75.01–75.17.

Bond validation cases are heard in circuit court. *See* Fla. Stat. § 75.01. Because market conditions can change rapidly, the court is required to act "with the least possible delay." *See* Fla. Stat. § 75.07.

The plaintiff in a bond validation case is the government entity that wants to issue the bonds. *See* Fla. Stat. § 75.04. The defendants are "the state and the several property owners, taxpayers, citizens and others having or claiming any right, title or interest in property to be affected." *See* Fla. Stat. § 75.05. Liberal intervention is permitted. *See* Fla. Stat. § 75.07.

Appeals go directly to the Florida Supreme Court. *See* Fla. Stat. § 75.08. As the constitution makes clear, the court must hear such appeals. *See* Art. V, § 3(b)(2) ("When provided by general law, [the court] shall hear appeals from final judgments entered in proceedings for the validation of bonds or certificates of indebtedness."). For a further discussion, see Ch. 15 of this book.

Government bonds come to court with a presumption of validity. *See Noble v. Martin County Health Facilities Authority, Florida*, 682 So. 2d 1089

(Fla. 1996). Moreover, in deciding whether to validate them, the courts limit themselves to three questions: 1) does the plaintiff have bonding authority?; 2) are the bonds being issued for a legal purpose?; and, 3) have all of the necessary constitutional and statutory pre-requisites been met? *See Roper v. City of Clearwater*, 796 So. 2d 1159 (Fla. 2001) (rejecting taxpayer's argument that city lacked the authority to issue bonds for a spring training baseball complex). Thus, the courts do not consider whether the bonds are affordable, constitute a sound investment, or represent a wise use of the public's money. *See Sebring Airport Authority v. McIntyre*, 783 So. 2d 238 (Fla. 2001); *State v. Inland Protection Financing Corp.*, 699 So. 2d 1352 (Fla. 1997); *Penn v. Pensacola-Escambia Governmental Center Authority*, 311 So. 2d 97 (Fla. 1975).

Once a bond is validated, most future lawsuits are cut off:

> If the judgment validates such bonds, certificates or other obligations . . . and no appeal is taken within the time prescribed, or if taken and the judgment is affirmed, such judgment is forever conclusive as to all matters adjudicated against plaintiff and all parties affected thereby, . . . or to be affected in any way thereby, and the validity of said bonds, certificates or other obligations or of any taxes, assessments or revenues pledged for the payment thereof, or of the proceedings authorizing the issuance thereof, including any remedies provided for their collection, shall

never be called in question in any court by any person or party.

Fla. Stat. § 75.09.

Lawsuits that are not cut off can go forward, but the plaintiff must file an "affidavit of good faith." *See* Fla. Stat. § 75.17. In it, the plaintiff must attest "that the action is not filed for delay" and must set forth "with particularity why the objection was not made as part of the validation action." *Id*.

The costs of a bond validation lawsuit are borne by the plaintiff. *See* Fla. Stat. § 75.12. When it finds it "equitable" to do so, however, the court can shift the costs to the "taxpayer, citizen, or other person [who] contests the action or intervenes." *Id*.

PART VI

CHANGING THE CONSTITUTION

CHAPTER 23
AMENDMENTS

A. OVERVIEW

Art. XI sets out the constitution's amending process. As § 5(a) makes clear, all proposed amendments must be submitted to the people at either a general or special election.

To pass, an amendment must be approved by 60% of the voters. *See* Art. XI, § 5(e). However, an amendment authorizing a new state fee or tax must be approved by 2/3 of the voters. *See* Art. XI, § 7.

The group Keep Our Constitution Clean has proposed a 2020 constitutional amendment that would require future amendments to be passed at two consecutive elections (the current margins would apply at both elections). *See Advisory Opinion to the Attorney General re Voter Approval of Constitutional Amendments*, SC19–1911 (Fla.).

Past and proposed amendments can be traced by consulting:

1) The Florida Division of Elections' web site (https://dos.myflorida.com/elections/laws-rules/constitutional-amendments/). Its data goes back to 1978.

2) Ballotpedia's "List of Florida Ballot Measures" web site (https://ballotpedia.org/List_of_Florida_ballot_measures). Its data goes back to 1886.

3) Jo Dowling's *Florida's Constitutions: The Documentary History*, which can be found in the background papers to the 1998 Constitution Revision Commission at Florida State University. Its data covers the period 1838 to 1998.

B. TERMINOLOGY

In *Smathers v. Smith*, 338 So. 2d 825, 829 (Fla. 1976), the Florida Supreme Court observed: "[An] amendment . . . alter[s], modif[ies] or change[s] the substance of a single section of the Constitution . . . [while a] revision . . . restructures an entire class of governmental powers or rights." In everyday discourse, however, the words "amendment" and "revision" are used interchangeably. *See Florida Hometown Democracy, Inc. v. Cobb*, 953 So. 2d 666 (Fla. 1st Dist. Ct. App. 2007).

C. STATISTICS

The 1838 constitution was amended six times in 16 years.

No amendments were made to either the 1861 constitution or the 1865 constitution.

The 1868 constitution was amended 14 times in 18 years.

The 1885 constitution was amended 157 times in 81 years.

The 1968 constitution has been amended 134 times in 50 years.

Popular voting on constitutional amendments began with the 1868 constitution. Since the adoption of the 1885 constitution, 402 amendments have been proposed, of which 291 have passed.

Percentage-wise, the largest margin of victory occurred in 1896, when an amendment increasing the powers of justices of the peace was approved 8,327 to 459 (94.8%–5.2%). The smallest margin of victory occurred in 2004, when an amendment allowing slot machines at pari-mutuel facilities in Broward and Miami-Dade Counties was approved 3,631,261 to 3,512,181 (50.8%–49.2%).

The largest margin of defeat occurred in 1942, when an amendment granting tax exemptions to businesses was rejected 19,176 to 58,773 (24.6%–75.4%). The smallest margin of defeat occurred in 1998, when an amendment expanding local property tax breaks was rejected 1,754,747 to 1,766,490 (49.8%–50.2%).

Over the years, nearly every aspect of the Florida Constitution has been amended. Since 1968, the subjects that have appeared on the ballot the most have been bonds and taxes (35% of all proposals); courts (15%); and education (6%). Gambling, health care, and voting rights also have made frequent appearances.

Compared to other states, Florida is at the high end when it comes to constitutional amendments. Between 2006 and 2014, for example, 683 amendments were proposed nationwide, of which 482 passed. This works out to 14 proposed, and 10 passed, amendments per state. Florida's numbers are more than double: 33 and 22.

The U.S. Constitution presents a very different statistical picture. Since its adoption in 1789, there have been only 33 proposed amendments, of which 27 have passed.

D. BALLOT PATHWAYS

In Florida, there are five ways for a proposed amendment to reach the ballot:

1) By a joint legislative resolution. *See* Art. XI, § 1.

2) By a proposal from the Constitution Revision Commission ("CRC"). *See* Art. XI, § 2.

3) By a citizens' initiative petition. *See* Art. XI, § 3.

4) By a constitutional convention. *See* Art. XI, § 4.

5) By a proposal from the Taxation and Budget Reform Commission ("TBRC"). *See* Art. XI, § 6.

No state has more amendment methods than Florida and many have only one or two.

Like all states, Florida's constitution leaves the governor entirely out of the amendment process. *See Collier v. Gray*, 157 So. 40 (Fla. 1934) (en banc). The U.S. Constitution's amendment process similarly omits the president. *See* Art. V (permitting only Congress and the states to propose changes).

1. LEGISLATURE

The 1838 constitution authorized the Florida Legislature to amend the constitution by a 2/3 vote. This power was omitted from the 1861 constitution and has not appeared in any subsequent constitution. Nationally, only Delaware's constitution still allows legislators to make changes without voter input.

The Florida Legislature has been permitted to place constitutional amendments on the ballot since 1868. To date, it has done so 347 times (257 of its proposals have been approved). Since 1868, 83.4% of all proposed constitutional amendments have come from the legislature.

Forty-nine states allow their legislatures to propose constitutional amendments (Delaware is the lone exception). In 35 states (including Florida), the legislature can place an amendment on the ballot after passing it once. In 10 states, the legislature must pass the proposal twice before putting it on the ballot. Four states have mixed systems: the proposal can go on the ballot after one passage with a supermajority or after two passages with simple majorities.

To place an amendment on the ballot, the Florida Legislature must pass a "joint resolution agreed to by three-fifths of the membership of each house. . . . The full text of the joint resolution and the vote of each member voting [must] be entered on the journal of each house." *See* Art. XI, § 1.

2.   CONSTITUTION REVISION COMMISSION

Since 1968, the constitution has required the CRC to meet on a regular schedule (initially 10 years but now every 20 years) and propose such amendments as it deems appropriate. *See* Art. XI, § 2(c). No other state has such a body.

In 1988, when the TBRC was created, budget and tax matters were omitted from the CRC's jurisdiction. Both were restored in 1996.

Each CRC has 37 members: the attorney general; 15 persons appointed by the governor; nine appointed by the president of the senate; nine appointed by the speaker of the house; and three appointed by the chief justice of the supreme court with the "advice" of the other justices. *See* Art. XI, § 2(a). The CRC's chair is selected by the governor. *See* Art. XI, § 2(b). Vacancies are filled in the same manner as appointments. *Id.* As part of its work, the CRC must hold public hearings. *See* Art. XI, § 2(c).

The first CRC met in 1978 and proposed eight amendments, all of which were rejected (several of its ideas, however, were adopted at later elections). As a result, in 1980 the legislature tried to abolish the CRC but was unsuccessful.

The second CRC met in 1998. It proposed nine amendments, of which eight were adopted. The one that failed would have expanded local property tax breaks. As explained above, it was rejected by the smallest margin in Florida's history.

The third CRC met in 2018. It proposed eight amendments (identified on the ballot as Amendments 6–13). The seven that made it to the ballot all passed. Prior to the election, Amendment 8, dealing with charter schools, was struck from the ballot because its title and summary were misleading. *See Detzner v. League of Women Voters of Florida*, 256 So. 3d 803 (Fla. 2018). In contrast, the title and summary of Amendment 13 (banning dog racing) were found to be proper. *See Department of State v. Florida Greyhound Association, Inc.*, 253 So. 3d 513 (Fla. 2018).

The 2018 CRC was notable for its aggressive "bundling" of unrelated proposals to ensure that its less popular ideas passed. Although the constitution limits both legislative bills and citizens' petitions to "one subject," see Art. III, § 6 and Art. XI, § 3, this requirement does not appear in Art. XI, § 2. As a result, the Florida Supreme Court refused to strike any of the CRC's proposals because of bundling. *See County of Volusia v. Detzner*, 253 So. 3d 507 (Fla. 2018) (Amendment 10); *Department of State v. Hollander*, 256 So. 3d 1300 (Fla. 2018) (Amendment 6); *Detzner v. Anstead*, 256 So. 3d 820 (Fla. 2018) (Amendments 7, 9, and 11).

The only amendment proposed by the 2018 CRC that did not end up in court was Amendment 12. It reasonably combined a proposal concerning legislative lobbying with one prohibiting officials from using their offices to gain "disproportionate benefits."

Since the election, some lawmakers have called for a ban on bundling while others have revived the idea of a constitutional amendment abolishing the CRC. *See* H.B. 303 and H.J.R. 301. Both suggestions are expected to be vigorously debated during the legislature's 2020 session. Assuming, however, that the CRC survives, it will next meet in 2038.

3. CITIZENS' INITIATIVE

Art. XI, § 3 was added to the constitution as part of the 1968 revision. It permits citizens to propose amendments to the constitution, an option not found in any previous Florida constitution. In 1911, Rep. Thomas West (D-Milton) proposed adding a citizens' initiative provision to the constitution. Immediately after it approved the idea, the senate changed its mind. *See Crawford v. Gilchrist*, 59 So. 963 (Fla. 1912).

Currently, 18 state constitutions have citizens' initiative provisions, although the exacting requirements in some states (*e.g.*, Illinois, Massachusetts) make such amendments rare. The first state to allow citizens to propose amendments was Oregon (1902). The most recent state to add such a provision is Mississippi (1992).

Florida does not permit citizens to propose statutes (21 states do). (Rep. West's 1911 proposal included such a provision.) As a result, many of Florida's citizens' initiatives read like statutes and would be more appropriate as legislation.

The process for a citizens' initiative is spelled out in Art. XI, § 3:

> The power to propose the revision or amendment of any portion or portions of this constitution by initiative is reserved to the people, provided that, any such revision or amendment, except for those limiting the power of government to raise revenue, shall embrace but one subject and matter directly connected therewith. It may be invoked by filing with the custodian of state records a petition containing a copy of the proposed revision or amendment, signed by a number of electors in each of one half of the congressional districts of the state, and of the state as a whole, equal to eight percent of the votes cast in each of such districts respectively and in the state as a whole in the last preceding election in which presidential electors were chosen.

Additional requirements are contained in Art. IV, § 10; Art. V, § 3(b)(10); Art. XI, § 5(b)–(c); and Fla. Stat. §§ 100.371 and 101.161.

As originally written, Art. XI, § 3 did not limit initiatives to one subject. It did, however, restrict them to a single section. As a result, a proposal to replace the state's bicameral legislature with a unicameral one was struck from the ballot because multiple constitutional sections would have been affected. *See Adams v. Gunter*, 238 So. 2d 824 (Fla. 1970).

In response to *Adams*, Art. XI, § 3 was amended in 1972 to permit revisions of multiple sections, so long as only one subject is involved. As explained below, since 1994 Art. XI, § 3 has allowed initiatives limiting the government's revenue powers to address multiple subjects.

In 1976, Gov. Reubin Askew, upset over the legislature's repeated refusal to toughen the state's weak financial disclosure rules, led the first successful initiative (resulting in Art. II, § 8). This outcome caused the legislature to turn against initiatives.

In 1986, the legislature persuaded voters to add Art. IV, § 10 and Art. V, § 3(b)(10). As a result, the attorney general must request, and the supreme court must issue, an advisory opinion on any initiative that collects 10% of the total number of signatures needed to appear on the ballot. Since 2004, the constitution has required such opinions to be issued "no later than April 1 of the year in which the initiative is to be submitted to the voters."

In 2002, 2004, and 2006, the legislature convinced the public to add further conditions. As a result, initiative petitions must be: 1) accompanied by a financial impact statement; 2) filed by February 1 of the year in which they are to be voted on (other types of amendments have much later deadlines); and, 3) approved by 60% of the voters rather than by a simple majority (although this change applies to all amendments, it was specifically aimed at initiatives). A discussion of these requirements appears later in this chapter.

The Florida Legislature's hostility is not unique. Since 2006, the legislatures in Montana, Nebraska, Nevada, Oklahoma, and Oregon also have made it more difficult for initiatives to succeed.

In 2019, the Florida Legislature enacted two new roadblocks. *See* H.B. 5 (Fla. Laws ch. 2019–64). First, paid petition gatherers now must register with the state. Second, such gatherers no longer can be paid by the signature (instead, they must be paid by the hour, which is more expensive). When asked about these restrictions, Gov. Ron DeSantis said he felt they did not go far enough: "We've let too much policy go into the constitution. If you want to do policy through an initiative, it should be a statutory initiative." As explained above, Florida does not permit citizens to propose statutory initiatives.

To date, 28 citizens' initiatives have been adopted. In 2018, for example, two initiatives passed. The first restored the voting rights of former felons. *See Advisory Opinion to the Attorney General re: Voting Restoration Amendment*, 215 So. 3d 1202 (Fla. 2017), now Art. VI, § 4(a)–(b) (discussed in Ch. 3 of this book). The second placed new restrictions on casino gambling. *See Advisory Opinion to the Attorney General re: Voter Control of Gambling in Florida*, 215 So. 3d 1209 (Fla. 2017), now Art. X, § 30 (discussed in Ch. 13 of this book).

Other constitutional provisions that owe their existence to initiative petitions include: Art. I, § 27 (banning gay marriages); Art. II, § 9 (declaring English Florida's official language); Art. X, § 15 (authorizing a state lottery); Art. X, § 20 (prohibiting workplace smoking); Art. X, § 23 (allowing slot machines in Broward and Miami-Dade Counties); and Art. X, § 29 (legalizing medical marijuana).

To ensure there is statewide support for a petition, sponsors must collect signatures from voters in at least half of Florida's congressional districts. Currently, Florida has 27 congressional districts (the 2020 census is expected to increase this number to 29). The signatures needed in each district is 8% of the voters who voted in that district in the last presidential election. In Florida's largest congressional district (the Fourth, which includes all of Jacksonville), this means 34,256 signatures. In Florida's smallest congressional district (the 24th, which includes a sliver of Miami), this means 21,599 signatures. These numbers will change after the 2020 presidential election.

A sponsor also must obtain signatures equal to 8% of the total number of Floridians who voted in the last presidential election. Currently, this works out to 766,200 signatures. This number also will change after the 2020 presidential election.

In the 1976 election (as explained above, the first in which an initiative was successful), a total of 206,270 signatures were needed. Since then, the total number of signatures needed has nearly quadrupled due to Florida's on-going population boom:

Elections	Signatures Needed
1978 & 1980	256,653
1982 & 1984	298,743
1986 & 1988	342,939
1990 & 1992	363,886
1994 & 1996	429,428
1998 & 2000	435,329
2002 & 2004	488,722
2006 & 2008	611,009
2010 & 2012	676,611
2014 & 2016	683,149
2018 & 2020	766,200

The 8% district and statewide requirements cannot be waived for any reason. *See Floridians Against Expanded Gambling v. Floridians for a Level Playing Field*, 945 So. 2d 553 (Fla. 1st Dist. Ct. App. 2006), *review granted*, 952 So. 2d 1189 (Fla.), *review dismissed*, 967 So. 2d 832 (Fla. 2007).

Signatures remain valid for two years (until 2011, there were good for four years). *See* Fla. Stat. § 100.371(3). As they are collected they are turned in to the county supervisors of elections, who verify them and report the totals to the state's Division of Elections. *Id.* Not all signatures will be verified— some will be rejected as illegible or fraudulent, or because they come from persons who are not registered Florida voters. *See Browning v. Florida*

Hometown Democracy, Inc., PAC, 29 So. 3d 1053 (Fla. 2010). As a result, many sponsors set a goal of one million signatures. To reach this number, they normally hire firms that specialize in gathering signatures. Until the 2019 changes discussed above, such companies typically charged $5 per signature, making the total cost of signature collection $5 million. With the 2019 changes, this figure is expected to rise to $8 million.

Canvassers normally set up tables at shopping malls, stadiums, supermarkets, and other high-traffic areas. However, Fla. Stat. § 100.371(7) states:

> No provision of this code shall be deemed to prohibit a private person exercising lawful control over privately owned property, including property held open to the public for the purposes of a commercial enterprise, from excluding from such property persons seeking to engage in activity supporting or opposing initiative amendments.

Signatures are verified pursuant to Fla. Stat. § 99.097. Election supervisors are permitted to charge 10 cents, or their actual cost, whichever is less, for each signature they verify. *See* Fla. Stat. § 99.097(4). A hardship exemption exists for sponsors who cannot pay. *See id*.

When the number of verified signatures reaches 10% "of the number of electors [needed] statewide and in at least one-fourth of the congressional districts," the secretary of state notifies the attorney general. *See* Fla. Stat. § 15.21. Pursuant to Art. IV,

§ 10, and Fla. Stat. § 16.061, the attorney general then requests an advisory opinion from the Florida Supreme Court. Under Art. V, § 3(b)(10), the court must, "subject to [its] rules of procedure, permit interested persons to be heard on the questions presented[.]"

In reviewing an initiative petition, the court examines the proposal's ballot title and summary and checks to make sure that it covers only "one subject and matter directly connected therewith."

The single subject language in Art. XI, § 3 is stricter than the language applicable to legislative bills (Art. III, § 6). Its purpose, however, is the same: to prevent "logrolling" and ensure that the various components have "a logical and natural oneness of purpose[.]" *Fine v. Firestone*, 448 So. 2d 984, 990 (Fla. 1984). As previously explained, initiative petitions seeking to limit the government's ability to raise revenue are permitted to cover more than one subject.

During its review, the court does not consider whether the proposal is constitutional or represents sound public policy. *See Weber v. Smathers*, 338 So. 2d 819 (Fla. 1976). As a result, it had no trouble during the 2016 election cycle approving two diametrically-opposed solar energy proposals, one pushed by the energy industry and the other championed by consumers. *See Advisory Opinion to the Attorney General re Rights of Electricity Consumers Regarding Solar Energy Choice*, 188 So. 3d 822 (Fla. 2016); *In re Advisory Opinion to the Attorney General re Limits or Prevents Barriers to*

Local Solar Electricity Supply, 177 So. 3d 235 (Fla. 2015).

Once the court approves a proposal, its sponsor typically starts active campaigning. If there is strong opposition, further money must be raised for advertising. The two 2018 initiatives, for example, faced only token opposition. Nevertheless, Floridians for a Fair Democracy spent $21.5 million on its felons' rights amendment and Voters in Charge spent $46 million on its casino amendment (a new state record—as explained in Ch. 13 of this book, nearly all the money came from Disney and the Seminole Indian tribe).

Initiative petitions are not limited to Floridians— anyone can propose them using a "front man." And because they can be funded by "dark money," there often is no way to tell who is behind a given initiative:

> *[South Florida] Sun Sentinel* reporters Skyler Swisher and Aric Chokey . . . wrote last week that "at least $21 million in dark money— political spending that can't be traced to its original source—has flooded initiatives vying for the 2020 ballot, leaving voters with no way to know who is really advocating for them."

> Some of that money appears, perhaps by intent, to be making it more difficult for other sponsors to hire the canvassers they need.

> As the reporters found, two ballot initiatives have been funded entirely by secret donors: "Keep Our Constitution Clean" and "Florida Citizen Voters."

The "Keep Our Constitution Clean" campaign calls for submitting all proposed amendments to voter approval in two successive elections, rather than in only one as now. It has raised $5.5 million entirely in dark money. If the lid could be lifted, it wouldn't be surprising to find the same corporate lobbies currently openly opposing initiatives to raise Florida's minimum wage or allow consumers to choose their electric energy providers.

The "Florida Citizen Voters" campaign would amend the Constitution to specify that only citizens can vote. That's already the law . . . so why the amendment? No one but its sponsors knows, yet it has reported $8.3 million in dark money and has gathered more than the 766,200 signatures needed to make the 2020 ballot. It is registered to a UPS Store near Jacksonville.

One plausible suspicion is that Republican money is being invested in an issue that would help draw Donald Trump voters to the polls. Another likely theory is that its purpose is to starve other initiatives of the paid canvassers they need to hire. . . .

A succession of Supreme Court cases, beginning in 1976 and culminating in the infamous *Citizens United* decision of 2010, equates free spending with free speech and allows corporations to spend without limit by simply pretending not to coordinate with candidates. Short of amending the U.S. Constitution, there is no way for either Congress or the Florida Legislature to put a lid on the money.

The Legislature could, however, pry open the secrecy, simply by forbidding campaign sponsors to accept money from sources that don't make public where they get theirs. The law should also require that contributions, including those from such secondary sources, be reported online when received.

Until that's done, voters should be intensely suspicious of any initiative funded by dark money. . . .

"Dark Money" Corrupts Ballot Petition Process, S. Fla. Sun-Sentinel, Dec. 5, 2019, at 13A.

4.   CONSTITUTIONAL CONVENTION

As noted in Ch. 1 of this book, in 1838 the territorial council called Florida's first constitutional convention, which drafted Florida's first state constitution. Later conventions produced Florida's 1861, 1865, 1868, and 1885 constitutions.

The 1968 constitution (which was drafted by the legislature rather than by a constitutional convention) transferred the right to call conventions from the legislature to the people. *See* Art. XI, § 4. As a result, a convention now involves four discrete steps: 1) a citizens' petition requesting a convention; 2) an election to decide whether to hold a convention; 3) a second election to choose the convention's delegates; and, 4) a third election to approve or reject the delegates' proposed constitution. Given these requirements, Florida seems unlikely to ever hold another constitutional convention.

Since 1776, there have been 235 state constitutional conventions in the United States; the most recent one occurred in Rhode Island in 1984. Forty-three state constitutions allow conventions to be called (seven provide two methods for doing so while Montana's constitution has three). Two state constitutions (Pennsylvania and Vermont) do not mention conventions, although both have been interpreted to allow them. Five states (Arkansas, Indiana, Mississippi, New Jersey, and Texas) have no mechanism for calling a convention.

In 30 states, the legislature can call a constitutional convention, although in 25 of these states voter approval also is needed. In 14 states, the question of whether to hold a convention is placed on the ballot at designated intervals: 10 years (five states), 16 years (one state), or 20 years (eight states). In four states (including Florida), voters can call a convention.

To date, there has been only one federal constitutional convention (in 1787). To call such a convention, a request must be made by 2/3 of the country's legislatures (*i.e.*, 34 states). *See* Art. V. At present, efforts are being made to hold conventions to: 1) add a balanced budget amendment to the U.S. Constitution (sought by 28 states, including Florida); 2) limit the powers of the federal government (12 states, including Florida); and, 3) overturn *Citizens United v. Federal Election Commission*, 558 U.S. 310 (2010) (five states). If such a convention is ever held,

Florida will be ready—in 2014, it passed detailed rules for selecting its delegates. *See* Fla. Stat. §§ 11.93–11.9352.

5. TAXATION AND BUDGET REFORM COMMISSION

The final method for placing a constitutional amendment on the ballot is by having the TBRC recommend it. The TBRC was added to the constitution in 1988.

Originally, the TBRC was to meet once every 10 years. In 1998, this schedule was changed to once every 20 years. To date, the TBRC has met twice (1992, 2008). The next meeting of the TBRC will occur in 2028.

Each TBRC is composed of 25 voting members and four non-voting ex officio members. *See* Art. XI, § 6(a). Voting members are appointed by the governor (11), president of the senate (7), and speaker of the house (7). *Id.* The four non-voting members must come from the legislature, with the president selecting two senators (one of whom must be a member of the minority party) and the speaker selecting two representatives (one of whom must be a member of the minority party). *Id.* Vacancies are filled in the same manner as appointments. *See* Art. XI, § 6(b).

The TBRC's chair is selected by the voting members from among themselves. *See* Art. XI, § 6(c). The TBRC sets its own rules of procedure. *Id.* The

TBRC may hold public hearings as it deems necessary. *See* Art. XI, § 6(e).

The mission of the TBRC is set out in § 6(d):

> The commission shall examine the state budgetary process, the revenue needs and expenditure processes of the state, the appropriateness of the tax structure of the state, and governmental productivity and efficiency; review policy as it relates to the ability of state and local government to tax and adequately fund governmental operations and capital facilities required to meet the state's needs during the next twenty year period; determine methods favored by the citizens of the state to fund the needs of the state, including alternative methods for raising sufficient revenues for the needs of the state; determine measures that could be instituted to effectively gather funds from existing tax sources; examine constitutional limitations on taxation and expenditures at the state and local level; and review the state's comprehensive planning, budgeting and needs assessment processes to determine whether the resulting information adequately supports a strategic decisionmaking process.

In addition to constitutional amendments, the TBRC can "propose to the legislature . . . statutory changes related to the taxation or budgetary laws of the state." *Id.* The decision to recommend a constitutional change requires the approval of 2/3 of the TBRC's voting members. *See* Art. XI, § 6(c).

Although some observers had hoped that the TBRC would be allowed to examine any issue potentially affecting the state's finances, the Florida Supreme Court has rejected this idea:

> We find that the plain reading of the term "state budgetary process" is clear and unambiguous—TBRC's jurisdiction to propose constitutional amendments does not extend to a subject solely because the State will expend funds on that subject or because it could affect the State's expenditures. TBRC's authority to propose constitutional amendments directly to the voters is constitutionally limited to two scenarios: if the proposal addresses taxation or the process by which the State's budget is procedurally composed and considered by the Legislature.

Ford v. Browning, 992 So. 2d 132, 139–40 (Fla. 2008).

To date the TBRC has proposed seven amendments, of which five have passed. *See* Ch. 20 of this book.

E. ADOPTION

Art. XI, § 5 sets out the mechanics for elections involving constitutional amendments. Its provisions are augmented by Florida's election code. *See, e.g.,* Fla. Stat. §§ 101.161 (requiring all proposed amendments to have ballot titles and summaries) and 101.171 (requiring copies of proposed constitutional amendments to be available at all voting locations).

1.   BALLOT TITLES AND SUMMARIES

Under Fla. Stat. § 101.161(1), ballot titles are limited to 15 words and ballot summaries cannot exceed 75 words. These limits do not apply to amendments proposed by the legislature. *Id. See also Sancho v. Smith*, 830 So. 2d 856 (Fla. 1st Dist. Ct. App.), *review denied*, 828 So. 2d 389 (Fla. 2002).

The Florida Supreme Court has stressed that ballot titles and summaries must be accurate and clear. *See Armstrong v. Harris*, 773 So. 2d 7 (Fla. 2000), *cert. denied*, 532 U.S. 958 (2001). They do not, however, need to point out every consequence that might result from an amendment's approval. *See Advisory Opinion to the Attorney General re Physician Shall Charge the Same Fee for the Same Health Care Service to Every Patient*, 880 So. 2d 659 (Fla. 2004).

For examples of deficient ballot language, see *Detzner v. League of Women Voters of Florida*, 256 So. 3d 803 (Fla. 2018) (amendment proposed by the CRC); *Florida Department of State v. Mangat*, 43 So. 3d 642 (Fla. 2010) (legislature); *Florida Department of State v. Slough*, 992 So. 2d 142 (Fla. 2008) (TBRC); *Advisory Opinion to the Attorney General, re Amendment to Bar Government from Treating People Differently Based on Race in Public Education*, 778 So. 2d 888 (Fla. 2000) (citizens' initiative).

2.   FILING DEADLINES

Proposals coming from the legislature or a constitutional convention must be filed with the state at least 90 days before the general election at which they are to be voted on. *See* Art. XI, § 5(a). By a 3/4 vote, the legislature can move up this timeline by calling a special election. *Id.* Such an election cannot take place until at least 90 days have elapsed from the date of filing. *Id.*

The CRC and the TBRC must file their proposals "not later than one hundred eighty days prior to the next general election." *See* Art. XI, §§ 2(c) and 6(e). *See also In re Advisory Opinion of the Governor Request of November 19, 1976 (Constitution Revision Commission)*, 343 So. 2d 17 (Fla. 1977) (choosing to ignore the fact that Art. XI, § 5(a) applies its 90-deadline to the CRC—a drafting mistake now also extended to the TBRC).

In contrast, initiative petitions must be filed "no later than February 1 of the year in which the general election is held." *See* Art. XI, § 5(b); Fla. Stat. § 100.371(1). This 270-day requirement was added in 2004 to make it tougher for initiative petitions to appear on the ballot. (Because supervisors have 30 days to verify signatures, as a practical matter initiative petitions must be filed by January 1.)

Additionally, an estimate of an initiative's cost must be prepared by a panel of experts known as the "Financial Impact Estimating Conference." *See* Art. XI, § 5(c); Fla. Stat. §§ 100.371(5) and 101.161(1). This requirement was added in 2002 and was spurred by the 2000 bullet train amendment (discussed later in this chapter). The legislature previously had passed a law requiring initiatives to be accompanied by financial impact statements, but the statute was struck down in *Smith v. Coalition to Reduce Class Size*, 827 So. 2d 959 (Fla. 2002), for improperly burdening the initiative process.

The cost statements prepared to date can be found at http://edr.state.fl.us/Content/constitutional-amendments/index.cfm. At one time, fiscal impact statements were examined by the Florida Supreme Court as part of its overall review of an initiative. In *Advisory Opinion to the Attorney General re: Raising Florida's Minimum Wage*, 2019 WL 6906963 (Fla. 2019), however, the court concluded that it lacked the power to do so. As a result, statements now must be challenged "in circuit or county court . . . by [means of a] declaratory judgment action. . . ." *Id.* at *6 n.4.

3. PUBLICATION

All proposed amendments must be published twice in each county. *See* Art. XI, § 5(d). The first publication must occur 10 weeks before the election, while the second must occur six weeks before the election. *Id.* On both occasions, the publication must appear in a local newspaper of general circulation. *Id.*

In *State v. State Board of Education of Florida*, 467 So. 2d 294 (Fla. 1985), the Florida Supreme Court held that the failure to follow these rules in two small counties could be overlooked because even without their votes, the election's outcome would have been the same. Similarly, in *Florida Hometown Democracy, Inc. v. Cobb*, 953 So. 2d 666 (Fla. 1st Dist. Ct. App. 2007), notices that were published in the ninth and sixth weeks, instead of the 10th and sixth and weeks, were deemed valid.

4. MARGIN OF APPROVAL

To be adopted, amendments must be approved by at least 60% of the voters. *See* Art. XI, § 5(e). Previously, only a simple majority was required. In 2006, the threshold was raised to make it tougher for all amendments, but especially those proposed by citizens. The 2002 pregnant pig amendment, see Art. X, § 21 (discussed in Ch. 4 of this book), largely was responsible for this change.

Florida is the only state that has a supermajority requirement for all constitutional amendments. Four states have limited supermajority requirements. Colorado (55%) requires a supermajority for proposals that add language to the constitution. Minnesota (3/5) and New Hampshire (2/3) require a supermajority to call constitutional conventions. New Mexico (3/4) requires a supermajority for votes involving specific constitutional sections (*i.e.*, bilingual teachers, educational rights of children of Spanish descent, racial and religious equality, and voter qualifications—changes to the last two also must be approved by 2/3 of each county's voters).

Florida increases its approval threshold to 2/3 if the amendment authorizes a new state fee or tax. *See* Art. XI, § 7. This change was proposed by an initiative petition in 1994 but was struck from the ballot by the Florida Supreme Court because, by including both fees and taxes, it violated the single-subject requirement. *See Advisory Opinion to the Attorney General re Tax Limitation*, 644 So. 2d 486 (Fla. 1994) (*Tax Limitation I*). However, after the single-subject requirement was made inapplicable to initiatives limiting the government's ability to raise revenue, the proposal was permitted to appear on the 1996 ballot. *See Advisory Opinion to the Attorney General re Tax Limitation*, 673 So. 2d 864 (Fla. 1996) (*Tax Limitation II*).

5.   EFFECTIVE DATE; SEVERANCE; CONFLICTS

Amendments become effective "on the first Tuesday after the first Monday in January following the election, or on such other date as may be specified in the amendment or revision." *See* Art. XI, § 5(e). *See also Fuchs v. Wilkinson*, 630 So. 2d 1044 (Fla. 1994).

Amendments that require no implementing legislation are "self-executing." When an amendment is not self-executing, it remains inoperative until such legislation is passed. In *Gray v. Bryant*, 125 So. 2d 846 (Fla. 1960), the court held that an amendment is self-executing if it

> lays down a sufficient rule by means of which the right or purpose which it gives or is intended to accomplish may be determined, enjoyed, or protected without the aid of legislative enactment. If the provision lays down a sufficient rule, it speaks for the entire people and is self-executing.

Id. at 851. *See also Advisory Opinion to the Attorney General re Extending Existing Sales Tax to Non-Taxed Services Where Exclusion Fails to Serve Public Purpose*, 953 So. 2d 471 (Fla. 2007) (reaffirming *Gray's* test).

An amendment that is not self-executing often will set a deadline for legislative action. For example, a 1990 amendment proposing a three-day waiting period for handgun purchases included a provision giving the Florida Legislature one year to enact the necessary regulations. *See* Art. I, § 8(b)–(c) (discussed in Ch. 8 of this book).

In recent years, it has become routine for proposed constitutional amendments to include language making it clear they are effective immediately, are self-executing, and are severable. In 2018, for example, Art. X, § 30 (restricting casino gambling) was added. Its final two paragraphs state:

(d)   This section is effective upon approval by the voters, is self-executing, and no Legislative implementation is required.

(e)   If any part of this section is held invalid for any reason, the remaining portion or portions shall be severed from the invalid portion and given the fullest possible force and effect.

For a further discussion of effective dates and implementing deadlines, see Ch. 24 of this book. For a further discussion of severability, see *Ray v. Mortham*, 742 So. 2d 1276 (Fla. 1999) (holding that constitutional amendments should be severed when doing so is both needed and possible).

To the extent that an amendment conflicts with an existing constitutional provision, the amendment, being later in time, controls. *See Floridians Against Casino Takeover v. Let's Help Florida*, 363 So. 2d 337 (Fla. 1978).

F.   INOPERATIVE PROVISIONS

1.   REJECTED PROVISIONS

Since the adoption of the 1968 constitution, 51 proposed amendments (27.6%) have been rejected by the voters. Among the more surprising provisions that have gone down to defeat are a 1970 amendment that would have given 18-year-olds the right to vote; a 1976 amendment that would have limited the number of full-time government workers to 1% of the state's population and part-time workers to 10%; and a 1978 amendment that would have outlawed sex-based discrimination.

2.   JUDICIALLY-INVALIDATED PROVISIONS

Four constitutional provisions are unenforceable because they run afoul of federal law:

1)   The ban on same-sex marriages, see Art. I, § 27 (due to *Obergefell v. Hodges*, 135 S. Ct. 2584 (2015)—prior to *Obergefell*, 31 states, including Florida, had adopted such bans).

2)   The term limits on U.S. senators and U.S. representatives, see Art. VI, § 4(c)(5)–(6) (due to *U.S. Term Limits, Inc. v. Thornton*, 514 U.S. 779 (1995)).

3)   The exclusion of non-property owners from local bond referendums, see Art. VII, § 12(a) (due to *City of Phoenix, Arizona v. Kolodziejski*, 399 U.S. 204 (1970)).

4) The requirement that the Florida Legislature not vote on proposed amendments to the U.S. Constitution until after an intervening election, see Art. X, § 1 (due to *Trombetta v. State of Florida*, 353 F. Supp. 575 (M.D. Fla. 1973)).

In addition, the provision making English Florida's official language, see Art. II, § 9, almost certainly is unenforceable because of the First and 14th Amendments. *See* Ch. 2 of this book.

3. REPEALED PROVISIONS

Since the adoption of the 1968 constitution, multiple provisions have been repealed. Oddly, two still appear in the constitution. Art. III, § 18 requires the legislature to prescribe "[a] code of ethics for all state employees and nonjudicial officers." As the section's footnote explains: "This section was repealed effective January 5, 1999. . . . Identical language . . . was enacted [as] § 8(g), Art. II . . . [in] 1998."

In 2000, voters added Art. X, § 19. It required the state to build a "bullet train" system linking Florida's five largest urban areas. *See Advisory Opinion to the Attorney General re Florida Transportation Initiative for Statewide High Speed Monorail, Fixed Guideway or Magnetic Levitation System*, 769 So. 2d 367 (Fla. 2000). (Bullet trains travel at speeds of 160–200 miles per hour. In contrast, most passenger trains in the United States top out at 60 miles per hour.) In 2004, § 19 was repealed after the public learned its cost ($50 billion). *See Advisory Opinion to the*

Attorney General re Repeal of High Speed Rail Amendment, 880 So. 2d 624 (Fla. 2004), and *Advisory Opinion to the Attorney General re Repeal of High Speed Rail Amendment*, 880 So. 2d 628 (Fla. 2004).

Following the 2004 vote, a footnote was added to § 19 explaining that it had been repealed. In 2018, the text was deleted but the footnote was kept as an aid to readers. In the meantime, a private company called Brightline/Virgin Trains USA has sought to fill the gap by building a "higher speed" rail system (110 miles per hour). At present, it runs from Miami to West Palm Beach; by 2022, it is expected to expand to Orlando. *See* https://www.gobrightline.com/.

CHAPTER 24
SCHEDULES

A. OVERVIEW

In constitutions, a "schedule" is used to indicate when a new provision goes into effect. It also may address issues likely to arise during the period between passage and implementation and preserve specific elements of the superseded provision.

Except for the 1861 constitution, all of Florida's constitutions have had schedules. While the 1838 schedule transitioned Florida from a territory to a state, subsequent schedules have served as bridges from one constitution to the next. *See, e.g.*, Art. XII, § 17 of the 1968 constitution, which provides: "This schedule is designed to effect the orderly transition of government from the Constitution of 1885, as amended, to this revision and shall control in all cases of conflict with any part of Article I through IV, VII, and IX through XI herein."

B. MAIN SCHEDULE

When the 1968 constitution was adopted, its schedules were placed in Art. XII. *See City of Tampa v. Birdsong Motors, Inc.*, 261 So. 2d 1 (Fla. 1972). As new provisions have been added to the constitution, Art. XII has grown. As a result, it now accounts for 20% of the constitution's verbiage.

C. OTHER SCHEDULES

The articles dealing with the judiciary (Art. V) and local governments (Art. VIII) both have their own schedules. *See* Art. V, § 20 and Art. VIII, § 6. In addition, three sections have their own schedules:

Art. II, § 8 (ethics in government) contains a schedule in paragraph (i).

Art. V, § 12 (disciplining of judges) contains a schedule in paragraph (f).

Art. X, § 15 (state-operated lotteries) contains a schedule in paragraph (c).

D. "EFFECTIVE DATE" LANGUAGE

Some sections of the constitution do not have a schedule. Instead, they simply state when they take effect:

Art. I, § 8(c) (handgun purchase waiting periods, passed 1990): "The legislature shall enact legislation implementing subsection (b) of this section, effective no later than December 31, 1991. . . ."

Art. I, § 25 (taxpayers' bill of rights, passed 1992): "This section shall be effective July 1, 1993."

Art. I, § 26(b) (attorney compensation in medical malpractice lawsuits, passed 2004): "This Amendment shall take effect on the day following approval by the voters."

Art. VII, § 5(c) (estate, inheritance, and income taxes, passed 1971): "This section [paragraph 5(b), authorizing a corporate income tax] shall become effective immediately upon approval by the electors of Florida."

Art. IX, § 1(a) (classroom size, passed 2002): "[The] legislature shall make adequate provision to ensure that, by the beginning of the 2010 school year, there are a sufficient number of classrooms. . . ."

Art. IX, § 1(c) (universal pre-kindergarten, passed 2002): "The early childhood education and development programs provided by reason of subparagraph (b) shall be implemented no later than the beginning of the 2005 school year. . . ."

Art. X, § 6(c) (eminent domain, passed 2006): "Private property taken by eminent domain pursuant to a petition to initiate condemnation proceedings filed on or after January 2, 2007 [shall require]. . . ."

Art. X, § 14 (retirement system benefits, passed 1976): "A governmental unit responsible for any retirement or pension system . . . shall not after January 1, 1977, provide any increase . . . unless. . . ."

Art. X, § 16(h) (fishing nets, passed 1994): "This section shall take effect on the July 1 next occurring after approval hereof by vote of the electors."

Art. X, § 20(d) (workplace smoking, passed 2002): "In the next regular legislative session occurring after voter approval of this section or any amendment to this section, the legislature shall adopt legislation to implement this section and any amendment to this section . . . having an effective date no later than July 1 of the year following voter approval."

Art. X, § 21(g) (pregnant pigs, passed 2002): "This section shall take effect six years after approval by the electors."

Art. X, § 23(d) (slot machines, passed 2004): "This amendment shall become effective when approved by vote of the electors of the state."

Art. X, § 24(c) (minimum wage, passed 2004): "Six months after enactment, the Minimum Wage shall be established at an hourly rate of $6.15."

Art. X, § 25, note 1 (reporting of adverse medical incidents, passed 2004): "This amendment shall be effective on the date it is approved by the electorate."

Art. X, § 26, note 1 (loss of license for repeated medical malpractice, passed 2004): "This amendment shall be effective on the date it is approved by the electorate."

Art. X, § 27(d) (tobacco use prevention, passed 2006): "This amendment shall become effective immediately upon approval by the voters."

Art. X, § 28(a) (land acquisition, passed 2014): "Effective on July 1 of the year following passage of this amendment by the voters. . . ."

Art. X, § 29(d)(1)–(2) (medical marijuana, passed 2016): Requires the Florida Department of Health to promulgate implementing regulations "no later than six (6) months after the effective date of this section" and begin issuing patient ID cards and registering treatment centers "no later than nine (9) months after the effective date of this section."

Art. X, § 30(d) (casinos, passed 2018): "This section is effective upon approval by the voters. . . ."

Art. X, § 31(f) (death benefits for survivors of first responders and military members killed in action, passed 2018): "This section shall take effect on July 1, 2019."

Art. XI, § 7 (new taxes and fees, passed 1996): "This section shall apply to proposed constitutional amendments relating to State taxes or fees which appear on the November 8, 1994 ballot, or later ballots. . . ."

Art. X, § 32, which outlaws betting on dog racing and was passed in 2018, has both a schedule and an effective date. *See* Art. X, § 32 ("After December 31, 2020, a person authorized to conduct gaming or pari-mutuel operations may not race greyhounds or any member of the *Canis Familiaris* subspecies in connection with any wager for money or any other thing of value in this state. . . .") *and* Art. XII, § 39

("The amendment to Article X, which prohibits the racing of or wagering on greyhound and other dogs, and the creation of this section, shall take effect upon the approval of the electors.").

E. SILENT PROVISIONS

When a constitutional amendment contains neither a schedule nor an effective date, determining when it becomes operational can be tricky. If it is "self-executing," it is effective immediately. If it is not self-executing, it must await the passage of implementing legislation. *See* Ch. 23 of this book.

F. DELETION

Once a constitutional provision is operational, there is no reason to keep its schedule in the constitution. Recognizing this fact, Art. XII, § 11 states:

The legislature shall have power, by joint resolution, to delete from this revision any section of this Article XII, including this section, when all events to which the section to be deleted is or could become applicable have occurred. A legislative determination of fact made as a basis for application of this section shall be subject to judicial review.

As is obvious, this provision only applies to Art. XII. However, Art. V, § 20(i) and Art. VIII, § 6(h) both contain their own deletion language.

With respect to the three section-specific schedules, only the one authorizing state-operated lotteries contains a deletion mechanism. *See* Art. X, § 15(c)(1) ("[This] schedule may be amended by general law.").

The drafters of the 1968 constitution clearly expected the legislature to remove transitional items as they became obsolete. To date, however, it has ignored this task. Perhaps this is just as well, for litigants and the courts occasionally look to the schedules for guidance. *See, e.g., Bentley v. State ex rel. Rogers*, 398 So. 2d 992 (Fla. 4th Dist. Ct. App. 1981) (finding that schedule consolidating courts preserved requirement that mental competency decisions be made only by judges).

INDEX

References are to Pages